Lost Treasures of the Bible

Lost Treasures of the Bible

*Understanding the Bible
through Archaeological Artifacts
in World Museums*

Clyde E. Fant *&* Mitchell G. Reddish

WILLIAM B. EERDMANS PUBLISHING COMPANY
GRAND RAPIDS, MICHIGAN / CAMBRIDGE, U.K.

Published 2008 by
Wm. B. Eerdmans Publishing Co.
2140 Oak Industrial Drive N.E., Grand Rapids, Michigan 49505 /
P.O. Box 163, Cambridge CB3 9PU U.K.

Printed in the United States of America

14 13 12 11 10 09 08   7 6 5 4 3 2 1

Library of Congress Cataloging-in-Publication Data

Fant, Clyde E.
    Lost treasures of the Bible: understanding the Bible through archaeological
    artifacts in world museums / Clyde E. Fant & Mitchell G. Reddish.
        p.   cm.
    Includes bibliographical references and indexes.
    ISBN 978-0-8028-2881-1 (cloth: alk. paper)
    1. Bible — Antiquities.   I. Reddish, Mitchell Glenn, 1953-   II. Title.

BS621.F37   2008
220.9′3 — dc22

                                      2008019792

www.eerdmans.com

Contents

CONTENTS

Ancient Biblical Texts

Illustrations

Color Plates — Following Page 228

Preface and Acknowledgments

This book can be seen as a map to the lost treasures of the Bible. Not buried beneath desert sands or hidden in remote mountain caves, these treasures are lost in the endless halls and countless glass cases of the scattered museum collections of the world. They can be seen, but only if one knows where to go and what to look for — and, especially, if one knows why they are true treasures of the Bible.

In one sense, these artifacts have been lost at least twice. They were first lost to the modern world before being discovered by archaeologists. Many have remained lost to the majority of visitors to museums, either because their existence simply is not known or because the significance of their rich contribution to biblical understanding is not recognized.

Since one of the purposes of this book is to assist museum visitors who are interested in the Bible, the book provides the location, size, and inventory number of each featured object (with a few rare exceptions when that information was not available). The different indices at the back of the book should inform the reader of specific objects to watch for in various museums.

Perhaps the best part about this particular treasure map, however, is that it is not necessary to travel abroad to use it. Armchair travelers can discover for themselves spectacular antiquities not often seen — and, even more rarely, understood — by the hardiest of tourist travelers. This book can transport its readers to many countries, take them to major cities and remote towns, and explain the meaning of these fascinating objects for an understanding of biblical times and texts.

The choice of the artifacts included here is necessarily selective, due to the thousands of objects related to the biblical world that are in world museums. By "biblical objects" we mean both those items directly connected with biblical characters or history and artifacts that provide an understanding of the background and context of that world, including literary parallels. We have attempted to include the most significant and interesting of such objects that are currently on display in museums and available for viewing by the general public. Regrettably, some notable items had to be omitted simply because they are not accessible to the general public.

Throughout the book, the dates given for various rulers are the dates of their reigns, unless otherwise indicated. We have chosen to use B.C.E. and C.E. for all dates. C.E. (Common Era) refers to the period of time common to Judaism and Christianity and is equivalent to A.D. The abbreviation B.C.E (Before Common Era) refers to the same period conventionally designated as B.C.

The book is generally arranged in chronological order corresponding to the history of ancient Israel and early Christianity. In some cases, artifacts from one time period shed light on events or literature of an earlier or later period of biblical history. For example, the tablet containing the Legend of Aqhat, which dates to the fourteenth century B.C.E., may help explain the title character of the book of Daniel, whose narrative setting is during the Babylonian exile of the sixth century B.C.E. The article on the Legend of Aqhat, therefore, appears in the section of the book dealing with the Babylonian Exile. One section of the book, "Poetry and Wisdom Literature," varies slightly from this arrangement. The articles in this section pertain to specific literary genres, examples of which come from various periods in ancient Israel. In every case, however, an initial description of the artifact, which provides the history of its discovery and historical importance, is followed by an analysis of its significance for biblical interpretation. In that way, it is our hope that preachers, teachers, and students of the Bible will be enriched in their understanding of the biblical story.

A caveat or two may be in order. American designations for floors in buildings are frequently different from those used elsewhere in the world. For instance, what are considered the first floor, second floor, and third floor by people in the United States are labeled ground floor, first floor, and second floor in many other countries. In the book, the floor designations follow the customs of the country in which the museum is located. The arrangement of the Louvre can be especially confusing to first-time visitors. The museum contains three wings — Richelieu, Sully, and Denon — spread over four levels — entresol (lower ground floor), ground floor, first floor, and second floor. Each wing of each floor is divided into sections, numbered 1 through 10, going from the Richelieu Wing to the Denon Wing. In the book, objects in the Louvre are located by room number, floor, wing, and section number. (The section numbers are not included on the floor plan of the museum that is distributed at the Louvre information desk. The section numbers are displayed in the signs in each room, however.

A special word of advice should be given about the inventory numbers for items in the British Museum. The museum has recently changed the name of the Department of the Ancient Near East to the Department of the Middle

East. As a result, objects in that collection now begin with the prefix ME, instead of the former ANE or WA. Although some placards in the museum may still carry the older prefixes, we have used the prefix ME for all of these objects (at the suggestion of the museum).

As this book was in its final stages, the Israel Museum closed the Bronfman Archaeology Wing for a major renovation, not to be reopened until 2009-10. When the museum reopens, many of the objects will likely be displayed in different rooms from those in which they were displayed during our visits. Thus, in order not to mislead any readers, we chose not to include room numbers for objects in the Israel Museum. Objects are described as being in the Bronfman Archaeology Wing.

If you plan on making a trip specifically to see a particular object, it would be wise to e-mail or telephone the museum to be sure it is currently on exhibition. Furthermore, museums are forever shifting exhibitions, moving objects, and renumbering rooms and items. A particular example of this is the closing of rooms 88-89 in the British Museum. At the time the research for this book began, these rooms displayed, among other objects, various artifacts from the Assyrian Empire. Recently, however, these rooms have been closed and are no longer public spaces. The objects on display in these rooms eventually will be relocated elsewhere. Since at the time of this writing the objects have yet to be relocated, we have continued to list their locations as rooms 88-89. In any museum, if you cannot locate an object, ask. Museum personnel are genuinely interested in assisting visitors. Also, if — as is frequently the case — a particular room is closed when you are visiting (a lack of adequate staff is sometimes the cause), ask when the room will be open again. Sometimes we found that a courteous inquiry will even enable you to enter a closed room briefly to see something important to you.

Finally, if this needs to be said, this is not one of those books that will twist the facts or ignore evidence in a misguided attempt to "prove" the Bible. (Yes, Virginia, there are such books.) We have the conviction that a book that has proved itself as the foundation of the faith of countless millions over many centuries does not need our help.

It is really impossible to thank adequately all the persons who have helped make this work possible. Over the past several years we have traveled to every museum whose objects are described here, and more, often on repeated trips. From Egypt to Israel to Turkey — unfortunately we were blocked from Iraq and Iran — to the islands of the Mediterranean, to Europe, and to museums in our own country, we have felt something of the excitement of those who first found these historic treasures. Again and again we have been assisted by helpful museum personnel, as well as other archaeologists and scholars, in locating and understanding the particular artifacts we were researching. Beyond that, however, we are indebted to the scores of writers and specialists of many nations whose books and articles we consulted to analyze the history and significance of these artifacts of biblical history.

In specific, we would first of all express our appreciation to Sam Eerdmans, whose initial and sustained enthusiasm for this project was so important in its development. Linda Bieze, Managing Editor at Eerdmans, has skillfully guided this book through the publication process, answering numerous questions from the authors along the way. Klaas Wolterstorff, Production Manager at Eerdmans, provided valuable assistance and guidance in the illustrations for the book. Professors Carol Newsom of Candler School of Theology at Emory University and Jonathan Reed of the University of La Verne were gracious in discussing various aspects of this work with us as it developed. We also are grateful for the support of Stetson University in making this work possible. Several individuals at Stetson deserve special mention: President H. Douglas Lee; Grady Ballenger, Dean of the College of Arts and Sciences, who encouraged us and provided some much appreciated grant money for the project; the College of Arts and Sciences Advisory Board, which generously provided support from its Fund for Faculty Development; our colleagues in the Department of Religious Studies; Lisa Guenther, Administrative Specialist in the Department of Religious Studies; the staff of the Dupont-Ball Library, and especially Susan Derryberry, Inter-Library Loan Coordinator, for her generous assistance in procuring numerous books and articles, and Sims Kline, Reference Librarian, for his skill in locating the unlocatable. We also express gratitude to James Ridgway Jr. of Educational Opportunities Tours and Ünver Gazez of Azim Tours in Turkey for advice and assistance with travel arrangements. Necdet (Net) Özeren deserves a word of thanks, too, for excellent service as a guide and driver on several of our trips to Turkey.

While many family members and friends have encouraged us and expressed interest in this project, our wives — Cheryl and Barbara — deserve our greatest thanks for their encouragement, patience, and understanding — and most especially, remaining married to us! — throughout our travel and research for this book.

Abbreviations

B.C.E.   Before Common Era (same time period as B.C.)
C.E.   Common Era (same time period as A.D.)

Collections of Ancient Texts

ANET   *Ancient Near Eastern Texts Relating to the Old Testament.* James B.
               Pritchard, ed. 3rd ed. with Supplement. Princeton: Princeton
               University Press, 1969.
COS   *The Context of Scripture.* William W. Hallo, gen. ed., and K. Lawson
               Younger Jr., assoc. ed. 3 vols. Leiden: E. J. Brill, 1997-2002.
DOTT   *Documents from Old Testament Times: Translated with Introductions
               and Notes by Members of the Society for Old Testament Study.*
               D. Winton Thomas, ed. New York: Harper & Row, Harper
               Torchbooks, 1958. Reprint, with new foreword and bibliography by
               K. C. Hanson, Eugene Ore.: Wipf & Stock Publishers, Ancient Texts
               and Translations, 2005.

Biblical Books, Including the Apocrypha

HEBREW BIBLE/OLD TESTAMENT			
		Ezra	Ezra
Gen.	Genesis	Neh.	Nehemiah
Exod.	Exodus	Esther	Esther
Lev.	Leviticus	Job	Job
Num.	Numbers	Ps./Pss.	Psalms
Deut.	Deuteronomy	Prov.	Prov
Josh.	Joshua	Eccles.	Ecclesiastes
Judg.	Judges	Song of Sol.	Song of Solomon
Ruth	Ruth	Isa.	Isaiah
1-2 Sam.	1-2 Samuel	Jer.	Jeremiah
1-2 Kings	1-2 Kings	Lam.	Lamentations
1-2 Chron.	1-2 Chronicles	Ezek.	Ezekiel

Dan.	Daniel	Bel	Bel and the Dragon
Hos.	Hosea	1-2 Macc.	1-2 Maccabees
Joel	Joel	3-4 Macc.	3-4 Maccabees
Amos	Amos	Pr. of Man.	Prayer of Manasseh
Obad.	Obadiah		
Jon.	Jonah	**NEW TESTAMENT**	
Mic.	Micah	Matt.	Matthew
Nah.	Nahum	Mark	Mark
Hab.	Habakkuk	Luke	Luke
Zeph.	Zephaniah	John	John
Hag.	Haggai	Acts	Acts
Zech.	Zechariah	Rom.	Romans
Mal.	Malachi	1-2 Cor.	1-2 Corinthians
		Gal.	Galatians
APOCRYPHA		Eph.	Ephesians
Tob.	Tobit	Phil.	Philippians
Jth.	Judith	Col.	Colossians
Add. Esth.	Additions to Esther	1-2 Thess.	1-2 Thessalonians
Wisd. of Sol.	Wisdom of Solomon	1-2 Tim.	1-2 Timothy
Sir.	Sirach (Ecclesiasticus)	Titus	Titus
Bar.	Baruch	Philem.	Philemon
1-2 Esd.	1-2 Esdras	Heb.	Hebrews
Let. of Jer.	Letter of Jeremiah	James	James
Pr. of Azar.	Prayer of Azariah and	1-2 Pet.	1-2 Peter
	the Song of the Three	1-2-3 John	1-2-3 John
	Jews	Jude	Jude
Sus.	Susanna	Rev.	Revelation

List of Selected Rulers

Dates indicate the dates of the rulers' reigns. Due to fragmentary and inconsistent data, many of the dates given are approximate. Unless otherwise indicated, all dates are B.C.E.

Egypt
Ahmenhotep III (ca. 1390-1353)
Akhenaten (ca. 1353-1336)
Ramesses II (ca. 1279-1213)
Merneptah (ca. 1213-1204)
Shoshenq I (Shishak) (ca. 945-924)
Taharqa (Tirhakah (690-664)

Assyria
Ashurnasirpal II (883-859)
Shalmaneser III (858-823)
Tiglath-pileser III (744-727)
Shalmaneser V (726-722)
Sargon II (721-705)
Sennacherib (704-681)
Esarhaddon (680-669)
Ashurbanipal (669-627)

Babylonia
Merodach-Baladin II (721-710)
Nabopolassar (625-605)
Nebuchadnezzar II (604-562)
Evil-Merodach (561-560)
Nerigilissar (559-556)
Labashi-Marduk (556)
Nabonidus (555-539)

Persia
Cyrus II (559-530)
Cambyses II (529-522)
Bardia (522)
Darius I (521-486)
Xerxes I (485-465)
Artaxerxes I (465-424)
Xerxes II (424)
Sogdianus (424)
Darius II (423-405)
Artaxerxes II (404-359)
Artaxerxes III (358-338)
Arses (Artaxerxes IV) (337-335)
Darius III (335-330)

Damascus (Aram)
Rezon (ca. 950)
Ben-Hadad I (ca. 900)
Hazael (ca. 842)
Ben-Hadad II (ca. 810)
Rezin (ca. 740)

Israel
(United Monarchy)
Saul   ca. 1020-1000
David   ca. 1000-960
Solomon   ca. 960-932

Israel **(Northern Kingdom)**	**Judah** **(Southern Kingdom)**
Jeroboam I (932-911)	Rehoboam (931-915)
	Abijah/Abijam (915-913)
Nadab (911-910)	Asa (913-873)
Baasha (910-887)	
Elah (887-886)	
Zimri (886)	
Omri (886-875)	
Ahab (875-854)	Jehoshaphat (873-849)
Ahaziah (854-853)	
Jehoram/Joram (853-842)	Jehoram/Joram (849-842)
Jehu (842-815)	Ahaziah (842)

Athaliah (842-837)

Jehoahaz (815-799)

Jehoash/Joash (836-797)

Joash/Jehoash (799-784)

Amaziah (797-769)

Jeroboam II (784-744)

Azariah/Uzziah (769-741)

Zechariah (744)

Shallum (744)

Menahem (744-735)

Jotham (741-735)

Pekahiah (735-734)

Ahaz (735-726)

Pekah (734-731)

Hoshea (731-722)

Hezekiah (726-697)

Destruction of Samaria in 722

Manasseh (697-642)

Amon (640)

Josiah (640-609)

Jehoahaz (609)

Jehoiakim (609-598)

Jehoiachin (598)

Zedekiah (598-587)

Destruction of Jerusalem in 587

Hellenistic Rulers

Alexander the Great (336-323)

Syria	Egypt
Seleucus I Nicator (305-281)	Ptolemy I Soter (305-282)
Antiochus III (223-187)	Ptolemy V Epiphanes (204-180)
Antiochus IV Epiphanes (175-164)	Cleopatra VII (51-30)

Herodian Rulers

Herod the Great, king of Judea, territory eventually expanded to include all of Palestine and parts of Transjordan (37-4 B.C.E.)

Archelaus, ethnarch of Judea, Samaria, Idumea (4 B.C.E.–6 C.E.)

Herod Antipas, tetrarch of Galilee and Perea (4 B.C.E.–39 C.E.)

Philip, tetrarch of Batanea, Trachonitis, Auranitis, and Gaulanitis (4 B.C.E.-34 C.E.)

Herod Agrippa I, king of Batanea, Trachonitis, Auranitis, and Gaulanitis (37-44 C.E.); later also given territory of Galilee and Perea (39 C.E.) and Judea and Samaria (41 C.E.)

Herod Agrippa II, king of Chalcis (50-53 C.E.); king of Batanea, Trachonitis, and Gaulanitis (53-ca. 93 C.E.); given parts of Galilee and Perea in 54 C.E.; also had control over the Jerusalem temple and the right to appoint the high priests

Roman Emperors (during the biblical period)

Augustus (27 B.C.E.–14 C.E.)

Tiberius (14-37 C.E.)

Gaius Caligula (37-41 C.E.)

Claudius (41-54 C.E.)

Nero (54-68 C.E.)

Galba (68-69 C.E.)

Otho (69 C.E.)

Vitellius (69 C.E.)

Vespasian (69-79 C.E.)

Titus (79-81 C.E.)

Domitian (81-96 C.E.)

Nerva (96-98 C.E.)

Trajan (98-117 C.E.)

Hadrian (117-138 C.E.)

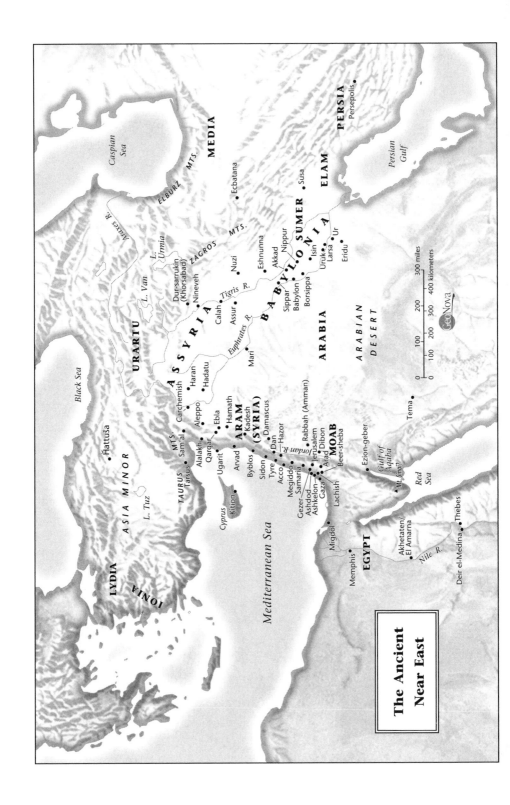

The Ancient
Near East

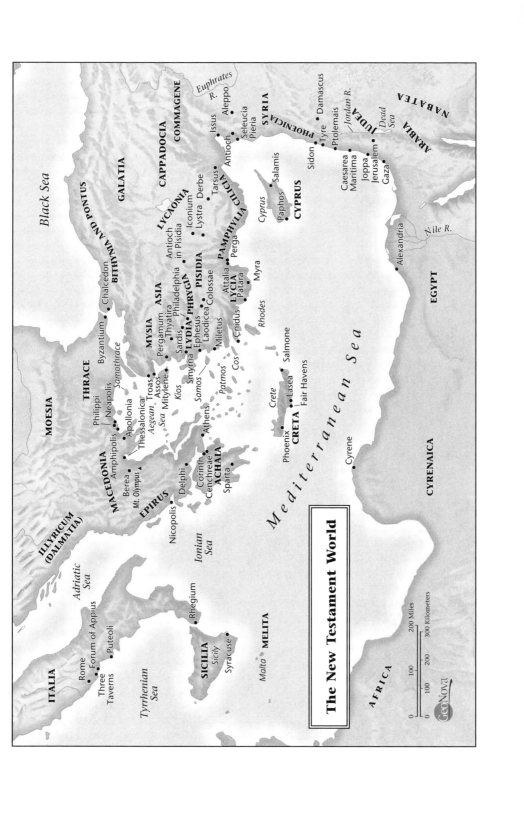

The New Testament World

Creation and Flood Stories

Enuma Elish, the Epic of Creation

Clay tablet

- ▷ Size: 21.30 cm. (8.38 in.) high; 6.35 cm. (2.5 in.) wide
- ▷ Writing: Akkadian language in cuneiform script
- ▷ Provenance: Nineveh (Kuyunjik, in modern Iraq)
- ▷ Date: Seventh century B.C.E.
- ▷ Present location: British Museum (room 55)
- ▷ Identification number: ME K3473

The *Enuma Elish* has sometimes been called the Babylonian Epic of Creation and is probably the best known of the ancient Mesopotamian creation stories. Yet, the creation episode is only incidental to the story contained in the text. The major purpose of the story was not to present an account of creation, but to describe and justify the rise of Marduk to the position of chief god of the Babylonian pantheon. The title by which the story is known, *Enuma Elish,* comes from the two opening words of the text and is translated as "when on high."

The *Enuma Elish* account consists of approximately 1100 lines of text on seven tablets. Copies of the text have been discovered at various sites in ancient Mesopotamia (including Nineveh, Ashur, Uruk, and Kish) and at Sultantepe in Turkey. Whereas the earliest known copy of the text is from around 900 B.C.E., the actual date of the composition of *Enuma Elish* is not clear. Previously many scholars argued for a date of composition during the Old Babylonian period (2017-1595 B.C.E.); now, however, most would date it later, sometime between the fourteenth

1. Fragments of tablet three of *Enuma Elish*

3

and eleventh centuries B.C.E. Since the statue of Marduk was recovered from Elam during the reign of Nebuchadnezzar I (1126-1105 B.C.E.), some scholars have argued for the story's composition during his reign. Part of the story line of *Enuma Elish* seems to have been adapted from an earlier Akkadian myth, the Myth of Anzu. The tablet on display in the British Museum (ME K3473; see fig. 1) is one of several tablets of *Enuma Elish* owned by the museum. It was part of a collection of tablets of *Enuma Elish* discovered in the middle of the nineteenth century at the site of Ashurbanipal's library in ancient Nineveh. This particular tablet, broken into four pieces with additional pieces missing, is tablet three of the seven-tablet story. The text, written on both sides of the long, narrow tablet, consists of a total of 138 lines. It was copied down during the time of Ashurbanipal during the seventh century B.C.E.

The myth begins with a description of the creation of the gods by Apsu (the water under the earth) and Tiamat (the sea):

> When on high no name was given to heaven,
> Nor below was the netherworld called by name,
> Primeval Apsu was their progenitor,
> And matrix-Tiamat was she who bore them all,
> They were mingling their waters together,
> No cane brake was intertwined nor thicket matted close.
> When no gods at all had been brought forth,
> None called by names, none destinies ordained,
> Then were the gods formed with the(se two.)[1]

Four generations of deities were produced. The gods who were created were too noisy, however, and disturbed Apsu, who plotted to eradicate them. When the gods heard of the plot, one of them, Ea, killed Apsu and built his dwelling upon him. In this dwelling, Marduk, son of Ea, was born. Soon Marduk, while playing with the four winds his grandfather Anu had formed and given to him, created a wave, whose turbulent motion disturbed the watery Tiamat and upset some of the other gods. Prodded by some of these gods, Tiamat gave birth to monstrous creatures to wage war against Marduk and the gods who were aligned with him. Tiamat took Qingu (or, Kingu) as her new consort, entrusted him with the tablet of destinies, and made him the king over all the gods. When Ea and Anu shrank back from fighting against Tiamat, Marduk stepped forward and agreed to combat her, on the condition that he would be recognized as the supreme god of the pantheon. When the assembly of the gods agreed to his condition, Marduk set out and confronted Tiamat and her forces. Tiamat was no match for the mighty Marduk:

1. "Epic of Creation," translated by Benjamin R. Foster (*COS* 1.111:391).

4

Tiamat and Marduk, sage of the gods, drew close for battle,
They locked in single combat, joining for the fray.
The Lord spread out his net, encircled her,
The ill wind he had held behind him he released in her face.
Tiamat opened her mouth to swallow,
He thrust in the ill wind so she could not close her lips.
The raging winds bloated her belly,
Her insides were stopped up, she gaped her mouth wide.
He shot off the arrow, it broke open her belly,
It cut to her innards, it pierced the heart.
He subdued her and snuffed out her life,
He flung down her carcass, he took his stand upon it.[2]

After defeating Tiamat, Marduk defeated the monstrous creatures and other forces aligned with Tiamat, including Qingu, from whom he took the tablet of destinies. Marduk then returned to the body of Tiamat, and from her corpse he created the universe:

He made firm his hold over the captured gods,
Then turned back to Tiamat whom he had captured.
The Lord trampled upon the frame of Tiamat,
With his merciless mace he crushed her skull.
He cut open the arteries of her blood,
He let the North Wind bear (it) away as glad tidings.
When his fathers saw, they rejoiced and were glad,
They brought him gifts and presents.
He calmed down. Then the Lord was inspecting her carcass,
That he might divide(?) the monstrous lump and fashion artful things.
He split her in two, like a fish for drying,
Half of her he set up and made as a cover, heaven.
He stretched out the hide and assigned watchmen,
And ordered them not to let her waters escape.[3]

In the sky, which he made from half of Tiamat's corpse, Marduk set the stars and the moon. With her other half he formed the earth: from her eyes, he made the Tigris and Euphrates flow, while from her udders he formed the mountains. All the gods then proclaimed the sovereignty of Marduk, who next proposed to create humans to do labor for the gods so that the gods could rest.

2. "Epic of Creation" (*COS* 1.111:398).
3. "Epic of Creation" (*COS* 1.111:398).

Specifically, the task of humans was to provide food each day for the gods. Marduk stated,

> I shall compact blood, I shall cause bones to be,
> I shall make stand a human being, let "Man" be its name.
> I shall create humankind,
> They shall bear the gods' burden that those may rest.[4]

Ea suggested that one of the gods be killed and his remains be used to form humans. That plan was adopted, Qingu was killed, and Ea used Qingu's blood to create humans. In appreciation for what Marduk had done, the gods constructed his temple in Babylon, at the completion of which Marduk threw a banquet for all the gods. During the banquet the other gods heaped elaborate praise upon Marduk, pledging their loyalty to him and bestowing upon him fifty names of honor.

Biblical Significance

Several aspects of the *Enuma Elish* myth have been claimed as parallels to and even sources for the biblical creation accounts. Many of these supposed parallels, however, have not held up to closer scrutiny. Scholars today, while admitting the Mesopotamian flavor of much of the biblical creation stories, are often cautious about claiming literary dependence (especially direct dependence) of the biblical writers upon the Mesopotamian myths. Even so, there are some intriguing similarities between *Enuma Elish* and the biblical versions of creation. Even the way the stories begin has a similar ring: "When on high no name was given to heaven" *(Enuma Elish);* "In the beginning when God created the heavens and the earth" (Gen. 1:1); "In the day that the LORD God made the earth and the heavens, when no plant of the field was yet in the earth and no herb of the field had yet sprung up" (Gen. 2:4b-5). In *Enuma Elish*, Marduk creates the world by splitting Tiamat, the primeval waters (depicted sometimes as having a physical body with human/animal parts, other times presented as a watery mass). With half of her, Marduk creates a cover that is the heaven or the sky. In Genesis 1:6-8, God separates the waters by means of the sky during the second day of creation: "And God said, 'Let there be a dome in the midst of the waters, and let it separate the waters from the waters.' So God made the dome and separated the waters that were under the dome from the waters that were above the dome. And it was so. God called the dome Sky." Creation in *Enuma Elish* culminates with the creation of humans, whose ap-

---

4. "Epic of Creation" (*COS* 1.111:400).

pearance provides for rest for the gods. In Genesis 1:26–2:3, humans are the final act of creation, after which God rests on the seventh day.

The biblical writers may very well have been influenced by the *Enuma Elish* and other Mesopotamian stories. Yet, important differences between the biblical accounts and *Enuma Elish* should not be overlooked. The violence of the creative act in *Enuma Elish* is absent from the Genesis stories, where God creates through divine command and through crafting the world. Furthermore, the creation of humans in Genesis (and especially in Psalm 8) is an act to be celebrated. Humans are the crowning act of God's creation. In *Enuma Elish*, humans are created to be a slave-like labor force for the gods. Finally, the monotheistic (or, at least, henotheistic; belief that other gods exist, but worship of only one) view of the biblical writers required that the God of Israel alone, not many gods, was responsible for bringing the world and humans into existence.

Sumerian Creation Myths

Clay tablets

▷ Size: AO 4153 — 8.5 cm. (3.35 in.) high, 9 cm. (3.54 in.) wide; AO 6020 — 12.13 cm. (4.78 in.) high, 6.4 cm. (2.52 in.) wide; AO 6715 — 12.7 cm. (5 in.) high, 6.35 cm. (2.5 in.) wide; AO 6724 — 9.06 cm. (3.57 in.) high, 7 cm. (2.76 in.) wide; AO 7036 — 14.3 cm. (5.63 in.) high, 10.7 cm. (4.21 in.) wide
▷ Writing: Sumerian language in cuneiform script
▷ Provenance: Lower Mesopotamia (modern Iraq)
▷ Date: Early second millennium B.C.E.
▷ Present location: Louvre (room 3, ground floor, Richelieu Wing, section 3)
▷ Identification numbers: AO 4153, AO 6020, AO 6715, AO 6724, AO 7036

These five tablets are displayed together in a case in the Louvre. Each represents a different Sumerian myth related to the creation of the world or the creation of humanity. In the texts of three of these tablets, the main god who figures in each of the myths is Enki, the Sumerian god of the subterranean fresh waters and god of wisdom. The tablet with the identification number AO 6020, acquired by the Louvre in 1912, is known as Enki and the World Order (see fig. 2). Several copies of this tale, dated to the early part of the second millennium B.C.E., have been found. The myth consists of 467 lines, most of which are well preserved. The tablet on display in the Louvre does not contain

**2. Clay tablet (AO 6020) containing portions of
the creation myth Enki and the World Order**

the entire myth but includes the
end of the myth. The first part of
the myth consists of praise of Enki
by the poet and hymns of self-
praise by Enki.

The myth then tells of Enki
traveling to various places (Sumer,
Ur, Meluhha, and Dilmun) to con-
fer blessings upon them, before
pronouncing curses on the enemies of Sumer. The next part of the
myth describes Enki's actions that
bring about the fertility and pro-
ductiveness of the waters and the
soil. In sexual imagery, the text portrays Enki as filling the Euphrates
and Tigris Rivers with his semen.
He then stocks the marshland with
fish and reeds and appoints a god
over them. Next he erects a holy
shrine in the sea and places a goddess in
charge. His next act is to call forth the rain clouds and appoint a god to be in
charge of them. After Enki has provided the Tigris and Euphrates for irrigation and rain water for the earth, he then attends to the various aspects of human needs and culture (agriculture and food production, building of houses,
abundant vegetation, wild and domestic animals, and weaving of cloth), creating and ordering the world.

After each of his creative activities, Enki appoints one of the deities to be in
charge of these various areas, with the sun god Utu being put in charge of the entire universe. The last part of this myth focuses on the goddess Inanna, who feels
slighted that she has not been given important powers and functions. Inanna
complains bitterly that other deities, particularly her sisters, have been given certain responsibilities and powers for maintaining the order of the world, yet she
has been slighted. Enki responds by reminding Inanna of her impressive powers
and activities and praising her. The final few lines of the text are missing.[1]

1. For a translation of this myth, see Samuel Noah Kramer and John Maier, *Myths of Enki,
the Crafty God* (New York: Oxford, 1989), pp. 38-56.

Another Sumerian creation myth involving Enki is called Enki and Ninhursag (also known as the Dilmun Myth). Three copies of this text are known, including the fragmentary tablet in the Louvre (AO 6724) that was acquired by the museum in 1914. The text, as reconstructed from the three copies, totals 278 lines and actually seems to be two myths that have been joined. The text begins with a passage extolling the purity and holiness of Dilmun (modern Bahrain in the Persian Gulf). Dilmun is in an unfinished, precreation state. When Ninsikila, a goddess of Dilmun, complains that the city lacks fresh water, Enki provides the city with water, which results in the farms and fields producing an abundance of grain. The text then describes Enki's sexual escapades, beginning with his impregnation of the goddess Ninhursag (also called Nintu in the text). She gives birth after nine days to the goddess Ninmu. Enki then has sex with his daughter Ninmu, who becomes pregnant and gives birth nine days later to Ninkurra. When his granddaughter Ninkurra comes out to the river bank, Enki impregnates her as well. As a result, Ninkurra becomes pregnant and gives birth to a daughter, Uttu.[2]

The Louvre text differs at this point from the other copies of this myth. In the Louvre fragment, an extra generation is described: Ninkurra gives birth not to Uttu, but to Ninimma, who gives birth to Uttu, after becoming pregnant by Enki. Part of the subsequent text is missing, but apparently Uttu is warned about Enki by Ninhursag, who tells her to stay in her house until Enki offers her gifts of cucumbers, apples, and grapes. Enki then waters the land, bringing forth produce which he presents to Uttu, who allows him to fondle and sexually penetrate her. Uttu does not become pregnant, however, because Ninhursag takes Enki's semen from her and from it produces eight plants, which Enki then eats. Angered at Enki's eating of the plants, Ninhursag curses him and vows not to look upon him again until he is dead. Enki becomes gravely ill, hurting in eight parts of his body. Ninhursag is convinced (by a fox) to return to Enki, whereupon she gives birth to eight deities, related somehow to the parts of Enki's body that were in pain, thus healing him. The last god to be born is Ensag, on whom Enki bestows the lordship of Dilmun.

The third creation myth with Enki describes the creation of humans. Called Enki and Ninmah, the text of approximately 141 lines has been reconstructed from several tablets and fragments, although several gaps and breaks in the text still prevent a full understanding of the myth. The Louvre fragment of Enki and Ninmah (AO 7036) was acquired in 1917 from an antiquities dealer,

2. For a translation of this myth, see "Enki and Ninhursag: A Paradise Myth," in *ANET*, pp. 37-41; or, Samuel Noah Kramer and John Maier, *Myths of Enki, the Crafty God* (New York: Oxford, 1989), pp. 22-30; or, Thorkild Jacobsen, *The Harps That Once . . . : Sumerian Poetry in Translation* (New Haven: Yale University Press, 1987), pp. 181-204.

and thus its provenance is unknown. The opening words of the myth provide the setting:

> In those days, in the days
>> when heaven and earth were [created],
> In those nights, in the nights
>> when heaven and earth were [created],
> In those [years], in the years
>> when the fates [were decreed],
> When the Anunna-gods were born,
> When the goddesses were taken
>> in marriage,
> When the goddesses were distributed
>> in heaven and earth,
> When the goddesses were inseminated,
>> became pregnant and gave birth,
> The gods who baked their daily-bread,
>> (and) set therewith their tables —
> The senior gods did oversee the work,
>> while the minor gods were bearing the toil.
> The gods were digging the canals,
>> were piling up their silt in Harali;
> The gods were dredging the clay,
>> they were complaining about their (hard) life.[3]

Moved by the tears and complaints of the gods about their hard work, Nammu, the primeval mother goddess, goes to Enki and suggests that he create a substitute worker who can relieve the gods of their toil. At Enki's direction and with the goddess Ninmah (another name for Ninhursag) serving as her helper (midwife?), Nammu produces humanity from the moist clay of Abzu, the subterranean fresh waters. At this point in the text, an originally separate story seems to have been joined to the first story. The setting for the second story is a banquet at which both Enki and Ninmah become inebriated from drinking too much beer. They enter into a contest that involves one deity making handicapped or deformed humans from the moist clay of Abzu and the other deity decreeing a function for the created individual. The end of the second story is badly damaged and missing, but the final lines leave no doubt that Enki has prevailed over Ninmah. The closing lines proclaim, "Ninmah did not equal the great lord Enki/Father Enki, your praise is sweet."[4]

---

3. "Enki and Ninmaḫ," translated by Jacob Klein (*COS* 1.159:516).

4. "Enki and Ninmaḫ" (*COS* 1.159:516).

The creation myths in the other two tablets on display in the Louvre do not feature Enki. In tablet AO 6715, a fragmentary tablet containing only a portion of the myth, creation is presented as the result of a cosmic marriage between heaven (An) and earth, a motif found in other Mesopotamian myths. As a result of the sexual union of An and earth, the fertile earth produces an abundance of vegetation. The text describes the event:

> Vast Earth adorned her body with precious metal and lapis-lazuli.
> She adorned herself with diorite, chalcedony, carnelian (and) elmeshu.
> [Heaven] clothed the plants in beauty, stood by their majesty.
> Pure [Ea]rth made herself verdant in a clean place for pure An.
> An, high Heaven, consummated marriage with vast Earth,
> He implanted the seed of the heroes Tree and Reed in (her womb).
> Earth, the good cow, received the good seed of An.
> Earth gave herself to the happy birth of the plants of life.
> Earth joyously produced abundance; she exuded wine and honey.[5]

The major focus of this text is not really creation, but a debate between Tree and Reed about who is superior. The creation account serves to describe the origin of the two debaters, whose growth and debate would have been narrated in the remainder of the text.

Tablet AO 4153 preserves only a portion of the introduction to a Sumerian myth about the creation of the world. The surviving text provides the setting; the subsequent action, however, is missing. The setting seems to be right before or after the separation of earth and sky from their sexual union; thus this text, like the previous one, was shaped by the idea of cosmic marriage. According to the text, the setting is a time before the birth of the gods, before there was any vegetation, and before the sun and moon were created. Unfortunately nothing more is preserved on this tablet, which apparently continued with an account of the creation of the gods, plants, and celestial luminaries.

Biblical Significance

Like other ancient creation stories (see the articles on *Enuma Elish* and the Epic of Atrahasis), these Sumerian myths provide an interesting background against which to read the biblical narratives of creation. The most well-known biblical

---

5. Richard J. Clifford, *Creation Accounts in the Ancient Near East and in the Bible,* The Catholic Biblical Quarterly Monograph Series 26 (Washington, D.C.: The Catholic Biblical Association of America, 1994), p. 26.

creation accounts are those found in Genesis 1 and Genesis 2. Yet other references to God's creative and ordering activity are found throughout the Hebrew Bible, including in many of the psalms (among them, Psalms 8; 19; 33; 65; 74; 90; 95; 102; 104; 136; and 148), in the book of Proverbs (3:19-20; 8:22-31), in the book of Job (9:1-10; 10:8-12; 26:5-14; 28:23-27; 33:6; 36:24–37:24; 38:1–39:30; 40:6–41:34), and throughout Isaiah 40-55, often known as Second Isaiah. Whether the Sumerian creation stories directly affected the ways in which the biblical writers expressed their understandings of the origin of the world and humanity is difficult to answer, but several interesting comparisons and contrasts can be made. Sumerian writers and biblical writers both thought of creation of the world and creation of humans as the products of divine activity. Both could describe humans as being created from dust (Gen 2:7) or clay (Job 33:6; Enki and Ninmah). On the other hand, whereas some Sumerian myths depicted creation as resulting from sexual activities of the gods, the biblical writers never talked of creation in those terms, perhaps because such imagery would have required that God have a consort, which was something avoided by the biblical writers. In the myth of Enki and Ninmah, humans are created as a source of workers to relieve the gods from wearisome labor. The biblical writers do not cite a specific reason for the creation of humans, but humans are not created as a workforce for God. A major difference between the Sumerian accounts and the biblical stories of creation, one that is obvious but still important, is that the Sumerian accounts were filled with many deities, whereas for the Hebrew writers, the God of Israel was solely responsible for creating the world.

The Epic of Atrahasis

Clay tablet

▷ Size: 25 cm. (9.84 in.) high; 19.4 cm. (7.64 in.) wide
▷ Writing: Akkadian language in cuneiform script
▷ Provenance: Sippar (Abu Habbah, in modern Iraq)
▷ Date: Seventeenth century B.C.E.
▷ Present location: British Museum (room 56)
▷ Identification number: ME 78941

Although this tablet is often called "The Babylonian Story of the Flood" (as it is so labeled in the British Museum), the ancient flood story is only one part of this Babylonian tale. The Epic of Atrahasis, as it is usually known, tells the story of the creation of humanity and the early history of humanity, including the attempt by the gods to destroy their troublesome creation by means of a flood. The story begins before the creation of humanity, when the more powerful gods (the Anunna-gods) force the lower gods (the Igigi-gods) to do all the physical labor.

> When gods were man,
> They did forced labor, they bore drudgery.
> Great indeed was the drudgery of the gods,
> The forced labor was heavy, the misery too much:
> The seven(?) great Anunna-gods were burdening
> The Igigi-gods with forced labor.[1]

Weary from the laborious task of digging the rivers and canals, the lesser gods revolt, march upon the house of Enlil and demand that they be relieved of their forced labor. In response, the Anunna-gods decide to create humans to serve as a labor force. The birth goddess Nintu (also called Mami) is summoned and given the task of creating humans, a task she completes with the help of the god Enki.

> They summoned and asked the goddess,
> The midwife of the gods, wise Mami:
> "Will you be the birth goddess, creatress of mankind?
> Create a human being that he bear the yoke,
> Let him bear the yoke, the task of Enlil,
> Let man assume the drudgery of god."
> Nintu made ready to speak,
> And said to the great gods:
> "It is not for me to do it,
> The task is Enki's.
> He it is that cleanses all,
> Let him provide me the clay so I can do the making."
> Enki made ready to speak,
> And said to the great gods:
> "On the first, seventh, and fifteenth days of the month,
> Let me establish a purification, a bath.
> Let one god be slaughtered,

1. "Atra-ḫasis," translated by Benjamin R. Foster (*COS* 1.130:450). (The *COS* text of "Atra-ḫasis" is a slightly altered reprint of the text in Benjamin R. Foster, *Before the Muses: An Anthology of Akkadian Literature*, vol. 1 [Bethesda, Md.: CDL Press, 1993], pp. 158-183.)

Then let the gods be cleansed by immersion.
Let Nintu mix clay with his flesh and blood.
Let that same god and man be thoroughly mixed in the clay.
Let us hear the drum for the rest of time,
From the flesh of the god let a spirit remain,
Let it make the living know its sign,
Lest he be allowed to be forgotten, let the spirit remain."
The great Anunna-gods, who administer destinies,
Answered "yes!" in the assembly.
On the first, seventh, and fifteenth days of the month,
He established a purification, a bath.
They slaughtered Aw-ilu, who had the inspiration, in their assembly.
Nintu mixed clay with his flesh and blood.
<That same god and man were thoroughly mixed in the clay.>
For the rest [of the time they would hear the drum],
From the flesh of the god [the] spi[rit remained].
It would make the living know its sign,
Lest he be allowed to be forgotten, [the] spirit remained.
After she had mixed that clay,
She summoned the Anunna, the great gods.
The Igigi, the great gods, spat upon the clay.
Mami made ready to speak,
And said to the great gods:
"You ordered me the task and I have completed (it)!
You have slaughtered the god, along with his inspiration.
I have done away with your heavy forced labor,
I have imposed your drudgery on man."[2]

Humans eventually multiply on the earth to the point where their noise becomes a great irritant to the gods. In order to squelch the noise the gods decide to wipe out humanity. Their initial attempts, through plague, drought, and starvation, do not succeed because each time Enki warns Atrahasis, who is one of the humans, and advises him on how the people can avoid destruction. Finally, the gods decide to destroy humanity by means of a great flood. Once more, Enki warns Atrahasis, this time instructing him to build a boat in preparation for the flood, which would begin in seven days. When the boat is finished, Atrahasis takes aboard his family, his possessions, the birds, the cattle, the wild creatures, and other animals. The great storm lasts for seven days and nights, destroying all humanity except Atrahasis and his companions. Soon

2. "Atra-ḫasis" (COS 1.130:451).

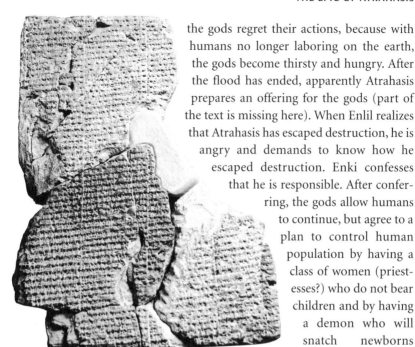

the gods regret their actions, because with humans no longer laboring on the earth, the gods become thirsty and hungry. After the flood has ended, apparently Atrahasis prepares an offering for the gods (part of the text is missing here). When Enlil realizes that Atrahasis has escaped destruction, he is angry and demands to know how he escaped destruction. Enki confesses that he is responsible. After conferring, the gods allow humans to continue, but agree to a plan to control human population by having a class of women (priestesses?) who do not bear children and by having a demon who will snatch newborns from their mothers.

3. Fragmentary copy of tablet one of the Epic of Atrahasis

The best preserved edition of the Epic of Atrahasis comes from the Old Babylonian period, written around 1635 B.C.E. This version of the tale was written on three tablets, with a total of approximately 1245 lines of text. These tablets can be dated rather precisely because each tablet bears the name of the scribe who wrote it (Ku-Aya) and the time of its composition during the reign of the Babylonian king Ammisaduqa. These tablets were apparently discovered at the site of ancient Sippar in modern Iraq. Four copies of portions of the first tablet are owned by the British Museum; one copy of part of tablet two is in the possession of the Library of J. Pierpont Morgan in New York, while part of another copy is owned by the Museum of the Ancient Orient in Istanbul; and part of one copy of tablet three is owned by the British Museum, with another part of the same tablet in the Museum of Art and History in Geneva, Switzerland. In addition to these Old Babylonian versions, portions of the story were also found on tablet fragments at Ras Shamra and Nippur from the Middle Babylonian period, at Nineveh from the Neo-Assyrian period, and on a couple of fragments from the Neo-Babylonian period. Thus, this story was known throughout Mesopotamia and even beyond for much of the second millennium B.C.E. Although the earliest extant copies date to the seventeenth century B.C.E., how much earlier the story originated is not known. The tablet on display in the British

Museum (ME 78941) contains the majority of the first tablet of the epic, although portions of the tablet are damaged.

Biblical Significance

The Epic of Atrahasis is of interest to students of the Bible because, like Genesis, this ancient narrative contains stories about the creation and early existence of humanity and about a primeval flood with a lone survivor and his family. Unlike Genesis, however, the Epic of Atrahasis concentrates on the creation of humanity alone and does not describe the creation of the rest of the world. Several interesting similarities and differences can be noted between the two accounts. In the Atrahasis Epic humans are created as a labor force to relieve the gods of this burden; neither of the Genesis versions (1:1–2:3 and 2:4-25) provides a reason for the creation of humanity. In the Atrahasis Epic humans are made from clay, mixed with the blood and flesh of a slaughtered god; in one of the Genesis versions, "the LORD God formed the man from the dust of the ground, and breathed into his nostrils the breath of life" (2:7). The Epic of Atrahasis explains that the flood occurred because the noise from all the people was bothering the gods; the Genesis story attributes the flood to God's regret at having made humans because they had become so wicked (6:11-13). In both accounts, one man (Atrahasis in the Mesopotamian story; Noah in the Genesis account) receives advance divine warning of the flood and is instructed to build a boat to escape, which he does, taking into the boat with him his family and a variety of animals. After the flood, the hero in each account makes an offering.

Whereas the question of dependence between the Mesopotamian stories and the Genesis stories is not uniformly answered by scholars, many scholars have concluded that the Genesis account is indebted to some extent to the Mesopotamian traditions, especially the flood stories. If that is the case, the ancient Hebrew writers recast these polytheistic tales within a monotheistic framework and interpreted the actions of people as having ethical consequences.

The Epic of Gilgamesh

Clay fragment containing portions of tablet 11

▷ Size: 15.24 cm. (6 in.) high; 13.33 cm. (5.25 in.) wide; 3.17 cm. (1.25 in.) thick
▷ Writing: Akkadian language in cuneiform script
▷ Provenance: Nineveh (Kuyunjik, in modern Iraq)

▷ Date: Seventh century B.C.E.

▷ Present location: British Museum (room 55)

▷ Identification number: ME K3375

The story of Gilgamesh was widely known throughout the ancient Near Eastern world. Gilgamesh, the main character in these tales, was the king of the Sumerian city of Uruk who ruled around 2600 B.C.E. A ruler named Gilgamesh likely actually existed (his name appears in the ancient Sumerian King List), but the stories preserved about him in these texts are more legendary than historical. These stories, which stressed the wisdom and heroic accomplishments of Gilgamesh, circulated for centuries in oral form, being shaped and adapted in the retelling before being written down. Known widely throughout the ancient Near East, Gilgamesh tales have been discovered at various sites in ancient Mesopotamia (including Nineveh, Nippur, Ashur, and Uruk), as well as at Emar in upper Syria, at Hattusa (the capital of the ancient Hittites in modern Turkey), and at Megiddo in ancient Canaan. The Megiddo fragment (IAA 1955-2), a portion of tablet 7 dated to the fourteenth century B.C.E., can be seen in the Israel Museum (Bronfman Archeology Wing). Copies of tablet 1 (OIM A29934), tablet 2 (OIM A3444), and tablet 3 (OIM A22007) are on display in the Mesopotamian Gallery of the Oriental Institute Museum of the University of Chicago.

How early these separate Gilgamesh tales were collected and woven together to form the continuous narrative referred to as the Gilgamesh Epic is unknown. Portions of at least three major editions of the epic have survived: one from the Old Babylonian period (2017-1595 B.C.E.), one very fragmentary version from the Middle Babylonian period (around 1200 B.C.E.), and one from the Neo-Assyrian period (934-612 B.C.E.). Eventually, the Gilgamesh Epic comprised twelve tablets. Unfortunately, no complete set of the twelve tablets has been found. Scholars have pieced together the Gilgamesh Epic from fragmentary versions of the tales discovered in various locations.

4. Tablet eleven of the Epic of Gilgamesh

The most complete version of the Gilgamesh Epic comes from the library of King Ashurbanipal of Assyria (ruled 669-627 B.C.E.), discovered in his palace at Nineveh. These twelve fragmentary tablets, which contain the Neo-Assyrian version of the story, are written in the Akkadian language in cuneiform script and date from the seventh century B.C.E. Although the tablets were discovered during the excavations at Nineveh led by Austin Henry Layard and later by Hormuzd Rassam during the middle of the nineteenth century, their contents were not widely known until 1872 when George E. Smith, an assistant in the British Museum, was examining the numerous cuneiform tablets possessed by the museum that had been discovered by Layard and Rassam. "The fragments of clay tablets were of all sizes," he later wrote, "from half an inch to a foot long, and were thickly coated with dirt, so that they had to be cleaned before anything could be seen on the surface."[1] Adept at reading cuneiform texts, Smith recognized in one of the tablets (tablet 11) a story about an ancient flood, similar to the biblical story of Noah. His announcement of this discovery to the public, in a paper presented to the Society of Biblical Archaeology in England on December 3, 1872, created much excitement. The large fragment on display in the British Museum is a portion of tablet 11. The fragment contains lines 55-106 and 108-269. Smith subsequently carried out excavations in Nineveh. Amazingly, on May 14, 1873, after only one week of digging at Nineveh, Smith found the tablet fragment that contained the major portion of the seventeen lines that had been missing from tablet 1.

In the Gilgamesh Epic the hero, whose father was Lugalbanda, king of Uruk in lower Mesopotamia, and whose mother was the goddess Ninsun, is described as being two-thirds god and one-third human. Gilgamesh meets Enkidu, who becomes his friend and companion in adventure. In one of their major exploits, Gilgamesh and Enkidu defeat Humbaba (or, Huwawa), the terrifying guardian of the cedar forest. When Humbaba pleads for his life, offering to become the servant of Gilgamesh, Enkidu advises the hero not to allow the fierce monster to live. The two adventurers kill Humbaba and cut off his head. In the next episode, the goddess Ishtar is attracted to Gilgamesh, but rather than accept her overtures, he rebuffs her with insults. Furious at such treatment, Ishtar asks for help from the god Anu, who responds by sending the Bull of Heaven to attack Gilgamesh and Enkidu. Once more the two heroes are successful and slay the bull. The other gods become angry not only at the slaying of the bull, but also at the insults that Enkidu subsequently casts upon Ishtar. After meeting in council, the gods decree that Enkidu must die. Thereafter, Enkidu weakens and soon dies, recounting before his death a dream he

---

1. George Smith, *Assyrian Discoveries: An Account of Explorations and Discoveries on the Site of Nineveh, during 1873 and 1874* (New York: Scribner, Armstrong & Co., 1875), p. 13.

had of the Underworld. Gilgamesh mourns the loss of his friend and struggles with the prospect of his own mortality. In search of immortality and the meaning of life, Gilgamesh sets off to find Utnapishtim, the survivor of the great flood who was granted immortality by the gods.

Tablet 11 begins with Gilgamesh asking Utnapishtim how he came to acquire eternal life. Utnapishtim responds by recounting for him the story of the flood. When the council of the gods decided to send the destructive flood, one of the gods, Ea, gave advance warning to Utnapishtim and instructed him to build a large boat, which when completed contained seven stories and was built like a large cube, almost two hundred feet tall and covering approximately one acre. Utnapishtim loaded the boat with all his possessions, his relatives, skilled craftsmen, and animals. For six days, a storm so fierce that it frightened even the gods unleashed a torrential rain that flooded the land, killing all the people. On the seventh day the storm abated, and the boat came to rest on Mount Nimush (or, Mount Nisir), usually identified with Pir Omar Gudrun in the Zagros Mountains, north of the city of As Sulaymaniyah, Iraq. For seven more days, Utnapishtim remained in the boat atop the mountain.

> When the seventh day arrived,
> I sent forth and set free a dove.
> The dove went forth, but came back;
> Since no resting-place for it was visible, she turned round.
> Then I sent forth and set free a swallow.
> The swallow went forth, but came back;
> Since no resting-place for it was visible, she turned round.
> Then I sent forth and set free a raven.
> The raven went forth and, seeing that the waters had diminished,
> He eats, circles, caws, and turns not round.
> Then I let out (all) to the four winds
>   And offered a sacrifice,
> I poured out a libation on the top of the mountain.
> Seven and seven cult-vessels I set up,
> Upon their pot-stands I heaped cane, cedarwood, and myrtle.
> The gods smelled the savor,
> The gods smelled the sweet savor,
> The gods crowded like flies about the sacrificer.[2]

Then one of the gods, Enlil, went on board the boat and granted eternal life to Utnapishtim and his wife:

---

2. "The Epic of Gilgamesh," translated by E. A. Speiser (*ANET*, 94-95).

Holding me by the hand, he took me aboard.
He took my wife aboard and made (her) kneel by my side.
Standing between us, he touched our foreheads to bless us:
"Hitherto Utnapishtim has been but human.
Henceforth Utnapishtim and his wife shall be like unto us gods.
Utnapishtim shall reside far away, at the mouth of the rivers!"
Thus they took me and made me reside far away, at the mouth
      of the rivers.[3]

After recounting this story, Utnapishtim tells Gilgamesh that he must stay awake for six days and seven nights, which is apparently a test. Gilgamesh falls asleep immediately and sleeps for seven days, thus failing the test. Upon awakening, he pleads with Utnapishtim:

[What then] shall I do, Utnapishtim,
    Whither shall I go,
[Now] that the Bereaver has laid hold on my [members]?
In my bedchamber lurks death,
And wherever I se[t my foot], there is death![4]

Before Gilgamesh departs in his boat, Utnapishtim tells him about a secret plant that can grant Gilgamesh new life. Gilgamesh then succeeds in diving deep into the sea and retrieving the plant. Soon thereafter, before Gilgamesh is able to benefit from the plant, a serpent, attracted by the fragrance of the plant, steals it from him. Grieving over his failure to attain immortality, Gilgamesh, along with his boatman, returns to the city of Uruk, bringing tablet 11 to a close. Tablet 12 is likely a later addition to the Gilgamesh Epic, since in this tablet Enkidu is still alive. In tablet 12 Enkidu volunteers to descend to the Underworld to retrieve two objects that Gilgamesh has lost. Once he has descended, however, Enkidu is not able to return because the Underworld seizes him. Gilgamesh pleads with the god Ea, who intercedes with Nergal, chief god of the underworld. Nergal then opens a hole in the earth, allowing the spirit of Enkidu to ascend and meet with Gilgamesh and report to him on the world of the dead.

The eleventh tablet of the Gilgamesh Epic is closely related to the Atrahasis Epic. In fact, the story of the flood in the Gilgamesh Epic is likely an adaptation of some version of the Atrahasis story. (The details of the Gilgamesh version are sufficiently different from the known text of the Atrahasis Epic that

3. *ANET*, p. 95.
4. *ANET*, p. 96.

the author of the Gilgamesh story was perhaps working from a different version of the Atrahasis Epic.) In one place in the Gilgamesh flood story, the hero of the flood, Utnapishtim, is actually called Atrahasis (which means "the exceedingly wise").

Biblical Significance

The Gilgamesh Epic created much popular interest when its contents were published, primarily because of the similarities between the story of Utnapishtim and the biblical story of Noah and the flood found in Genesis 6–9. Among the similarities often noted are the advance notice of the flood given to one individual (Utnapishtim and Noah), the instructions to build a boat, preservation of the hero's family and the animals aboard the boat, the boat coming to rest atop a mountain, the sending out of birds after the flood to determine if the world was habitable, and the offering of sacrifices after the flood. Although the differences between the two stories may be too great to support a theory of direct literary dependence, most scholars are convinced that the biblical flood narrative is to some degree dependent upon ancient Mesopotamian flood narratives. The biblical writer has taken a well-known story of a great flood and adapted it to fit his or her own religious worldview. While no copies of the Gilgamesh flood story yet have been found in ancient Palestine, clearly some of the Gilgamesh tales were known in the area, however, as evidenced by the discovery at Megiddo of a fourteenth-century fragment of tablet 7 of the Gilgamesh Epic.

Connections between other tablets of the Gilgamesh Epic and biblical literature have also been suggested, most notably with the book of Ecclesiastes. The concern with human mortality and the note of despair and pessimism that occupy Gilgamesh are also themes in Ecclesiastes. One particular passage from the Gilgamesh Epic that has echoes in Ecclesiastes is in tablet 10 when Gilgamesh meets the ale-wife Siduri and tells her of his quest to become immortal. In the Old Babylonian version of the story, Siduri tells Gilgamesh that his quest will not succeed. Rather than continuing to pursue this journey that will inevitably end in failure, he should return home and enjoy what he has in life. She states,

> Gilgamesh, whither rovest thou?
> The life thou pursuest thou shalt not find.
> When the gods created mankind,
> Death for mankind they set aside,
> Life in their own hands retaining.
> Thou, Gilgamesh, let full be thy belly,

Make thou merry by day and by night.
Of each day make thou a feast of rejoicing,
Day and night dance thou and play!
Let thy garments be sparkling fresh, thy head be washed; bathe thou
    in water.
Pay heed to the little one that holds on to thy hand,
Let thy spouse delight in thy bosom!
For this is the task of [mankind]![5]

This passage from Gilgamesh is often compared to the conclusion reached by the author of Ecclesiastes:

> Go, eat your bread with enjoyment, and drink your wine with a merry heart; for God has long ago approved what you do. Let your garments always be white; do not let oil be lacking on your head. Enjoy life with the wife whom you love, all the days of your vain life that are given you under the sun, because that is your portion in life and in your toil at which you toil under the sun. (9:7-9)

Sumerian King List

Clay prism

▷ Size: 20 cm. (7.87 in.) high; 9 cm. (3.54 in.) wide
▷ Writing: Sumerian language in cuneiform script
▷ Provenance: Larsa in Babylonia (in modern Iraq)
▷ Date: ca. 1800 B.C.E.
▷ Present location: Ashmolean Museum of Art and Archaeology, University of Oxford, Oxford, England
▷ Identification number: AN 1923.444

Fifteen copies of the Sumerian King List have survived. These copies, most dated to the eighteenth century B.C.E., contain many variations in their contents. The most extensive list is the one preserved on this clay prism now in the Ashmolean Museum in Oxford, England. Sometimes known as the Weld-Blundell Prism (named after Herbert Weld-Blundell who donated the prism

5. *ANET,* p. 90.

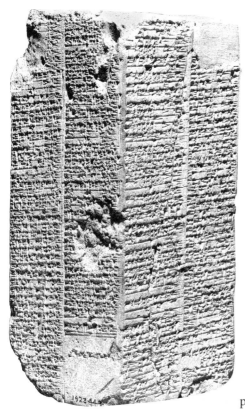

5. The Weld-Blundell Prism containing the Sumerian King List

to the museum), this four-sided prism is inscribed in two columns of text on each of its four sides. The inscription contains a list of the kings of various cities of Sumer prior to "the flood," a brief reference to the flood, and a list of kings after the flood. The first king is Alulim, king of Eridu; the last king in the Weld-Blundell list is Sin-magir, king of Isin. (Another version of the list adds one more name, Damiq-ilishu, the last king of Isin, who ruled 1816-1794 B.C.E.). The length of the reign of each king is given, which in many cases is unrealistically long. The reigns of the pre-flood kings range from 36,000 years to 18,600 years, whereas the post-flood reigns are much lower, ranging from 1500 years to 2 years.

Some of the copies of the Sumerian King List do not contain the list of the pre-flood kings. This portion of the list is usually considered to be a secondary addition and may have originated from a different source. (The pre-flood list is a part of the prism in the Ashmolean Museum.) The various copies of the Sumerian King List not only differ in whether or not they contain the pre-flood kings, but also in the order of the dynasties, the lengths of the reigns of certain kings, the names of the kings, and the number of kings. These variations indicate that the Sumerian King List had a complex history of composition and transmission. The variant versions probably came from a single original version composed around 2000 B.C.E. or earlier.

In the list, one king at a time is cited as a ruler in the land of Sumer, giving the impression that that king was the ruler of all of Sumer. Altogether, the Weld-Blundell Prism lists 134 kings ruling from eleven different cities. By presenting the kings in this manner, the author of the list was propagating the fictional idea that the land of Sumer had always been united under one ruler and that kingship had been divinely established. The suggestion has been made that the original purpose of the creation of the king list was to justify the reign of a particular king by showing that his kingship was the only legitimate kingship. Several interesting items appear in the list of kings: Gilgamesh, the hero-king of the Epic of Gilgamesh, is listed as one of the post-flood kings, as also is Etana, the central character of the Legend of Etana; the occupations of many of the kings are given (including boatman, jeweler, metal smith, shepherd, leatherworker, and priest); and one of the kings listed is a woman — "Ku-Ba'u, the woman tavern keeper."

The excerpt of the Sumerian King List given below follows mainly the wording of the Weld-Blundell Prism, with some portions corrected or added from other versions. The excerpt contains the listing of the pre-flood kings and the first few kings after the flood (paragraph divisions are not in the Sumerian original):

> After kingship had descended from the heavens, (the seat of) kingship was in (the city of) Eridu. In Eridu Alulim became king and reigned for 28,800 years. Alalgar reigned for 36,000 years. (In sum) two kings reigned for 64,800 years. Eridu was abandoned and its kingship was taken to (the city of) Badtibira.
>
> In Badtibira, Enmeluana reigned for 43,200 years; Enmegalana reigned for 28,800 years; Dumuzi, the shepherd, reigned for 36,000 years. (In sum) three kings reigned for 108,000 years.
>
> Then Badtibira was abandoned and its kingship was taken to (the city of) Larak. In Larak, Ensipaziana reigned for 28,800 years. (In sum) 1 king reigned for 28,800 years.
>
> Then Larak was abandoned and its kingship was taken to (the city of) Sippar. In Sippar Enmendurana became king and reigned for 21,000 years. (In sum) 1 king reigned for 21,000 years.
>
> Then Sippar was abandoned and its kingship was taken to (the city of) Shuruppak. In Shuruppak, Ubar-Tutu became king and reigned for 18,600 years. (In sum) 1 king reigned for 18,600 years.
>
> In five cities eight kings reigned for 385,200 years. Then the flood swept over (the land).
>
> After the flood had swept over (the land and) kingship had (once again) descended from the heavens, (the seat of) kingship was in (the city of) Kish. In Kish, Gishur became king and reigned for 1,200 years. Kullassina-bel reigned for 900 years. Nangish-lishma reigned for 670 (?) years. Endarahana reigned for 420 years, 3 months, and 3½ days, Babum . . . reigned for 300 years, Pu'annum reigned for 840 years, Kalibum reigned for 960 years, Kalumum reigned for 840 years, Zuqaqqip reigned for 900 years, Atab reigned for 600 years, Mashda, the son of Atab, reigned for 840 years,

Arwi'um, the son of Mashda, reigned for 720 years. Etana, the shepherd, who flew to the heavens and made fast all the foreign lands, became king and reigned for 1,500 years.[1]

Biblical Significance

The Sumerian King List is of interest to students of the Bible for at least two reasons: its mention of a major flood and the incredibly long reigns attributed to the kings. The brief mention of the flood in the Sumerian King List is reminiscent of the biblical flood story involving Noah (Genesis 6). Admittedly, the Sumerian King List gives no details of the flood, but the Sumerian flood, like the biblical flood, was viewed as an event of tremendous proportions, covering the land. The flood serves as a dividing line: the institution of kingship had to be reinstated after the flood, and kings are listed as being prior to the flood or after the flood. An ancient Sumerian version of the flood has been found that has many similarities with the flood story in tablet eleven of the Gilgamesh Epic and with the Atrahasis Epic, all of which have certain affinities with the Genesis flood story. (See the articles on the Atrahasis Epic and the Gilgamesh Epic.) Some readers have understood the flood reference in the Sumerian King List, as well as the flood stories from Mesopotamian literature, as evidence for a worldwide flood, which is then seen as support for the historicity of the biblical flood account. Such conclusions are not warranted by the evidence, however. At most, one can say that the idea of a massive, ancient flood was widespread in antiquity. Whether such a flood actually occurred, however, is another matter. Stories and folk tales of major floods would not be unexpected in Mesopotamian traditions, since Mesopotamia (the land "between the rivers") lay between the Tigris and Euphrates Rivers, both of which were prone to flooding between February and May. Since this portion of the biblical narrative postdates the Mesopotamian traditions (the final form of this portion of Genesis is usually dated to the fifth century B.C.E., although its oral or written sources may be dated as much as six hundred years earlier), it is conceivable, if not likely, that the biblical writer has borrowed and adapted Mesopotamian flood traditions. Such borrowing could have occurred through intermediate traditions or directly from contact with Mesopotamian traditions during the period of the Babylonian exile of the people of Judah.

The other connection between the Sumerian King List and the Bible is the listing of the reigns of the kings, comparable to the genealogies in Genesis 5

---

1. "Sumerian King List," translated by Piotr Michalowski, in *The Ancient Near East: Historical Sources in Translation,* ed. Mark W. Chavalas (Malden, Mass.: Blackwell Publishing, 2006), p. 82.

and 11. In both the Sumerian and biblical lists, approximately ten generations are listed prior to the flood. In both, the reigns or life spans are exceptionally long (longer in the Sumerian list, where the longest reign is 36,000 years compared to the longest life span in Genesis of 969 years). In both traditions the time spans decline and generally are longer before the flood than after. Obviously, these chronological listings are not to be taken literally, even if that is how the original author and readers/hearers would have understood the numbers. For the Sumerian King List, the lengths of reigns seem to have been derived from astronomical or mathematical calculations. The incredibly long reigns, particularly for the pre-flood rulers, were possibly used to enhance the status of the kings, who are often described in the list as divine or semi-divine rulers. The biblical writer was likely indebted to this Mesopotamian tradition of incredibly long ages for ancestral, heroic persons. If so, the biblical writer (or the sources he used) exercised tremendous restraint, lowering the time spans from tens of thousands to hundreds. The purpose served by these long and decreasing life spans in Genesis is not clear. Perhaps the biblical writer, by mimicking Mesopotamian traditions of long time spans, sought to enhance the Hebrew tradition. Or, perhaps the declining ages was intended to make a theological point: the result of human sin and disobedience was a shortening of the human life span.

Israel's Ancestral, Exodus, and Settlement Periods

Ram Caught in a Thicket

Statuette of gold, silver, copper, lapis, shell, and coral

▷ Size: 40 cm. (15.8 in.) high
▷ Provenance: Ur, the Great Death Pit; modern Iraq
▷ Date: Early Dynastic III (2600–ca. 2350 B.C.E.)
▷ Present location: British Museum (room 56)
▷ Identification number: ME 122200

After these things God tested Abraham. He said to him, "Abraham!" And he said, "Here I am." He said, "Take your son, your only son Isaac, whom you love, and go to the land of Moriah, and offer him there as a burnt offering on one of the mountains that I shall show you." So Abraham rose early in the morning, saddled his donkey, and took two of his young men with him, and his son Isaac; he cut the wood for the burnt offering, and set out and went to the place in the distance that God had shown him. On the third day Abraham looked up and saw the place far away. Then Abraham said to his young men, "Stay here with the donkey; the boy and I will go over there; we will worship, and then we will come back to you." Abraham took the wood of the burnt offering and laid it on his son Isaac, and he himself carried the fire and the knife. So the two of them walked on together. Isaac said to his father Abraham, "Father!" And he said, "Here I am, my son." He said, "The fire and the wood are here, but where is the lamb for a burnt offering?" Abraham said, "God himself will provide the lamb for a burnt offering, my son." So the two of them walked on together.

When they came to the place that God had shown him, Abraham built an altar there and laid the wood in order. He bound his son Isaac, and laid him on the altar, on top of the wood. Then Abraham reached out his hand and took the knife to kill his son. But the angel of the Lord called to him from heaven, and said, "Abraham, Abraham!" And he said, "Here I am." He said, "Do not lay your hand on the boy or do anything to him; for now I know that you fear God, since you have not withheld your son, your only son, from me." And Abraham looked up and saw a ram, caught in a thicket by its horns. Abraham went and took the ram and offered it up as a burnt offering instead of his son. So Abraham called that place "The Lord will provide"; as it is said to this day, "On the mount of the Lord it shall be provided." (Gen. 22:1-14)

In the late fall of 1927, the archaeologist Leonard Woolley uncovered spectacular discoveries in the ancient city of Ur that made headlines all over the world. It was his sixth season of digging on an expedition jointly sponsored by the British Museum and the University of Pennsylvania. In 1922 he had sailed from London to Basra in southern Iraq, then on to Baghdad where he obtained an excavation permit to lead the work of excavating for evidence of ancient Mesopotamian civilization. On November 2, Woolley arrived at Ur where he was met by his foreman, Hamoudi, who had worked with Woolley at Carchemish. Conditions were primitive in the area, so his team lived in tents until they built a mud-brick excavation house.

By 1923 Woolley had completed his survey of the area and decided to begin excavation around the ruins of the ancient ziggurat, or step-temple. (The "pyramids" of Mexico are step-temples.) The crew began their exploration by digging two large trenches, called trench A and trench B. Many precious objects were discovered in trench A, immediately named the "gold trench." The trenches also yielded evidence of ancient tombs. But Woolley thought his team lacked sufficient experience to excavate these tombs, so he decided to wait for a future season. Over the next three seasons he and his crew excavated several temples, buildings, and private houses, but no tombs.

During the course of these early excavations, a sensation was created by the announcement that Woolley had found evidence of a great flood of biblical proportions. Sumerian legends told of a great deluge in antiquity, and Woolley's digging uncovered eleven feet of silt, which he said "would probably mean a flood not less than twenty-five feet deep." He estimated that such a flood would cover an area about 300 miles long and 800 miles wide: "The whole of the fertile land between the Elamite mountains and the high Syrian desert would disappear, every village would be destroyed, and only a few of the old cities, set high on their built-up mounds, would survive the disaster."[1] For the Sumerians, "the Flood" of the legends was the only flood that really mattered, "what we call Noah's flood."[2] Naturally, such statements caused a sensation in England and elsewhere. But Woolley knew that this flood nevertheless was localized: "It was not a universal deluge; it was a vast flood in the valley of the Tigris and the Euphrates which drowned the whole of the habitable land between the mountains and the desert; for the people who lived there that was all the world."[3]

In his fourth season Woolley decided to begin excavating some of the 1800 tombs he had previously discovered. Among them were sixteen he named the "royal tombs" because of their size, their use of stone, and the value of the objects found within. In one of them, tomb PG 779, he discovered the so-called

---

1. Leonard Woolley, *Excavations at Ur* (New York: Thomas Y. Crowell Co., n.d.), p. 36.

2. Woolley, *Excavations at Ur*, p. 34.

3. Woolley, *Excavations at Ur*, p. 36.

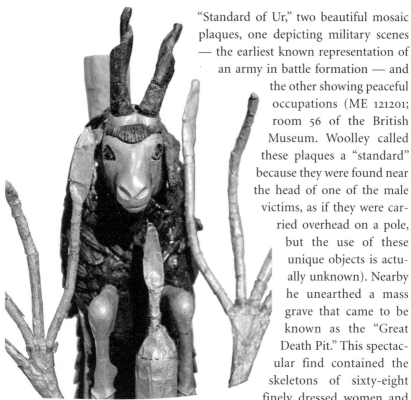

6. Detail of the figure the "Ram Caught in a Thicket" from Ur

"Standard of Ur," two beautiful mosaic plaques, one depicting military scenes — the earliest known representation of an army in battle formation — and the other showing peaceful occupations (ME 121201; room 56 of the British Museum. Woolley called these plaques a "standard" because they were found near the head of one of the male victims, as if they were carried overhead on a pole, but the use of these unique objects is actually unknown). Nearby he unearthed a mass grave that came to be known as the "Great Death Pit." This spectacular find contained the skeletons of sixty-eight finely dressed women and six men, probably guards. Small cups were found beside each; apparently they died after taking poison, ceremonial victims of some ritual. Likely they were slain to provide attendants for a prominent ruler or priest in the afterlife. Their bodies were laid in orderly fashion, surrounded by many valuable objects. An ancient game board was also found in the pit (originally of wood, long disintegrated, covered with mosaic squares of bone, shell, lapis lazuli, and red limestone in a matrix of bitumen) with seven disc-shaped playing pieces, black and white, for two players. Woolley dubbed it the "Royal Game of Ur," and today it can be seen in the British Museum (ME 120834; room 56).

Other spectacular objects found by Woolley include the silver head of a lion with eyes of shell and lapis, perhaps intended as a magic talisman; jewelry, golden utensils, and an elaborate headdress of gold, lapis, and carnelian belonging to the lady/queen Puabi. The magnificent musical instruments known as the "Great Lyre" (again, a pair of matching objects, now in the British Museum [ME 121198a; room 56] and the University of Pennsylvania Museum [B17694]) were discovered in the "King's Grave." These beautiful lyres, made of wood and inlaid ivory, with a golden bull's head on the front, were found crushed together by the ancient collapse of the tombs and eventually were separated during conservation. But it was in the western corner of this same pit that two of the most spectacular objects of archaeology were discovered: a pair of twin figures that Woolley named the "ram caught in a thicket" after the biblical story of Abraham and Isaac. These two beautiful statuettes were so crushed into the earth that it was difficult to discern how to begin their conservation. Luckily, one was in profile while the other was face up, enabling archaeologists better to determine their original form. Woolley wrote of this find:

> When we found them, both statues were in very sorry plight. The wood had decayed to nothing, the bitumen was dried powder, the plaster of Paris reduced to irregular lumps and pellets; one figure was lying on its side, crushed absolutely flat so that the shell curls of the two flanks touched each other and the animal was a mere silhouette distorted by pressure, the other, standing upright, preserved some of its roundness but had been telescoped together and the legs had been broken off from the body, flattened and twisted. Nothing except the earth around them kept the fragments of the lapis and shell inlay in position, and if that position were once lost, there would have been no guide at all for the restoration of the figure; the whole thing was therefore solidified with hot wax poured liberally on, and then bands of waxed muslin were applied to every exposed part until the ram was as securely wrapped up as a mummy and could be lifted from the earth.[4]

The ram pictured here (see also plate 1) is in the British Museum; its twin is in the University of Pennsylvania Museum of Archaeology and Anthropology in Philadelphia (inventory number 30-12-702). Originally Woolley had shaped their backs with the same curvature, believing the two figures to be identical. Recently, however, during extensive restoration by the University of Pennsylvania it was determined that the ram in their possession originally stood in a more upright position, which would enable its front hooves to rest naturally on the branches of the tree in a more secure position. It has now been restored to its original form.

Both of the rams are beautifully made with a complex mixture of precious materials. Their heads and legs are of gold leaf, as are the trees and flowers; the ears are of copper. The bellies of the rams were originally of silver, which has disintegrated. The fleece on the bodies is of white shell; the fleece on the shoulders and the horns is lapis lazuli. The rams stand on a base of silver that is cov-

---

4. Woolley, *Excavations at Ur*, pp. 84-85.

ered with mosaics of lapis, shell, and red limestone. The core of the figures originally was wooden, but the wood had long since disintegrated. Apparently the posts extending upwards through the backs of the rams were intended to hold a pair of bowls, and if so, the rams likely stood on small tables.

Although the figures are reminiscent of Abraham's ram, they are actually he-goats; and they are not "caught in a thicket," but nibbling on the upper branches of a tree, the sacred tree often portrayed in Mesopotamian religion. (This pose is often seen among the various gazelles and browsing animals of Africa.) The flowers of the tree also are symbolic. These stylized rosettes represent Inanna, the goddess of fertility, love, and war. Each of them has eight points, and the same form is found in many contexts in Mesopotamia, even as much as four hundred years earlier. The symbolism of the shape, however, is unknown. Kings are often portrayed with the sacred tree, and Woolley believed that these tombs belonged to nobility. Other theories have suggested they served as a burial place for priests and priestesses.

Biblical Significance

Since these figures clearly do not represent "the ram caught in a thicket" of the Genesis story — as Woolley knew; he only said they were reminiscent of the Abraham story — that connection cannot be their biblical significance. What, then, do they tell us? All of these magnificent finds of Sir Leonard Woolley (he was knighted following his final season at Ur) may be dated to the Early Dynastic III period, 2600–ca. 2350 B.C.E., and modern scholars would not place the time of Abraham so early. (Competing theories range from 2200 to 1000 B.C.E.) Nevertheless, the discoveries at Ur are a significant indication of an amazing level of cultural sophistication in an early period in the locale identified as the birthplace of the father of the Hebrews. If Abraham and his family came from Ur, a city of such considerable cultural advancement, to the tents of the land of Canaan, it further dramatizes the biblical story of his sacrificial following of the promises of an unknown God.

The Rosetta Stone

Granodiorite stela

> ▷ Size: 114.4 cm. (45.04 in.) high; 72.3 cm. (28.46 in.) wide; 27.9 cm (10.98 in.) thick
> ▷ Writing: Egyptian hieroglyphic; demotic (cursive Egyptian); Greek

▷ Provenance: Fort St. Julien, el-Rasid (Rosetta), Egypt
▷ Date: 196 B.C.E.
▷ Present location: British Museum (room 4)
▷ Identification number: EA 24

The Rosetta Stone is the most visited object in the enormous British Museum, viewed by millions of visitors since it was first displayed to the public in 1802. It has been called "the most famous piece of rock in the world." Unlike many famous ancient artifacts, such as the King Tut treasures, the fame of the Rosetta Stone does not derive from its intrinsic value or beauty, nor from the message of its inscription, as is the case, for example, with the Code of Hammurabi. Yet this inscription has yielded incalculable value for an understanding of ancient history, as it provided the key to unlocking the mystery of Egyptian hieroglyphics. As a result, scholars have been able to decipher the meaning of countless historical writings previously lost to civilization.

The inscription itself is unremarkable, a flattering decree issued by the priests of Memphis that granted a royal cult to the young King Ptolemy V, only thirteen years old at the time, in exchange for certain favors. It was written in three languages, representing the languages used by the powerful and literate groups of Egypt at that time: hieroglyphics, understood and used only by the priestly class; demotic, the cursive script used by the literate population at that time; and Greek, the language of the ruling government. Since ancient Greek was a language understood by modern scholars, the discovery of the Rosetta Stone enabled them to compare the Greek letters against the hieroglyphic signs and therefore solve the mystery of hieroglyphics.

That task, however, was by no means easily accomplished. Two remark-

7. The Rosetta Stone

able scholars, one French and one English — Jean-François Champollion and Thomas Young (nicknamed in his day, Thomas "Phenomenon" Young) — each contributed to the translation of the stone and the understanding of hieroglyphics. Like any two scientists who mutually make a great discovery, each believed himself the first to solve the ancient riddle, as Young's memorial in Westminster Abbey specifically claims. Nevertheless, both played a vital role in the eventual success of the translation.

The stone as we have it today is not complete; it is missing its upper portion, which likely contained traditional symbols and decorations depicting the king among the gods. Its shape no doubt was typical of such stelae, rounded and tombstone-like at the top. The missing portion would have added another 35 cm. (13.78 in.) to its height. The stone broke along a seam of pink granite within it, perhaps when toppled by irate Coptic monks during the Christian religious reforms following the decree of Emperor Theodosius closing all Egyptian temples in 392 c.e. Or it may have been broken during subsequent transport or use, as most of the valuable stone was stripped from the empty temples and used elsewhere.

Where the stela was originally located is unknown, but it was not at Rosetta (el-Rashid); that city was founded later on alluvial land that did not exist at that time. We do know, according to the inscription itself, that it was to be placed in a temple next to an image of the pharaoh. (One suggestion has been the royal city of Sais, which was a celebrated site of ancient wisdom.) Because the inscription had certain propagandistic values — it magnifies the virtues of the pharaoh and his contributions to the nation — most likely it would have been erected at the base of an outer wall within the temple compound, in a semipublic area where it could be viewed by at least the higher-ranking portion of the population. The back of the stone is also rough and unfinished, unlike the polished surface at the front, further indication that it was designed to be viewed from only one side. Its base is quite flat, suggesting that it was made to rest on a flat surface such as a courtyard floor.

The stone's journey after its removal is also unknown, but eventually it came to Rashid where it became part of the construction material for a fortress being built by the Mamluk ruler of Egypt at that time, Sultan Qaitbay (1468-1495 c.e.). Over the centuries the fortress fell into ruin, and the Rosetta Stone might never have been discovered except for an accident of history. The French under Napoleon invaded Egypt in 1798 to make war against the ruling Ottoman Turks and the British who supported them. In July of 1799, as they were preparing fortifications in the old Qaitbay fortress, now named Fort Julien, the stone was discovered in a portion of an ancient wall. Napoleon had brought some 150 scientists and scholars along with the military as part of his colonial ambitions, and the soldiers had been alerted to be on the watch for valuable historical objects, including inscriptions. The stone immediately was brought to the attention of a young French officer of the engineering battalion, Pierre François Xavier Bouchard, who recognized its worth as a historical artifact. In spite of repeated searches, no pieces of the missing portion of the stela were discovered then or have ever been found since.

The fortunes of war turned against the French, and the Rosetta Stone came into the possession of the English in 1801. Subsequently King George III donated it to the British Museum in 1802 with these words painted on its left side: "Captured in Egypt by the British army in 1801"; and on its right side, "Presented by King George III." Originally the stone was displayed on a horizontal angle, supported at its base and sides, without any cover over it. White chalk was pressed into the engraved letters for ease of reading, and wax then was applied to the surface for protection. Though visitors were not allowed to touch the stone's surface, eventually the decision was taken to protect it by glass. For almost two centuries the stela remained in the same position, essentially unchanged. In 1917, during World War I, it was hidden fifty feet underground in a tube station for two years to protect it from bombing. In 1999 conservation work was done to clean the stone of the dust and dirt accumulated over the centuries that had left it blackened. Following this cleaning, the stone was placed in an upright position for the first time since it was displayed originally in Egypt, and it is in this position that visitors see it today.

Biblical Significance

Coptic Christians in Egypt regarded hieroglyphics as a language of idolatrous and evil superstition. The Coptic language had become the tongue of Christian Egypt, and the persecutions of the Hebrews in Egypt as portrayed in the Bible caused fierce animosity among Egyptian Christians toward anything connected with the ancient religion of Egypt. Later Arab scholars, however, developed an interest in hieroglyphics and made various significant observations concerning them. By the time Western scholars began to scrutinize these texts, all knowledge of how to translate them had been lost. After the discovery of the Rosetta Stone and its subsequent translation, this knowledge was put to use by biblical scholars eager to know more about the religious ancestry of both Christians and Jews.

Neither the inscription itself nor the king of the Rosetta Stone has any relevance for the biblical story. Nevertheless, without it vital facts that are essential to an understanding of the Bible would have been lost. One of the most critical pieces of information derived from hieroglyphic texts was found on the Merneptah inscription, often called the "Israel Stela" (see the article "Merneptah Stela [or, Israel Stela]") that is the earliest existing mention of Israel. It correctly identifies Israel as a people rather than an organized nation at that time, thanks to an understanding of hieroglyphic prefixes known as determinatives that identify the categories of words. The date of this inscription has proved vitally important for scholars by establishing a benchmark for identifying the emergence of the Hebrew people in Palestine. Furthermore, though it does not place Israel or the family of Joseph in Egypt, this inscription is the oldest connection of Egypt with the ancestors of the Jewish nation.

Although the Merneptah inscription is the most dramatic of the biblical insights gained from hieroglyphics, it is by no means the only such example. The chronology of early Egyptian history was established in large part through the lists of pharaohs and their deeds that were inscribed on their mortuary temples and elsewhere, and there is virtually no possibility of gaining background information on the earliest story of the Hebrew people without it.

Amarna Tablets

Clay tablets

▷ Size: Various; see text below
▷ Writing: Dialects of Akkadian, in cuneiform script
▷ Provenance: Ancient Akhetaten, el-Amarna, Egypt
▷ Date: ca. 1365-1335 B.C.E.
▷ Present location: British Museum (rooms 55 and 57)
▷ Identification numbers: ME E29832 (tablet EA 299), ME E29844 (tablet EA 252), ME E29855 (tablet EA 245), ME E29831 (tablet EA 228), ME E29848 (tablet EA 330), ME E29785 (tablet EA 9), ME E29793 (tablet EA 23), and ME E29836 (EA 323). (The longer numbers are the British Museum numbers; the shorter are the standard tablet numbers.)

Sometime around the year 1887, Egyptian peasants living on the plains of el-Amarna unearthed a large cache of clay tablets in the ancient city of Akhetaten, which briefly served as the capital of Egypt during the reign of Amenhotep IV (Amenophis IV, also known as Akhenaten). By 1907, 358 tablets had been discovered and made their way into the collections of various museums. Since that time the number of tablets has reached 382; one tablet was discovered as recently as 1979. Of this number, 350 are letters. The remainder comprises various genres (myths, word lists, etc.). The tablets generally range in size from ca. 5 cm. wide by 6.5 cm. high (2 in. by 2.5 in.) to ca. 9 cm. wide by 23 cm. high (3.5 in. by 9 in.). Today this collection is spread among several world museums, including the Egyptian Museum in Cairo (fifty tablets), the British Museum (ninety-five tablets), and the Louvre (seven tablets). The majority of the Amarna tablets are in the Vorderasiatisches Museum (Museum of Ancient Near Eastern Art, Pergamum Museum), Berlin (203 tablets). Tablets on display at the time of this writing, in addition to the eight at the British Museum, include three at the Louvre (AO 7098 [tablet EA 365], AO 7096 [tablet EA 366], and AO 7094 [tablet EA 364]) — all in room D, ground floor, Sully Wing, section 4); one at the Ashmolean Museum, Oxford (AN 1893.1-41 [408]; tablet EA 43; room 6); and an unnumbered group at the Egyptian Museum in Cairo (room 3).

The letters in this collection were sent to the Egyptian pharaoh, Akhenaten, and stemmed from two sources: various vassals of Egypt in neighboring states, and his fellow kings in Babylonia, Syria (Mitanni), Asia Minor (Hatti; the Hittites), Cyprus (Alashiya), and Arzawa (a small state in southwest Asia Minor). Some forty of the letters came from the kings, the remainder from various vassal authorities. Remarkably, these important letters only spanned about thirty years, and perhaps less than that. They have provided, however, the finest existing resources for understanding the relationships between these rulers. Even more importantly, from the biblical point of view, they give us additional insight into a mysterious group in Palestine, the *habiru*. Both these features combine to provide further clues for understanding the social and political situation in the land of Canaan at the beginning of the biblical period.

The Amarna letters show that the "Great Kings," as they liked to call themselves, composed an early version of the "old boys' club." They addressed one another as "brother," and spoke of their wives as "sisters" (which, of course, in some cases was literally true!). One might think they were all one big, happy family, and that was a fiction they sought to maintain. Lesser rulers — for example, in Palestine — were spoken of as "servants." No serious diplomatic negotiations are dealt with in these tablets; that was left either to face-to-face meetings or was handled through diplomatic representatives. The business of these texts almost exclusively concerned gifts wanted or sent, travel plans for themselves or their queens, or complaints and requests from lesser officials.

The matter of gifts was especially touchy. If a ruler felt he had received a gift of lesser value than one he had sent the pharaoh, he would grumble about it in his next letter. All of the rulers outside of Egypt desired gold as their present from the pharaoh, since none of them had gold mines in their territories. In exchange, they sent valuables from their own region. For example, in the case of Cyprus (Alashiya), copper ingots were much desired and often sent. From Asia Minor and Mesopotamia, horses — especially expensive and valuable — were prized, and lapis lazuli was a common gift to the neighboring states. Vari-

8. An assortment of Amarna tablets

ous other precious and semiprecious stones, as well as rare varieties of wood, were frequently included in the gifts exchanged among the rulers.

These presents might be sent on the occasion of the birth of a child, the ascension to the throne by a ruler, or virtually any excuse to prime the pump for a return gift by the recipient. For example, on one occasion the ruler of Cyprus included a small amount of ivory among his gifts to the pharaoh. That is especially odd, since the primary source of ivory in the ancient world was Egypt where there was certainly no scarcity of it. The point of including a token amount of ivory was to prompt the pharaoh to send him a substantial amount of ivory in his return gift.

All of these games had a serious purpose. The kings considered such gifts essential as ongoing proof of mutual standing in the "club" of the Great Kings. To be snubbed suggested an implication of inferiority and perhaps trouble on the horizon. Likewise, these presents were important domestically to display their power to their courts. Of course, the utilitarian value of certain gifts is evident as well: gold was necessary to fund operations, horses and chariots essential for warfare, and beautiful objects important to decorate their extravagant palaces.

Equally significant were the plans for travel between the states, a great deal more of which went on than previously suspected. Face-to-face meetings helped solidify relationships. Daughters also were sent by the kings to become the wives of their "brothers." The Egyptians, however, would not permit any foreign male to marry one of their princesses, for fear a foreigner would become ruler of Egypt; and as they were "divine" monarchs descended from the gods, that was not a possibility. (Later an exception would be made in the case of Alexander the Great — principally because he had an army behind him — but also because he suffered from the delusion, or at least allowed others to believe, that he also was a descendant of the gods.) Of course, Egypt's exclusivity in this matter was a sore point with the other rulers.

The letters from the vassals are even more revealing than the letters between equals. Whereas the kings showed little of themselves or daily events in their letters, the vassals' letters were full of them. Of course, they mostly complained about oversights, or perceived slights, from the pharaoh or his officials or sought to undermine other servants to ingratiate themselves with the king. In truth, they usually were attempting to divert attention from the real subject that frequently concerned the pharaoh, their tardiness in sending the tax revenues they owed him.

But one topic that occurs often in this correspondence is the danger posed from the group known as the *habiru*. In fact, the Amarna letters have become a chief source of knowledge concerning these people, whose name has often been connected with the early ancestors of Israel, the Hebrews. The *habiru* are mentioned in several of the letters that are on display in room 57 of the British Museum, which are discussed below.

The other three letters on display in the British Museum, in room 55, do not deal with the *habiru*. Tablet ME E29785 (EA 9) was sent to the pharaoh (either Amenhotep IV or Tutankhamen) by Burnaburrias, a king of the Kassite dynasty of Babylon, asking for more gold to be sent to him and requesting that the pharaoh not deal with the Assyrians who have come to him. The Assyrians are his (Burnaburrias's) vassals and have come on their own, not with his authority. They are thus to be sent away empty-handed. Burnaburrias reminds the pharaoh that his ancestor, Kurigalzu, had remained loyal to the Egyptians and refused to join with the Canaanites in a revolt against the Egyptians. Tablet ME E29793 (EA 23), is from Tushratta, king of Mitanni, to Amenhotep III. One of the people Tushratta mentions in the opening greeting is his daughter, who is one of the pharaoh's wives. The purpose of the letter is to inform the pharaoh that Tushratta has sent a statue of the goddess Shausha (Ishtar) to Egypt at the goddess's request. The Mitanni king requests that the statue be returned after due honor has been accorded the goddess. The other Amarna letter in room 55, ME E29836 (EA 323), is a letter from Yidya, who was king of

Ashkelon, informing the pharaoh that the pharaoh's order for glass had been filled and the glass sent.

Biblical Significance

A repeated theme in the letters of the vassals was the threat of an outcast group called the *habiru* (also spelled *'apiru* [*'Apiru*]). The meaning of the term is uncertain, but these people were found in Palestine and every land bordering on it. Who were they?

The lavish wealth referred to in the exchange of letters between the Great Kings is partly responsible for the genesis of the *habiru*. As the city-states grew and flourished, the kings demanded more and more labor to support their enterprises. As in the case of Ramesses II himself, and later on Israelite soil with King Solomon, peasant farmers were forced into labor camps for extended periods (the corvée). As the kings grew in wealth, poverty increased among the peasants, who had less time to work their own land. Unable to pay their debts, many of them were forced into indentured servitude, if not prison or outright slavery.

As a result, increasingly the poor fled their native lands for a life in the wilderness. There they joined informal bands of people like themselves for mutual support and protection. Naturally, among this group also could be found a variety of thieves, violent criminals, and dangerous political exiles. Some of these *habiru* groups raided villages and occasionally threatened Egyptian outposts seeking supplies and arms. Not surprisingly, they were not a welcome presence anywhere.

In the Amarna tablet ME E29832 (EA 299), the Egyptian ruler in Gazru (Gezer) pleads with the pharaoh for military assistance:

> To the king, my Lord, my god, the Sun, the Sun [f]rom the sky: Message of Yapahu, the ruler of Gazru, your servant, the dirt at your feet, the groom of your horses. Truly I fall at the feet of the king, my lord, my god, and my Sun, the Sun from the sky, 7 times and 7 times, on the stomach and on the back. I have listened to the words of the messenger of the king, my lord, very carefully. May the king, my lord, the Sun from the sky, take thought for his land. Since the 'Apiru [*habiru*] are stronger than we, may the king, my lord, <g>ive me his help, and may *the king*, my lord, get *me* away from the 'Apiru lest the 'Apiru destroy us.[1]

1. William L. Moran, ed., *The Amarna Letters* (Baltimore: The Johns Hopkins University Press, 1992), pp. 340-41. In the text, [ ] indicates restored text, < > indicates omission by the scribe, and italics indicate the translation is doubtful.

This period was one in which Egypt was preoccupied with domestic affairs, and therefore its wider empire came under severe strain due to instability and insurrection.

How do these *habiru* relate to the biblical Hebrews, or do they? That question has never been definitively answered. The words themselves seem to have a linguistic connection, but that is not absolutely certain, either. What we can say for sure is that the two groups are not identical. The *habiru* extended across several nations long before the Hebrews appeared in Israel and therefore cannot be equated with the Hebrews of the early chapters of the Bible. Nevertheless, when the descendants of Abraham, Isaac, and Joseph appeared in Palestine — by whatever means — they certainly would have been regarded as *habiru* by the local inhabitants, and just as unwelcome.

Furthermore, many of these letters were sent from familiar biblical cities in the Palestine district of Egyptian control. Tablet ME E29855 (EA 245) is from Megiddo, as is one tablet in the Louvre (AO 7098 [EA 365]). Tablet ME E29831 (EA 228) is from the ruler of Hazor, Abdi-tirshi, asserting his fidelity to the pharaoh and assuring him that all is in good order in his city. Similarly, Shipti-Ball of Lachish assures the pharaoh of his loyalty (ME E29848 [EA 330]). In a familiar note in these letters, King Biridiya of Megiddo accuses another ruler, the king of Acco, of treasonous conduct by his releasing of Labayu, whom he refers to as one of the *"habiru"* (figurative; similar to our use of "terrorist"), instead of sending him captive to Egypt (ME E29855). In yet another tablet, Yapahu, ruler of Gezer, begs the pharaoh for help in defending his city against *habiru* raids (ME E29832 [EA 299]).

Most interesting is the letter from Labayu himself to the pharaoh. In tablet ME E29844 (EA 252) he is identified as the ruler of Shechem, in the central hill country of Palestine, which apparently had been a power base for some *habiru* activities. Labayu may have been in league with the *habiru*, since he had to deny that he knew of his son's "consorting" with the *habiru* (EA 254) and agreed to hand him over to the pharaoh. (In EA 246, Biridiya had accused the two sons of Labayu of giving money to the *habiru* to wage war against him.) But Labayu insists that he had not violated the pharaoh's orders by capturing a certain town; he was only striking in self-defense: "When an ant is struck, does it not fight back and bite the hand of the man that struck it?"[2] (For further information on the *habiru*, see the "Biblical Significance" section of the article on the Treaty of Kadesh.)

In summary, the discovery of the Amarna tablets has been important in clarifying the sociological setting in which the ancestors of Israel first appear in the pages of the Bible.

---

2. Moran, p. 305.

Akhenaten: Stela and Panel, Adoration of the Aten

Painted limestone

▷ Size: Stela — 44 cm. (17.32 in.) high, 39 cm. (15.35 in.) wide; panel — 53 cm. (20.87 in.) high, 48 cm. (18.90 in.) wide

▷ Provenance: Tell el-Amarna

▷ Date: ca. 1353-1336 B.C.E.

▷ Present location: Egyptian Museum in Cairo (room 3, ground floor)

▷ Identification number: Stela — JE 44865; panel, TR — 10.11.26.4

The figures depicted in the stela and panel represent a fascinating and intriguing period in Egyptian history, the reign of Amenhotep IV (Amenophis IV), now known as Akhenaten (ca. 1353-1336 B.C.E.). For the first — and only — time in Egyptian history, the nation officially recognized only one god: Aten, the sun disk. All other gods were declared false, their temples were closed, and many of their images destroyed. The pharaoh who led this remarkable religious revolution would later be declared a heretic and every vestige of his reign would be destroyed. Who was this radical pharaoh, and what led to these dramatic changes? Furthermore, was this "monotheism before Moses," and did the theories of Akhenaten influence the religion of the Hebrews?

Nothing has been discovered from the early life of the young Pharaoh Amenhotep IV to indicate the promptings that led to his revolutionary ideas. His early official names indicate loyalty to the god Amun-Re. But in the second year of his reign he constructed a temple to Aten — an exceedingly minor god in the Egyptian pantheon — on the eastern side of the great temple complex at Karnak and named it *Gempaaten*, "the Aten is found." Built of small sandstone blocks from a quarry north of Aswan, this temple would later be dismantled and its blocks reused in various projects elsewhere. (Today archaeologists are reassembling many of these stones to gain valuable insights into this mysterious period.) Subsequently, he would change his name to Akhenaten, "Aten is well pleased." In the sixth year of his rule, Akhenaten moved his capital from Thebes to a ten-mile stretch of land on the east side of the Nile at a place now known as Tell el-Amarna. There an entire city was constructed, with elaborate dwellings for nobility, a magnificent royal palace, and an enormous, open-air temple to Aten, appropriate for worship of a sun god. He named his capital city Akhetaten, "Horizon of the Sun Disk." Akhenaten functioned both as king and high priest, prophet of Aten and sole intermediary between the one god and all of Egypt. In fact, the people of Egypt were forbidden to worship Aten directly; they were to worship Akhenaten, and he would represent them before the god.

9. Stela depicting Pharaoh Akhenaten with his wife and three daughters

In this sense, his powers exceeded any pharaoh before or since — and that, indeed, was a principal point of his revolution.

Yet it is impossible to say to what degree Akhenaten acted out of philosophical and religious motivations and to what degree from political shrewdness. Closing the great temple at Karnak alone put six thousand priests out of work, out of power, and most importantly, out of the ability to levy taxes on the peasants for support of the temple. That scenario was repeated countless times throughout all Egypt. Imagine the fury of the religious hierarchy — cult leaders who had been rivals now found common cause in their hatred of this "heretical" pharaoh. Little wonder that Akhenaten's revolution did not survive his generation. For generations, however, pharaohs had fumed over the increasing power of the priests, at times ordering them to cease and desist from levying taxes and threatening to send troops if they did not, because the empire was struggling with its own finances. Akhenaten's bold moves thus effectively terminated the greatest rival to the power of the pharaoh; that much is certain.

Nevertheless, images such as these portrayed in the beautiful stela and panel indicate another side of the story. The touching scene in the stela of the pharaoh and his family, Nefertiti ("the beautiful woman has come") and their three daughters, seated beneath the beneficent rays of Aten is remarkable in many ways. No pharaoh ever was shown in such a gentle family setting. Akhenaten seems to have coupled a genuine love for a philosophical, gracious, peaceful life — at times even to the neglecting of border threats from the rootless peoples known as the *habiru* — with his shrewd political acumen. (Some of the Amarna letters plead repeatedly for military reinforcements; they seem to have been ignored. At the same time, in another letter the ruler of Assyria complains because his ambassador was forced to stand beneath the burning sun for hours in the temple courtyard during ceremonies worshiping Aten.)

Scenes such as these make it evident that the revolution in religion during the Amarna period was matched by a revolution in art. The formalism and strictness of the previous periods was transformed into more human, and eventually, more realistic art. Early in his reign, the figure of Akhenaten — always peculiar, with its elongated features and swollen body — was more exaggerated; toward the end of his reign, his portrayal and that of his family softened and yielded to a more naturalistic appearance. (Scholars and scientists have pursued the question of some possible disease or genetic deformity accounting for the shape of his skull and body, but the general consensus has favored a deliberate stylistic exaggeration of body tendencies rather than physical causes.)

In both the stela and the panel, the sun's rays terminate in small, open hands. They receive offerings of food and lotus flowers from the pharaoh and his family. They also extend to them the *ankh,* symbol of life, and the *was,* symbol of prosperity. Only the pharaoh and his family enjoyed these gifts. This stela served as a shrine for worship of the pharaoh in a private home; the panel was designed as a portion of the decoration for the royal tomb. In both, the figure of Akhenaten is incised more deeply than the others, indicating his greater authority (though the queen in the panel is depicted as the same size as the king). The daughters touch their parents, reach for an earring, and hold one another's hand. The serenity of these scenes is palpable. No doubt that

peace was a dream of Akhenaten. But with his actions toward the religious authorities, his death would end all the dreams of the new kingdom.

Biblical Significance

Biblical scholars generally do not regard the Amarna period as especially relevant to the biblical period. Therefore in the various texts and collections referencing biblical objects, little from this era will be found.

10. Panel showing Pharaoh Akhenaten and his family

The one notable exception is the collection of ancient documents known as the Amarna tablets. These letters yield important insights into the troublesome folk known as *habiru* (see the article "Amarna Tablets"). Yet what, if any, relevance is there in this material from the biblical standpoint? And what of the so-called "monotheism" of the pharaoh, Akhenaten? Is it some sort of precursor of later biblical monotheism?

With reference to the first question, what we learn from the Amarna tablets only points to the unsettled lives of displaced persons, sometimes raiding various prosperous cities of the established order. Nevertheless, they do highlight the extreme gulf fixed between the rich and poor in that world and the oppression that forced these people to leave the security of their cities. To be a rootless wanderer, without home or country, has always been a miserable existence in world history, but in that era it was even worse than usual. Ancient cities, to say the least, were not welcoming of strangers, who were invariably regarded with suspicion as either criminals or spies. These *habiru* of the tablets were not the Hebrews we encounter in the Old Testament, but similarly they were peasants without a homeland and in the same country where the ancestors of the Jews would appear sometime within the next century. As such, they show us the struggles of displaced persons against the established and more powerful forces in the land, struggles that would be mirrored in the early experience of the children of Abraham in the Promised Land.

As to the "monotheism" of Akhenaten, his "theism" has been questioned (that is, belief in a divine being rather than an abstract force). At first he did refer to the Aten by such terms as "father" and later, "king of the gods." Other intriguing terms are used, too: "The One," "the Light," "the Universal," and "the One who was within King Akhenaten." Nevertheless, Aten was the sun disk itself (some would say, more especially, the rays from the disk). As such, the worship of Aten would be directed toward an object rather than toward a divine being as in theistic belief. At this distance, however, it is impossible for us to measure to what degree personal characteristics of the Aten may have prevailed over the image of the sun disk itself. Likely such fine distinctions were never made. Akhenaten did see the figure of Aten as the sole god of every land and wished for that unity of religion across the Egyptian empire, not merely within Egypt itself. Of course, this would have resulted in greater subservience to Akhenaten himself. Again, we do not know, nor can we understand, the full motivations of the pharaoh in establishing his unique religion.

In spite of certain similarities between the two beliefs, many factors have convinced scholars that any resemblance between Atenism and Mosaic faith is coincidental. The differences between the two religious views are much greater than their similarities. For example, only Akhenaten and his family were allowed either to pray or sacrifice to the one god, Aten, unlike the Mosaic requirements of the worship of Yahweh; everyone else worshiped Akhenaten as the mediator of Aten on earth. That is hardly a precedent for later Israelite monotheism. Whatever arrangement of favor existed between humans and the Aten extended strictly to the pharaoh and his family, unlike the covenant of God with all the people of Israel. Furthermore, Aten had a visible image; Yahweh did not. Even allowing for the more primitive practices and traditions in the day of Moses than in the later experiences of the Jews, these differences, and many others, are too significant to ignore.

Finally, it is important to remember that every vestige of this Egyptian "monotheism" was obliterated, as was every other memory of Akhenaten and his notions, prior to the exodus era. Of course, it is possible that these early Hebrews somehow might have been told of this unique history. In terms of their own faith-origin, however, it is far more likely that they knew and recited their own tradition of an ancestor-figure who worshiped an invisible, singular god and wandered into the land of Canaan following his equally unique, passionate vision — Abraham, father of the Hebrew people.

The Birth Legend of Sargon

Clay tablet

- ▷ Size: 9.5 cm. (3.74 in.) high; 8.4 cm. (3.31 in.) wide
- ▷ Writing: Akkadian language in cuneiform script
- ▷ Provenance: Nineveh (Kuyunjik, in modern Iraq)
- ▷ Date: Seventh century B.C.E.
- ▷ Present location: British Museum (room 55)
- ▷ Identification number: ME K3401 + Sm. 2118

Three individuals named Sargon were rulers in Mesopotamia in ancient times. The person who is the subject of the legend on this tablet was the king of Akkad (or, Agade) ca. 2334-2279 B.C.E. The other two were Sargon I (ruled ca. 2000 B.C.E.) and Sargon II (721-705 B.C.E.), both of whom were kings of Assyria. The tablet pictured here is one of three partial tablets owned by the British Museum that contain portions of the birth legend of Sargon of Akkad. The larger portion of this tablet fragment (ME K3401, along with two other fragments from different copies of the text) was found by Austen Henry Layard and his archaeological team ca. 1850 at Nineveh (modern Kuyunjik).

In 1874, George Smith, exploring the ruins of Ashurbanipal's library at Nineveh, discovered an additional fragment. This last fragment, given the identification number Sm. 2118, was a portion of the lower tablet of ME K3401, to which it has now been joined. The front (or, obverse) side of this tablet preserves parts of twenty-seven lines of writing. The reverse side of the tablet is missing. Certain aspects of the language and content of the text of this tablet have convinced a number of scholars that the legend was likely created during the first millennium B.C.E., perhaps at the direction of Sargon II as a way of glorifying his namesake, and thus himself as well. The legend, written in autobiographical style, describes the birth of Sargon of Akkad to a high priestess, who because of her role was forbidden to bear children. That situation would explain the claim in the text that she gave birth to him "in secret" and why she abandoned him in a basket. Found and raised by a "drawer of water" who owns an orchard, Sargon eventually works in his adopted father's orchard. The goddess Ishtar, however, takes note of him, and he becomes king over "the black-headed folk" (the people of Mesopotamia), ruling for fifty-five years.

The first half of the text, as reconstructed from the three tablets, reads as follows:

> I am Sargon the great king, king of Agade.
> My mother was a high priestess, I did not know my father.
> My father's brothers dwell in the uplands.
> My city is Azupiranu, which lies on Euphrates bank.
> My mother, the high priestess, conceived me, she bore me in secret.
> She placed me in a reed basket, she sealed my hatch with pitch.
> She left me to the river, whence I could not come up.
> The river carried me off, it brought me to Aqqi, drawer of water.
> Aqqi, drawer of water, brought me up as he dipped his bucket.
> Aqqi, drawer of water, raised me as his adopted son.
> Aqqi, drawer of water, set (me) to his orchard work.
> During my orchard work, Ishtar loved me,
> Fifty-five years I ruled as king.
> I became lord over and ruled the black-headed folk.[1]

The Louvre possesses a fragment from an Old Babylonian copy of a Sumerian text that dealt with legends about Sargon. Originally the tablet (AO 7673) consisted of four columns of text, two on each side of the tablet. Unfortu-

---

1. "The Birth Legend of Sargon of Akkad," in Benjamin R. Foster, *Before the Muses*, vol. 2 (Bethesda, Md.: CDL Press, 1993), p. 819.

nately, all that has survived is a corner of the tablet containing parts of the first and fourth columns of the text. A portion of the remaining text contains partial lines describing the origin of Sargon in terms similar to the opening of the birth legend on the British Museum tablet. Thus the Louvre tablet likewise originally told the story of the birth and upbringing of Sargon.

Biblical Significance

The similarities between the Birth Legend of Sargon and the biblical account of the birth of Moses (Exod. 2:1-10) are obvious. They both describe a newborn child who is secretly placed by his mother in a basket made of reeds and sealed with pitch. The basket is then set in a river, where it is discovered by someone who takes the child and raises him as his adopted son. In the case of Sargon, the child grows up to become king. In the case of Moses, the child is

raised in the royal court, but flees the court when he grows up. Such legends were widespread in the ancient world, containing the "rags to riches" motif of an infant exposed to die who is rescued, adopted, and grows up to become a king or hero figure. In the opinion of many scholars the biblical author has borrowed and adapted the Sargon legend (or a similar legend) to present the story of the birth of Moses. While there are significant differences between the two stories (Moses is not abandoned to die; after discovery, Moses is nursed by his own mother until old enough

11. Fragmentary clay tablet containing a portion of the Birth Legend of Sargon

to be weaned; Moses is rescued by a princess, not a peasant), the major elements of the stories are similar. Using elements common to various legends, such as that of Sargon, the biblical writer creatively and skillfully told the story of the birth of Moses, God's exceptional deliverer of the enslaved Hebrews.

The Mummy of Ramesses II

Mummified body of Ramesses II

▷ Size: ca. 170 cm. (67 in.) long
▷ Provenance: Deir el-Bahri /Thebes, Egypt
▷ Date: 1213 B.C.E.
▷ Present location: Egyptian Museum, Cairo (Mummy Room, room 49, upper floor)

Afterward Moses and Aaron went to Pharaoh and said, "Thus says the LORD, the God of Israel, 'Let my people go, that they may celebrate a festival to me in the wilderness.'" But Pharaoh said, "Who is the LORD, that I should heed him and let Israel go? I do not know the LORD, and I will not let Israel go." (Exod. 5:1-2)

The slight figure of the mummified remains of Ramesses II gives little indication of the power once wielded by this longest reigning Pharaoh in Egyptian history. For some sixty-seven years (ca. 1279-1213 B.C.E.), Ramesses II was the most powerful ruler in the Near East. He had inherited the kingdom from his illustrious father Seti I. His grandfather, Ramesses I, a military man who had apparently seized the throne, established the Nineteenth Dynasty and then moved the capital to the northeast delta region of the Nile, their ancestral homeland. During his reign, Ramesses II built more extensively than any other pharaoh, including such spectacular projects as the temple at Abu-Simbel and

12. The mummy of Ramesses II

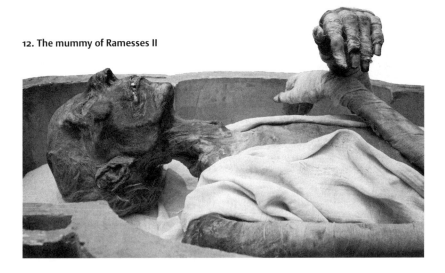

the completion of the Great Hypostyle Hall at Karnak. As a military man, he was noted for his personal bravery and daring. He boasted of defeating the Hittites at the battle of Kadesh, but in fact he barely escaped a humiliating defeat. The result was a mutual nonaggression pact between the Egyptians and the Hittites, the first of its kind in world history.

The mummy of Ramesses II now rests in the new Mummy Room of the Egyptian Museum in Cairo where it is viewed by thousands of visitors each year. For many years, due to the strict religious policies of Egypt, bodies of the dead could not be put on public display and therefore these mummies were stored in a basement room. Now these ancient pharaohs and their queens are one of the central attractions of the museum. (For those who are interested, the lid of the coffin in which Ramesses was buried also is in the museum [JE 26214; gallery 49, upper floor]. It was found at the Deir el-Bahri cache, with an inscription telling of the pharaoh's reburial, although the coffin may have belonged originally to one of his predecessors.)

In order to preserve the mummies from grave robbers who frequently plundered the royal tombs, they were moved by priests around 930 B.C.E. from their original resting places in the Valley of the Kings to the tomb at Deir el-Bahri, which originally had belonged to a high priest of Amun. There they remained until discovered in 1881 by Emile Brugsch, assistant director of the Egyptian Antiquities Service. Altogether, forty mummies and thirty-six coffins were found, comprising pharaohs, queens, and high officials from the Seventeenth to the Twenty-second Dynasties.

Brugsch described the body of Ramesses II as lying in a "modest tomb, with his arms folded," a position in which he still rests today. His left arm, however, is slightly raised now, as if gesturing — the only one of the mummies so postured — which gives the body an animated appearance. (When the mummy was unwrapped for study at the beginning of the twentieth century, the scientists clustered about the body sprang back in alarm when the long-compressed arm of Ramesses suddenly extended.) Viewers of the mummified body of Ramesses immediately notice his hooked nose and red hair. The nose is typical of the Ramesses dynasty, as it is in the line of the Austrian Hapsburgs. Chemical analysis has revealed that the color of his hair is due to henna that had been applied to the white hair of his old age. But further examination of the roots of the hair showed that its natural color in his youth was red, and that this also was a family trait, as seen in his father, Seti I, and some of his own descendants.

Ancient Egyptian documents claimed that Ramesses II lived to ninety-nine years of age. Modern estimates, however, place his age somewhere around ninety, still an extremely advanced age for his time. His mummy shows that he stood approximately 5 ft. 7 in. tall, although he may have been an inch or two taller in his youth; tests showed that Ramesses suffered from serious bone degeneration from arthritis, particularly in his hips. He also had significant hardening of the arteries in his lower legs, and one scan revealed a dental infection severe enough to have killed him.

Biblical Significance

If Ramesses II is the hated pharaoh of the biblical exodus account, then obviously his mummy is of enormous interest to readers of the Bible. But was he that pharaoh? The answer to the question depends upon the most likely date for the Hebrews to have been in Egypt. Assuming that the biblical record does yield evidence of at least some of the ancestors of later Israel spending a sojourn in Egypt, when was that time? (For a discussion of the question of Israel being in Egypt at all, see the articles on the Merneptah Stela and the mud brick of Ramesses.)

First of all, throughout the exodus account the Bible gives us no name for the oppressor of the Hebrews, always referring to him merely as "the Pharaoh." That is not particularly unusual, especially for a ruler with such a lengthy reign as Ramesses II. Furthermore, no rulers are ever named by their opponents in any documents or inscriptions from that period anywhere in the Near East, unless they have been taken captive. (Ironically, the names of the lowly midwives who delivered the baby Moses are named in the Bible — Puah and Shiphrah — but not the king of Egypt! Cf. Exod. 1:15.) From a theological perspective, however, the intent of the biblical writer is clear; the emphasis of the narrative is on the name of God, which Moses had been given, not on the name of the Pharaoh. Nevertheless, the absence of a specific name for the pharaoh of the exodus has caused endless debate among biblical and archaeological scholars, which shows no signs of abating.

Although the Bible does not provide sufficient evidence for a conclusive date for the period of the exodus, recent archaeological studies have yielded significant, if not conclusive, information as to the likely pharaoh. Some fundamentalist writers have insisted on dating the exodus at 1447 B.C.E., based on a variety of biblical chronologies and genealogies. But the discovery of the Merneptah stela (see that article), together with recent excavations that date the cities of Pithom and Rameses in the Nile Delta (Exod. 1:11) to the period of Ramesses II; and Palestinian excavations that decisively rule out Israelite occupation in Canaan prior to the Iron Age (ca. 1200 B.C.E.), along with the description of conditions in Canaan during the time of Ramesses II as found in the Anastasi Papyrus I — all these put the Hebrews in Egypt at that time and make Ramesses II the pharaoh of the exodus.

Mud Brick of Ramesses II

Mud brick made with straw

▷ Size: 38 cm. (14.96 in.) long; 19 cm. (7.5 in.) wide; 12.8 cm. (5 in.) deep
▷ Provenance: Thebes, Egypt
▷ Date: Reign of Ramesses II (ca. 1279-1213 B.C.E.)
▷ Present location: British Museum (room 61)
▷ Identification number: EA 6020

This small, undistinguished lump of Nile mud with a straw binder rests on a glass shelf amid numerous other objects in the British Museum. Virtually unnoticed by thousands of passersby, this brick bears the faint cartouche of the great pharaoh, Ramesses II. During his lengthy reign Ramesses engaged in more building than any pharaoh, before or since. Countless millions of these mud bricks were used in his various construction projects. Many of them were used in the building of temples to form the inner core of walls; later, stone would be added to the exterior. When he built his store cities, Rameses and Pithom, such bricks were used in abundance. Incredible as it may seem today, if this brick is typical of the usual practice, Ramesses II would have had his name stamped on every one of them. This custom was not unique to Egyptian pharaohs. Ancient Mesopotamian rulers such as Nebuchadnezzar followed the same practice as they, too, used millions of bricks in their building projects. Brick stamps for this purpose also have been found in the ancient Near East. In comparison with bricks used elsewhere, however, Egyptian bricks were unique in that they used chopped straw in their composition to stabilize them. Perhaps the higher percentage of clay in the bricks of other countries made straw unnecessary, while the alluvial soil that made up a portion of the Egyptian bricks required it for a binder.

Two factors clearly identify this particular brick as having been used in con-

structing one of the royal buildings of Ramesses II. The first, of course, is the imprint of the pharaoh's cartouche. Mud bricks were commonly used for ordinary houses, but only bricks for official proj-

13. Mud brick with name of Ramesses II

ects — temples and royal residences — could bear the mark of the ruler. The second identifier is the size of the brick. Smaller bricks were used in private projects than those used by the government. This brick is 38 cm. (14.96 in) long. Bricks used for official buildings measured 35 cm. (13.80 in.) to 45 cm. (17.71 in.) in length; bricks for private construction usually measured 30 cm. (11.8 in.) in length.

The use of mud brick for building in Egypt began sometime in the Late Dynastic Period. Enormous quantities of these bricks were used in the construction of both public and private buildings. The process of brick making in ancient Egypt is well documented by a wooden model from Beni Hasan of brick makers at work, but more especially in pictures from the tomb of Rekhmire, the vizier of Thutmose III (ca. 1479-1425 B.C.E.). These workers, the inscription tells us, were taken as prisoners of war from the "South Lands" (Nubia) and the "North Lands" (Syria-Canaan). They are shown digging mud with hand tools, mixing water into it, packing it into wooden frames on the ground, and then measuring the straightness of the wall they are constructing. Also in the process, chopped straw is mixed into the mud to stabilize it. All of this is being done under the watchful eye of supervisors with a stick or rod in their hands. This information comports well with the biblical account in the book of Exodus of the experience of the Hebrews serving in the work crews of the pharaoh.

Another example of a mud brick stamped with the cartouche of Ramesses II can be seen in the Oriental Institute Museum of the University of Chicago. This brick (OIM 1347; Egyptian Gallery) was found at Thebes where it had been used in the construction of the pharaoh's mortuary temple (the Ramesseum).

Biblical Significance

That same day Pharaoh commanded the taskmasters of the people, as well as their supervisors, "You shall no longer give the people straw to make bricks, as before; let them go and gather straw for themselves. But you shall require of them the same quantity of bricks as they have made previously; do not diminish it, for they are lazy; that is why they cry, 'Let us go and offer sacrifice to our God.' Let heavier work be laid on them; then they will labor at it and pay no attention to deceptive words."

So the taskmasters and the supervisors of the people went out and said to the people, "Thus says Pharaoh, 'I will not give you straw. Go and get straw yourselves, wherever you can find it; but your work will not be lessened in the least.'" So the people scattered throughout the land of Egypt, to gather stubble for straw. The taskmasters were urgent, saying, "Complete your work, the same daily assignment as when you were given straw." And the supervisors of the Israelites, whom Pharaoh's taskmasters had set over them, were beaten, and were asked, "Why did you not finish the required quantity of bricks yesterday and today, as you did before?" (Exod. 5:6-14)

These verses from the book of Exodus encapsulate the experience of the Hebrews as part of the slave-labor force of Egypt. Many records document the use of forced labor in the building of government projects. Labor camps at such sites as Rameses and Pithom comprised both prisoners of war and indigenous workers. Even as early as the Old and Middle Kingdoms, quotas for brick making were often established, though rarely reached. The Louvre Leather Roll (1275-1274 B.C.E., during the reign of Ramesses II) documents one such shortfall, and Papyrus Anastasi IV (end of the thirteenth century) reports the complaint of one official that the surrounding area was lacking in both men to make bricks and straw for them. Finally, unlike the experience of the Hebrews, it was a common practice for some workers occasionally to be given time off for religious holidays to make sacrifices and offer prayers to their gods.

Nevertheless, since there is no hard evidence as yet on the ground in Egypt to prove the presence of the specific ancestors of Israel at that time (Nineteenth Dynasty or earlier), the matter must remain somewhat open-ended and controversial. However, numerous facts are well established: by the time of Ramesses II, Semites by the thousands had been present in Egypt for many years; forced labor camps were well-known; taskmasters, such as those reported to be over the Hebrews, were a known supervisory group at that time; captives and foreigners were employed in brick making on official projects; quotas were established for workers, and they and their supervisors were disciplined if those quotas were not met. Therefore, although proof of the presence of the ancestors of Israel, whatever their number, does not exist, the biblical record in this instance is consistent with the history of Egypt during the Ramesside era.

The Treaty of Kadesh

Baked clay tablet

▷ Size: (One tablet composed of two fragments) 13.8 cm. (5.43 in.) high, 17.6 cm. (6.93 in.) wide; 9.2 cm. (3.62 in.) high, 4 cm. (1.57 in.) wide
▷ Writing: Akkadian language in cuneiform script

▷ Provenance: Ancient Hattusa in modern Turkey

▷ Date: ca. 1270 B.C.E.

▷ Present location: Museum of the Ancient Orient, Istanbul (Anatolia Hall)

▷ Identification number: Bo 10403 + 6549 + 6674

The tablet pictured here is unique in the history of the ancient world. These unimpressive clay fragments contain a record of the first mutual non-aggression pact ever established between nations. Today, an enlarged copy of this document hangs in the entrance of the United Nations Building in New York.

Egyptian fears over the territorial ambitions of the Hittites, masters of central Asia Minor (modern-day Turkey) and northern Syria, coupled with news of a large Hittite force moving south, led Pharaoh Ramesses II to lead an army northward to block their advance. The result was the battle of Kadesh (Syria), one of the most historic battles of ancient times. After a bitter four-day fight, the Egyptian army under Ramesses withdrew to Egypt, and the army of the Hittites, led by King Muwatallis II, returned home to Turkey. Subsequently, these rulers agreed on a pact that would freeze in place their mutual territories in the region. Yet historical records show that the matter was not so simple, and the details involved hold important ramifications for the history of the

14. Fragments of the tablet containing portions of the Treaty of Kadesh

biblical lands — caught, as usual, in the middle.

For many years Egypt had taken for granted its control in the region of Syria-Palestine, remaining largely indifferent to local problems except where the collection of tribute was involved. Gradually, however, the Hittite Empire extended its interests into northern Syria. When it expanded its territory to include Kadesh, Ugarit, and various northern Syrian states as vassals (ca. 1340-1300 B.C.E.), Egypt at first made no moves to oppose it. But with the greatly increased strength of the Nineteenth Dynasty in Egypt, both Seti I and Ramesses II had ambitions to include northern Syria under their influence. The final result of Egypt's subsequent re-

peated incursions into Hittite territory was the battle of Kadesh. The account of the fight was preserved in extraordinary detail in Egypt where Ramesses had the battle depicted on the northern wall of the temple at Abu Simbel, as well as on the first pylon of the Luxor temple and the second pylon of the Ramesseum. Likewise, two written narrative accounts, known as The Bulletin and The Poem (actually, another form of war narrative), retained the details.

In May of 1274 B.C.E., in the fifth year of his reign, Ramesses II led an army through Gaza and Canaan into southern Syria. (The troops of Ramesses included Sherdens, part of the ancient Sea Peoples who had settled in Gaza — the biblical Philistines.) The pharaoh's four divisions of soldiers were each named for an Egyptian god-protector. Ramesses himself led the division of Amun, followed by the divisions of Re, Ptah, and Seth, in that order, and the pharaoh and his division began to encamp upon a knoll southwest of Kadesh. False information given to them by two Hittite spies disguised as bedouin had led them to believe that Muwatallis had withdrawn with his army, out of fear, far to the north in Syria, to the city of Aleppo. In fact, the Hittite army lay in concealment on the northeast side of Kadesh. But Egyptian scouts soon captured two Hittite spies, who revealed the truth after being beaten. An alarm was sent to the following troops to hasten.

As the division of Re was preparing to cross a ford of the Orontes River approximately one mile to the south, they were suddenly attacked by a large detachment of Hittite heavy chariots (large, relatively slow-moving chariots, but carrying four heavily-armed warriors — the tank support of ancient warfare), perhaps as many as one to two thousand; accounts vary. Routed by the attack, the Egyptian division fled to the command camp, hotly pursued by the Hittites, where Ramesses and his generals were in the midst of hurried discussions on the situation. Wholesale panic ensued. For a while, Ramesses apparently fought alone, and — at least, according to his own account — with remarkable skill and valor. He was able to rally his division somewhat, though his accounts say he was abandoned by everyone except his chariot driver. The arrival of the other divisions, plus the timely intervention of another Egyptian army unit that had been trailing along the western coast, rescued him from a dire situation. As for the Hittites, they had failed to commit their infantry quickly enough because they had been caught on the wrong side of the river and thus were not able to deliver what likely would have been the crushing blow to Ramesses.

The following day the armies engaged in a bloody battle that resulted in serious losses to both sides. Although the Hittites had lost almost all of their chariots, their army was at least twice the size of that of Ramesses. By the end of the day the armies had fought each other to a stalemate, and both sides went home claiming victory.

Muwatallis sought a treaty on the spot with Ramesses, but Ramesses was having none of it. It would be the twenty-first year of the pharaoh's reign, after numerous unsuccessful forays against the Hittites in southern Syria and under increasing pressure from the Assyrians, before Ramesses would agree to a treaty. By this time Hatussilis III had become king of the Hittites, and it was he who signed the treaty. The terms of the Treaty of Kadesh called for both nations to respect their existing borders and spheres of influence, to cease from future hostilities, and to mutually support one another in case of attack by any foe:

(17-21) [Behold], we will create our [peace]ful brotherhood, far better than the peaceful brotherhood of Egypt and Ḫatti from old times. . . .

(22-24) Ramses, Beloved of Amon, Great King, King of Egypt, shall never attack Ḫatti for the purpose of taking anything from it. So shall Ḫattušili, Great King, King of Ḫatti, never attack Egypt for the purpose of taking anything from it.

(27-30) Now if an external enemy comes upon Ḫatti, then Ḫattušili, <Great King>, [King of Ḫatti], will write to me, saying: "Come to my aid against him." Then R[amses, Be]loved of Amon, Great King, King of Egypt, will send his army and chariotry, and they will kill [his enemy], avenging Ḫatti.

(33-36) And if an external enemy comes against Egypt, then Ramses, beloved of Amon, [King] of Egypt, your brother, will write to (you), Ḫattušili, King of Ḫatti, his brother, saying: "Come to my aid against him." So Ḫattušili, King of Ḫatti, will send his army and chariotry, and he will kill my enemy.[1]

The actual recording and transmission of this historic document was complex. According to the document itself, the treaty was to be written "upon a tablet of silver" (now lost; however, the clay-tablet version of the treaty that survives describes the front and back of the silver treaty as stamped with images of the gods Seth and Re). It was written in Akkadian and preserved in two versions. The version written in Hatti was sent to Egypt, where it was translated into Egyptian and then inscribed in hieroglyphics on the walls of Ramesses' temples. The Egyptians then wrote a version that was sent to Hattusa, where it was copied on the clay tablet that remains. This tablet is broken; the larger fragment has forty-five lines, the smaller piece, twenty-eight

1. Yoram Cohen, "The Hittite-Egyptian Treaty" in *The Ancient Near East: Historical Sources in Translation,* ed. Mark W. Chavalas (Malden, Mass.: Blackwell, 2006), pp. 245-46.

lines. The translation we have today is from this tablet, modified and clarified in places by the hieroglyphic inscriptions in Egypt.

Of course, like many treaties over the ensuing centuries, these provisions were not always followed. Nevertheless, for the time in question, the existence of such an agreement at all is remarkable.

Biblical Significance

The events described above occurred long before the existence of the formal nation of Israel. Nevertheless, repercussions from them could be felt centuries later in Palestine. Because of their preoccupation with Syria, the Hittites could not adequately defend their northern borders, and it was from this direction that more primitive tribes eventually overran them. As for Egypt, the end of the Nineteenth Dynasty marked the waning of Egyptian supremacy in the region. Thus, in spite of their pledges to support one another against enemies, their days in the "club of the great powers" were numbered. The relative vacuum in Syria created by the fading superpowers on its borders allowed a few cities there to flourish and grow rich. A primary example is the city of Ugarit, where class distinctions developed that had never existed before. Those employed by the government were known as "people of the king"; all others were called "the sons of Ugarit." (Echoes of these class distinctions could be heard centuries later as the aristocracy of Israel would speak derisively of their poor as "the people of the land.")

As the king demanded increased labor for his building projects, the poor villagers were forced to leave their farming and join the labor pool. With less time to work their crops, they had increasing difficulty paying their onerous taxes. The rich got richer and the poor got debts. These villagers were forced to take out loans they were unable to repay. The kings who demanded such labor did not abolish debts as had been the practice in the early second millennium, and debt-slavery became common. The same situation also obtained in the few other cities of any size in the area.

A laborer who saw not only himself but also his family condemned to a life of indentured servitude had but one option — flee from both his debts and his homeland. The result was an increasing number of men and women in the Syro-Palestinian area who were displaced and rootless, outcasts from society. Many of them became semi-nomadic, living together in wandering bands in the more remote places. They were feared, of course, by the city dwellers, though later their services as labor would again be needed in the cities. These conditions existed across Palestine and even into the former territories of the Hittites. The term of derision used to designate these wandering folk was *habiru.*

Although no direct connection has ever been established between the He-brews, as a people, and the *habiru* (except, perhaps, in the word linguistically), obvious similarities exist. Even David in the 10th century B.C.E., who fled from Saul, was able to organize a band of displaced men (certainly, a form of *habiru*) around him in the wilderness of Judah. At least this much may be said of the Hebrew/*habiru* question: no doubt, regardless of the source of origin of the early ancestors of Israel, the city dwellers in Canaan regarded the Hebrews as *habiru* and felt about them much as the elite city dwellers of ancient Syria felt about the debtors and political exiles of that time who also had fled into the wilderness to make a new life for themselves.

The Law Code of Hammurabi

Diorite stela

▷ Size: 2.25 m. (7.38 ft.) high; 65 cm. (2.13 ft.) wide
▷ Writing: Akkadian language in cuneiform script
▷ Provenance: Susa, in modern Iran
▷ Date: ca. 1760 B.C.E.
▷ Present location: Louvre (room 3, ground floor, Richelieu Wing, section 3)
▷ Identification number: Sb 8

In the 12th century B.C.E., the Elamites took this spectacular monument from the temple of the Babylonian god Shamash in Sippar to the acropolis of the city of Susa, where it was exhibited along with other trophies of their defeat of the Baby-lonians. There it remained until discovered by a French archaeological expedition in 1901-02, led by Jacques de Morgan. The stela was then taken to its final resting place in the Louvre Museum in Paris, where it has remained one of the most fa-mous objects of ancient history. The figures on the upper portion of the stela de-pict Hammurabi receiving his commission from Shamash, god of justice, who extends to him the ring and rod, symbols of authority and justice. The laws them-selves are written in columns below these figures, on both sides of the stela.

In addition to its beauty as a work of art in itself, the initial sensation created by this find was the result of two factors. Initially it was believed that these 282 laws, known as the Code of Hammurabi, constituted the world's oldest law code. Even though subsequent research has determined that there were similar legal codes in neighboring states that preceded it — the code of Ur-Nammu of the city of Ur, home place of Abraham, dates to ca. 2100 B.C.E. (discussed below) — these laws nonetheless remain the most extensive and polished of any such documents. Many experts also have doubted that this work actually constituted a regularly functioning legal code, at least not one in the modern sense. Other legal texts from the same era do not reveal references to it, as, for example, one might find later legal references to a Napoleonic code of law. Furthermore, its prologue and epilogue give the inscription a distinctly propagandistic flavor. In them Hammurabi seeks to assure the gods, as well as his people, that he will maintain order and ensure justice. Yet the code is nonetheless surprisingly detailed, dealing with specifics of property law, family law, and even regulating wages and fees.

Hammurabi (1792-1750 B.C.E.) actually was not so much a creator of a new law code as he was a preserver of traditional, received order. His work no doubt introduced certain additions and reforms of earlier precepts, but its principal objective was to maintain stability within the stratified social order of Babylonia. The code therefore makes clear that it is to remain as a permanent statute to be followed by subsequent rulers. To some degree Hammurabi was successful in this demand; some fifty manuscripts, from his era to the middle of the first millennium, reveal that subsequent scribes studied and copied all or parts of the laws, prologue, or epilogue of the code.

A second reason for the intense interest in this discovery centered on its similarity to the laws of Moses in the Hebrew Scriptures. Particularly noted was the

15. Stela containing the Law Code of Hammurabi

"eye for an eye" section of the laws. That subject will be discussed in the subsequent section on the relevance of the code to the biblical record.

In the epilogue of the document, Hammurabi stresses his role as the "shepherd" of his people, one who has not been "careless or negligent toward humankind," but who has "made the people of all settlements lie in safe pastures" in the role entrusted to him by his god Marduk.[1] Therefore individuals are encouraged to seek out this monument when they are seeking justice:

1. "The Laws of Hammurabi," translated by Martha Roth (*COS* 2.131:351). (The *COS* text is a slightly altered reprint of the text in Martha T. Roth, with a contribution by Harry A. Hoffner Jr., *Law Collections from Mesopotamia and Asia Minor*, ed. Piotr Michalowski, Society of Biblical Literature Writings from the Ancient World, no. 6, 2nd ed. [Atlanta: Society of Biblical Literature, 1997], pp. 121, 128, and 134.)

> May any wronged man who has a case come before the statue of me, the king of justice, and may he have my inscribed stela read aloud to him, thus may he hear my precious pronouncements and may my stela reveal the case for him; may he examine his case, may he calm his (troubled) heart, (and may he praise me).[2]

The inscription closes with a lengthy section of curses upon any who would defy these laws or deface the image of the king.

In addition to the stela, other copies of Hammurabi's law code are also known to exist. In ancient times, copies of the law code were made by scribes as a writing exercise. An example of one of these clay tablets (AO 7757) is on display in room 3, ground floor, Richelieu Wing, section 3, of the Louvre. This fragmentary tablet was found in Nineveh in the library of the Assyrian king Ashurbanipal (eighth century B.C.E.). In the same case with this fragment is another clay tablet (AO 10237), consisting of 120 lines of cuneiform script. The text on this tablet, dated to the eighteenth century B.C.E., appears to be an earlier version of the prologue than that found on the stela. Another clay tablet containing the Law Code of Hammurabi can be seen in the Museum of the Ancient Orient in Istanbul (Ni 2358; Mesopotamia Hall). This tablet, from the eighteenth century B.C.E., was discovered at Nippur (in modern Iraq).

Another collection of Mesopotamian laws known as the Laws of Ur-Nammu (or, Ur-Namma) was developed either during the reign of King Ur-Nammu (2112-2095 B.C.E.) or his son Shulgi (2094-2047 B.C.E.). Ur-Nammu founded the Third Dynasty of Ur, uniting the city-states of southern and northern Mesopotamia, and he also is remembered for building the spectacular ziggurat (stepped "pyramid" temple) of Ur, part of which is still standing today. Only the prologue to this collection and some thirty-seven laws, many fragmentary, have been discovered on partial tablets. Similar to the style of other law codes from this area, the prologue is used to establish Ur-Nammu as a mighty ruler and giver of justice. Some phrases in the prologue strongly resemble expressions in the Hebrew prophets, particularly the prophet Isaiah. For example, the prologue to the laws states:

> I did not deliver the orphan to the rich. I did not deliver the widow to the mighty. I did not deliver the man with but one shekel to the man with one mina (i.e., 60 shekels). I did not deliver the man with but one sheep to the man with one ox. . . . I established justice in the land.[3]

---

2. "The Laws of Hammurabi" (*COS* 2.131:351).

3. Roth, *Law Collections from Mesopotamia and Asia Minor,* pp. 16-17.

In the book of Isaiah, similar concepts occur: "Seek justice, rescue the oppressed, defend the orphan, plead for the widow" (Isa. 1:17). Likewise, "He will not grow faint or be crushed until he has established justice in the earth" (Isa. 42:4). The prologue to the laws also refers to the establishing of standardized weights and measures by the king; honest weights and measures are a concern of the Hebrew Torah as well:

> You shall not have in your bag two kinds of weights, large and small. You shall not have in your house two kinds of measures, large and small. You shall have only a full and honest weight; you shall have only a full and honest measure, so that your days may be long in the land that the LORD your God is giving you. (Deut. 25:13-15)

The laws of Ur-Nammu predate the Code of Hammurabi by more than three hundred years, and it might be expected that they would be harsher than the laws that followed them. In fact, many authorities have noted that quite the opposite seems to be the case. Rather than the familiar "eye for an eye, tooth for a tooth" (*lex talionis;* law of retaliation) in both the Code of Hammurabi and the Hebrew Scriptures, these laws say:

> 18 If [a man] cuts off the foot of [another man with . . .], he shall weigh and deliver 10 shekels of silver.
> 22 If [a man knocks out another man's] tooth with [. . .], he shall weigh and deliver 2 shekels of silver.[4]

In other words, the laws of Ur-Nammu did not specify retributive justice (retaliation) for wrongs, but rather economic compensation.

A damaged tablet containing parts of the law code of Ur-Nammu is preserved in the Museum of the Ancient Orient in Istanbul, Turkey (Ni 3191; Mesopotamia Hall; see fig. 16).

Biblical Significance

The similarity between many of the specific laws in the Mosaic code and the code of Hammurabi is striking, so much so that intense analysis has been made of the two. The regulation most often cited is the "eye for an eye" law of both codes, the so-called law of retaliation *(lex talionis)*. Babylonian society was divided into three classes — free men/nobles *(awīlu)*, commoners, and

---

4. Roth, *Law Collections from Mesopotamia and Asia Minor*, p. 19.

slaves — and penalties in the law are adjusted accordingly, although the distinction between the first two classes is not completely clear:

> Law 196: If an *awīlu* should blind the eye of another *awīlu,* they shall blind his eye.
>
> Law 197: If he should break the bone of another *awīlu,* they shall break his bone.
>
> Law 200: If an *awīlu* should knock out the tooth of another *awīlu* of his own rank, they shall knock out his tooth.[5]

The similarities with the biblical code are immediately apparent: "Anyone who maims another shall suffer the same injury in return: fracture for fracture, eye for eye, tooth for tooth; the injury inflicted is the injury to be suffered" (Lev. 24:19-20).

Numerous other laws are either identical, or nearly identical. Yet it should be pointed out that though many of the biblical laws deal with the same legal issues, their remedies are most often quite different. One set of laws in both codes, however, because of their unusual nature, has been singled out as pointing to literary dependence on the part of the later biblical regulations.

The Code of Hammurabi:

> Law 250: If an ox gores to death a man while it is passing through the streets, that case has no basis for claim.
>
> Law 251: If a man's ox is a known gorer, and the authorities of his city quarter notify him that it is a known gorer, but he does not blunt (?) its horns or control his ox, and that ox gores to death a member of the *awīlu*-class, he (the owner) shall give 30 shekels of silver.
>
> Law 252: If it is a man's slave (who is fatally gored), he shall give 20 shekels of silver.[6]

The biblical regulations of "the law of the ox":

> When an ox gores a man or woman to death, the ox shall be stoned, and its flesh shall not be eaten; but the owner of the ox shall not be liable. If the ox has been accustomed to gore in the past, and its owner has been warned but has not restrained it, and it kills a man or woman, the ox shall be stoned, and its owner also shall be put to death. . . . If the ox gores a male or female

---

5. "The Laws of Hammurabi" (*COS* 2.131:348).
6. "The Laws of Hammurabi" (*COS* 2.131:350).

slave, the owner shall pay to the slave-owner thirty shekels of silver, and the ox shall be stoned. (Exod. 21:28-29, 32)

On first reading the two regulations sound nearly identical. The essential difference in their details, however, marks the essential difference between these codes. Babylonian regulations uniformly focus on the economic impact imposed by the actions of one person upon another; biblical regulations, while usually addressing the economic effects of a violation, emphasize the violation of the moral code of God. So in this case, the death of the innocent party results in more than a simple fine. The negligent owner is put to death and, indeed, by stoning, a regulation specified for an act against God. A human being has been killed by the negligence of another, and the value of a human life exceeds that of mere monetary value and cannot be corrected by a simple fine.

16. Fragmentary clay tablet containing portions of the Law Code of Ur-Nammu

The form of laws themselves suggests the same conclusion. The laws of Hammurabi are all casuistic: "If . . . then." The Levitical regulations are often casuistic, but many are also apodictic: "You shall . . . you shall not." Babylonian law had no sense of divine morality, because the gods themselves were not involved with questions of morality. To "establish justice," in the Babylonian term, meant to secure order and prevent chaos in society. Therefore the laws of Hammurabi are not prescriptive, but strictly regulative. The biblical laws also pertain to the individual and society, but the source of these laws and the motivation to obey them came from a desire to conform society to the image of the holy God. Moses is said to have received his laws from God. Although on the stela Hammurabi stands before Shamash, the god of justice, he is not said to be receiving these laws from Shamash, but rather presenting himself and his regulations to the god as evidence of his commitment to maintaining the stability of the state.

Whether the biblical laws of the Torah were dealing coincidentally with the same set of circumstances as the Babylonian laws, thereby accounting for their similarity, or whether the knowledge of such laws since the time of Abraham, and before, influenced their form cannot be established with certainty. What is evident, however, is that in the biblical laws, as in every biblical narrative of the Hebrew Scriptures, God is at the center. The people of Israel were to be holy and just, not merely to establish or maintain the stability of the state, but because they served a holy and righteous God.

Middle Assyrian Laws, Tablet A

Clay tablet

- ▷ Size: 32 cm. (12.60 in.) high; 20.5 cm. (8.07 in.) wide
- ▷ Writing: Akkadian language in cuneiform script
- ▷ Provenance: Ashur (modern Qal'at Shergat, Iraq)
- ▷ Date: Twelfth century B.C.E.
- ▷ Present location: Museum of the Ancient Near East, Pergamum Museum, Berlin (room 11)
- ▷ Identification number: VAT 10000

Between 1903 and 1913, a German archaeological team under the direction of the architect Walter Andrae conducted excavations at the ancient Assyrian city-state of Ashur on the Tigris River. The Assyrians had located this stronghold on an outcrop of limestone above a fork in the river, which gave it natural protection against enemies. Andrae's principal excavations were carried out in the vicinity of the temples and palaces on the northern side of the city. There he began his work with the Germans' typical methodology of cutting trenches across the site from east to west at intervals of one hundred meters, according to the grid lines of his survey. He and a colleague, Robert Koldewey, had previously worked for four years on the extensive site of ancient Babylon. In Babylon they had devoted most of their time to the buildings and architecture of the site, but little to any inscriptions that were uncovered. At Ashur, however, Andrae discovered that unraveling the complicated layers of the various structures erected over many years would be virtually impossible without the use of the chronology of inscriptions. Therefore, by sheer necessity, greater attention was given by the team to written materials.

As it happened, Ashur proved to be exceptionally rich in clay tablets and other inscriptions. Though the Assyrians themselves were not particularly given to literary pursuits, they were avid in their collecting of the writings of others, particularly Babylonian texts. (The relationship between the two nations may be compared to the later attraction of the Romans for Greek learning.) The library of Tiglath-pileser I (1114-1076 B.C.E.), as it is known today because of the number of its texts that can be dated to his reign — though it likely was begun as early as the reign of Ashur-urballit I (1363-1328 B.C.E.) — is the earliest and one of the most complete libraries in all of Mesopotamia prior to the great library of Nineveh with its 20,000-30,000 cuneiform tablets that was established by King Ashurbanipal (ca. 669-627 B.C.E.).

Among the many discoveries of the German archaeologists were the tablets known as the Middle Assyrian Laws (MAL), the principal ones of which are called tablets A, B, and the tablet known as C+G. Of these three, tablet A is by far the most complete. It lists fifty-nine statutes, virtually every one of which concerns women, with strict rules and brutal punishments. Tablet B contains twenty regulations regarding landed property and inheritance, and tablet C+G specifies laws for other types of property, particularly pledges and deposits.

17. Tablet A of the Middle Assyrian Laws

(These latter two tablets are extremely fragmentary, as are the other eleven fragmentary tablets that compose the collection.)

Although most of the regulations in Tablet A are directed toward the behavior of women, it does have one law (A 20) that treats male homosexual conduct (which was regarded as effeminate), the punishment for which is as harsh as that prescribed for women who committed violations: "If a man sodomizes his comrade and they prove the charges against him, they shall sodomize him and they shall turn him into a eunuch." (This assumes the convicted party is the active partner in the affair. He is then subjected to the same dishonor he has imposed upon his neighbor. The root of the word that is translated "to sodomize" literally means "I want to fornicate with you," to initiate illicit sex; "sodomize" is derived from the context.)[1] An associated law concerns a false rumor of male homosexual conduct. The party who made the assertion but is unable to prove it is treated with equal harshness: "They shall strike that man fifty blows with rods; he shall perform the king's service for one full month; they shall cut off his hair [or beard]; moreover, he shall pay 3600 shekels of lead" (A 19).

The preponderance of the legal code in tablet A, however, is concerned with the conduct of women. These laws reveal the total male domination of the female in Assyrian culture, as well as the degree to which the imperial court dictated the conduct of all citizens in marital and sexual relations. Most of these regulations are concerned with married women and the daughters of the upper classes, but there are also statutes for unmarried women, prostitutes, and widows. Social deportment is strictly regulated. In general, married women and widows must have their heads covered; single women must veil their faces but not cover their heads. Female slaves, concubines, and prostitutes must neither cover their heads nor veil their faces. Extreme penalties awaited those who violated these regulations: "Slave women should not be veiled, and he who should see a veiled slave woman shall seize her and bring her to the palace entrance; they shall cut off her ears; he who seizes her shall take her clothing" (A 40). Penalties were likewise harsh for any man who saw such violations and failed to report them:

> If the man should see a veiled slave woman but release her and not seize her, and does not bring her to the palace entrance, and they then prove the charges against him and find him guilty, they shall strike him fifty blows with rods; they shall pierce his ears, thread them on a cord, tie it at his back; the one who informs against him shall take his garments; he shall perform the king's service for one full month. (A 40)

Punishment for many crimes was frequently mutilation. A woman who stole something from an individual would have her ears cut off by her husband or her nose cut off by the victim (A5). If a man kissed the wife of another man, he would be mutilated: "They shall draw his lower lip across the blade (?)

---

1. All quotations from the Middle Assyrian Laws, Tablet A, are from Martha T. Roth, with a contribution by Harry A. Hoffner Jr., *Law Collections from Mesopotamia and Asia Minor,* ed. Piotr Michalowski, Society of Biblical Literature Writings from the Ancient World, no. 6, 2nd ed. (Atlanta: Society of Biblical Literature, 1997), pp. 153-94.

of an ax and cut it off" (A 9). Forcible rape — at least of a noble woman — was punishable by death (A 12).

Some laws were designed to protect the possessions of a man — including his wife, and any children who might be born to her. If a man had been captured in war, his wife must remain single for two years; after that, she might marry. But should her husband subsequently return he could take her back as his wife, though any children born in the interim would remain the property of the second husband (A 45). Abortion was punished with particular cruelty: "If a woman aborts her fetus by her own action, and they then prove the charges against her and find her guilty, they shall impale her, they shall not bury her" (A 53).

A final, and perhaps most telling, indication of the total subservience of wives to their husbands is the last, "catch-all" clause of the laws: "In addition to the punishments for [a man's wife] that are [written] on the tablet, a man may [whip] his wife, pluck out her hair, mutilate her ears, or strike her, with impunity" (A 59). These Assyrian laws could scarcely be considered an advance on the Code of Hammurabi, though they came some six centuries later (see the article "The Law Code of Hammurabi").

18. Clay tablet containing part of the New Hittite Laws

Another interesting comparison may be made between the harshness of the Assyrian laws and the Hittite laws that preceded them in the region. The Hittites, whose capital was at Hattusa (Central Anatolia; modern Turkey), dominated the region in earlier centuries, once even conquering mighty Babylon some seven hundred miles distant. Their oldest laws, the Old Hittite (OH) laws (ca. 1650-1500 B.C.E.), were later revised in the New Hittite (NH) laws (ca. 1500-1180 B.C.E.). These revisions show considerable softening from the harshness of the older regulations, unlike the Middle Assyrian laws that would follow them one hundred years or more later. For example, a Hittite law concerning land and planting rights demonstrates the difference between the two eras:

> 166 If anyone sows his own seed on top of another man's seed, his neck shall be placed upon a plow. They shall hitch up two teams of oxen: they shall turn the faces of one team one way and the other team the other. Both the offender and the oxen will be put to death, and the party who first sowed the field shall reap it for himself. This is the way they used to proceed.

> 167 But now they shall substitute one sheep for the man and two sheep for the oxen. He shall give thirty loaves of bread and three jugs of . . . beer and reconsecrate (the land?). And he who sowed the field first shall reap it.[2]

The clay tablet pictured in figure 18 contains part of the New Hittite laws from the thirteenth century B.C.E. and is located in the Archaeological Museum in Istanbul, Turkey (second floor; inventory number Bo. 2094 CBA [KBo VI 4]).

Biblical Significance

Scholars have devoted considerable attention to the question of the relationship, if any, of the earlier law codes of the Mediterranean region to the laws of the Hebrew Scriptures. The similarity between many of the laws in the Mosaic code and other codes is, in many places, striking, so that the biblical regulations are under continuous comparison with those of their neighbors. For example, in the Hittite laws, a virtual parallel exists to the levirate law of the Hebrew Scriptures, which says:

> When brothers reside together, and one of them dies and has no son, the wife of the deceased shall not be married outside the family to a stranger. Her husband's brother shall go in to her, taking her in marriage, and performing the duty of a husband's brother to her. (Deut. 25:5)

The Hittite law (193) reads: "If a man has a wife, and the man dies, his brother shall take his widow as wife."

Whether the laws of the early Hebrews were dealing coincidentally with the same set of circumstances as faced by other societies, accounting for

---

2. All quotations from the Hittite Laws are from Martha T. Roth, with a contribution by Harry A. Hoffner Jr., *Law Collections from Mesopotamia and Asia Minor,* ed. Piotr Michalowski, Society of Biblical Literature Writings from the Ancient World, no. 6, 2nd ed. (Atlanta: Society of Biblical Literature, 1997), pp. 213-40.

their similarity, or whether knowledge of those previous laws influenced their form cannot be established with certainty. Such comparative studies face considerable difficulties. In the first place, the meaning of the individual law codes themselves is anything but certain. Before the regulations in one code can be compared with another, obviously the meaning of the first has to be determined. Even within one nation, and much more across centuries and other cultures, considerable differences clearly are present. Another problem arises because it is not certain that all such legal collections were actual law codes, that is, applied in case law, or that many of these regulations were ever carried out in everyday life. For example, it has been pointed out concerning the Mosaic laws that there are virtually no examples of them being applied in actual situations in the Bible. Therefore the question has been raised whether they were "private" codes, i.e., religious ideals, rather than official court law. Nevertheless, such seeming barriers have not prevented many scholars from attempting to make comparisons between law collections.

Since most of the Middle Assyrian Laws in tablet A concern women, inevitable comparisons have been made with the corresponding biblical regulations. Specifically, the question has been raised as to whether the biblical laws are indeed any improvement over the treatment of women in the Assyrian code. Earlier treatments of that question — all by men — found the biblical laws superior, at least by modern standards. Recently, more critical studies — including those of several women scholars — have questioned those conclusions. One example given is the legislation in Deuteronomy 22:22-29 and Leviticus 20:10. Most biblical interpreters regard these laws as dealing with adultery, and the penalty prescribed for both parties is death. One writer believes this harsh penalty is really because the acts involved are actually rape, but she suspects the law came about as the result of "androcentric jealousy" on the part of the husband, who wanted to punish the woman whether or not she had given consent to the act. Other laws are seen as being less absolute. She adds, "Interestingly, some ancient Near Eastern laws mention similar cases but they always prescribe a wider range of penalties than in the Deuteronomic law," citing Middle Assyrian Law Tablet A, regulation 15. Other biblical passages likewise are compared unfavorably.[3]

The availability today of such ancient law codes as the Middle Assyrian Laws

3. Suzanne Scholz, "Reconstructing Rape for the 'Olden Days': The Challenge of Biblical Rape Laws in Biblical Studies" (paper presented at the conference on "The Rhetorics of Identity: Place, Race, Sex and the Person," University of Redlands, Redlands, Calif., January 2005), p. 8.

has facilitated such studies, as well as the controversies involved, and certainly the comparative analysis of the Mosaic code appears to be nowhere near completion.

Merneptah Stela (or, Israel Stela)

Granite stela

▷ Size: 3.18 m. (10.43 ft.) high; 1.63 m. (5.35 ft.) wide
▷ Writing: Hieroglyphics
▷ Provenance: Western Thebes, Egypt
▷ Date: ca. 1208 B.C.E.
▷ Present location: Egyptian Museum, Cairo (ground floor, gallery 13)
▷ Identification number: JE 31408

From the standpoint of Egyptian history, the Merneptah Stela is a rather insignificant document. From the standpoint of biblical history, however, it is one of the most significant objects ever discovered. This inscription contains the first mention of Israel outside the Bible. Found in 1896 by Sir Flinders Petrie in western Thebes, the stela remains a key document in uncovering the earliest origins of Israel. Today it sits in a side alcove of the Egyptian Museum, and, not surprisingly, unlabeled as to its historic significance for the history of the people of Israel. The significant portion of this remarkable text reads:

> The (foreign) chieftains lie prostrate, saying, "Peace." Not one lifts his head among the Nine Bows. Libya is captured, while Hatti is pacified. Canaan is plundered, Ashkelon is carried off, and Gezer is captured. Yenoam is made into non-existence; Israel is wasted, its seed is not; and Hurru is become a widow because of Egypt. All lands united themselves in peace. Those who went about are subdued by the king of Upper and Lower Egypt . . . Merneptah.[1]

In the summer of the fifth year of his reign, Merneptah, the thirteenth son of Ramesses II, began a major military campaign into Libya. Since he ruled for ten years, beginning in 1213 B.C.E., Merneptah's attack on Libya would have occurred in 1208 B.C.E. His encounter with the people identified as "Israel" likely took place prior to that, perhaps 1211-1208 B.C.E. The stela is principally concerned

---

1. "The (Israel) Stela of Merneptah," translated by James K. Hoffmeier (*COS* 2.6:41).

19. The Merneptah Stela (or, the Israel Stela)

with the Libyan campaign; twenty-three of its twenty-eight lines address that subject. The "Nine Bows," who do not "lift their heads," is a traditional Egyptian identification of its surrounding enemies. These all are either captured, destroyed, or pacified ("Hatti," the Hittites, having been neutralized by the mutual non-aggression pact established by his father following the famous battle of Kadesh, Syria).

In lines 26-27, however, the subject changes. The stela refers to a people, Israel, that is "wasted" and whose "seed is not." The word "Israel" is preceded by a determinative, an Egyptian grammatical symbol that indicates an ethnic group rather than a nation or city. (The other places referred to are preceded by a second determinative that is indicative of organized states or cities.) That designation is entirely appropriate for this period in the history of the Israelites, prior to the monarchy. The size and number of this group are not indicated. But the close proximity in the text of the "Hurru," an Egyptian term for Syria, may indicate that Israel is significant enough to be compared with the Syrians.

Biblical Significance

The absence of any archaeological evidence in Egypt of the presence of the Israelites has posed considerable difficulties for understanding the Bible's account of Israel's origins. No material remains of the Hebrews or Egyptian written records have ever been found that would place the Hebrew people in Egypt. True, Semites — various peoples of Semitic origin, known as Asiatics to the Egyptians — were abundant in Egypt, both as captives and immigrants, long before the time of the biblical account. Later, following the several invasions of Israel by the Assyrians and Babylonians, there is considerable evidence of Jews in Egypt. But nothing yet has been uncovered in Egypt that specifically indicates that the early ancestors of Israel were ever there.

On the one hand, that fact would seem to relegate the stories of Joseph, their later bondage and hard labor, and the leadership of Moses to the realm of folklore. Many scholars regard them as exactly such. On the other hand, other scholars ask why a proud people such as the Jews would fabricate a less than flattering tale of their origins, particularly one that involved subjugation and abject slavery by a hated enemy. They also point in the biblical stories to countless details of life in the time of the Nineteenth Dynasty, the Ramesside period, which are exactly correct, many of which no longer obtained in the post-captivity period when Jews were in Egypt. Even the name of their great deliverer, Moses, is a pure Egyptian name.

How can these differences be reconciled? No definitive answer is as yet possible, and, given the great antiquity of these accounts, may never be. Some facts, however, are clear. Israel based its most important celebration, the Passover, on this story. Many elements in its temple and cult plainly are heavily influenced by archaic Egyptian practices. Furthermore, the story of Egyptian bondage is not a story of the capture and deportation of one nation by another, such as was the case in the Assyrian deportation of the northern tribes of Israel or the Babylonian captivity of Judah. The story of Joseph is the story of one Semitic man (Jacob) and his family coming to Egypt during a famine, a practice well known in Egyptian history. These simple people likely had no significant cultural remains to deposit on Egyptian soil; what would one look for? Given their long sojourn in Egypt, it might be expected that they would assume much of Egyptian culture. This was not a nation transplanted to foreign soil, as was Israel's deportation by the Assyrians, or when the people of Judah were transported to a colony in Tel-Abib, by the river Chebar, in Babylonia. This was only an extended family of pastoralists from somewhere in Canaan, centuries before Israel emerged as a nation.

Finally, what the Merneptah Stela reveals is that a people referred to as "Israel" by a son of Ramesses — whatever their number or nature — was in existence in Canaan/Palestine prior to 1208 B.C.E. That alone makes this a record of critical importance in any attempt to unravel the mystery of the origins of the nation of Israel.

Calf Statuette and Model Shrine

Silver-plated bronze statuette with pottery shrine

▷ Size: Calf statuette — 11 cm. (4.3 in.) long, 10.5 cm. (4.1 in.) high; shrine — 25 cm. (9.8 in.) high, 12 cm. (4.7 in.) wide

▷ Provenance: Tel Ashkelon, Israel
▷ Date: Middle Bronze Age, ca. 1550 B.C.E.
▷ Present location: Israel Museum (Bronfman Archaeology Wing)
▷ Identification numbers: calf statuette — IAA 1990-1119; shrine — IAA 1990-1120

In the summer of 1990, the site of ancient Ashkelon, located on the coast of the Mediterranean approximately forty miles south of Tel Aviv, yielded numerous important archaeological discoveries. It was the sixth season of the Leon Levy Expedition, sponsored by the Harvard Semitic Museum. Professor Lawrence Stager of Harvard University, director of the expedition, uncovered a statuette of a silver calf, an image associated with the worship of Baal or El, chief gods in the Canaanite religion, housed in a ceramic shrine. It was found on the outskirts of the city on the slope of an enormous rampart, or glacis, a semicircle of earthworks around the city nearly a mile long. This passive defense protected the city on all sides except at the sea itself, where a steep bluff provided natural protection. By the end of the Middle Bronze Age, the approximate time of the calf and shrine, the rampart had reached a height of fifty feet. Its base was seventy feet thick; this feature was intended to make tunneling through the walls of the city more difficult. The steep, forty-degree slope of the glacis originally had been constructed of mud bricks, but later it was rebuilt of fieldstones and made more difficult to ascend by a smooth coating of clay.

At the top of the rampart, the mud brick wall of the city was pierced by a gateway more than eight feet wide and twelve high, flanked by mud brick towers, which even today remain to a height of nearly twenty feet. At one time this arched passageway was so long that a stone-lined, plaster-covered barrel vault — the oldest ever discovered — was needed to support this structure of the gate. All in all, the appearance of this formidable defense must have been imposing to any traveler who approached the outskirts of this vast city of some 150 acres and approximately 15,000 inhabitants. All the evidence of Ashkelon during the first half of the second millennium B.C.E. indicates its power and importance during this pinnacle of Canaanite culture.

Near the bottom of the rampart, along a road that led from the nearby harbor to the monumental gate at its crest, the archaeologists found the calf and its shrine buried in the debris of an ancient storeroom where they had been hidden for safekeeping shortly before the destruction of the city in 1550 B.C.E. The bull calf, just old enough to have developed horns, is made of bronze composed of only two to five percent tin; the remainder is copper. The animal was once coated with pure silver leaf, remnants of which remain in various body creases. The body itself was cast solid, along with two of its legs. The horns, ears, tail, left hind leg and right foreleg were made separately. These two legs were riveted in place; the remaining parts were made of forged copper and inserted into the body. When discovered, the calf was complete except for one horn, and the right foreleg was detached from the body. At one time the statuette was mounted on a small platform, but that has disappeared. This spectacular find weighs nearly a pound.

The ceramic model shrine that housed the calf has a beehive shape with a flat bottom and a small button or knob on the roof. The doorway in the shrine is just large enough to admit the calf. Marks on the doorjambs of the shrine indicate that clay doors had once been affixed to them.

Because of the location where this treasure was discovered, it is possible that the shrine and its calf once resided in a wayside sanctuary where travelers could make an offering to Baal prior to entering the city. Lawrence Stager, excavator of these objects, writes:

> A merchant approaching the Canaanite city from the Mediterranean on the road leading up from the sea would have been dwarfed by the imposing earthworks and towering fortifications on the northern slope of the city. About 300 feet along his ascent from the sea, he might have paused to make an offering at the Sanctuary of the Silver Calf, just off the roadway to the right — nestled in the lower flanks of the ramparts. Farther up the road to the east, the merchant would have entered the vast metropolis of Askelon through the city gate on the north.[1]

Baal Hadad, the Canaanite version of Baal, was often pictured standing on the back of a bull, with a club raised in his hand, poised to strike the earth with lightning (see the article "Stela of Baal of the Lightning"). Since much of Ashkelon's economy was dependent on trade from the sea, it would be natural for Baal, the storm god as well as the god of fertility, to have a prominent place in their worship. Visitors to the city would have been eager to show respect to the presiding god of the area and secure his blessing. Whether or not the calf and its shrine were used in this manner, their existence establishes the presence of a cult in Canaan that utilized the bull-calf symbol as an object of worship prior to the establishment of an Israelite presence in the land.

Biblical Significance

The notion of a calf associated with worship appears early in the Hebrew Scriptures. In Exodus 32, Aaron is condemned for making a golden calf from

---

1. Lawrence E. Stager, "When Canaanites and Philistines Ruled Ashkelon," *Biblical Archaeology Review* 17, no. 2 (March/April 1991): 24.

jewelry given by the restless Hebrew people who had grown impatient waiting for Moses to descend from Mount Sinai. He then built an altar and proclaimed "a festival to the Lord," which quickly degenerated into an orgiastic cult celebration. (The bull is an ancient symbol of fertility, which apparently is suggested by the actions of the people.) When Moses came down from the mountain, he pulverized the calf image, mixed the powder with water, and compelled the people to drink it. In Numbers 5:16-28, a similar ritual was forced upon women who were suspected of adultery. A priest would administer a potion of water mixed with dust from the floor of the tabernacle to the suspected woman. If she were guilty, these "bitter waters" would cause her to miscarry or be incapable of childbearing. Adultery is also a frequent term in the Hebrew Scriptures for religious infidelity or apostasy (Jer. 3:8-9; Hos. 9:1).

God's disapproval of Aaron's actions on this occasion was so severe that he would have been killed except for the intervention of Moses (Deut. 9:20). He was not the only one brought under condemnation, however. Moses himself was rebuked, and according to Exodus 32:27 Moses ordered the Levites to kill anyone involved in the worship of the calf, including even their closest relatives. As a result, 3,000 Israelites were put to death, and for their faithfulness the Levites were consecrated for all time as Yahweh's servants. A remarkably similar incident is told in 1 Kings 12:26-33 concerning two golden calves which were set up at the sanctuaries of Bethel and Dan by Jeroboam, first king of the northern kingdom of Israel after the division of the nation following the death of Solomon (932 B.C.E.). Virtually every incident in this story parallels the earlier story in Exodus, so much so that some connection between the two can scarcely be doubted. Either Jeroboam revived an ancient cult from the days of Aaron, his role model in all cultic activities — he even named his two sons after Aaron's eldest sons — or the writer of 1 Kings used the narrative in Exodus 32 to shape his telling of the story of Jeroboam's cult of

20. Bronze statuette of a calf and a clay model shrine

the calf, which was a threat to the temple in Jerusalem, and of Yahweh's stern disapproval of the apostate northern kingdom.

The prophets also knew of worship of the calf image. Hosea rebuked "Ephraim" (the northern kingdom) for its making of silver calf images and their worship of them:

> When Ephraim spoke, there was trembling;
>> he was exalted in Israel;
>> but he incurred guilt through Baal and died.
> And now they keep on sinning,
>> and make a cast image for themselves,
> idols of silver made according to their understanding,
>> all of them the work of artisans.
> "Sacrifice to these," they say.
>> People are kissing calves!
> Therefore they shall be like the morning mist
>> or like the dew that goes away early,
> like chaff that swirls from the threshing floor
>> or like smoke from a window. (Hos. 13:1-3)

Philistine Cult Stand with Musicians

Pottery stand

- ▷ Size: 34.7 cm. (13.66 in.) high; 14.2 cm. (5.59 in.) wide (at base)
- ▷ Provenance: Ashdod, Israel
- ▷ Date: Tenth century B.C.E.
- ▷ Present location: Israel Museum (Bronfman Archaeology Wing)
- ▷ Identification number: IAA 1968-1182

Cult stands have been found surprisingly often in the Near East. These cylindrical stands were most likely used for offerings to the gods, offerings either of burning incense or drink (libations); sometimes grain offerings and small cakes were placed there as well. A few representations from the region depict a worshiper pouring liquid into a bowl on top of such a stand in which some plant is growing, which likely represents an offering on behalf of fertility for the land.

The earliest of these stands (3800-3400 B.C.E.) were made of stone or bronze, as well as some of clay. The greatest number of such cult objects, particularly in terms of biblical history, date from the early Iron Age (1200-900 B.C.E.). These later stands, like the one pictured here, were almost exclusively of clay. Usually such stands were constructed of two pieces, having a cylindrical or cone-shaped base or pedestal with a bowl resting on its top; occasionally these parts were molded in one piece. Some of the pedestals are solid but many are fenestrated, that is, having windows or openings in their sides. Whether or not these openings represent more than mere decoration is uncertain.

This particular stand is unusually interesting because of the musicians it portrays. Such depictions are known from Phoenician tombs from the seventh and eighth centuries B.C.E. This stand, however, is the first representation of a musical ensemble ever found in Israel. As recently as 1957 it was said, "Of the instruments themselves [of biblical times] not a single example has as yet come to light, and from the pre-Hellenistic period no native representation of a Palestinian instrument survives."[1]

Five musicians are depicted around the base of the stand. The players in this orchestra stand in the window openings; four of them are modeled in the round, with their bodies merging into the base. The fifth musician is cut out of the wall of the vessel, with his features subsequently molded and added. Each is playing an instrument: one plays a frame-drum; another plays a stringed instrument, probably a lyre (of which only a portion is preserved); two play double-pipes; and one plays a cymbal. Above the musicians three rectangles hold crude, incised images of animals. The stand gives evidence of having been covered with a white slip, and the bowl above shows faint traces of a red and black lattice pattern. This kind of decoration, a mixture of ancient Mycenaean and Canaanite traditions, is typical of Philistine ceramics.

21. A clay Philistine cult stand decorated with figures of musicians

1. C. H. Kraeling and L. Mowry, "Music in the Bible," *The New Oxford History of Music, 1: Ancient and Oriental Music*, ed. E. Wellesz (London: Oxford University Press, 1957), p. 295.

Biblical Significance

All the instruments shown on the stand are well known in the Bible: the drum, sometimes mistakenly translated as "tambourine" (2 Sam. 6:5; Jer. 31:4), the lyre (1 Chron. 25:3; Isa. 5:12), the pipes (Jer. 48:36; Matt. 9:23), and the cymbal (Ezra 3:10; Ps. 150:5), as well as others. The most interesting biblical connection with this stand, however, is found in 1 Samuel 10:5. Samuel, the great prophet-priest, last of the ancient judges of Israel, tells Saul, the newly anointed choice of God as king of Israel:

> After that you shall come to Gibeath-elohim, at the place where the Philistine garrison is; there, as you come to the town, you will meet a band of prophets coming down from the shrine with harp [*nevel;* a large lyre], tambourine [*tof;* frame drum], flute [*halil;* double pipe], and lyre [*kinnor*] playing in front of them; they will be in a prophetic frenzy.

Musical instruments were commonly used among such groups of ecstatic prophets to induce trances and other states of ecstasy. The musicians depicted on this stand probably were part of a similar Philistine cult, but perhaps their role was more similar to the Levitical singers and instrumentalists in 2 Chronicles 5:12-13:

> All the levitical singers, Asaph, Heman, and Jeduthun, their sons and kindred, arrayed in fine linen, with cymbals, harps, and lyres, stood east of the altar with one hundred twenty priests who were trumpeters. It was the duty of the trumpeters and singers to make themselves heard in unison in praise and thanksgiving to the LORD, and when the song was raised, with trumpets and cymbals and other musical instruments, in praise to the LORD,
>
> "For he is good,
>   for his steadfast love endures forever,"
>
> the house, the house of the LORD, was filled with a cloud.

Whatever the function of these musicians, this ancient object reveals an interesting and unique insight into cultic practices by these near neighbors of Israel during the period of the early monarchy.

Stela of Baal of the Lightning

Limestone stela

- ▷ Size: 1.42 m. (4.66 ft.) high; 50 cm. (19.69 in.) wide; 28 cm. (11.02 in.) deep
- ▷ Provenance: Ugarit (Ras Shamra, in modern Syria)
- ▷ Date: Fifteenth-thirteenth century B.C.E.
- ▷ Present location: Louvre (room B, ground floor, Sully Wing, section 4)
- ▷ Identification number: AO 15775

This limestone stela was one of the impressive discoveries made by Claude F. A. Schaeffer, the French archaeologist who led the first major excavations at Ras Shamra, Syria, site of ancient Ugarit. Discovered in 1932, this stela was part of the large collection of ancient Ugaritic items found at Ras Shamra. The stela was found in the sanctuary just to the west of one of the two large temples excavated on the acropolis of the city. Because of the discovery of this representation of Baal near the temple, the temple has been identified as a temple of Baal. In addition to this stela, major finds at Ras Shamra include various ancient buildings (temples, palaces, fortress, and residential quarters), streets, other stelae, and a large collection of cuneiform documents.

The relief on the stela depicts Baal standing with legs apart, with his right hand raised over his head holding a club ready to release a lightning storm upon the earth. In his left hand he holds a spear whose sharpened head is pointed downward. The upper end of the shaft of the spear forks into several branches. Some scholars have interpreted this as a stylized representation of lightning. Other scholars have understood the branched shaft as representing a growing plant, symbolizing the effects of the nourishing rain which Baal gives to the earth through the thunderstorm. Baal wears a conical headdress with two horns protruding from the front. He is bearded, and his hair hangs below his shoulders, ending in two curls. He wears a loin cloth or kilt, with a dagger stuck in his waistband. The god stands on a platform (an altar?) upon which are depictions possibly of the mountainous home of Baal and the waves of the sea. Under his left arm and between his left leg and the shaft is a small figure, often interpreted as a representation of the king of Ugarit, symbolizing his protection by Baal.

Baal was the Canaanite god of storm and fertility. The Semitic word "baal" means "lord" or "owner." (Since a wife was considered the property of her husband, "baal" could also be used to mean "husband.") Although the generic meaning of "baal" was sometimes applied to various gods in the ancient world, Baal came to be used as the name for the storm god. His real name was appar-

22. Stela with a relief of the Canaanite storm god Baal

ently Haddu to the Canaanites (Hadad to the Amorites and Aramaeans, and Adad to the Mesopotamians), the name which appears in some of the ancient texts. Our greatest source of information about Baal comes from the Ugaritic texts that were discovered at Ras Shamra. Although El was the chief god in the Ugaritic pantheon, Baal was the most prominent and active god. Since in the semiarid climate of Canaan all life was dependent upon the water provided by precipitation, proper acknowledgement and worship of Baal was important. As the storm god, Baal ruled over the winds, lightning, thunder, rain, snow, and dew. He was described as "the rider of the clouds." Lightning was his weapon and thunder was his voice. Because the precipitation that he provided nourished the earth, made the crops grow, and watered the livestock, Baal was seen as a god of fertility. His home was said to be on Mt. Zaphon (modern Jebel el-Aqra), the highest mountain in Syria.

A variety of other representations of Baal (or Hadad) can be seen in several museums. Included among these are:

1. Another stela, made of basalt, in the Louvre (AO 13092; room 6, ground floor, Richelieu Wing, section 3) that depicts Hadad standing on the back of a bull. He has a beard, long hair, and wears a horned headdress. In each hand he holds a shaft with a three-pronged fork on each end, representing lightning bolts. This stela, found at Hadatu (modern Arslan Tash in Syria), dates to the eighth century B.C.E. Made of basalt, it is 1.36 meters (4.46 feet) tall and .54 meters (1.77 feet) wide.

2. A stela in the Museum of the Ancient Orient in Istanbul (Mesopotamia Hall) that shows the storm god Hadad. This stela (7816), from the ninth century B.C.E., was found in the palace of Nebuchadnezzar in Babylon, where it had been brought as war booty after a campaign by the Babylonian king against one of the Late Hittite kingdoms.

3. A collection of small statuettes of Baal in the Louvre in a display case in room B, ground floor, Sully Wing, section 4, including three from the fourteenth-twelfth centuries — AO 11598 (bronze and gold; from Minet el-

Beida near Ras Shamra; see fig. 23); AO 17329 and AO 17330 (bronze; from Ras Shamra); and AO 18511 (bronze with helmet in stone and horns in gold; from Ras Shamra).

4. A small bronze figurine of Baal in the Oriental Institute Museum of the University of Chicago. Located in the Megiddo Gallery, this figurine (OIM A22467) was found at Megiddo and is dated to the Late Bronze Age (1550-1200 B.C.E.).

Biblical Significance

Baal figures prominently in the Hebrew Bible. Of all the gods in the ancient world, Baal was the one who was the most tempting for the ancient Israelites to worship. As the Hebrew people settled in the land of Canaan, they lived among a people for whom Baal was the most important god. Since Baal was the god of storm and rain who made the crops grow and provided water for the live-stock, Baal was seen also as the god of fertility. The temptation to be a

23. Bronze statuette of Baal (AO 11598)

part of the cult of Baal was strong for the Israelites, for they, too, wanted to ensure the fertility of their crops and livestock, and even of themselves. During the settlement and monarchical periods of Israel's history, the worship of Baal continued to be a problem, according to the biblical writers. Numerous texts recount the practice and dangers of Baal worship, as well as occasions when the people rejected Baal worship (Num. 25:1-9; Deut. 4:3; Judg. 2:11, 13; 3:7; 6:25-32; 8:33; 10:6, 10; 1 Sam. 7:4; 12:10; 1 Kings 19:18; 22:53; 2 Kings 3:2; 10:18-29; 11:18; 17:16; 23:4-5; 2 Chron. 17:3; 23:17; 24:7; 28:2; 34:4; and Ps. 106:28). The most famous episode in the Hebrew Bible of a clash between the worship of Baal and Yahweh is the story of the contest on Mt. Carmel between Elijah, the prophet of Yahweh, and the prophets of Baal. This story, recounted in 1 Kings 18, is the culmination of the conflict between Elijah and the king and queen of Israel, Ahab and Jezebel, who were major promoters of Baal worship.

Aside from Elijah, the Hebrew prophets who voiced the strongest condemnations and warnings against the cult of Baal were Hosea and Jeremiah. Hosea, the eighth-century prophet to the northern kingdom of Israel, condemned the people for their worship of Baal and their relying on Baal for fertility and prosperity. They wrongly attributed their success to Baal, instead of to Yahweh, who was really the source of all Israel's blessings and prosperity (2:8). In sexual imagery that appropriately described a people who had become involved in the worship and rituals of the fertility cult of Baal, Hosea accused the people of going after new lovers (2:13), committing adultery (4:13-14), and having "played the whore" (4:12). Over a century later, the prophet Jeremiah charged the people of the southern kingdom of Judah with similar transgressions. He claimed that the prophets of Judah "prophesied by Baal" (2:8), while the people made "offerings to Baal" (7:9), had "gone after the Baals" (9:14), and had even built altars to Baal where they could "burn their children in the fire as burnt offerings to Baal" (19:5; cf. 32:35).

(For additional information about Baal, as well as the biblical significance of Baal, see the articles "Cylinder Seal of El and Baal" and "Myths of the Baal Cycle.")

Cylinder Seal of El and Baal

Cylinder seal made of hematite, with the mounting made of gold

- ▷ Size: Seal — 22 mm. (.87 in.) high; 10 mm. (.39 in.) diameter; seal with gold mounting — 42 mm. (1.65 in.) high; 14 mm. (.55 in.) diameter
- ▷ Provenance: Unknown
- ▷ Date: Eighteenth century B.C.E.
- ▷ Present location: Louvre (room C, ground floor, Sully Wing, section 4)
- ▷ Identification number: AO 1634

Two major types of seals were used in the ancient world — stamp seals and cylinder seals. Stamp seals, which were the earliest seals, have a flat or slightly convex surface into which the design was carved. Cylinder seals, as the name implies, are short cylinders with the design carved all around the outside of the cylinder. The design was engraved into the seal in reverse, so that when the seal was used a raised impression in the correct sequence was left in the soft clay. Impressions with a stamp seal were made by stamping the soft surface with the seal; impressions with a cylinder seal were made by rolling the cylinder across the surface of the wet clay. Cylinder seals were usually hollow tubes, generally made of stone, and worn on a string around the neck or from the wrist or pinned to one's clothing. Some of the cylinder seals were more elaborate and had gold or silver caps on one or both ends and a wire loop on one end. The designs on seals might represent depictions of the gods, scenes from everyday life, hunting scenes, sports activities, warfare, mythological or legendary scenes, ritual activities, or geometric designs. Seals could include inscriptions along with the design or contain an inscription alone. The inscriptions often included the name of the owner of the seal.

Although the date for the first use of cylinder seals is unknown, evidence of cylinder seal impressions has been found as early as ca. 3700 B.C.E. People used cylinder seals to leave impressions on clay for sealing containers (jars, sacks, baskets, and boxes), on lumps of clay placed on door latches of storerooms, on clay tags, and on cuneiform clay tablets and their envelopes. The purpose of the seal was to guarantee that the contents of a container or room had not been tampered with, to show ownership, or to guarantee the authenticity of a document. This latter use became one of the major purposes for cylinder seals. Seals were used to mark letters, receipts, official orders, treaties, loans, deeds and other legal or administrative documents. Not only were there official and government seals, including royal seals, but people of all walks of life owned seals, including merchants, craftsmen, soldiers, cooks, and priests. Some seals belonging to women have been found. During the first millennium B.C.E., when the use of clay tablets and cuneiform writing began to wane and they were replaced by the use of papyrus and ink, the use of cylinder seals also declined. Stamp seals became the more common way of leaving an authoritative impression on a lump of clay.

24. Cylinder seal with a scene of the gods El and Baal

The cylinder seal shown here (fig. 24), dated to the eighteenth century B.C.E., was acquired by the Louvre in 1887. The seal is made of hematite, with the cap on each end and the loop at the top made of gold. The seal would have been hung by the loop on a necklace or bracelet, or perhaps attached by a chain from the loop to a pin on the clothing. The scene inscribed on the seal depicts two Syrian gods, El and Baal, facing each other. Standing on the left on the tops of mountains is the storm god Baal, portrayed in typical fashion, with legs apart, wearing a pointed headdress and a kilt, holding a mace in his up-raised right hand, and a spear or lightning bolt in his left hand. The cuneiform inscription to the left of Baal reads, "Haqata, son of Patala, servant of Hadni-Addu." The latter individual was the chief of a town in Syria who is mentioned in the royal archives from Mari.

Opposite Baal is El, the supreme god of the Canaanite pantheon. El is shown here similar to Ea, the Mesopotamian god of water, with streams of water and fish. In Canaanite mythology, El was the head of the divine pantheon. He was the primordial father of the gods and of humans, the creator and the "father of years." Known as "El the Kind, the Compassionate," he was the wise judge and ruler over the council of gods. El's wife was Asherah (also known as Athirat), the mother of the gods.

Much of our information about El and Baal comes from the Ugaritic cunei-form tablets found at Ras Shamra. An example of one of these Ugaritic texts, now in the Louvre, is called The Birth of the Gracious and Beautiful Gods (also known as A Ritual Theogony of the Gracious Gods, or The Birth of Dawn and Dusk). This text is a narrative poem that tells of the exuberant sexual activity between El and two goddesses, Athirat and Rahmay (some scholars interpret the text to refer to only one goddess). The two goddesses become pregnant and give birth to Shahar and Shalim, whose names mean "dawn" and "dusk." Either these two gods or a subsequent group of gods that are born (scholars disagree over how to interpret the text) are referred to as the "gracious gods." The text is on a clay tablet, AO 17189, in room B, ground floor, Sully Wing, section 4.

An impressive, small statue of El (see plate 2) is on display in the Megiddo Gallery of the Oriental Institute Museum of the University of Chicago. This figurine (OIM A18316) is made of bronze, overlaid with gold leaf. Dated to around 1300 B.C.E., the figurine was discovered during excavations at Megiddo. El is seated and wears a conical hat.

Biblical Significance

As Canaanite gods, both Baal and El have contacts with the biblical world. Baal is mentioned frequently in the Hebrew Bible, and worship of Baal was a major temptation to the people of Israel during their settlement in Canaan and afterwards. El, however, as a specific name for a Canaanite god, is rarely if ever used in the Bible. The word "el" was used in almost every ancient Semitic language, including Ugaritic and Hebrew, as a generic word for "god." Thus, in the Hebrew Bible the word "el" can refer to any god, Israelite or non-Israelite. In order to make the identification specific, the ancestors of the ancient Israelites attached epithets or locations to the word: El-Elyon (God Most High), El-Olam (God Everlasting), El-Bethel (God of Bethel), El-Shaddai (God Almighty, or God of the Mountains). Whereas originally these terms may have designated local or tribal deities, by the time the Bible was written, these terms were understood as variant ways of referring to Yahweh, the God of Israel. Eventually El, and its plural form Elohim, was used as the name for Israel's God, even supplanting the use of Yahweh. This was a natural development when monotheism became the dominant view among the Jewish people. If there are no other gods, then "god" can function as the specific designation for the only deity.

Although the ancient Israelites did not identify Yahweh with other gods, some of the descriptions or epithets of the Canaanite god El (as well as Baal) likely influenced Israel's understanding and depiction of Yahweh. Two examples of this possibility can be mentioned. Exodus 34:6 includes a self-description of Yahweh as "a God merciful and gracious," a description that may be a conscious or unconscious reference to the epithet for the Canaanite god, "El, the Kind, the Compassionate," which is found in some Ugaritic texts. A second example is Daniel 7:9-14, which describes a vision of God sitting in judgment. In this passage God is called "the Ancient of Days" and is described as having hair like pure wool. Scholars have often noted how similar this description of God is to the descriptions of El that appear in the Ugaritic texts, where he is an aged, grey-haired god who is called the "father of years" and who functions as a judge.

(For additional information about the Canaanite deities and their significance for biblical studies, see the articles "Myths of the Baal Cycle" and "Stela of Baal of the Lightning.")

Myths of the Baal Cycle

Clay tablets

▷ Size: AO 16640 — 12.2 cm. (4.8 in.) high, 9.9 cm. (3.9 in.) wide; AO 16641/AO 16642 — 14.5 cm. (5.71 in.) high, 15.6 cm. (6.14 in.) wide; AO 16636 — 26.5 cm. (10.43 in.) high, 19.5 cm. (7.68 in.) wide

▷ Writing: Ugaritic language in cuneiform script

▷ Provenance: Ugarit (Ras Shamra, in modern Syria)

▷ Date: ca. fourteenth century B.C.E.

▷ Present location: Louvre (room B, ground floor, Sully Wing, section 4)

▷ Identification numbers: AO 16640; AO 16641/AO 16642; and AO 16636

One of the major archaeological sites discovered in the Middle East during the twentieth century was at Ras Shamra in Syria. Ras Shamra was the site of the ancient city of Ugarit, capital city of the kingdom of Ugarit that flourished from the fifteenth to the twelfth centuries B.C.E. (The site had been occupied for several millennia prior to that, however.) Excavations of the tell at Ras Shamra began after a farmer accidentally uncovered a tomb at the nearby port of Minet el-Beida in 1928. From 1929 to 1970, Claude F. A. Schaeffer directed the French excavations at Ras Shamra. Excavations have continued since then under the direction of the French, and in the last two decades by a joint French and Syrian endeavor. Among the most important discoveries at Ras Shamra was a collection of six broken tablets that contain myths about the god Baal. These tablets, commonly known as the Myths of the Baal Cycle (or, the Baal-Anat Cycle), were discovered by Schaeffer during the early years of the excavations in the remains of a building on the acropolis that has been labeled the House of the High Priest. These tablets were produced during the fourteenth (or possibly thirteenth) century B.C.E., although the stories themselves are much older. The name of the scribe responsible for the writing of

25. Tablet six of the Myths of the Baal Cycle (AO 16636)

these tablets, and perhaps the compilation and arrangement of the myths, was Ilmilku, whose name appears in the colophon, or ending inscription, of tablet six. (The only other tablet on which a colophon has survived is tablet four, where the name is damaged but was almost certainly Ilmilku because of the similarity in wording between the colophons on tablets four and six.)

The six tablets contain stories featuring Baal (transliterated as Ba'lu in the translation cited below), Anath, El ('Ilu), Yamm, and Mot (Môtu). Although some uncertainty exists about the exact order of the events described in the six tablets, and especially whether the first two tablets even belong to the cycle, the majority view that the tablets present a continuous collection of episodes of the gods is followed here. The first two tablets describe the struggle between Baal, god of storm and fertility, and Yamm, the sea god. Yamm sends messengers to El, the chief god, demanding that Baal be turned over to him. When El agrees, Baal refuses, and a battle ensues between Baal and Yamm. With the assistance of special weapons built by the craftsman god Kothar-wa-Hasis, Baal is victorious and succeeds in killing and dismembering Yamm. (The remainder of tablet two is missing.) After a passage describing Anath's violent destruction of certain of her enemies and an enigmatic reference to her previous defeat of Yamm, tablets three and four focus on the need for Baal to have a palace and the attempts by Baal and his consort Anath to convince El of this need. Finally, at the urging of his consort, the mother goddess Athirat, El agrees, and Kothar-wa-Hasis builds a palace for Baal.

The final part of the cycle of myths, found in tablets five and six, concerns the battle between Baal and Mot, the god of death and the underworld. Lured to the underworld realm of Mot, Baal dies. (The part of the text that apparently described the death of Baal is missing.) The text describes Mot as a ravenous mouth — "My throat is the throat of the lion in the wasteland, and the gullet of the 'snorter' in the sea"[1] — and Baal's descent to the underworld as entering the insides of Mot — "Ba'lu will enter his insides, (will go down) his mouth like a roasted olive, (like) the produce of the earth and the fruit of (its) trees."[2] When El hears of Baal's death he wails and cuts himself in mourning. Anath responds likewise, then goes in search of Baal's body and buries it. Athirat nominates another god to take Baal's place, but he is not tall enough to fill Baal's throne. Anath goes to Mot and demands that he return Baal to her. Mot describes for her his conquest of Baal:

I went searching
    every mountain to the heart of the earth,

---

1. "The Ba'lu Myth," translated by Dennis Pardee (*COS* 1.86:265).
2. "The Ba'lu Myth" (*COS* 1.86:266).

every hill to the heart of the fields.
There were no humans for me to swallow,
   no hordes of the earth to swallow.
I arrived at the best part of the earth, the pasture land,
   at the most beautiful field on the edge of death's realm.
(There) I met up with Mighty Ba'lu,
   I took him as (I would) a lamb in my mouth,
   he was destroyed as a kid (would be) in my crushing jaws.[3]

Anath remains with Mot for months, pressing him for the return of Baal. Finally she attacks the fearsome god of the underworld:

She seizes Môtu, son of 'Ilu:
   with a knife she splits him,
   with a winnowing-fork she winnows him,
   with a fire she burns him,
   with grindstones she pulverizes him,
   in the field she sows him;
The birds eat his flesh,
   the fowl finish off his body parts,
   flesh(-eaters) grow fat on flesh.[4]

El is greatly concerned about the death of Baal, for with his death, a drought has hit the earth because Baal, the god of storm, no longer provides water for the crops. In a dream El sees the return of the fertility of the earth, which he interprets as a sign that Baal is once more alive. Baal does indeed return and reclaim his throne. A battle ensues between Baal and Mot, a contest in which the two combatants are almost equally matched:

They eye each other like finished (warriors),
   Môtu is strong, Ba'lu is strong;
They butt each other like wild bulls,
   Môtu is strong, Ba'lu is strong;
They bite each other like snakes,
   Môtu is strong, Ba'lu is strong;
They trample each other like running (animals),
   Môtu falls, Ba'lu falls.[5]

3. "The Ba'lu Myth" (*COS* 1.86:270).
4. "The Ba'lu Myth" (*COS* 1.86:270).
5. "The Ba'lu Myth" (*COS* 1.86:272).

Finally, after the sun god Shapash intercedes and warns Mot that El will not allow him to remain as king of the underworld if he persists in his struggle with Baal, Mot concedes defeat.

The tablet labeled AO 16640 in the Louvre is a fragmentary tablet that likely originally contained two columns of text on each side of the tablet. This tablet is tablet two in the Baal Cycle. Only two columns of text survive, one column on each side (columns one and four), plus a few lines of column two. An additional fragment (AO 16640a) containing one column of text is thought to be a part of this same tablet, although it does not physically join the larger portion. Items AO 16641 and AO 16442 are two fragments of the same tablet, what is referred to above as tablet five. They were found in different years, 1930 and 1931. The tablet originally contained six columns, three columns on each side of the tablet. Most of columns three and four (on the right hand side of the tablet), as well as part of the top and bottom of the tablet, is missing. The tablet labeled AO 16636 (see fig. 25) is pieced together from two fragments, the bottom half found in 1930 and the other fragment in 1933. Almost all of columns one and six are preserved on the tablet, whereas approximately half of the remaining columns is missing. This tablet is the sixth of the Baal Cycle tablets.

Biblical Significance

Baal, the son of El and the god of storm and fertility, occurs frequently in the Hebrew Bible (see the articles "Stela of Baal of the Lightning" and "Cylinder Seal of El and Baal"). Several aspects of his portrayal in the Myths of the Baal Cycle are of interest for biblical studies. Many of the attributes, titles, and actions associated with Baal in the Ugaritic literature were also applied by the biblical writers to Yahweh, the god of Israel. For example, one of the descriptive titles used of Baal in the Baal Cycle is "Cloud-Rider," reminiscent of the description of Yahweh as the one "who rides upon the clouds" (Ps. 68:4; cf. Deut. 33:26; Ps. 104:3). This depiction of Baal is also likely the ultimate source for the description of "one like a human being coming with the clouds of heaven" in Daniel 7:13, a description that is associated with Jesus in the New Testament (Mark 13:26; Rev. 1:7). Passages in the Hebrew Bible that portray Yahweh as being enthroned over the water or subduing the seas (Psalms 29; 89:9-10; 93) appear to have borrowed imagery from the myth of Baal defeating Yamm (the Hebrew word for sea is "yam") and then being enthroned as king. Furthermore, biblical writers applied images of storms, lightning, and thunder to Yahweh, similar to the depictions of Baal, the Canaanite storm god (Pss. 29:3-9; 97:2-4).

In tablet five of the Baal Cycle, Baal is told,

When you smite Lôtan, the fleeing serpent,
   finish off the twisting serpent,
   the close-coiling one with seven heads.
The heavens wither and go slack
   like the folds (?) of your tunic.[6]

Lôtan, the mythological sea serpent or dragon of the Ugaritic myths, appears in the Hebrew Bible as Leviathan, the sea monster who is defeated by Yahweh (Job 7:12; Ps. 74:12-15; Isa. 27:1; see also Job 3:8; 41:1-34; and Ps. 104:26, where Leviathan also appears). In Psalm 74 the defeat of Leviathan occurs at creation; in Isaiah 27:1 his defeat will be a future event. The author of Revelation further adapted the Leviathan creature for his seven-headed dragon in Revelation 12:3 and the seven-headed beast in 13:1 and 17:3.

Athirat, the wife of El, is mentioned several times in the Hebrew Bible, where her name has been altered to Asherah (1 Kings 15:13; 18:19; 2 Kings 21:7; 23:4; the plural form, "Asherahs" or "Asheroth," appears in Judg. 3:7). Asherah is also used for the name of the wooden cult-object, perhaps a wooden pole, associated with the goddess (see, as examples, Deut. 16:21; Judg. 6:25-30; 1 Kings 14:15, 23; 16:33; 2 Kings 13:6; 17:16; 18:4; 21:3; Jer. 17:2; Mic. 5:14).

Furthermore, the Canaanite god of death, Mot, may be behind some of the depictions of death in the Hebrew Bible. The Hebrew words for "to die" and "death" are *mot* and *mawet,* the same root form as the Ugaritic word for death that is the name of the god of death. Some passages in the Hebrew Bible that personify death (or Sheol, the place of the dead) as having a mouth and a voracious appetite were possibly adaptations of the mythological image of Mot with the enormous mouth and appetite. Habakkuk 2:5, describing the wealthy, says, "They open their throats wide as Sheol; like Death they never have enough" (cf. Job 18:13-14; Ps. 141:7; Prov. 1:12; 27:20; 30:15-16; Isa. 5:14).

---

6. "The Ba'lu Myth" (*COS* 1.86:265).

The Period of the Monarchy

Gezer Calendar

Soft limestone tablet

▷ Size: 11.1 cm. (4.37 in.) high; 7.2 cm. (2.83 in.) wide
▷ Writing: Proto-Hebrew
▷ Provenance: Gezer (modern Tel el-Jazari in Israel)
▷ Date: Tenth century B.C.E.
▷ Present location: Archaeological Museum, Istanbul (third floor)
▷ Identification number: 2089 T

> Two months of ingathering. Two months of sowing. Two months
>   of late sowing (*or* spring growth).
> Month of pulling flax.
> Month of barley harvest.
> Month when everything [else] is harvested.
> Two months of pruning [vines].
> Month of summer fruit.[1]

> Abiya (A personal name, written sideways in the margin)

Regarded as the work of a schoolboy on a practice tablet, the seven lines of the Gezer Calendar have an importance far beyond their content. Scholars generally refer to this agricultural calendar as the oldest existing example of the Hebrew language, an archaic southern Palestinian dialect previous to the later, dominant Jerusalem dialect. (Because of its variances with later inscriptions, some authorities would regard the writing as a South Canaanite dialect rather than proto-Hebrew, and the abecedary from Tel-Apheq as the earliest example of Hebrew lettering.) The name "Abiya," the short form of the biblical name "Abijah," establishes the writer as an Israelite.

This important document was found in 1908 by the archaeologist R. A. S. Macalister, working on behalf of the Palestine Exploration Fund, at the site of ancient Gezer in Israel. Positive identification of the site was made possible by the discovery of several engraved rock inscriptions (first century B.C.E.) in Hebrew with the words "boundary of Gezer"; another of these stones was found recently. Macalister's work in stratigraphy (determining the layers from which artifacts come, and thus their date) was primitive, even for his time, and there-

---

1. "The Gezer Calendar," translated by J. Mauchline (*DOTT,* p. 201).

26. Inscribed stone known as the Gezer Calendar

fore precise dating of the tablet is not possible. Recent consensus generally assigns a date to the tenth century B.C.E.

Although the tablet generally has been regarded as the efforts of a schoolboy learning to write, some scholars see it as a text used in scribal training; the varying forms of the letters are seen only as evidence of an early date. Because of the rhythmic nature of the words, other scholars understand these words as a device for learning the months, much like "thirty days hath September. . . ." Another hypothesis views the inscription as a "blessing tablet" to be placed in the local shrine as a visible prayer to Yahweh for a favorable harvest.

Both sides of the tablet show evidence of use. The soft limestone readily allowed reuse by scraping away the older lettering, so the tablet is technically a palimpsest (writing surface used more than once after previous writing has been erased, often incompletely). Fragments of some previous words still remain on the calendar, complicating its translation. The content, however, plainly is describing the year in terms of agricultural seasons, which emphasizes the close connection of the lives of the ancient Hebrews to the land. This calendar begins, not with the beginning of the farming cycle, but in the fall, the traditional beginning of the year in ancient Israel.

One theory has described this tablet as an official document somehow related to the taxation of agricultural products. But the crudeness of the lettering, coupled with the numerous variations in the formation of repeated letters, makes it most likely that the document was not produced in official circles but as a practice exercise in writing.

Biblical Significance

The principal importance of the Gezer Calendar is its connection to the Hebrew language. Linguists continue to reference it in studies of the origin of the language of the Old Testament/Hebrew Scriptures. But the calendar's designation of agricultural periods also corresponds to many texts in the biblical record.

This calendar starts not in late winter or spring with the beginning of the farming cycle, but in the fall, the end of the agricultural cycle, which was the traditional beginning of the year in ancient Israel (Exod. 23:16). The "ingathering" of grain and olives (August-October) at the "turn of the year" had to occur before the "early rains," usually at the end of October or the beginning of November (Exod. 34:22). "Ingathering" in the Bible refers to the harvesting of summer fruit, grapes and olives, in that order, from August to November. Plowing and sowing of grain followed (November-December) once the ground had softened. The months of "late sowing" (January-February) were those that served for the planting of summer crops, such as beans, lentils, and millet (Ezek. 4:9). Flax was harvested in March; Hosea refers to it (Hos. 2:5, 9). Rahab hid the Hebrew spies under stalks of flax on her rooftop (Josh. 2:6). (Flax had to first dry in the sun before it could be made into a fiber.) Barley was harvested in April (Ruth 1:22), and the remaining crops in May. June and July were the months for pruning in the vineyards, and in August, figs were gathered (2 Sam. 16:1).

Mesha Stela (Moabite Stone)

Black basalt stela

- ▷ Size: 1.15 m. (45.28 in.) high; 60-80 cm. (23.6–31.5 in.) wide
- ▷ Writing: Moabite language
- ▷ Provenance: Dhiban (ancient Dibon), Jordan
- ▷ Date: ca. 835 B.C.E.
- ▷ Present location: Louvre (room D, ground floor, Sully Wing, section 4)
- ▷ Identification number: AO 5066

The story of the discovery of the Mesha Stela, also known as the Moabite Stone, reads like a good adventure tale. In the middle of the nineteenth century, F. A. Klein, who was from the Alsatian city of Strasbourg, was serving as an Anglican missionary in Palestine. In the summer of 1868 he set out on a mission trip from Jerusalem and traveled by horseback to the area of Moab in modern Jordan. Even though the Transjordan region was officially a part of the Ottoman Empire at the time, it was in reality under the control of various bedouin tribes. Travel in the region was unsafe for outsiders. Thus Klein took along with him the son of the sheikh of the *Bani Sakhr* tribe as a traveling companion and protector that summer. On August 19, Klein arrived at a bedouin camp at Dhiban, where the members of the *Bani Hamidi* tribe treated him courteously. Late that afternoon the bedouin told Klein about an inscribed stone nearby that no European had ever seen. Curious, Klein accepted their offer to show him the stone. Arriving at the stone after a short walk, Klein examined the stone, made a sketch of it, and copied a few words of the text before darkness forced him to stop. He could not read the inscription, but sensed that it might be important.

When he returned to Jerusalem at the end of August, Klein reported his discovery to the German consul in the city, who began, with Klein's assistance, a prolonged attempt at negotiating a purchase of the stone from the bedouin, an effort that lasted over fifteen months. Word of the discovery soon leaked out to others in Jerusalem, including the Englishman Charles Warren and the Frenchman Charles Clermont-Ganneau. Warren hesitated to interfere with the attempts to acquire the stone. Clermont-Ganneau, however, made an offer to the bedouin to buy the stone and sent a young Arab man to Dhiban with instructions to make a paper squeeze of the stela. (A squeeze is made by placing a sheet of wet paper over the object and pressing the wet paper down into the inscription or carving on the stone. Once the paper dries and is removed, it contains an impression of the contents of the stone.) While he was at Dhiban, a fight broke out among the bedouin, and the young Arab had to flee, taking the still wet squeeze with him. In his haste, the squeeze was torn into several pieces and also crumpled. Disappointed with the poor condition of the paper impression, Clermont-Ganneau was still able to read enough of the inscription to realize its value.

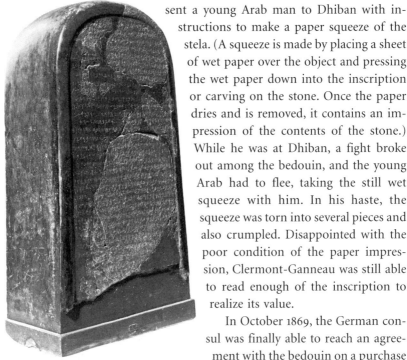

27. The Mesha Stela, also known as the Moabite Stone

In October 1869, the German consul was finally able to reach an agreement with the bedouin on a purchase price for the stela. However, another snag appeared. The stone would have to be transported through territory under the control of a different bedouin tribe, who refused permission for the stone's passage through their territory. When the Ottoman authorities attempted to intervene to allow transportation of the stone, the bedouin, who hated the Ottomans, destroyed the stone by heating it in a fire and then pouring cold water on it. As a result, the stela shattered into many pieces, which were taken by a number of bedouin families and placed in their granaries in the belief that the stone had powers to insure the fertility of their crops. With the stone destroyed, German interest in acquiring the stela seems to have waned. Warren and Clermont-Ganneau, however, attempted to purchase as many pieces of the stone as they could. Warren obtained eighteen fragments, and Clermont-Ganneau acquired thirty-eight fragments. (A German scholar bought an additional piece.) All fifty-seven fragments, containing approximately two-thirds of the inscription, were soon given to the Louvre. With the assistance of the paper squeeze, Clermont-Ganneau was able to assemble the broken pieces and reconstruct the stela for the Louvre.

The stela, made of black basalt, is rounded at the top and has a raised lip on the top and side edges, which frames the inscription. It stands 1.15 m. (45.28 in.) tall, with its width varying from 80 cm. (31.5 in.) at the bottom to 60 cm. (23.6 in.) at the top. The language of the inscription is Moabite, a language very similar to ancient Hebrew. The inscription consists of thirty-four lines of text, making it the longest inscription ever found on a monument in Palestine. Portions of the inscription are missing, including apparently a few additional lines of text at the end.

The stela was erected by Mesha, king of the land of Moab, in his capital city of Dibon (modern Dhiban) to commemorate his military victories and other accomplishments during his reign. Mesha placed the stone at the sanctuary which he built for Chemosh (or, Kemosh), the chief god of Moab, to whom Mesha attributed his success. Most scholars date the stela to around 835 B.C.E. during the latter part of Mesha's kingship.

The text of the inscription reads as follows (numbers in parentheses indicate line numbers):

I am Mesha, son of Chemosh- . . . , king of Moab, the Dibonite. My father was king over Moab thirty years and I became king after my father. And I made this sanctuary for Chemosh at Qrchh, [a sanctuary of] salvation; for he saved me from all the kings and let me see my desire upon my adversaries. Omri, (5) king of Israel, he oppressed Moab many days, for Chemosh was angry with his land. And his son succeeded him and he too said, "I will oppress Moab." In my days he spoke (thus), and I saw my desire upon him and upon his house, when Israel perished utterly for ever. And Omri had taken possession of the land of Medeba and [Israel] dwelt in it his days and half the days of his son, forty years; but Chemosh dwelt in it in my days. And I built Baal-meon and made in it the reservoir, and I built (10) Qaryaten. And the men of Gad had long dwelt in the land of Ataroth, and the king of Israel had built Ataroth for himself. But I fought against the town and took it and I slew all the people of the town, a spectacle for Chemosh and Moab. And I brought back from there the altar-hearth of David and I dragged it before Chemosh at Qeriyoth. And I settled there the men of Sharon and the men of Mchrt. And Chemosh said to me, "Go, take Nebo against Israel." And I (15) went by night and fought against it from the break of dawn till noon; and I took it and slew all: seven thousand men, boys, women, and [girls] and female slaves, for I had consecrated it to Ashtar-Chemosh. And I took from there the vessels of Yahweh and dragged them before Chemosh. And the king of Israel had built Jahaz and he dwelt in it while fighting against me. But Chemosh drove him out before me. And (20) I took from Moab two hundred men, all of them leaders, and led them up against Jahaz and took it to annex it to Dibon. I built Qrchh, the walls of the parks and the walls of the mound; and I built its gates and I built its towers; and I built the king's house; and I made both the reservoirs for water inside the town. And there was no cistern inside the town at Qrchh, so I said to all the people, "Make (25) yourselves each one a cistern in his house." And I had ditches dug for Qrchh by prisoners of Israel.[1]

The remainder of the inscription (lines 26-34) describes additional accomplishments during Mesha's reign, particularly his building activities. In these final lines also, Mesha claims that Chemosh instructed him to fight against the city of Horonaim. Line 31, not included in the excerpt given here, identifies who the inhabitants of Horonaim were. Unfortunately part of the inscription is missing. André Lemaire has argued that line 31 states that "the house of David" lived at Horonaim.[2] If his reading, which is disputed, is correct, then the Mesha Stela provides an important early inscriptional reference to the Davidic dynasty, similar to the Tel Dan inscription, both of which date to the ninth century B.C.E. (see the article "Tel Dan Inscription"). The phrase translated "altar-hearth of David" in line 12 of the translation above is a notoriously difficult passage to interpret, particularly the word translated as "David." Various other suggestions have been given for this word, including "chieftain," "uncle," "beloved," and "vessel." The meaning remains uncertain.

1. "The Moabite Stone," translated by E. Ullendorff (*DOTT*, pp. 196-97).
2. André Lemaire, "'House of David' Restored in Moabite Inscription," *Biblical Archaeology Review* 20 (1994): 30-37.

Biblical Significance

Moab, located east of Israel in the Transjordan region, was a traditional enemy of Israel. The name first occurs in the Bible in Geneses 19:30-38 where Moab is the name of a son of Lot whose conception resulted from an incestuous episode between a drunken Lot and his daughter (actually with both of his daughters). Moab's descendants, supposedly, were the Moabite people. This biblical etiology is best seen as a scurrilous slur against an enemy rather than as an accurate statement of the origin of the people of Moab. In the biblical story of the Hebrew people departing from Egypt and eventually settling in Canaan, part of their journey was through the land of Moab. One of the major locations where Moses taught the people the commandments and laws of God was Moab (Num. 35:1; 36:13; Deut. 29:1). Furthermore, the mountain from which he saw "the Promised Land" was in Moab, and he died and was buried in that land (Deut. 34:1-8).

The book of Judges describes conflict between the Israelites and the king of Moab, in which Israel was first defeated and subservient to the Moabites. After eighteen years of servitude, the Israelites under the leadership of Ehud revolted and defeated the Moabites (Judg. 3:12-30). During the early monarchical period, both Saul and David fought against Moab, with David succeeding in defeating them and requiring payment of tribute from them (1 Sam. 14:47; 2 Sam. 8:2). As one of the traditional enemies of Israel, Moab was singled out by several of the prophets — particularly Amos, Isaiah, and Jeremiah — as a future recipient of God's punishment.

With this history of animosity between Moab and Israel, one can understand why the accomplishment of Mesha's reign that receives the most attention in the stela inscription is his overthrow of Israel's domination of Moab. According to the text, Moab had been oppressed by Israel for forty years until Mesha successfully revolted against Israel and reclaimed Moabite territory. This rebellion against Israel occurred when "the son of Omri" (apparently Ahab) reigned as king of Israel. The biblical version of Mesha's revolt is told in 2 Kings 3, which states that when Mesha rebelled, a coalition of the kings of Israel, Judah, and Edom led their armies against Moab. (The Bible does not describe how Moab first came under the control of Omri and his successors.) The coalition armies were on the verge of victory over the Moabites, when Mesha, in an apparent act of desperation, sacrificed his oldest son as a burnt offering. Then, according to the biblical text, the coalition armies halted their attack on Mesha: "Great wrath came upon Israel, so they withdrew from him and returned to their own land" (2 Kings 3:27).

Since the Mesha inscription and the biblical account are written from opposing viewpoints, not surprisingly several discrepancies or even contradictions appear when the two versions are compared. For example, there appears to be a chronological problem. Whereas the Mesha inscription states that the rebellion occurred during the reign of Omri's son, the biblical account claims that it took place when Jehoram, grandson of Omri, was king. Scholars have suggested several ways to resolve this difference, such as proposing that "the son of Omri" should not be taken literally, but should be understood as a reference to a descendant of Omri, specifically Ahaziah or his brother Jehoram (also called Joram), grandsons of Omri. Another proposal is that the revolt actually occurred, or at least began, during the reign of Ahab, as stated in the inscription. The biblical writer, then, would have shifted the focus to Jehoram in order to highlight his failure as a king. Regardless of whether the details of the biblical account or the Mesha Stela version are correct, both attest that Moab, which had been subjugated by the Omride dynasty of Israel, gained its freedom from Israelite control during the reign of Mesha.

Also of interest is the way in which the stela inscription describes Mesha's victory. In language reminiscent of that of the biblical writers, Mesha views Moab's initial subjection to Israel as a result of the god Chemosh's anger at the people of Moab. Then when Mesha is successful, he attributes the victory to Chemosh. Furthermore he explains his actions as the result of direct guidance and commands from his god: "Go, take Nebo against Israel." Readers who are familiar with biblical historical narratives can easily see the similarities.

Two aspects of the stela's description of Mesha's conquest of Nebo are noteworthy. First, Mesha claims that when he took Nebo, he completely slaughtered all its inhabitants, for he "had consecrated" it to Chemosh. (Chemosh is mentioned in the Hebrew Bible in several places: Num. 21:29; Judg. 11:24; 1 Kings 11:7, 33; 2 Kings 23:13; Jer. 48:7, 13, 46.) The word translated "had consecrated" is the word *herem*, the same word that is used numerous times in the Hebrew Bible to describe the Israelites' similar practice of total annihilation of a city or town during a divinely sanctioned war. In the Hebrew Bible, to put a city under the ban *(herem)* meant that all the inhabitants of the city were to be exterminated and that no spoils of war could be taken; everything was consecrated to Yahweh for destruction. (See, for example, 1 Sam. 15:1-33.) Second, Mesha claims that from Nebo he took "the vessels of Yahweh." This statement contains the earliest known reference outside the Bible to the name of Israel's god, Yahweh.

Finally, all of Israel's connections to Moab were not negative. The book of Ruth tells the story of a man from Bethlehem who went and lived with his wife in the land of Moab during a time of famine in Canaan. While in Moab, their two sons married Moabite women. After the father died, his wife, Naomi, and a widowed daughter-in-law, Ruth, traveled back to Bethlehem. Eventually Ruth married again and bore a son, the grandfather of King David. Thus, according to the biblical account, the great-grandmother of David, Israel's greatest king, was a Moabite.

Tel Dan Inscription

Basalt stela fragments

▷ Size: Fragment A: 32 cm. (12.6 in.) high; 22 cm. (8.66 in.) wide
     Fragment B1: 20 cm. (7.87 in.) high; 14 cm. (5.51 in.) wide
     Fragment B2: 10 cm. (3.94 in.) high; 9 cm. (3.54 in.) wide
▷ Writing: Aramaic
▷ Provenance: Tel Dan, Israel
▷ Date: Ninth century B.C.E.
▷ Present location: Israel Museum (Bronfman Archaeology Wing)
▷ Identification number: IAA 1993-3162; IAA 1996-125

Archaeological excavations at Tel Dan, the site of the ancient city of Dan, located at the foot of Mt. Hermon in northern Israel, were begun in 1966. In July 1993 an archaeological team from the Hebrew Union College–Jewish Institute of Religion in Jerusalem was doing further excavations at the site when the surveyor of the expedition spotted an inscribed stone fragment that had been reused in an ancient wall. This fragment, known as fragment A, was determined to be part of a larger stela that had been smashed in antiquity. In June of the following year, the members of the team found two additional inscribed fragments, designated B1 and B2. All three fragments originally belonged to the same monument. Fragment B2 can be joined to the bottom of B1, and together they seem to be the left side of a portion of the stela, while fragment A is the right side. A gap exists, however, between fragments B1/B2 and fragment A, with the result that a few intervening letters or words are missing. Fragments B1/B2 contain eight partial lines of text, whereas fragment A contains thirteen partial lines. If the fragments have been correctly arranged in relation to one another, then the text on B1/B2 is a continuation of the text on fragment A. The inscription, written in the Aramaic language, is clearly legible, with almost all the words separated by a dot between the words. The face and one of the sides of the stone, which was a local basalt stone, had been smoothed for carving the inscription on the stone. Unfortunately, the remainder of the inscription has not yet been found.

The reconstructed text, as translated by Avraham Biran and Joseph Naveh, is given below. (Conjectural emendations are enclosed in brackets; numbers indicate the lines of text on the fragments.)

1. [. . .   . . .] and cut [. . .   ]
2. [. . .] my father went up [against him when] he fought at [. . .]
3. And my father lay down, he went to his [ancestors] (*viz.* became sick and died). And the king of I[s-]
4. rael entered previously in my father's land. [And] Hadad made me king.
5. And Hadad went in front of me, [and] I departed from [the] seven [. . .-]
6. s of my kingdom, and I slew [seve]nty kin[gs], who harnessed thou[sands of cha-]
7. riots and thousands of horsemen (or: horses). [I killed Jeho]ram son of [Ahab]
8. king of Israel, and [I] killed [Ahaz]iahu son of [Jehoram kin-]
9. g of the House of David. And I set [their towns into ruins and turned]
10. their land into [desolation . . .   ]
11. other [. . .   and Jehu ru-]
12. led over Is[rael . . .   and I laid]
13. siege upon [. . .   ][1]

The site where the city of Dan was located had been inhabited at least since the fifth millennium B.C.E. Sometime during the fourth millennium the site seems to have been abandoned for nearly a thousand years, after which it was settled once more during the third millennium B.C.E. A large settlement, known as Laish, existed here for approximately three hundred years (ca. 2700–ca. 2400 B.C.E.) and then ceased for some unknown reason. During the second millennium the site was again resettled. One of the most impressive remains from this period uncovered by archaeologists is a triple-arched, mud brick gate. Archaeological evidence points to a destruction of the city during the twelfth century B.C.E., a destruction that was possibly related to the conquest of the area by the Israelite tribe of Dan, mentioned in Joshua 19:40-48 and Judges 18, at which time the city was renamed Dan. Around the middle of the eleventh century, the city was destroyed again, but was soon rebuilt. During the ninth century, according to 1 Kings 15:16-20, Ben-hadad, king of Aram-Damascus, invaded Israel. Among the cities which he conquered was Dan. The city recovered, although it contin-

---

1. Avraham Biran and Joseph Naveh, "The Tel Dan Inscription: A New Fragment," *Israel Exploration Journal* 45, no. 1 (1995): 13.

28. Inscription from Tel Dan mentioning the "House of David"

ued to be faced with threats from Ben-hadad and his successor Hazael until the beginning of the eighth century, when the Arameans were defeated by Assyria. When Assyria conquered the northern kingdom of Israel in the latter half of the eighth century B.C.E., the city of Dan apparently fell victim to the Assyrians, as evidenced by a destruction layer caused by fire dated to the second half of the eighth century.

In the inscription, the author claims that Hadad (the Semitic storm god) had made him king. He further boasts that he had killed the king of Israel and the king of the house of David. Even though the names of the kings of Israel and Judah are only partially preserved, enough letters are present for the kings to be identified with a high degree of certainty as Jehoram of Israel and Ahaziah of Judah. The Aramean king at this time, likely responsible for setting up this victory stela, was Hazael, who took over as king ca. 842 B.C.E.

Biblical Significance

The discovery of fragment A in 1993 created a sensation because of its reference to the "House of David." This was the first time that any reference to the royal name "David" or "House of David" had been found in any inscription or non-biblical literature. A minority of scholars have argued that the phrase *bytdwd,* translated as "House of David," has been mistranslated. Other suggestions have been that the phrase means "house of Dod" (a reference to an otherwise unknown god) or "house of vessels" or that the phrase *bytdwd* is a reference to some geographical location. In spite of these challenges, most scholars have concluded that "house of David" is the most plausible reading of the text. Because some minimalist scholars have argued that no historical David ever existed as king of Israel, this discovery helps reinforce the case in support of the historical David.

If, as has been suggested above, the king who is the subject of this inscription is Hazael, two problems arise. First, both the biblical texts and Assyrian records mention that Hazael was not of royal descent, but was a usurper of the throne. The Assyrian records call him the "son of a nobody" (see the article "Ivory Plaque Mentioning Hazael"), while 2 Kings 8:7-15 describes how he came to the throne after killing his predecessor, Ben-hadad. Yet, in the inscription, the author makes reference to his father three different times in ways that seem to indicate that his father was a king. How can this be reconciled with the biblical and Assyrian claims that he was a usurper? Some scholars have suggested that the apparent references to his predecessor as his father may have been Hazael's attempt to legitimate his kingship by claiming royal kinship, even though none existed. Others have suggested that, since any background information about Hazael is unknown, perhaps he actually was related in some way to the royal family in Damascus, or that he was the son of the ruler of another land. Without more information, this conundrum must remain unsolved. On the other hand, the claim that the god Hadad had made him king may be understood as support for the idea that the author of the text was a usurper, since by claiming divine warrant for his kingship he was seeking legitimacy for his kingship that he could not claim by kinship.

The second problem related to identifying the king of the inscription with Hazael is the author's claim that he was the one who killed the king of the north and the king of the south, that is Joram (or, Jehoram) and Ahaziah. According to 2 Kings 9–10, Jehu, a general in Joram's army, was responsible for their deaths, not Hazael. Actually, this problem arises whether the author of the inscription is Hazael or any other person, except Jehu. Yet, almost certainly Jehu is not the author of the text, for he would hardly claim that the god Hadad had made him king. One proposed solution is that perhaps Jehu was an ally of Hazael and that Hazael saw Jehu as his agent in assassinating the two kings. Another suggestion has been that the biblical writer, writing long after the events had taken place, confused the historical events and mistakenly attributed the killing of the two kings to Jehu, associating the deaths of Joram and Ahaziah during their battle against Hazael with the revolt of Jehu in which he killed the descendants of the house of Omri (see 2 Kings 10). Once again, information currently does not allow a definite answer to the dilemma.

Ivory Plaque Mentioning Hazael

Fragmentary ivory plaque

▷ Size: Joined pieces — 7.9 cm. (3.11 in.) long, 2 cm. (.79 in.) high; separate piece — 3.2 cm. (1.26 in.) long, 1.9 cm. (.75 in.) high

▷ Writing: Aramaic language
▷ Provenance: Hadatu (Arslan Tash, in modern Syria)
▷ Date: End of the ninth century B.C.E.
▷ Present location: Louvre (room C, ground floor, Sully Wing, section 4)
▷ Identification number: AO 11489

Ivory, derived from elephant or hippopotamus tusks, was a popular material for carving in the ancient world, particularly for luxury items. It was used to make a variety of objects, including small boxes, figurines, combs, handles (for mirrors, knives, fans, etc.), and inlays and veneers for wall and furniture decorations. This small ivory plaque was discovered in 1928 in Arslan Tash in northern Syria (ancient Hadatu) by a French archaeological expedition led by F. Thureau-Dangin and A. Barrois. The ivory was part of a large assortment of ivories found at the site of an eighth-century B.C.E. palace that once belonged to the Assyrian governor. It is thought to be part of a decoration or an ivory veneer for a bed. The Aramaic inscription on the plaque is possibly a dedicatory inscription, or perhaps a description inscribed by a royal official to indicate the place of origin of the object. The ivory is broken into three pieces. Two of the pieces fit together; the other piece does not join them but is a separate piece (that is, part of the plaque between the pieces is missing). As normally arranged, the two joined pieces are the second and third pieces, and the other piece is first. (The first piece is on the right, since Aramaic is written from right to left.) The total inscription on the three pieces is usually reconstructed to read, "This . . . has . . . son of Amma engraved for our lord Hazael in the year. . . ."[1] The ivory plaque, along with the other ivories discovered at Arslan Tash, is thought to be part of the booty from Damascus brought to ancient Hadatu by the Assyrians after the conquest of Damascus by Tiglath-pileser III in 732 B.C.E.

The state of Aram (or Aram-Damascus), which was located in southern Syria with its capital at Damascus, flourished between the tenth and eighth centuries B.C.E. The area was occupied for a while during the eleventh century by troops of King David of Israel, but by the time of Solomon had removed itself from Israelite control. By the middle of the ninth century, Aram had become one of the most powerful states in the region of Syria-Palestine. When the Assyrian army under Shalmaneser III began to advance against the Syro-Palestinian states, Aram was the leader of a coalition of states (including the northern kingdom of Israel) that temporarily limited the Assyrian westward expansion.

Hazael was the king of Aram from ca. 842 to ca. 810 B.C.E. According to the

---

1. John C. L. Gibson, *Textbook of Syrian Semitic Inscriptions,* vol. 2: *Aramaic Inscriptions* (Oxford: Clarendon Press, 1975), p. 5.

29. A small ivory plaque mentioning King Hazael of Damascus

Bible (2 Kings 8:7-15), Hazael had been a high official in the royal court of the Aramean king. After assassinating the king ca. 842 B.C.E., Hazael seized the throne for himself. Hazael is mentioned in the records of the Assyrian king Shalmaneser III, where he is referred to as "the son of a nobody," the common term for someone who had usurped power. During Hazael's reign, Aram became one of the most powerful states in the Syro-Palestinian area, covering much of southern Syria and Palestine.

Hazael is mentioned also on the Black Obelisk of Shalmaneser III (see the article on the Black Obelisk), where the Assyrian king boasts of his successes against Hazael on two different occasions. Even though Shalmaneser was successful in capturing some of the territory under Hazael's control, he failed to capture the city of Damascus. The kingdom of Aram-Damascus continued for another century before it fell completely to the Assyrians in 732 B.C.E.

Biblical Significance

Hazael appears on several occasions in the biblical narrative. The story of his murderous seizure of the throne is recounted in 2 Kings 8:7-15. The prophet Elisha had gone to Damascus when the king of Aram (Ben-hadad according to the text, likely to be identified with Hadadezer) was ill. When Hazael was sent to meet Elisha to inquire whether or not the king would recover from his illness, the prophet told Hazael that he would become the king of Aram. The next day, Hazael murdered the king by smothering him and claimed the throne. Hazael created major problems for both Israel and Judah. During Hazael's reign, Joram (also called Jehoram), king of Israel, and Ahaziah, king of Judah, fought against Hazael at a town in northern Israel. During the fight, Joram was wounded and had to retire from the battle (2 Kings 8:28-29). (See the article "Tel Dan Inscription.") Later, according to 2 Kings 10:32-33, Hazael attacked Israel and annexed Israelite territories to the east of the Jordan River. Shortly afterwards, he conquered the city of Gath on the Philistine coastal plain and even marched against Jerusalem. The king of Judah was able to spare the city by sending a large bribe from the temple and palace treasures to Hazael, perhaps rendering Judah a vassal to Hazael (2 Kings 12:17-18). During the reign of Jehoahaz as king of Israel, the biblical account states that God gave

Israel "repeatedly into the hand of King Hazael of Aram" and that Hazael "oppressed Israel all the days of Jehoahaz" (2 Kings 13:3, 22). The death of Hazael, which occurred ca. 800 B.C.E., is mentioned in 2 Kings 13:24. Approximately forty years later, the prophet Amos pronounced judgment against Damascus and the dynasty begun by Hazael, declaring that God would "send a fire on the house of Hazael" (Amos 1:4).

Samaria Ivories

Carved ivory pieces

▷ Size: Winged sphinx — 8.7 cm. (3.43 in.) high (including tenons at top and bottom), 7.1 cm. (2.8 in.) wide; lion attacking bull — 4.2 cm. (1.65 in.) high, 11.2 cm. (4.41 in.) wide (including tenon on the right side)
▷ Provenance: Samaria, Israel
▷ Date: Ninth-eighth century B.C.E.
▷ Present location: Israel Museum (Bronfman Archaeology Wing)
▷ Identification numbers: IAA 1933.2572 (winged sphinx); IAA 1933.2552 (lion attacking bull)

When the nation of Israel split into the northern kingdom of Israel and the southern kingdom of Judah during the tenth century B.C.E., the capital of the northern kingdom was established at Shechem, then at Penuel, and later at Tirzah (either consecutively or as co-capitals). When Omri became king in the early part of the ninth century B.C.E., he moved the capital to Samaria, which remained the political center of the northern kingdom until the destruction of the city by the Assyrians in 722 B.C.E.

Major excavations of the city of Samaria were carried out from 1908 to 1910 and from 1931 to 1935. Minor excavations occurred from 1965 to 1967 and another minor campaign in 1968. In addition to uncovering remains from the Hellenistic, Roman, and Byzantine periods, the excavators found remains of a palace and casemate wall attributed to the time of Omri; a building, tower, and wall (likely part of a gate system) from the time of Ahab; and buildings associated with the time of Jeroboam II. Among the most interesting objects found at Samaria was an assortment of approximately 12,000 pieces of ivory. Most of them were discovered during the excavations of 1931-1935, which was a joint Harvard University/Hebrew University/Palestine Exploration Fund expedition. The majority of the ivories were found on the acropolis between the walls of a building that was possibly an Israelite palace. They were located within a layer of burned material, indicating the destruction of the building. Some of the ivories themselves were badly burned. The ivories are often identified with the palace of Ahab in the ninth century B.C.E. The precise date of the ivories, however, cannot be ascertained, and some scholars would place them in the eighth century. For the most part, these ivory pieces, which were either polished or decoratively carved, were panels or parts of panels used to decorate walls or pieces of wooden furniture. Some of the ivory pieces were used for inlaid designs or veneer coverings, others were carved decorations, and some were fancy toilet articles. Some of the items had stone or glass inlays or gold foil. The designs of the ivory carvings represent Phoenician, Syrian, and Egyptian motifs or styles.

Scholars are divided over the question of whether these Samaria ivories were produced in a Palestinian workshop or whether they were produced elsewhere, such as in Phoenicia or Syria, which were famous for their ivory craftwork. Although ivory from wild boar's tusks and hippopotamus tusks was sometimes used for carving, by the first millennium elephant ivory was the preferred and most commonly used type of ivory in the ancient Near

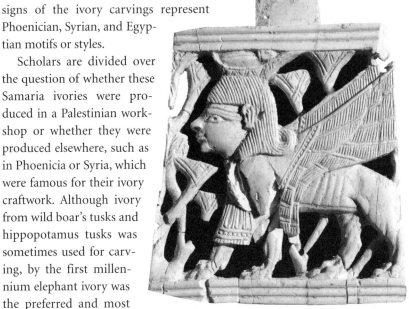

30. Ivory carving from Samaria of a winged sphinx

East. Asian elephants existed in Syria until sometime around the end of the eighth century B.C.E. Even when ivory from Asian elephants was available, artisans often preferred ivory from African elephants due to its being harder, more brilliant, and of finer grain than the Asian variety. Some of the ivory objects found at Samaria have been identified as African ivory. Ivory was highly prized in the ancient world and was an important commodity in trading.

Two of the small ivory plaques from Samaria on display in the Israel Museum depict a winged sphinx (IAA 1933.2572; see fig. 30) and a lion attacking a bull (IAA 1933.2552; see fig. 31). The human head of the sphinx wears an Egyptian-style double crown and has curled hair. The front part of the creature's lion-like body is dressed in a kilt. Its wings are spread and its tail is raised. Facing straight ahead, the sphinx stands in the middle of a thicket of lotus plants. A similar ivory plaque, found at Calah (modern Nimrud in Iraq), is displayed in room 57 of the British Museum (ME 134322). In the other plaque, part of which is missing, a lion is shown attacking a bull. The lion has sunk its teeth into the bull's throat, while it has reached its right forepaw around the bull and dug its claws into the top of the bull's neck. These plaques likely were used as inlays or decorations for furniture.

A small assortment of broken pieces of ivory from Samaria (ME L 31-48) is on display in the British Museum, room 57. Even though the ivories are fragmentary, they still give the viewer an idea of the types of carvings found on decorative ivories.

Biblical Significance

Several biblical passages refer to luxurious ivory items. According to 1 Kings 10:18, King Solomon made for himself "a great ivory throne, and overlaid it with the finest gold," likely referring to a throne decorated with ivory plaques and inlays such as those found at Samaria (cf. 2 Chron. 9:17). The author of 1 Kings, in recounting the death of King Ahab, mentions "the ivory house that he built" (1 Kings 22:39). For the writer to single out Ahab's "ivory house" probably means that it was especially impressive, or even scandalous, for its luxuriousness and opulence. If the numerous ivories found at Samaria were indeed decorations and coverings for the furniture and perhaps some of the walls of Ahab's palace, as some scholars have suggested, then one can understand why such an ornate building would have caught the biblical writer's attention. In a similar way, Psalm 45:8, which is an ode probably composed for a

31. Ivory carving from Samaria showing a lion attacking a bull

king's wedding, describes the royal buildings as "ivory palaces," meaning buildings decorated with ivory.

The prophet Amos, who was active around the middle of the eighth century B.C.E., condemned the social injustice and opulence of the wealthy people of Samaria. Not only did they have winter houses and summer houses, but they also lived in "houses of ivory" (3:15). In a later passage, Amos included the wealthy of Jerusalem in his condemnation as well. They, along with the powerful and wealthy of Samaria, indulged themselves with fine food and drink while lying "on beds of ivory," unconcerned about the troubles of the nation (6:4-6). For their arrogance and indifference, he warned, they would be the first to be carried away by their enemies (6:7).

The winged sphinx that is depicted in many of the carved ivories from the ancient world (such as IAA 1933.2572), as well as in other media (wall reliefs, sculptures, and jewelry), is one example of what is meant by the biblical term "cherub" or "cherubim" (plural). The cherubim are described as various winged, composite creatures, sometimes with the features of humans, lions, bulls, or eagles. Such composite beasts occur frequently in ancient Near Eastern, particularly Assyrian, art. The biblical texts describe the early tabernacle, as well as the temple in Jerusalem, as being extensively decorated with cherubim. They were woven into curtains and veils and carved into walls, panels, doors, and other objects (Exod. 26:1, 31; 36:8, 35; 1 Kings 6:29; 7:27-37). Two golden cherubim with outstretched wings adorned the top of the Ark of the Covenant (Exod. 25:18-22; 37:7-9), which was kept in the holy of holies, the most sacred part of the temple. In the temple, the ark rested underneath two enormous olivewood cherubim overlaid with gold (1 Kings 6:23-28; 8:6-7). The four living creatures pulling the throne-chariot of God that Ezekiel saw in his vision are somewhat cherub-like creatures (Ezek. 1:5-25; in Ezekiel 10 they become cherubim), as were also the four living creatures of Revelation 4. The latter were modifications of the creatures of Ezekiel's vision.

Nimrud Ivories

Carved ivory pieces

▷ Size: Woman at the window — 10.79 cm. (4.25 in.) high, 8.46 cm. (3.33 in.) wide; lioness and Nubian boy — 10.35 cm. (4.07 in.) high, 10.2 cm. (4.02 in.) wide

▷ Provenance: Calah (Nimrud, in modern Iraq)

▷ Date: Ninth-eighth century B.C.E.

▷ Present location: British Museum (room 57)

▷ Identification numbers: ME 118156 (woman at the window); ME 127412 (lioness and Nubian boy)

Nimrud is the modern name for the site of Calah, one of the ancient capitals of Assyria. It was the location for the palaces of several Assyrian kings, most notably Ashurnasirpal II, who was the first Assyrian king to establish his capital at Nimrud during the ninth century B.C.E. The site was first excavated by Austen Henry Layard, beginning in 1845. On the very first day of his diggings at Nimrud, Layard found the remains of two palaces, including the palace of Ashurnasirpal. On his second day, digging in the Northwest Palace of Ashurnasirpal, he made the first of what would become several discoveries of ivories at Nimrud, by Layard as well as by others. Between 1949 and 1952, M. E. L. Mallowan found a large number of some of the most impressive ivories from Nimrud. Many of these he discovered at the bottom of wells in the Northwest Place, where, after having been stripped of their gold, they apparently had been tossed by the soldiers who sacked the city, either at the death of Sargon II in 705 B.C.E. or at the end of the seventh century B.C.E. when Assyria collapsed. Another large find of ivories occurred during the 1854-1855 excavations at the site of the co-called "Burnt Palace" by W. K. Loftus. The most spectacular collection of ivories at Nimrud, however, was yet to be unearthed. From 1957 to 1963 David Oates directed the excavation of what he labeled "Fort Shalmaneser," a palace/arsenal complex built by Shalmaneser III in the middle of the ninth century and renovated and used by later kings until the fall of Assyria. One of the uses of this arsenal was as a storeroom for booty taken from captured territories. In the arsenal, stored in several of its rooms, Oates

32. Ivory carving from Nimrud with a scene of "the woman at the window"

discovered the largest collection of ivory objects from that time period ever found. The arsenal had apparently served as the main storage center for ivory objects amassed by the Assyrian kings during the ninth and eighth centuries. Additional discoveries of ivories occurred in subsequent years, including some by the Iraq Department of Antiquities. The ivories today are in several museums, including the British Museum and the Iraq Museum.

The ivories found at Nimrud came from various locations. Phoenicia and Syria were major producers of ivory work, and their products were traded throughout the ancient Near East. The Nimrud ivories contain representatives of both Phoenician and Syrian styles, many using Egyptian motifs in their designs. In addition to thin ivory pieces used as veneer for furniture, carved ivory pieces for inlays and decorations were discovered, as were also ivory objects such as combs, spoons, cosmetic boxes and bowls, horse ornaments, parts of figurines, and handles for mirrors and fly-whisks. Many of the ivory pieces were carved plaques for decorating furniture such as beds and chairs. Common subjects for the plaques were scenes of a cow and calf, human-headed sphinxes, winged guardians, bulls and stags, youths with a lotus plant, the birth of Horus, and "the woman at the window." Many of the plaques were originally overlaid with gold; some had inlays of glass or stone.

Among the Nimrud ivories on display in the British Museum is one with a scene popularly known as "the woman at the window" (ME 118156; see fig. 32). This motif is found on several ivory carvings, including ones discovered at Samaria, Arslan Tash (in Syria), and Nimrud. The British Museum possesses at least two ivories with this scene, only one of which is on display. The scene shows the head of a woman facing forward, looking out a window. The woman's hair (or wig) is cut in an Egyptian style. A balustrade with columns shaped like palm trees is underneath the window. The top and sides of the window have a triple-recessed design. Although the significance of this scene is uncertain, it has been suggested that it alludes to the cult of Astarte and that the woman represents Astarte or one of her devotees, depicted as a sacred prostitute. (Astarte was the Canaanite goddess of love and war and was the consort of Baal, god of storm and fertility. Some scholars have connected the woman with Ishtar, the Mesopotamian goddess, rather than Astarte.) Other examples of ivory with this scene, this time from Arslan Tash (ancient Hadatu in Syria), are displayed in the Louvre (AO 11459, AO 11460, AO 11461; room 6, ground floor, Richelieu Wing).

An especially interesting example of the Nimrud ivories in the British Museum is a small plaque showing a Nubian boy being attacked by a lioness, which has the boy's throat in its mouth (ME 127412; see plate 3). The ivory originally had a gold leaf overlay on much of the plaque and inlays of carnelian and lapis lazuli. The boy's hair was made of blackened ivory pegs whose tops had a gold overlay. The background of the scene is filled with papyrus and lotus plants. An identical but better preserved copy of this plaque is in the Iraq Museum. This matching pair probably decorated a piece of furniture.

Biblical Significance

If, as some scholars have suggested, the figure of "the woman at the window" does indeed relate to the cult of Astarte, then this scene connects to the numerous references to Astarte in the Hebrew Bible. When the Israelites settled in the land of Canaan, they were living among people who worshipped a variety of deities, including Astarte and her consort Baal. (The latter was particularly attractive, since he was the god responsible for bringing storms and rain. This precipitation made their crops grow and provided water for their livestock and ultimately made the earth fertile. In other Canaanite traditions, Anath is the consort of Baal in addition to or in place of Astarte.) In the Hebrew Bible, Astarte is known as Ashtoreth (or, Ashtaroth, the plural form). The biblical practice of spelling the name as Ashtoreth instead of Astarte is thought to be an intentional distortion of the name of the goddess by scribes who substituted the vowels from the Hebrew word for "shame" *(boshet)*. The author of 1 Kings gives a negative assessment of King Solomon, blaming his lack of faithfulness to Yahweh on his many foreign wives, who "turned away his heart after other gods" (11:4). Among the foreign deities whom he is accused of following is "Astarte the goddess of the Sidonians" (11:5, 33). Over three hundred years later, Josiah, king of Judah, destroyed the high place east of Jerusalem that Solomon "had built for Astarte the abomination of the Sidonians" (2 Kings 23:13). Elsewhere in the Hebrew Bible the plural form, Ashtaroth ("Astartes," NRSV), is used (Judg. 2:13; 10:6; 1 Sam. 7:3, 4; 12:10; 31:10). The plural may simply be a way of speaking of Canaanite goddesses in general, or it may refer to various local versions of Astarte.

Beyond the possible connection to Astarte, this scene is reminiscent of the biblical account of Jezebel, the queen mother, appearing in the window of the palace when Jehu entered the city of Jezreel. Jezebel appeared at the window adorned like a prostitute — "she painted her eyes, and adorned her head" (2 Kings 9:30) — perhaps hoping to seduce Jehu. Upon seeing Jezebel at the window, Jehu, who had led a coup that resulted in the deaths of the king of the northern kingdom of Israel and the king of the southern kingdom of Judah, ordered her servants to throw her down from the palace, which they did. As a result Jezebel died, bringing to an end one of the most infamous characters of the Hebrew Bible.

Furthermore, the biblical writers frequently used the image of an unfaithful wife or a prostitute as a way of referring to the unfaithfulness of the people to Yahweh (cf. Jer. 3:1-10; 4:30; Ezekiel 23; Hos. 4:15; 5:3-4; 9:1).

Like the Samaria ivories, the Nimrud ivories are examples of the ivory used for decorating walls and luxury items of furniture. Since the Nimrud ivories came from various spots throughout the Assyrian Empire, some of them could have come from Palestine, including Samaria. Thus these ivories, like the Samaria ivories, provide an illustration of the condemnation by the prophet Amos of the wealthy of Samaria who lived in "houses of ivory" (Amos 3:15) and lay on "beds of ivory" (6:4).

The Kurkh Monolith of Shalmaneser III

Limestone stela

▷ Size: 2.20 m. (7.22 ft.) high
▷ Writing: Akkadian language in cuneiform script
▷ Provenance: Kurkh (near Diyarbakir, Turkey)
▷ Date: ca. 852 B.C.E.
▷ Present location: British Museum (room 6a)
▷ Identification number: ME 118884

Shalmaneser III ruled as king of the Neo-Assyrian Empire from 858 to 823 B.C.E. Like his father, Ashurnasirpal II, who preceded him on the throne, Shalmaneser was a builder and an expander of his empire. Among his numerous building projects were the construction of an arsenal or fort ("Fort Shalmaneser") and the completion of a ziggurat begun by his father at Nimrud; the building of city walls, gates, and temples at Assur; repairs and new buildings at Nineveh; and the erection of huge cedar gates with bronze bands filled with scenes and texts at Imgur-Enlil (Balawat). Not content with the limits of his empire, Shalmaneser sent his armies to subjugate other lands, particularly to the west, bringing them under his control and inflicting destruction and terror on any who opposed him. Like rulers throughout history, Shalmaneser had his various accomplishments and victories inscribed on buildings, stelae, tablets, statues, clay prisms and cylinders, and other venues. This self-serving combination of propaganda and public relations is a boon to modern historians, for these ancient inscriptions, though filled with exaggerated boasts and biased accounts, still provide valuable information about ancient rulers and their kingdoms.

The Kurkh Monolith of Shalmaneser III was found at Kurkh (near Diyarbakir, Turkey) in 1861 by J. E. Taylor, who found there another monolith also, this one by Shalmaneser III's father, Ashurnasirpal II. (The monolith erected at Kurkh by Ashurnasirpal, ME 118883, is displayed adjacent to that of Shalmaneser in the British Museum.) The monolith from Shalmaneser is rounded at the top and contains a relief carving of the king standing with an upraised right arm before the symbols of the gods. The writing is inscribed on both the front and back sides of the stela. On the front, the inscription covers the major portion of the face of the stela, including over the picture of Shalmaneser, from his shoulders to below his feet. After a typical invocation of the gods, followed by the king's name, descriptive phrases, and genealogy, the inscription describes the military campaigns of the king year-by-year from 858 B.C.E. to 853 B.C.E. (The campaign of 854 B.C.E. is omitted.) The numerous scribal errors in the inscription suggest that the stela was carved in haste.

The last entry in the inscription describes the battle of Qarqar in Syria in 853 B.C.E. Shalmaneser faced a coalition of twelve states, led by Hadadezer of Aram. On three subsequent occasions (849, 848, and 845 B.C.E.), he would face this same coalition of armies arrayed against him; in his annals he claimed victory each time. On the Kurkh stela, Shalmaneser boasted:

I approached the city of Qarqar. I razed, destroyed and burned the city of Qarqar, his royal city. 1,200 chariots, 1,200 cavalry, (and) 20,000 troops of Hadad-ezer *(Adad-idri)* of Damascus; 700 chariots, 700 cavalry, (and) 10,000 troops of Irhulēni, the Hamathite; 2,000 chariots, (and) 10,000 troops of Ahab, the Israelite *(Sir'alāia);* 500 troops of Byblos; 1,000 troops of Egypt; 10 chariots (and) 10,000 troops of the land of Irqanatu (Irqata); 200 troops of Matinu-ba'al of the city of Arvad; 200 troops of the land of Usanatu (Usnu); 30 chariots (and) [ ],000 troops of Adon-ba'al of the land of Šianu (Siyannu); 1,000 camels of Gindibu' of Arabia; [ ] hundred troops of Ba'asa, (the man) of Bīt-Ruḫubi, the Ammonite — these 12 kings he took as his allies.

They marched against me [to do] war and battle. With the supreme forces which Aššur, my lord, had given me (and) with the mighty weapons which the divine standard, which goes before me, had granted me, I fought with them. I decisively defeated them from the city of Qarqar to the city of Gilzau. I felled with the sword 14,000 troops, their fighting men. Like Adad, I rained down upon them a devastating flood. I spread out their corpses (and) I filled the plain. <I felled> with the sword their extensive troops. I made their blood flow in the *wadis* (?) [ ]. The field was too small for laying flat their bodies (lit. "their lives"); the broad countryside had been consumed in burying them. I blocked the Orontes River with their corpses as with a causeway. In the midst of this battle I took away from them chariots, cavalry, (and) teams of horses.[1]

Biblical Significance

Among the kings who joined the coalition with Hadadezer of Damascus in Aram was Ahab, king of Israel. In fact, according to the number of troops, cavalry, and chariots supplied by each of the states, Israel, along with Damascus and Hamath, was one of the major partners in the coalition. Prior to the time of this coalition, Israel's relationship with Damascus had been troublesome, likely including border skirmishes between the two nations. According to 1 Kings 15:16-20, during the time when Baasha was king of Israel (910-887 B.C.E.), Aram-Damascus, under Ben-hadad I, broke its treaty with Israel, attacking and conquering part of the northern portion of Israel. In the following decades, particularly during the reigns of Omri and Ahab, relationships between the two nations must have improved significantly in order for them to have forged the alliance against the Assyrian threat represented by Shalmaneser III. (The writer of 1 Kings 20 and 22 recounts a war between Benhadad and Ahab. For various reasons, many scholars have suggested that this narrative actually describes a later conflict that occurred between Aram and Israel, arguing that the biblical writer has in-

33. The Kurkh Monolith of Shalmaneser III

serted the names of the Israelite king — and possibly the Aramean king, as well — into an originally anonymous narrative and misplaced it chronologically.)

The battle of Qarqar, described on the Kurkh Monolith, is not mentioned in the Hebrew Bible, which also never mentions Shalmaneser III. The biblical writers take no notice of the Assyrians until the reign of Tiglath-pileser III (in

---

1. "Kurkh Monolith," translated by K. Lawson Younger, Jr. (*COS* 2.113A:263-64).

the Bible sometimes called Pul, a form of his Assyrian nickname), who ruled Assyria from 744 to 727 B.C.E. As the Assyrian records clearly indicate, however, the Assyrians had been a growing threat to Israel and other Syro-Palestinian states for several decades prior to the time of Tiglath-pileser III. Shalmaneser's claim of victory at Qarqar, rather than being an accurate statement, is probably an exaggeration for propaganda purposes. The battle likely was a failure for Shalmaneser, or at best a draw, since he returns immediately to Assyria, has no further confrontations with the coalition, and does not return to Syria for four more years.

The Black Obelisk of Shalmaneser III

Black limestone obelisk

- ▷ Size: 1.98 m. (6.5 ft.) high; 45.08 cm. (17.75 in.) wide
- ▷ Writing: Akkadian language in cuneiform script
- ▷ Provenance: Calah (Nimrud in Iraq)
- ▷ Date: ca. 827 B.C.E.
- ▷ Present location: British Museum (room 6a)
- ▷ Identification number: ME 118885

In addition to the Kurkh Monolith described in the previous article, another of the inscribed artifacts from the reign of Shalmaneser III is the impressive object known as the Black Obelisk. Made of fine-grained black limestone streaked with white, this obelisk was discovered at Nimrud (ancient Calah) by Austin Henry Layard in 1846. Layard was responsible for the first archaeological excavations at Nimrud, unearthing spectacular finds beneath the mound at the site, including a pair of colossal winged bulls from the time of Shalmaneser III and the impressive wall panels from the palaces of Tiglath-pileser III and Ashurnasirpal II. The fortuitous discovery of the Black Obelisk was described by Layard as follows:

> I had business in Mosul, and was giving directions to the workmen to guide them during my absence. Standing on the edge of the hitherto unprofitable trench, I doubted whether I should carry it any further; but made up my mind at last, not to abandon it until my return, which would be on the following day. I mounted my horse; but had scarcely left the mound when a corner of black marble was uncovered, lying on the very edge of the trench.

This attracted the notice of the superintendent of the party digging, who ordered the place to be further examined. The corner was part of an obelisk, about seven feet high, lying on its side, ten feet below the surface.

An Arab was sent after me without delay, to announce the discovery, and on my return I found the obelisk completely exposed to view. I descended eagerly into the trench, and was immediately struck by the singular appearance, and evident antiquity, of the remarkable monument before me. We raised it from its recumbent position, and, with the aid of ropes, speedily dragged it out of the ruins. . . . The whole was in the best preservation; scarcely a character of the inscription was wanting; and the figures were as sharp and well defined as if they had been carved but a few days before.[1]

The obelisk is shaped like a ziggurat, with its top narrowing in steps. On each of its four sides are five panels that contain relief drawings depicting various individuals bringing tribute to the king. The main text of the inscription is written above and below the groupings of panels, while above each panel is a brief epigraph describing the scene in the panel. The inscription, which begins with an invocation of the various Mesopotamian gods and a listing of

34. The Black Obelisk of Shalmaneser III

the royal name and descriptive phrases for Shalmaneser III, boasts of the major military exploits and subjugations of the reign of Shalmaneser, listing them year by year from his first year through his thirty-first year. Because the last listing is for his thirty-first year, or 828 B.C.E., the obelisk was written in 828 or, more likely, 827 B.C.E.

1. Austin Henry Layard, *Nineveh and Its Remains* (New York: George P. Putnam, 1849), 1:281-82.

Of particular interest is the record of his campaign during the eighteenth year of his reign: "In my eighteenth regnal year, I crossed the Euphrates for the sixteenth time. Hazael of Damascus attacked to do battle. I took away from him 1,121 of his chariots, 470 of his cavalry together with his camp."[2] Hazael was the king of Aram (or Aram-Damascus) in modern Syria from ca. 842 to ca. 810 B.C.E. (see the article entitled "Ivory Plaque Mentioning Hazael"). Shalmaneser had invaded the land of Aram on four occasions (when Hadadezer was king) prior to the invasion listed here, and once again three years later: "In my twenty-first regnal year, I crossed the Euphrates for the twenty-first time. I marched to the cities of Hazael of Damascus. I captured 4 of his fortified settlements. I received the tribute of the Tyrians, the Sidonians, and the Byblians."[3] The invasion that occurred during Shalmaneser's eighteenth year (841 B.C.E.) is described in more detail in another one of Shalmaneser's inscriptions:

> In my eighteenth regnal year, I crossed the Euphrates for the sixteenth time. Hazael of Damascus trusted in the massed might of his troops; and he mustered his troops in great numbers. He made Mt. Saniru/Senir, a mountain peak, which (lies) opposite Mount Lebanon, his fortress. I fought with him. I decisively defeated him. I felled with the sword 16,000 of his troops, his fighting men. I took away from him 1,121 of his chariots, 470 of his cavalry, together with his camp. In order to save his life he ran away. I pursued after him. I confined him in Damascus, his royal city. I cut down his orchards. I marched to the mountains of Ḥaurāni. I razed, destroyed and burned cities without number. I carried away their booty without number. I marched to the mountains of Baʾli-rasi at the side of the sea. I erected a statue of my royalty there.
>
> At that time, I received the tribute of the Tyrians and the Sidonians, and of Jehu *(Ia-ú-a)*, (man of) Bīt-Humrî (Omri).[4]

The above-mentioned payment of tribute to Shalmaneser by Jehu, king of Israel, is depicted in the row of panels second from the top on each side of the obelisk. The panel on side A (see fig. 35) depicts Shalmaneser, beneath a parasol, along with four Assyrians, accepting the tribute from Jehu, who is prostrating himself on the ground before the king. (This relief is the only known, contemporary representation of an Israelite king.) The panels on the other three sides show two Assyrian officials receiving the tribute from a total of thirteen tribute bearers from Israel. The tribute bearers wear long garments with fringed cloaks over them, shoes with upturned toes, and soft, pointed

2. "Black Obelisk," translated by K. Lawson Younger (*COS* 2.113F:269).
3. "Black Obelisk" (*COS* 2.113F:269).
4. "Annals: Calaḥ Bulls," translated by K. Lawson Younger (*COS* 2.113C:267).

35. Detail of the Black Obelisk showing King Jehu of Israel offering tribute

caps. The inscription above the panels reads: "I received the tribute of Jehu *(Ia-ú-a)* (the man) of Bīt-Ḫumrî: silver, gold, a golden bowl, a golden goblet, golden cups, golden buckets, tin, a staff of the king's hand, (and) javelins(?)."[5] The identification of Jehu as "man (or, 'of the house') of Omri" (Bīt-Ḫumrî) is technically incorrect. Jehu was not a descendant of Omri, but in fact was the individual responsible for bringing the Omride dynasty to an end. The Assyrians, however, frequently referred to the rulers of a country by the name of the dynasty that was in power at the time of their first encounter with that country. Thus, Jehu is called "of the house of Omri" because the Omride dynasty had previously been the ruling dynasty.

Additional artifacts connected to Shalmaneser III, although having no direct biblical connection, are the Balawat Gates. The bronze bands of the gates (ME 124651–ME 124663), as well as a replica of the gates, are located in room 6b of the British Museum. Balawat (ancient Imgur-Enlil), located about ten miles northeast of Nimrud, was the site of an Assyrian royal palace. The impressive Balawat Gates were made of cedar, decorated with a series of bronze bands on which were carved inscriptions and various scenes in relief. The inscriptions describe Shalmaneser III's military campaigns between 858 and 850 B.C.E., while the scenes depict various aspects of those campaigns — cities under attack, soldiers in battle, prisoners led captive, punishment and slaughter of enemies (impaling of victims, decapitations, dismemberment), and payment of tribute. Although the wood of the gates had rotted by the time they were discovered, leaving only the bronze bands, the original height of the gates

---

5. "Black Obelisk" (*COS* 2.113F:270).

has been estimated at around 6.8 meters (22.3 ft.). Each of the sixteen bronze bands (eight on the outside of each door) was 27 cm. (11 in.) high. The remains of the gates were discovered in 1877 by Hormuzd Rassam, who also found there remains from similar gates from Ashurnasirpal II, the father of Shalmaneser III. (Some additional bronze bands from the Balawat Gates [AO 14038–AO 14048, AO22279–AO22281] are on display in the Louvre in room 6, ground floor, Richelieu Wing, section 3.)

Another object related to Shalmaneser is a small gold foundation document commemorating the restoration of the wall of the city of Ashur by Shalmaneser III. The document (OIM A2529) is on display in the Mesopotamian Gallery of the Oriental Institute of the University of Chicago. The Museum of the Ancient Orient in Istanbul contains a large basalt statue of Shalmaneser (4650; Mesopotamia Hall; see fig. 36), inscribed with his royal titles and the names and titles of his father and grandfather, who had also been Assyrian kings. The inscription also lists his military campaigns and conquests of several lands.

Biblical Significance

During the ninth century B.C.E., Israel, along with other nations and city-states in Syria-Palestine, began to be threatened by the expansionist ambitions of the Assyrian Empire. On several occasions, Israel joined forces with its neighbors, including Damascus, to try to contain the Assyrian threat (see the article "The Kurkh Monolith of Shalmaneser III"). After the death of Hadadezer and the usurpation of the throne by Hazael, this coalition of Syro-Palestinian kings seems to have collapsed. Around the same time Jehu, a former army commander, successfully led a coup against King Joram (also called Jehoram) of Israel and took over the throne. When Shalmaneser invaded Syria in 841 B.C.E., Hazael of Damascus suffered extensively at the hands of the Assyrians, although Shalmaneser was not able to destroy the city of Damascus or to remove Hazael as king. Jehu, rather than resist the Assyrians, submitted peacefully to Shalmaneser, offering him gifts as tribute, as clearly portrayed on the Black Obelisk. One benefit of this

36. Statue of Shalmaneser III

conciliatory gesture was that Assyria now provided protection for Israel against the growing threat of Hazael of Damascus, who could not risk an invasion of Israel while Assyria was still a strong foe. Once more, in 838 B.C.E., Shalmaneser led another campaign against the Aramean kingdom centered at Damascus. As had been the outcome three years earlier, Shalmaneser was able to inflict heavy losses on Hazael but had to stop short of totally defeating him. The survival of Hazael would be detrimental to Israel, for shortly after this last campaign by Shalmaneser, Assyria began to suffer internal problems and the empire declined, freeing Hazael to turn his attention toward Israel. According to the biblical narrative, Hazael became a ruthless and dreaded enemy of Israel, confiscating a large portion of Israel's territory (2 Kings 10:32-33; cf. 2 Kings 8:7-15; 13:3).

Apart from Jehu's bloody takeover of the Omride throne, including the subsequent slaughter of the Omride family and its supporters followed by the annihilation of the worship of Baal that had been introduced by the Omrides, the biblical writer gives little information about the reign of Jehu. The payment of tribute by Jehu to Shalmaneser that is depicted on the Black Obelisk does not appear in the biblical account of his reign. In fact, Shalmaneser III is never mentioned in the Bible, with the possible exception of Hosea 10:14, which alludes to a certain "Shalman" who destroyed Beth-arbel. At least one scholar has suggested that this is a reference to Shalmaneser III. Such identification, however, is purely speculative and has scant basis for support. Even if he is never explicitly named in the biblical texts, Shalmaneser III certainly affected the history of the people of Israel.

Shema Seal of Megiddo

Bronze seal replica (cast); original, jasper

▷ Size: 27 mm. (1.06 in.) high; 37 mm. (1.46 in.) wide; 17 mm. (.67 in.) thick
▷ Writing: Hebrew language
▷ Provenance: Megiddo, Israel
▷ Date: Eighth century B.C.E. (ca. 786-746 B.C.E.)
▷ Present location: Israel Museum, Jerusalem (Bronfman Archaeology Wing; replica)
▷ Identification number: Cast 230

Between 1903 and 1905, Gottlieb Schumacher, an American-born German engineer who lived in Haifa, began the first excavation at the site of Megiddo on behalf of the German Society for the Study of Palestine. Schumacher cut a

37. Bronze cast of the seal of Shema from Megiddo

trench twenty meters (65 ft.) wide from north to south across the site, as well as a number of smaller trenches, to begin his excavation. His exploration subsequently identified six different building levels and periods of occupation. In 1904 Schumacher made his greatest discovery in the vicinity of a gatehouse or tower (no. 1567 on Schumacher's plan), near the northern wall of a court-yard, approximately one meter (3 ft.) beneath the surface. There he uncovered a beautiful oval seal of jasper with a picture of a roaring lion in an aggressive pose, its tufted tail curled over its back. Below the lion was written an inscription in the ancient Hebrew script in use prior to the Babylonian captivity (587 B.C.E.): "[Belonging] to Shema, servant of Jeroboam." The seal was somewhat unusual in that it was not perforated in a fashion common to prominent individuals who carried such seals about their necks on a cord. The Shema seal may have been mounted in a ring whose precious metals were stripped from the discarded seal, or it may have been used in its present form as a stamp seal by the high official, Shema, "servant of Jeroboam," who was named on it. (In this use, the term "servant" does not indicate a menial laborer in the employ of the king, but rather is a specific title for a ranking palace official.)

Since Palestine was under the Ottoman Empire at that time, Schumacher sent the seal to the Turkish sultan in Constantinople. That was the last time anything is known of the seal. It apparently disappeared not long after it reached the collection of the sultan and its whereabouts today, if it still exists, remains unknown. Fortunately, a bronze cast had been made of the original, without which we would have no image of the seal.

The immediate question posed by the discovery of the Shema seal concerned its date. Which Jeroboam was intended on the inscription, Jeroboam I or Jeroboam II? Archaeologists and scholars from that time until the present day still have not agreed on the answer to that question, and it remains hotly debated. Schumacher, and many other scholars, were certain it belonged to the time of Jeroboam II. Recently that theory has been challenged by some archae-ologists, most notably David Ussishkin, who argues for an earlier date that would place it in the time of Jeroboam I, first king of the northern kingdom of Israel.[1] The preponderance of scholarly opinion, however, remains with the eighth-century date and Jeroboam II as the king named on the seal.

Biblical Significance

The discovery of the Shema seal is regarded as significant for a number of rea-sons, including what scholars see as artistic influences on the lion figure (whether Egyptian, as earlier believed, or Mesopotamian, and therefore later, as some recent scholars believe; all "roaring" lion figures are believed relatively late).[2] Furthermore, the use of precious jasper in the seal is one more bit of ev-idence, along with the substantial and impressive nature of the buildings near which it was found, of the prosperity of the northern kingdom during this pe-riod in Israel's history. The paleography of the inscription also continues to influence thinking — and provoke arguments — concerning the nature of early Hebrew writing. Finally, and perhaps most importantly, the seal has led to significant archaeological discussion, where a kind of circular argument re-volves about the seal: does the seal aid in determining the date of the struc-tures near where it was found, or do the structures and the strata where it was located determine the age of the seal? Since the seal itself is not unambiguous, nor is the location where it was found — at least not until now — scholarly opinion remains somewhat unsettled.

Nevertheless, the finding of any authentic object with the name of a biblical figure, much less a king of Israel, has great significance as external witness to the biblical account. As such, the Shema seal joins an elite group of objects and inscriptions that document the names of persons from the Bible.

Reliefs from the Central Palace of Tiglath-Pileser III at Nimrud

Carved alabaster panels

▷ Size: Panels are ca. 1.5–2.25 m. (ca. 5–7.5 ft.) high
▷ Provenance: Calah (Nimrud, in modern Iraq)

1. David Ussishkin, "Gate 1567 at Megiddo and the Seal of Shema, Servant of Jeroboam," in *Scripture and Other Artifacts: Essays on the Bible and Archaeology in Honor of Phillip J. King,* ed. Michael D. Coogan et al. (Louisville: Westminster/John Knox Press, 1994), p. 421.
2. Ussishkin, "Gate 1567," p. 420.

▷ Date: ca. 730-727 B.C.E.

▷ Present location: British Museum (rooms 6a and 8); the Louvre (room 6, ground floor, Richelieu Wing, section 3); and Museum of the Ancient Orient, Istanbul (Mesopotamia Hall)

▷ Identification numbers: See text below

Tiglath-pileser III ruled over the Neo-Assyrian Empire from 744 to 727 B.C.E. The period of approximately forty years immediately prior to Tiglath-pileser III's assumption of royal power in Assyria was a chaotic period of internal political instability and weakness. These internal problems were exacerbated by an external threat from the kingdom of Urartu, located in eastern Asia Minor with its center near Lake Van in modern Turkey, which took over part of the Assyrian territory and threatened to completely destroy the Assyrian Empire. The details of Tiglath-pileser's ascendancy to the Assyrian throne are unclear, but most scholars have concluded that he had not been directly in line for the throne. Rather, he likely was a usurper who took advantage of the chaotic situation in Assyria and staged a successful coup that allowed him to take over. Tiglath-pileser III proved to be a skillful ruler, able administrator, and powerful military leader. During his reign, he led a military campaign every year, except for one. As a result of these campaigns, he expanded and solidified the borders of his empire. His successes included defeats of Urartu, Babylon, Gaza, Israel, and parts of Syria (including Damascus), as well as areas to the east of Assyria. He also gained control of the Sinai. Many of these areas he was able to bring under his control without direct military conflict, forcing the lands to pay tribute to him.

Because he spent so much time on his military campaigns, Tiglath-pileser did not devote much of his time and effort to major construction projects. One of his building accomplishments, however, was a new palace at Calah (Nimrud), re-

38. Relief carving showing King Tiglath-pileser III in his chariot and a scene of the captured city of Astartu

ferred to as the Central Palace. The tell at Nimrud was first excavated by Austen Henry Layard, beginning in 1845, who successfully uncovered at the site the remains of the Central Palace of Tiglath-pileser III, the Southwest Palace of Esarhaddon, and the Northwest Palace of Ashurnasirpal II. Unfortunately, not much remained of the Central Palace, due in large part to Esarhaddon's pillaging of materials from the palace for his new building, the so-called Southwest Palace. Many of the carved stone reliefs that decorated the walls of the Central Palace were removed by Esarhaddon for reuse in his own palace. Some of these stone reliefs were found in the Southwest Palace, where Esarhaddon had them relocated; others were found by Layard stacked in the area of the Central Palace. The latter collection apparently had been intended for use in Esarhaddon's palace also, but had not been moved there yet. Of those panels that were found in Esarhaddon's palace, some were attached to the walls, while others were lying on the floor waiting to be put into place. Some were attached upside down, some were attached backwards (with the reliefs to the wall), and on some the relief carvings had been shaved down so they could be recarved. (Esarhaddon's palace was apparently destroyed prior to its completion.) The removal of these panels by Esarhaddon has created problems for modern historians trying to reconstruct the history of Tiglath-pileser III's reign because the annals of the king were inscribed on the panels. Since uncertainty sometimes exists about the correct ordering of the panels, in some cases the chronological order of the events described on the slabs is difficult to ascertain.

The relief pictured here (fig. 38), ME 118908 (British Museum, room 6a), is one of those found in Esarhaddon's palace after it had been removed from the palace of Tiglath-pileser III. The bottom part of the panel consists of a carving of Tiglath-pileser standing in a chariot with two attendants, one of whom holds a parasol over the king to shade him from the sun. The king is part of a royal procession. Above the procession, in the top panel, soldiers are marching captives and their livestock away from their captured city, which is shown as a citadel set on a hill or mound (possibly a tell). The inscription above the city identifies it as "Astartu," probably to be identified with Ashtaroth, a city mentioned in the Hebrew Bible in the northern Transjordanian area, located east of the Sea of Galilee in modern Jordan (see Deut. 1:4; Josh. 9:10). The records of Tiglath-pileser do not specifically mention his capture of this city, but he campaigned in this area on several occasions. This event possibly occurred during his final campaign in Syria-Palestine in 733-732 B.C.E.

The British Museum (room 8) contains several additional panels from Tiglath-pileser III's Nimrud palace, including a relief of the king (ME 118900). Three panels depict an Assyrian military campaign against several cities, probably in Babylonia because of the date palm trees in the scenes. One of these panels shows a city under siege by the Assyrians (ME 118902). On the right, the

Assyrians have built a siege ramp and are attacking the city walls with a batter-ing ram and archers. From atop the city walls archers are shooting arrows at the Assyrian soldiers. Several headless corpses lie on the ground. (Assyrians used literal "head counts" as a way of quantifying their victories.) In another panel (ME 118904), an Assyrian soldier holds a large body shield while two ar-chers take aim at a city under attack. Another relief (ME 118882) shows the evacuation of people and livestock from a captured city. In the center of the panel a scribe holding a clay tablet and a stylus records in Akkadian cuneiform the booty captured from the city as an officer dictates the list to him. Next to the scribe is another individual with a leather scroll, perhaps an artist record-ing the scene or, as has been suggested, another scribe recording the informa-tion in Aramaic.

Other panels from the Central Palace can be seen in the Louvre. In room 6 on the ground floor of the Richelieu Wing, section 3, is a relief panel portray-ing a standing Tiglath-pileser III (AO 19853). In the same room, other panels depict an archer and his shield-bearer (AO 19854), an Anatolian fortress (AO 19855), and a warrior carrying enemy heads that had been cut off (AO 19916). Also in room 6 are two small bulls from the time of Tiglath-pileser III (AO 11500 and AO 11501) that guarded the doors of the entrance to the temple of Ishtar in Hadatu (modern Arslan Tash).

In the Museum of the Ancient Orient in Istanbul (Mesopotamia Hall) are two partial relief slabs from Tiglath-pileser's palace at Nimrud. One of the slabs (inventory number 23) shows a man carrying a bow and being followed by some cattle, while the other one (inventory number 40) depicts the face of a man, likely a eunuch. The museum also contains a series of orthostats with re-lief carvings of scenes of Assyrian soldiers marching in procession (inventory numbers 7, 8, 9, 10, 11, 12, 13, 14, 15, 16, 17, and 18), the royal chariot and guards (1946 and 1848), and Syrians bearing tribute on their heads (1995 and 1982). All of these relief orthostats, which were found at Hadatu, are from the time pe-riod of Tiglath-pileser III.

Biblical Significance

During the ninth century B.C.E., Syria and Palestine had to deal with the ex-pansionist ambitions of the Assyrian Empire, particularly during the reign of Shalmaneser III. Soon after his death, however, the Assyrian Empire entered a period of decline, with the result that its hold over the Syro-Palestinian re-gion lessened. With the accession of Tiglath-pileser III to the throne, Assyria was able to reassert itself and once more dominate much of Syria and Pales-tine. This Assyrian threat forms the backdrop for several episodes in the He-brew Bible. When Tiglath-pileser took control in Assyria, the kings in Israel and Judah were Menahem and Uzziah (also called Azariah). According to 2 Kings 15:19-20, during the reign of Menahem, Tiglath-pileser invaded Israel, prompting Menahem to give "Pul a thousand talents of silver, so that he might help him confirm his hold on the royal power. . . . So the king of Assyria turned back, and did not stay there in the land." (In the Bible, Tiglath-pileser III is sometimes called "Pul," a variation of his Assyrian nickname, "Pulu.") The payment of tribute to Tiglath-pileser by Menahem is documented as well in some of the Assyrian king's inscriptions. This event likely occurred around 738 B.C.E.

The period of Tiglath-pileser's reign was a turbulent time for the Israelite kingdom. Various coups and assassinations resulted in quick turnovers on the throne. Menahem had taken the throne after he had murdered the previous occupant. After his death, his son ruled for only two years before he was assassinated by Pekah, who then took over. Although the details are not always clear and scholars disagree about the exact order of events and dates, sometime around 734 B.C.E. Tiglath-pileser led a campaign into Philistia. Then, apparently shortly afterwards, Pekah joined forces with Rezin, king of Damascus, in a revolt against Assyria and an invasion of Judah (2 Kings 16:5; 2 Chron. 28:5-15). This was the beginning of what is known as the Syro-Ephraimite war. (Ephraim was the name of one of the northern tribes located in Israel and was sometimes used for the name of the northern kingdom.) The purpose of this incursion into Judah was to pressure Ahaz, the king of Judah, to join Israel and Damascus in their anti-Assyrian alliance. Faced with the threat from Pekah and Rezin, Ahaz turned to Assyria and sought Tiglath-pileser's protection (2 Kings 16:7-8; 2 Chron. 28:20-21). As a result, Judah became a vassal state under the Assyrians. This move by Ahaz was contrary to the strong advice of the prophet Isaiah that Ahaz should not rely upon the Assyrians for help. The prophet assured Ahaz that Israel and Damascus would soon be wiped out and thus would no longer be a threat (Isa. 7:1-17; 8:1-10).

Tiglath-pileser then invaded Syria-Palestine, capturing portions of the northern part of Israel and carrying some of the people back to Assyria as captives (2 Kings 15:29). Pekah was assassinated by Hoshea, a pro-Assyrian Israelite who claimed the throne, and the state became a vassal of Assyria (2 Kings 15:30). The territory left for him to rule was greatly diminished, primarily only the area around Samaria, the capital of Israel. It is perhaps this pro-Assyrian move that saved Samaria — and the rest of the northern kingdom — from destruction by the Assyrians. (Tiglath-pileser, in his inscriptions, claims credit for placing Hoshea on the throne.) Damascus was not as fortunate, however, for Tiglath-pileser turned his wrath against the city, destroying it and putting Rezin to death (2 Kings 16:9). This conquest of Damascus occurred in 732 B.C.E.

During the remaining five years of Tiglath-pileser's reign, Hoshea and Ahaz were loyal vassals to the Assyrians, paying the required tribute and not attempting to break out from under Assyrian control. No further mention of Tiglath-pileser III occurs in the Hebrew Bible.

Annals of Tiglath-Pileser III

Baked clay tablet

▷ Size: 23.4 cm. (9.21 in.) high; 17.5 cm. (6.89 in.) wide
▷ Writing: Akkadian language in cuneiform script
▷ Provenance: Calah (Nimrud, in modern Iraq)
▷ Date: ca. 728 B.C.E.
▷ Present location: British Museum (formerly in room 89; check with museum personnel for current location)
▷ Identification number: ME K3751

Although labeled "Annals of Tiglath-pileser III," this clay tablet actually is a summary inscription; that is, it is not a year-by-year chronicle of the king's reign, but rather provides a resumé of the military and building accomplishments during the first seventeen years of his reign (until 728 B.C.E.). Tiglath-pileser III was one of the most successful kings of the Neo-Assyrian Empire, ruling from 744 to 727 B.C.E. (See the article "Reliefs from the Central Palace of Tiglath-Pileser III at Nimrud.") Only the top half of the tablet survives today, containing the beginning (on the front, or obverse, side) and ending (on the reverse side) of the inscription. The first part of the inscription summarizes the various conquests and military successes of Tiglath-pileser, listing the lands and cities he conquered, the destruction he caused, and the various types of tribute he received from submissive rulers. Among the rulers named who paid tribute are several Syro-Palestinian and Philistine rulers, including the kings of Ammon, Moab, Ashkelon, Judah, Edom, Gaza, and Tyre. Their payment to the Assyrian king included "gold, silver, tin, multi-colored garments, linen garments, red-purple wool, [all kinds of] costly articles, produce of the sea (and) dry land, the commodities of their lands, royal treasures, horses (and) mules broken to the yo[ke . . .]."[1]

The last part of the inscription describes in detail Tiglath-pileser's con-

---

1. "Summary Inscription 7," translated by K. Lawson Younger Jr. (*COS* 2.117D:289).

struction of his palace at Calah (modern Nimrud). The size of the palace, he claims, was to be larger than the palaces of his predecessors. Its doorways were made of ivory and various types of wood (including maple, boxwood, mulberry, cedar and juniper); its beams were made of cypress from Lebanon. Slabs of alabaster were placed under the doorways, while carved stone panels decorated the walls. Colossal bulls and lions guarded the entrances. The remains of the palace that Tiglath-pileser III built at Calah (the so-called Central Palace) were first excavated by Austen Henry Layard, beginning in November of 1845. Unfortunately, not much had survived for Layard to uncover, with the exception of several wall panels carved with scenes of Tiglath-pileser's military campaigns and inscribed with his annals. (See the previous article, "Reliefs from the Central Palace of Tiglath-Pileser III at Nimrud.")

Biblical Significance

One of the rulers listed in the inscription as bearing tribute to the Assyrian king is the king of Israel, who is mentioned by name as "Jehoahaz, the Judahite." Jehoahaz is the full name of Ahaz, king of Judah during the latter half of the eighth century. Ahaz was king when Pekah, king of Israel, and Rezin, king of Aram-Damascus, formed an alliance to revolt against Assyria (ca. 734 B.C.E.; 2 Kings 16). The two kings attacked Judah, apparently trying to force Ahaz to join forces with them in their rebellion against Tiglath-pileser. Rather than join with this Syro-Israelite coalition, Ahaz went to the Assyrian king and asked him for protection. As a result, Judah became a vassal state of the Assyrian Empire, subject to Assyrian control and required to pay annual tribute to the Assyrians. During the Assyrian campaigns of 733-732 B.C.E., Tiglath-pileser squashed the

Syro-Israelite revolt, captured Damascus, killed Rezin, and severely decreased the territory under Israel's control. The payment of tribute by the various kings from Syria, Palestine, and Philistia mentioned in the summary inscription

39. Clay tablet containing the annals of Tiglath-pileser III

on this tablet in the British Museum (ME K3751) likely reflects the Assyrian campaigns of 734-732 B.C.E.

Palace of Sargon II at Khorsabad

Stone wall reliefs and colossal bulls

▷ Size: Panels generally 3 m. (9 ft.) high; bulls ca. 4–4.5 m. (14-15 ft.) high
▷ Provenance: Dur-Sharrukin (Khorsabad, in modern Iraq)
▷ Date: ca. 645 B.C.E.
▷ Present location: Louvre (room 4, ground floor, Richelieu Wing, section 3); British Museum (room 10c); and the Oriental Institute Museum of the University of Chicago (Khorsabad Court and Assyrian Empire Gallery)
▷ Identification numbers: See text below

A major revolt against Shalmaneser V of Assyria took place in 722 B.C.E., reportedly because Shalmaneser had imposed taxes and corvée (forced labor) on the cities of Ashur and Haran, which had traditionally been free cities. As a result of the revolt, Shalmaneser was deposed, and Sargon II gained the Assyrian throne. (Shalmaneser either died or was killed around the time of the revolt.) He ruled from 721 B.C.E. until his death in battle in 705 B.C.E. The meager evidence is not clear, but Sargon was apparently not of royal birth and thus was a usurper of the throne. Many people opposed his accession, but Sargon succeeded in squashing his opposition, deporting 6,300 resisters to Hamath in Syria. The unsettled situation in Assyria that accompanied Sargon's gaining control of the throne provided the opportunity for a major rebellion in Syria and Palestine (including Samaria) against Assyrian control. After securing his position in Assyria, Sargon defeated the combined rebel forces at Qarqar in Syria in 720 B.C.E. He then marched south to reconquer Gaza and defeat an Egyptian army at Egypt's border, later even establishing an Assyrian garrison on the Egyptian border. After his defeat of the combined Syro-Palestinian forces, Sargon deported many of the residents of these territories and resettled them elsewhere. Samaria and Hamath in Syria are specifically mentioned as cities whose residents were deported. Later, Sargon also gained control over the cities of Philistia and the island of Cyprus, the first time Cyprus had come under Assyrian dominance (see the comments on the "Cyprus Stela" below).

Among his other military campaigns, which included conflicts with the

40. Stone panel with a relief of King Sargon II of Assyria and a high dignitary

Phrygians and Urartians, Sargon had to deal with Babylon, which had broken from Assyrian control during the confusion surrounding his accession to the Assyrian throne. Merodach-baladan II, the leader of one of the Chaldean tribes, had seized control of Babylon, a control which he was able to maintain with assistance from the Elamites. Sargon did not regain control over Babylon until twelve years later, when in 710 B.C.E. he was able to oust Merodach-baladan, who fled to Elam for safety. Merodach-baladan, however, continued to be a problem for Sargon and later for his successor Sennacherib, when he formed a coalition with other rulers in an attempt to revolt against Assyria. (A fragmentary tablet in the Louvre containing the annals of Sennacherib, AO 7747, describes one of Sennacherib's campaigns against Merodach-baladan. The tablet is located in room 6, ground floor, Richelieu Wing, section 3.) One of the rulers who joined Merodach-baladan in the revolt against Assyria was Hezekiah of Judah (see 2 Kings 20:12-19).

During his reign, Sargon completed several building projects, such as restoration of temples in Ashur, Nineveh, Babylon, and Uruk. His most impressive building project was the construction of an entirely new capital, the city of Dur-Sharrukin, or "Fort Sargon" (modern Khorsabad), located approximately fifteen miles north of Nineveh. In addition to a large ziggurat and several temples, the new city boasted a splendid palace, constructed of ivory, precious stones, and various types of wood. The walls of the palace were covered with large stone slabs that were decorated with scenes carved in relief.

The remains of Dur-Sharrukin were first excavated by Paul Emile Botta, the French consul to Mosul, from 1843 to 1844. Several tons of sculptures from Sargon's palace, including two colossal winged human-headed bulls (AO 19857 and AO 19858) and many wall reliefs, were sent to France for the Louvre. The second major excavation of the site occurred from 1852 to 1854 by Victor Thomas Place, who had been recently appointed the new French consul to Mosul. Place discovered even more rooms of the palace than Botta had. The sculptures and wall reliefs, along with other items he discovered, were packed in crates and shipped to Baghdad, where they joined artifacts excavated from Nimrud and Nineveh (for a total of over 235 cases). From Baghdad these items were to be shipped to Basra and eventually on to Paris and Berlin. Disaster struck, however, and most of the items never reached their intended destinations. In May 1855 the boat and rafts that were transporting the crates were attacked and plundered by a group of Arabs, resulting in the boat and one of the rafts being sunk. Most of the crates were lost and have never been recovered. Eighty of the cases and two large sculptures were saved; sixteen of these cases were objects from Khorsabad that were eventually delivered to the Louvre. The last large-scale excavation at Khorsabad was undertaken by the Oriental Institute of the University of Chicago from 1927 to 1934. The findings from this campaign were sent to the Oriental Institute or to the Iraq Museum in Baghdad. The British Museum was able to acquire several objects from Khorsabad by purchasing them from local excavators or through intermediaries; most were purchased from an English merchant living in Baghdad.

The Louvre contains an impressive display of numerous wall reliefs from Sargon's palace, mounted on the walls in room 4, ground floor, Richelieu Wing, section 3. The reliefs, which adorned both external and internal walls, depict large genies, foreign tributaries, the Assyrian king, officials, attendants, soldiers, and horses. Traces of red, blue, white, or black paint are sometimes discernible on the reliefs, indicating that the reliefs were originally painted, at least in part. Among the wall reliefs and sculptures on display are the following:

1. A relief depicting Sargon II and a high-ranking official (AO 19873/AO 19874; see fig. 40). In the relief, Sargon is standing with his left hand resting on the hilt of his sword and holding a long staff in his right hand. Traces of white paint appear on the king's eye and red paint on his crown. Facing the king is an unknown bearded individual who was likely an important Assyrian official. Because of similarities between the features of this individual and depictions of Sargon's son, the crown prince Sennacherib, this individual has sometimes been identified as Sennacherib. In spite of the similarities, however, scholars usually understand this figure as a depiction of an Assyrian official. (See the similar relief [ME 118822] in the British Museum, located in room 10c, which is almost a mirror image of the relief in the Louvre.) Another high-ranking bearded Assyrian official is depicted in AO 19875.

2. A series of panels showing the transport of cedar logs from Lebanon (AO

19888, AO 19889, AO 19890, and AO 19891). The scenes show groups of men on land hauling the logs and ships at sea transporting the logs. Lebanon was famous in the ancient world for its tall and straight cedar trees, which were prized for building purposes. Cedar was one of the types of wood Sargon used in building his palace at Khorsabad. When Solomon built the Jerusalem temple during the tenth century B.C.E., he requested and received cedar trees from the mountains of Lebanon as part of his building materials. (Cf. Isa. 37:24, where in his response to the threats of Sennacherib against Judah, the prophet Isaiah claimed, "By your servants you have mocked the Lord, and you have said, 'With my many chariots I have gone up the heights of the mountains, to the far recesses of Lebanon; I felled its tallest cedars, its choicest cypresses.'")

3. A large human figure holding a small lion in his left arm and a sickle-shaped sword in his right hand (AO 19862; see plate 4). The hero figure grasps the lion tightly, which appears to be struggling feebly to escape. This relief was situated between two other reliefs, each depicting a winged, human-headed bull (called a *lamassu*) moving away from the hero. One of the bulls (OIM A7369) is now displayed in the Khorsabad Court of the Oriental Institute Museum in Chicago. (A reproduction of it [AO 30043] is in the Louvre, adjacent to AO 19862. See plate 4.) The bull's head is turned facing the viewer. These panels were part of the decoration of one of the outer walls around the palace terrace, where, along with a matching set of reliefs, they flanked one of the entryways to the terrace. Similar compositions of bulls and a hero figure flanked several of the entrance gates to the city or the palace (see for example AO 19861, very similar to AO 19862. This panel came from

41. Two winged, human-headed bulls that guarded an entrance of the palace at Khorsabad

another gate.) The hero figure is not identified. Some have suggested that he is Gilgamesh, the Sumerian epic hero and king.

4. Colossal winged, human-headed bulls (AO 19857, AO 19858, AO 19859 in the Louvre; ME 118808 and ME 118809 in room 10c of the British Museum). These bulls (or *lamassus*) lined the inner walls of the gateways, one on each side. (A plaster reproduction of another *lamassu* from Khorsabad is also in room 4 in the Louvre [AO 30228].) Figure 41 shows AO 19857 and AO 19858 in the Louvre. Reliefs of genies were often adjacent to them. These bull sculptures, which faced straight ahead, were carved with five legs so that when viewed from the front they appear to be standing still; when viewed from the side they appear to be walking. The size of the bulls varies somewhat, but they are approximately 4.25 meters (14 feet) tall and 4.5 meters (14.75 feet) long and weigh around sixteen tons each. Originally carved from one block of stone, each of the bulls in the British Museum was sawn into several pieces for transport to the museum, where the sculptures were reassembled. Cuneiform inscriptions are carved between the legs of the animals. Crudely scratched into the base of ME 118809 is a grid for an ancient game known as the "Game of Twenty Squares," likely carved by palace guards or persons waiting to enter the palace. The colossal bull figures, as well as the genies, were symbols of protection, guarding the entrances.

The Oriental Institute Museum of the University of Chicago also exhibits some of the reliefs from the palace at Dur-Sharrukin. One set of panels (in the Khorsabad Court) originally came from the courtyard outside the throne room. The panels depict a pair of stallions being led by a groom (OIM A7358), Sargon and an attendant (OIM A7359) receiving tribute bearers (OIM A7360; the tribute bearers are badly damaged), and courtiers appearing before Sargon, led by an individual variously identified as his son, Sennacherib (the crown prince), or an Assyrian official (the panels from left to right are OIM A7368, OIM A7367, and OIM A7366). Other panels, in the Assyrian Empire Gallery, show scenes from a royal hunt (OIM A11254), Sargon in his chariot (OIM A11256), and a scene of a shrine (OIM A11255), as well as scenes of tribute bearers. In room 10c of the British Museum, in addition to the wall reliefs and bulls already mentioned, are several other items from Khorsabad, including a stone door sill carved to resemble a carpet (ME 118910), a part of an inscribed door sill listing some of Sargon's accomplishments (ME 135206), and a wall panel depicting a hunting scene (ME 118829).

In addition to these wall reliefs and sculptures, several museums display additional items pertaining to Sargon II. These would include:

1. An inscribed stela of Sargon (VA 968) in the Museum of the Ancient Near East, Pergamum Museum, Berlin (room 3). This stela, sometimes called the Cyprus Stela, was found in 1845 at Kition (modern Larnaca) on the island of Cyprus in the middle of the nineteenth century. Sargon sent the inscribed stone to Cyprus in return for gifts, perhaps tribute, that the people of Cyprus sent to him. The inscription, written on both sides of the stela, describes many of his accomplishments, including his military campaigns against Babylonia, Urartu, Media, and Syria, as well as the situation surrounding the making of the stela. The scene on the stela depicts Sargon standing, with the symbols of his gods carved in front of him.

2. A clay tablet (AO 5372) in room 6, ground floor, Richelieu Wing, section 3, of the Louvre. Written as a letter from Sargon to "Ashur, father of the gods," this tablet of four hundred thirty lines of text recounts in unusual detail the events of Sargon's eighth campaign (714 B.C.E.) when he defeated the Urartians (in Asia Minor, near Lake Van), pillaged their country, and sacked Mushashir, the sacred city of Urartu.

3. An inscribed altar in the Museum of the Ancient Orient in Istanbul (4784; Mesopotamia Hall). The provenance of this altar dedicated by Sargon is uncertain, but it perhaps came from Khorsabad. The altar is 1.04 meters (3.4 feet) tall. The top part of the solid stone altar is carved in a tripod shape, with each of its three legs ending in a lion's foot, all of which rests on a tripod base (still the same block of stone as the top part) with round posts for legs. The altar top is circular, with an inscription carved along its edge. The inscription reads, "To the Sebettu, the hero who has no rival, Sargon, king of the universe, viceregent of Babylon, king of Sumer and Akkad, has set up and dedicated (this altar)."[1] The Sebettu, to whom the altar was dedicated, was a group of identical protective gods of Mesopotamia ("Sebettu" means "seven"). A similar altar with the same inscription is in the Louvre (AO 19900; room 4, ground floor, Richelieu Wing, section 3), and another is owned by the Iraq National Museum in Baghdad.

4. Several objects from the palace of Sargon at Dur-Sharrukin, on display in a case in room 4, ground floor, Richelieu Wing, section 3, in the Louvre. These include four foundation documents with the same inscription, one of gold, one of silver, one of copper, and one of stone (AO 19933, AO 21371). These documents, along with others, were found in a stone box that had been buried under the foundation of Sargon's palace. The inscription, similar to that underneath the colossal winged bulls, describes the construction

---

1. Pauline Albenda, *The Palace of Sargon, King of Assyria: Monumental Wall Reliefs at Dur-Sharrukin, from Original Drawings Made at the Time of Their Discovery in 1843-1844 by Botta and Flandin* (Paris: Editions Recherche sur les Civilizations, 1986), p. 113.

of the city and the palace, gives the titles of Sargon, and issues warnings against anyone who would destroy the works of the king. Also in the case are various other items, including bricks from Dur-Sharrukin and a clay foundation document (N III 3156) with an inscription similar to that of AO 19933, AO 21371.

5. Numerous items at the Oriental Institute Museum of the University of Chicago from Dur-Sharrukin, including a nine-sided clay prism commemorating Sargon's founding of Dur-Sharrukin (OIM A17590; Mesopotamian Gallery); a basalt column base from a residence in the Khorsabad citadel (OIM A17558; Khorsabad Court); two clay bricks with the inscription "Palace of Sargon, king of the world, king of Assyria, viceroy of Babylon, king of Sumer and Akkad, builder of the city Dur-Sharrukin" (OIM A39949, Mesopotamian Gallery; and OIM A25449, Khorsabad Court); bronze bands from the temples to Shamash (OIM A12468) and to Nabu (OIM A12467, OIM A12469, OIM A12470), all in the Khorsabad Court; and glazed bricks from the temple to Sin (OIM A11810; Khorsabad Court).

6. A small barrel-shaped clay cylinder describing Sargon's renovation of the temple of Eanna in Uruk. This cylinder (VA 10955) is in room 11 of the Museum of the Ancient Near East, Pergamum Museum, Berlin.

Biblical Significance

The only mention of Sargon II in the Bible occurs in Isaiah 20:1 in a passing reference to his campaign against the Philistine city of Ashdod in 712 B.C.E. that begins with the words, "In the year that the commander-in-chief, who was sent by King Sargon of Assyria, came to Ashdod and fought against it and took it." The scant mention of Sargon belies the significant impact that this Assyrian king had on the biblical story. In several of his records, Sargon boasts that he was responsible for the capture of Samaria (the capital of the northern kingdom of Israel) and the deportation of its inhabitants. In spite of these claims, most scholars have concluded it was actually his predecessor, Shalmaneser V, who put Samaria under siege and finally conquered the city in 722 B.C.E., the same year that Shalmaneser died. After Samaria fell, the Assyrians deported a portion of the residents of the northern kingdom and resettled them in Assyria and Media. This removal of the Israelites, which may have begun during the time of Shalmaneser, probably took place over several years. Thus, Sargon was the king primarily responsible for the deportation to Assyria.

In place of the deported Israelites, Sargon resettled the northern kingdom with people from Babylon, Cuthah, northern Syria, and elsewhere. These new settlers continued to worship their native gods, a practice strongly condemned by the biblical writers. The eventual intermarriage of these foreigners with the

Israelites who had not been deported is the biblical explanation for the origin of the people called Samaritans. (The Samaritans, themselves, trace their ancestry prior to the period of the deportation and claim that they are direct descendants of the Israelite tribes of Ephraim and Manasseh, rather than a result of intermarriage with foreigners. They see themselves as Israelites who are the true worshippers of Yahweh.) According to Ezra 4, the Samaritans opposed and interfered with the rebuilding of the temple and walls of Jerusalem after the Babylonian exile. Relations between the Jews and Samaritans worsened over the next several centuries, with each side harshly denouncing the other. The Samaritans eventually built a religious sanctuary, which may or may not have included a temple (mentioned in literary sources, but archaeological evidence is uncertain), at Shechem at the base of Mt. Gerizim. The Jewish governor and high priest, John Hyrcanus, destroyed the Samaritan sanctuary at Shechem in 128 B.C.E. The animosity between Jews and Samaritans is also reflected in the New Testament, most famously in Jesus' parable of the Good Samaritan, in which surprisingly a Samaritan comes to the rescue of an injured Jew (Luke 10:25-37).

The Epitaph of Uzziah

Marble plaque

▷ Size: 35 cm. (13.8 in.) high; 34 cm. (13.4 in.) wide
▷ Writing: Aramaic language
▷ Provenance: Jerusalem
▷ Date: ca. 150 B.C.E. to 50 C.E.
▷ Present location: Israel Museum (Bronfman Archaeology Wing)
▷ Identification number: IMJ 68.56.38

In 1931, E. L. Sukenik, professor of archaeology at Hebrew University in Jerusalem (who became well-known several years later because of his role in the procurement, translation, and interpretation of some of the first Dead Sea Scrolls) was rummaging through an assortment of items in the Russian Orthodox monastery on the Mount of Olives in Jerusalem when he found this inscribed plaque. Written on the marble slab in Aramaic are the words: "Here were brought the bones of Uzziah, king of Judah. Do not open." The plaque is not actually from the time of Uzziah, who was king of Judah during the eighth century B.C.E.; rather, based on the style of writing, this grave marker is dated sometime during the Hasmonean or early Roman period (ca. 150 B.C.E. to 50 C.E.). It was apparently used to mark the reburial spot of the supposed bones of Uzziah some seven to eight hundred years after his death. The location from which the marker came is unknown. Although there is no way to authenticate the plaque's claim that it marked the reburial site of Uzziah's bones, there is no valid reason to deny that it came from the Hasmonean or early Roman periods. The tomb from which the bones were taken and reburied may not have been Uzziah's actual tomb but rather the tomb traditionally ascribed to him.

Uzziah, also called Azariah in some biblical texts, received a qualified positive assessment from the biblical writers. Although "he did what was right in the sight of the LORD, just as his father Amaziah had done" (2 Kings 15:3; 2 Chron. 26:4), Uzziah eventually succumbed to the sin of pride. Uzziah came to the throne as a teenager and experienced a lengthy reign, ruling from approximately 769 to 741 B.C.E. (The reign of fifty-two years claimed by the biblical writers, if accurate, likely includes the years when his son Jotham ruled with him or in his place.) Uzziah is credited with strengthening Judah's military, defeating several of its enemies, accomplishing several building projects in Jerusalem and elsewhere in Judah, and improving farming throughout the land.

Biblical Significance

Uzziah's reign as king overlapped with the careers of at least three important Hebrew prophets: Isaiah, Amos, and Hosea (Isa. 1:1; 6:1; Hosea 1:1; Amos 1:1). In a memorable passage, the prophet Isaiah connected his dramatic temple experience of being called to be a prophet with the year of Uzziah's death: "In the year that King Uzziah died, I saw the Lord sitting on a throne, high and lofty" (Isa. 6:1). Both Amos and Zechariah mention that during the time of Uzziah an earthquake struck Israel, which must have been a catastrophic event for it to have been so remembered (Amos 1:1; Zech. 14:5).

42. Stone plaque with an epitaph for King Uzziah of Judah

The biblical story of Uzziah may provide a clue for the reason for the reburial of the remains of Uzziah. According to 2 Kings 15:5, Uzziah was struck by God with leprosy (an imprecise term in the Bible for several skin diseases). The writer of 2 Kings gives no reason for this action by God against the king. The author of 2 Chronicles, however, gives a theological rationale for Uzziah's affliction: Yahweh was punishing Uzziah for his sinful pride that led him to enter the temple to make an offering on the incense altar, a task that belonged solely to the temple priests. Uzziah suffered from leprosy the rest of his life and was forced to live in a separate house and to turn the governance of the kingdom over to his son Jotham (2 Chron. 26:16-21). The Chronicler describes Uzziah's death: "Uzziah slept with his ancestors; they buried him near his ancestors in the burial field that belonged to the kings, for they said, 'He is leprous'" (2 Chron. 26:23). Because he was a leper, Uzziah appears not to have been buried in the royal cemetery, but only near it. This separate burial may have led to the discovery of his grave several hundred years later, at which time his bones were reburied and this marble plaque inscribed to mark the new burial spot. (For additional information about Uzziah, see the article "Seal of Shebnayau, Servant of Uzziah.")

Seal of Shebnayau, Servant of Uzziah

Stamp seal made of red limestone

▷ Size: 21 mm. (.83 in.) long; 16 mm. (.63 in.) wide; 11 mm. (.43 in.) thick
▷ Writing: Hebrew language
▷ Provenance: Unknown
▷ Date: Eighth century B.C.E.
▷ Present location: Louvre (room D, ground floor, Sully Wing, section 4)
▷ Identification number: AO 6216

This reddish-brown, oval-shaped stamp seal has two convex sides, each containing a different carving. The inscriptions and scenes on each side are encircled by a border of two lines with a row of dots between the lines. The scene on one side (Face A, shown in figure 43) depicts a man wearing a long garment, possibly of Assyrian style, and holding a staff or scepter in his left hand. His right arm is raised. The Hebrew inscription behind him reads, "Belonging to Shebnayau." (The name could also be read as Shubnayaw or Shebanyau.) The carving on the other side (Face B) has two winged solar discs, one at the top and one at the bottom. Between the two discs is a two-line inscription that reads, "Belonging to Shebnayau, servant of Uzziah." The term "servant" was commonly used as a title for a high royal official. This seal, then, belonged to a man named Shebnayau who was likely an official in the court of King Uzziah. Unfortunately, nothing more is known about Shebnayau. (In the clay impression from this seal shown in figure 43, the impression of Face B is upside down. For additional information about seals and their use in the ancient world, see the article "Cylinder Seal of El and Baal.")

Biblical Significance

The importance of this object for biblical studies is that it mentions Uzziah, who reigned as the king of Judah during the eighth century B.C.E. The dates and length of his reign are problematic, but his reign perhaps lasted from ca. 769 to ca. 741 B.C. (Some scholars would argue for a shorter reign, perhaps of less than twenty years; the biblical record, on the other hand, assigns him a longer reign, explicitly stating that he reigned fifty-two years [2 Kings 15:2; 2 Chron. 26:3], which is likely incorrect.) Two versions of his name are used by the biblical writers — Uzziah and Azariah. The reason for the two versions of his name (the author of 2 Kings uses both names for the king) is uncertain. A plausible suggestion has been that "Uzziah" was his throne name and "Azariah" was his personal name. According to the biblical account, Uzziah became king when he was only sixteen years old, following the assassination of his father, Amaziah (2 Kings 14:21; 15:2; 2 Chron. 26:1, 3). The author of 2 Kings gives few details of the reign of Uzziah, but remembers him as a king who "did what was right in the sight of the LORD" (2 Kings 15:3). The author of Chronicles, after repeating the positive evaluation of Uzziah, describes the king's successes in subduing his enemies, expanding the territory of his king-

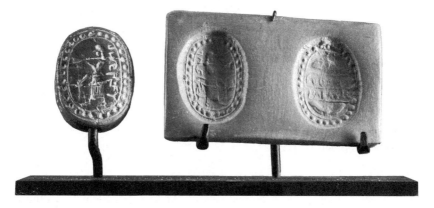

43. Stamp seal belonging to Shebnayau, a servant of King Uzziah of Judah

dom, building towns, enlarging and equipping the army, building towers for the city wall of Jerusalem, and enhancing the royal farms (2 Chron. 26:6-15).

Both the author of 2 Kings and the author of 2 Chronicles report that Uzziah eventually fell victim to leprosy, but only the Chronicler gives a reason for his affliction — the king's pride. According to the Chronicler, Uzziah entered the temple to make an offering on the incense altar, a task that was reserved for the priests alone. When a contingent of eighty priests confronted Uzziah over this violation, he became angry with them. Immediately, "a leprous disease broke out on his forehead" (26:19), and the king was ushered from the temple and no longer permitted to enter it, for he was now ritually impure. As a result of his condition, he was forced to live "in a separate house" (literally, a "house of freedom") the rest of his life, meaning either that he lived apart from other people or only that he no longer functioned as king. His son Jotham took over the reigns of government (2 Kings 15:5; 2 Chron. 26:21; for additional information about Uzziah, see the article "The Epitaph of Uzziah").

The name of the official to whom the seal belonged, Shebnayau, is similar to the name of the person who is called Shebna in 2 Kings 18–19 and Isaiah 22, 36–37. Any attempt, however, to identify these two people as the same person, while possible, is unlikely to be correct. The name "Shebna" and its variants were not uncommon and have been found in several other inscriptions. Furthermore, the title used here for Shebnayau, "servant," is different from the titles used for Shebna in the biblical texts (see the article "Shebna Inscription from Silwan").

Hezekiah's Tunnel Inscription

Inscribed stone slab

▷ Size: 32 cm. (12.6 in.) high; 69 cm. (27.16 in.) wide
▷ Writing: Hebrew language
▷ Provenance: Jerusalem
▷ Date: End of the eighth century B.C.E.
▷ Present location: Archaeological Museum, Istanbul (third floor)
▷ Identification number: 2195 T

In 1838 the American scholar Edward Robinson rediscovered a rock-cut tunnel running underneath part of the old City of David in Jerusalem. The tunnel, largely silted up, carried water from the Gihon Spring to the Pool of Siloam. More than forty years later, in 1880, a group of boys were playing in the water at the end of the tunnel when they discovered an inscription that had been carved into a prepared surface on the wall of the tunnel. The inscription was approximately ten meters (thirty-three feet) from the south end of the tunnel (near the Pool of Siloam) on the east wall of the tunnel. In 1890, the inscription was chiseled from the wall by vandals, which resulted in the inscription being broken into several pieces. The pieces were sold to an antiquities dealer, and shortly afterward, due to the intervention of some officials of the Ottoman Empire, the inscription was taken to the Archaeological Museum of Istanbul, where it remains today.

The inscription, six lines of text written in Old Hebrew, describes how the tunnel was excavated:

[The day of] the breach. ——— This is the record of how the tunnel was breached. While [the excavators were wielding] their pickaxes, each man towards his co-worker, and while there were yet three cubits for the brea[ch,]a voice [was hea]rd each man calling to his co-worker; because there was a cavity in the rock (extending) from the south to [the north].——— So on the day of the breach, the excavators struck, each man to meet his co-worker, pick-axe against pick-[a]xe. ——— Then the water flowed from the spring to the pool, a distance of one thousand and two hundred cubits. One hundred cubits was the height of the rock above the heads of the excavat[ors.][1]

The text indicates that the tunnel was dug by two teams, one working from each end, who cut their way through the bedrock underneath the city using pickaxes, wedges, and hammers. The most amazing part of this construction project is that the two groups of excavators, working underground, managed to meet. Even though several theories have been advanced, no one is certain how this engineering task was carried out. The workers knew when they were getting close to each other by the sound of the voices of the opposite crew. In three or four different places near the meeting point, corrections were made in the course of the tunnel to facilitate the meeting of the two halves of the tunnel. The inscription likely was written by the skillful engineer who accomplished this amazing construction feat. Since the inscription was not intended for public display (it was located approximately ten meters [thirty-three feet] from the

---

1. "The Siloam Tunnel Inscription," translated by K. Lawson Younger Jr. (*COS* 2.28:145-46). The solid lines in the text represent spaces in the inscription that apparently served to introduce a new piece of information. The format of the inscription presented here has been modified from that present in *COS*. The inscription is presented here in paragraph format, rather than in verse format as in *COS*.

end of the tunnel) and is anonymous, it is unlikely that the king or other official was responsible for the inscription. Rather, it was probably the work of the engineer, who was justly proud of his accomplishment. Thus the inscription is a "common person's" inscription, not a royal inscription. The text does not describe the total process of digging the tunnel; it is interested in only the final moment of triumph when the tunnel was completed. The place where the text was inscribed had been carefully smoothed and the inscription chiseled into the bottom half of the rectangular area. The top half of the prepared surface, which was never used, was probably intended for a relief carving of the engineer or a scene showing the moment when the two ends of the tunnel were joined.

The tunnel follows a winding course for approximately 533 meters (1750 ft.) — nearly a third of a mile. The course of the tunnel initially runs west from the Gihon Spring, then turns south for a long run, before turning west once more, and then taking a short southerly run again. (The beginning and ending of the tunnel are actually only 320 meters apart; the sinuous route taken by the excavators, however, resulted in the tunnel being 533 meters long.) The width of the tunnel is approximately .6 meters (2 ft.), and its height varies from around 1.5 to 5 meters (5 to 16.5 ft.); throughout most of the tunnel, the height is approximately 1.68 to 1.83 meters (5.5 to 6 ft.). The cold water from the Gihon Spring flows through the tunnel today at a depth of usually 2.5 to 3 feet. Visitors to Jerusalem can still walk the entire length of Hezekiah's Tunnel (as long as they do not mind getting wet).

Biblical Significance

Hezekiah, following in the steps of his father Ahaz, became king of Judah in 726 B.C.E. (some scholars date the beginning of his reign to 715 B.C.E.) and

44. Inscription commemorating the completion of Hezekiah's Tunnel

ruled for approximately twenty-eight years. During his reign he initiated a religious reform in Judah that included the removal of cultic objects associated
with the worship of other gods and the refurbishing of the Jerusalem temple.
Not only did he carry out a religious reform, but he also made political
changes in his vassal relationship to Assyria. The author of 2 Kings states that
Hezekiah "rebelled against the king of Assyria and would not serve him"
(18:7). Hezekiah's rebellion eventually led to an invasion of Judah by
Sennacherib and the Assyrian army in 701 B.C.E. Aware that his actions would
likely have serious repercussions, Hezekiah had made preparations for the
possible invasion. Specifically, "he made the pool and the conduit and brought
water into the city" in order that if Jerusalem were put under siege its inhabitants would still have water (2 Kings 20:20). These actions are described in
2 Chronicles also: "Hezekiah closed the upper outlet of the waters of Gihon
and directed them down to the west side of the city of David" (32:30). The author of the book of Sirach (also called Ecclesiasticus) provides an even fuller
account:

> Hezekiah fortified his city,
> > and brought water into its midst;
> he tunneled the rock with iron tools,
> > and built cisterns for the water.
> In his days Sennacherib invaded the country;
> > he sent his commander and departed;
> he shook his fist against Zion,
> > and made great boasts in his arrogance. (48:17-18)

Almost all scholars agree that the preparations of Hezekiah described in
these biblical passages included the excavation of the tunnel known today as
Hezekiah's Tunnel or the Siloam Tunnel. The prevailing thought has been that
the Gihon Spring was outside the city wall and the tunnel was necessary to
save the water supply. Yet recent excavations have shown that a second city
wall, which enclosed the Gihon Spring, already existed at the time of Hezekiah. Why then build the tunnel if the spring was already within the wall's protection? No one knows for sure, but perhaps Hezekiah was afraid that the
outer wall would not provide enough protection, so he built the tunnel for additional security to bring the water farther into the city.

The inscription on the tunnel wall would have been incised soon after the
tunnel was completed. Hezekiah and the people of Jerusalem were able to endure Sennacherib's siege of the city, in part no doubt due to the successful construction of this tunnel that brought water into the city. Hezekiah was indeed
forced to pay heavy tribute to Sennacherib, but the Assyrian army withdrew

and Jerusalem was spared. (See the article "The Taylor Prism" for additional information about the siege and its outcome.)

Horned Altar of Beer-sheba

Ashlar limestone blocks

▷ Size: 1.57 m. (5.15 ft.) high, and square; originally, ca. 2.67 m. (8.75 ft.) square
▷ Provenance: Tell Beer-sheba, Israel
▷ Date: ca. eighth century B.C.E.
▷ Present location: Israel Museum, Jerusalem (Bronfman Archaeology Wing)
▷ Identification number: IAA 1995-3877

In 1973 the Israeli archaeologist Yohanan Aharoni discovered a large horned altar at Tell Beer-sheba in southern Palestine. Until that time, the only other altar for burnt offerings that had been found in Israel was at Arad, due east of Beer-sheba; subsequently, important Israelite horned altars have been found at Megiddo and Dan. Unlike the altar at Arad, the Beer-sheba altar was not found intact. Its stones had been reused as part of a repaired wall belonging to a storehouse complex of the eighth century B.C.E. The curved altar horns were found beside one another in the wall, intact except for the point of one of the horns. Not all of the altar's foundation stones were recovered, however; approximately half of the stones remain missing. As a result, only the height of the altar can be determined with certainty. Yet the excavators were convinced that the original dimensions of the altar, as those of the altar at Arad, would have matched the dimensions specified in the Bible: five cubits square and three cubits high (Exod. 27:1). The horns at the corners also conformed to the biblical specifications given in the book of Exodus (27:2; 30:2) that the horns must be an integral part of the altar stones, that is, not a separate piece added on top of another stone but carved from the stone itself.

The origin and meaning of the horns at the corners of altars remain unknown, but examples are found in many ancient civilizations. In certain Near Eastern cultures (the Hittites, among others), horns represent the power of divinity. Some biblical scholars suggest that they may represent the original "standing stones" (massebot) that stood on the corners of the altar. Whatever their significance, they must have had particular sacred meaning since the blood of the sacrificial animal was to be sprinkled upon them seven times (Exod. 29:12; Lev. 16:18-19). Likewise, they are mentioned as the first item in the building of an altar (Exod. 27:2), and cutting them off desecrated an altar (Amos 3:14). In certain cases, a fugitive could obtain asylum by catching hold of them (1 Kings 1:50; but not in cases of murder, 1 Kings 2:28-34).

The altar at Beer-sheba does contain certain anomalies. Biblical regulations specified that altars should be made of uncut stones (Deut. 27:6; Josh. 8:31), whereas these stones are smoothed (ashlar). The texts in Joshua and Deuteronomy specify that iron tools are not to be used upon stones of an altar, but there has been some speculation that bronze tools may have been regarded as acceptable. On the other hand, Exodus 20:25 seems to forbid tools of any kind. Nevertheless, the Bible never mentions horns in connection with altars of unhewn stones. (Practically speaking, how could such horns be made?). Furthermore, only altars upon which animals are to be slain are specifically required to be unhewn. Altars also were used for grain offerings and for burning the fat of a slain animal, and these, like the smaller incense altars, apparently were not prohibited from being constructed of smoothed stones. Such altars were found in many places in Israel, nine being found in Megiddo alone and six others at Dan. One such horned altar from Megiddo is housed today in the Israel Museum, Jerusalem (IAA I.3567). These altars likely were used for offerings of small cakes of grain mixed with oil and possibly also for offerings of wine.

45. Large horned altar from Beer-sheba for burnt offerings

A second peculiarity of this altar was the carving of a crawling snake on one of the stones. This unique feature perhaps represented a fertility symbol, as it does in many parts of the Near East. On the other hand, Israel itself had precedence for such a symbol since the time of Moses (Num. 21:8-9). The staff that turned into a serpent before the pharaoh was a symbol of the power God gave to Moses (Exod. 7:8-15). Later, Moses made a bronze serpent in the wilderness, and those of the children of Israel who looked upon it and had been bitten by poisonous snakes were healed. Subsequently, the bronze serpent was venerated in the temple in Jerusalem prior to the reforms of Hezekiah (2 Kings 18:4).

As mentioned above, horned altars of a different sort were found at Megiddo. Too small to have been used for animal sacrifice, measuring approximately 29 cm. (11.42 in.) square and 68 cm. (26.77 in.) high, these altars must have been used for sacrifices of wine, incense, or grain meal mixed with oil (Lev. 7:12). One of these limestone altars is at the Oriental Institute of the University of Chicago (OIM A13201; Megiddo Gallery), whose archaeological team excavated it in 1926 at Megiddo. It was found in a stratum dated to the tenth century B.C.E. near large public structures that included a four-chambered gate and a casement wall, which some archaeologists date to the time of King Solomon.

Biblical Significance

The discovery of any horned altar as described in the Bible is significant in itself, particularly because of the correlation of the shape and dimensions of these altars with the biblical specifications. The altar at Beer-sheba raises interesting questions because of the ashlar stones used in its construction rather than the unworked fieldstones implied in the biblical texts, but more specifically because of the strange carving of a serpent on one of the stones.

The most suggestive implication of this discovery does not come from its construction or dimensions, but from its location and its dismantled state. After his discovery of the temple area at Arad, Yohanan Aharoni had posited the existence of a series of royal border sanctuaries and even suggested Beer-sheba as the most promising site for a second discovery. More recently, the find of the altar at Dan in the northern extremity of the country would seem to bear out his theory. But why was the altar at Beer-sheba not intact? Scholarly opinion now favors the view that the altar was dismantled as part of the reforms of King Hezekiah (ca. 726-697 B.C.E.). Hezekiah is portrayed in the Bible as a righteous king who restored the services of the Jerusalem temple and suppressed worship of other gods (2 Chronicles 29-31). Some evidence of these actions is found in 2 Kings 18:19-35. A messenger from Sennacherib, on the verge of the Assyrian siege of Jerusalem (701 B.C.E.), asks sarcastically if the people of Jerusalem intend to rely on the Lord alone for their protection, and if this is the Lord "whose high places and altars Hezekiah has removed, saying to Judah and to Jerusalem, 'You shall worship before this altar in Jerusalem'" (2 Kings 18:22). The twin implications of this remark suggest that Hezekiah had pulled down altars outside of Jerusalem, and that this action of centralization might prove a cause for dissent within the kingdom.

While Aharoni saw the disassembled altar at Beer-sheba as an example of this reform, another distinguished archaeologist, Yigael Yadin, dated the wall in which the altar stones were found more than 100 years later, at the time of the Babylonian invasion and destruction of the area (587 B.C.E.). This opinion set off one of the bitterest debates among the followers of both schools of thought in the history of biblical archaeological research. Currently, Aharoni's theory seems to have been sustained by subsequent inquiries, and the dismantled Beer-sheba altar remains as an example of the reforms of Hezekiah.

Sanctuary of Arad

"Holy of holies" from the Arad Sanctuary

▷ Size: See text below
▷ Provenance: Tell Arad, Israel
▷ Date: Eighth century B.C.E.
▷ Present location: Israel Museum, Jerusalem (Bronfman Archaeology Wing)

Between 1962 and 1967, the distinguished Israeli archaeologist Yohanan Aharoni excavated at the ancient fortress city of Arad in the desert region of the Negev (southern Israel). Even though Arad is mentioned only three times in the Bible (Num. 21:1-3; 33:40; and Josh. 12:14, all having reference to the Israelites' entry into the Promised Land), Arad was one of Israel's most important defenses in the south. The site gained its greatest prominence with the discovery of the first sanctuary to Yahweh ever found by archaeological excavation. (Because of the situation on the Temple Mount in Jerusalem, excavation of any remains of the ancient Jerusalem temples has been impossible.)

The history of Arad began in the Early Bronze Age (ca. 3400 to 2000 B.C.E.), and the lower city of Arad today represents the finest example of a Bronze Age settlement in Israel, if not in the world. That early city was destroyed, but later it was rebuilt by the Israelites upon the highest point of the site, its eastern hill, beginning in the tenth century B.C.E. Six successive Israelite fortresses were constructed on this location, each about 49 meters (160 ft.) long on each side, virtually covering the hilltop. The first of these fortresses was destroyed toward the end of the tenth century B.C.E., most likely by Shishak of Egypt in 926 B.C.E.

The excavations at Arad yielded numerous significant discoveries, including various important ostraca (pottery sherds with writing; see the article "Arad Ostracon Mentioning 'House of Yahweh'"). The most exciting of these finds, however, was a temple sanctuary, complete with a sacrificial altar, two limestone incense stands (or perhaps small altars), and, most surprising, a chamber that served as the holy of holies *(debir)*. The incense stands (IAA 1967-980 and IAA 1967-981), which are 39 cm. (15.35 in.) and 51 cm. (20.07 in.) high, stood at the entry to the holy of holies; within that chamber stood a smooth stela or standing stone. It had no marks or symbols on it, and it is impossible to know if it ever did. On either side of the holy of holies, on the main wall of the temple, were placed plaster benches, likely for offerings. Much of this inner sanctuary is now on display in the Israel Museum in Jerusalem.

The sanctuary area in general consisted of a large courtyard, some nine meters (30 ft.) square, paved with small wadi stones. At the west end of this area stood the main hall, and within it, the holy of holies. The courtyard also contained in its center a sacrificial altar, built to the specifications of various altars in the Torah. It was made of unworked stones (Exod. 20:25) and measured exactly "five cubits long and five cubits broad" (Exod. 27:1; approximately 2.3 meters [7.5 ft.] square). The remains of an earlier al-

46. Incense stands from the sanctuary at Arad

tar served as a step at the foot of this new altar. Unlike the altar at Beer-sheba, this Arad altar had no horns at its corners; whether any such horns ever existed (perhaps of plaster or other materials) is unknown. A large slab of flint lay on top of the altar, complete with plaster grooves, which collected the blood and fat from the sacrifices. There was no evidence of burnt offerings, such as soot stains or burn marks, as at Beer-sheba. Two shallow bowls were found at the foot of the altar with an abbreviated inscription that meant "set apart for the priests." (These containers probably were used for the portion of the sacrifices designated for the priests.) An incense burner was discovered in a small room to the west of the sacrificial altar. This burner consisted of a small bowl, trimmed with leaf-like decorations, designed to fit onto a hollow stand also decorated with leaves. Opposite the entrance to the courtyard on its southeast end, a stone basin likely once held a metal water container for ablutions (washings) by the priests.

The rectangular main hall (*heykhal*, or holy place) at the west end of the courtyard faced to the east, with a door in the middle of its long wall. As such, it resembles more the "broad wall" temples of the Canaanites than it does the "long wall" temple in Jerusalem with its entry door on the shorter wall. (Some scholars also have suggested that the arrangement of the temple at Arad might have been influenced by the general plan of the Israelite "four-room house," which had a broad room at the rear of the house and three long rooms perpendicular to it on the front.) The Jerusalem temple of Solomon seems to have gotten its greater influence from the megaron (long-room) temples of northern Syria and Phoenicia, which would be logical, given Solomon's use of Phoenician skilled workmen in its construction (1 Kings 5). Against the back wall of the main hall stood the small holy of holies, within a niche that projected out from the back wall. Later additions extended the main hall of the temple approximately two feet to the north, and this extension was further expanded into the courtyard, creating a long storage room for ritual vessels and other implements.

Biblical Significance

The discovery of this temple sanctuary outside of Jerusalem was exciting to scholars for many reasons. For the first time there was evidence of a significant location for worship outside of the central place of worship in Jerusalem, so designated since the time of David. Scholars knew that such centers existed, but this discovery enabled them to date specifically one such locale and to compare it with the temples constructed by Solomon and Herod. The finding of an altar made to the exact specifications of the Old Testament was also a first. But the most surprising discovery was that of the holy of holies, an innermost sanctuary of Yahweh, and one most certainly not presided over by the high priest of Jerusalem. All of this evidence served to cement the long-held view that the biblical standards of orthodoxy were the ideal, but by no means the uniform, practices of Israel. The deviations from this norm that are occasionally described in the Bible also were seen to be more widespread and persistent than once believed.

The archaeology of the strata at the Arad sanctuary was so complex that conclusions as to dating proved especially difficult. The original excavators first described the sanctuary as originating in the tenth century B.C.E. and continuing into the seventh century B.C.E., when it was destroyed during the reforms of King Josiah. Some later archaeologists, particularly David Ussishkin, challenged this dating, moving the founding of the complex into the late eighth or even seventh century. Consensus today favors the conclusions of the second intense study of the site conducted by one of its original excavators, Ze'ev Herzog. He became convinced that the site indeed did not originate in the tenth century B.C.E., but in the eighth century. But he also denied that the site had any seventh-century existence. According to Herzog, the sanctuary had a relatively brief existence entirely within the eighth century and likely fell during the reforms of King Hezekiah, as did its neighboring sanctuary at Beersheba (see the article "Horned Altar of Beer-sheba").

One question, however, does not seem to be answered in any of the theories of the dismantling of the sanctuary. If indeed the zeal of Hezekiah or Josiah terminated the Arad place of worship, why was anything at all left of the worship center and, most particularly, its holiest place, the holy of holies? Nonetheless, due to the condition of the site at this point, it is highly unlikely that additional clarifications of the strata and details concerning the Arad temple will ever be forthcoming.

Shebna Inscription from Silwan

Inscribed limestone rock

- ▷ Size: 1.32 m. (4.33 ft.) long; ca. 26 cm. (10.24 in.) high
- ▷ Writing: Hebrew language
- ▷ Provenance: Silwan (Jerusalem), Israel
- ▷ Date: Eighth-seventh century B.C.E.
- ▷ Present location: British Museum (room 57)
- ▷ Identification number: ME 125205

The discovery of a tomb inscription in the vicinity of Jerusalem attributed to Shebna, an official in the court of King Hezekiah, presents one of the most fascinating stories — and mysteries — of biblical archaeology. Who exactly was Shebna, and what was the story behind his elaborate tomb?

47. Inscription from the tomb of Shebna at Silwan

In 1870 Charles Clermont-Ganneau, a French government official, discovered two inscriptions in the façade of a rock-hewn tomb on the main
street of the village of Silwan (or, Siloam), across the valley east of Jerusalem.
Clermont-Ganneau had already made an important contribution to biblical
research by the impression ("squeeze") he had made of the Mesha stela prior
to its destruction by Arab bedouin (see the previous article, "Mesha Stela").
His work in examining and analyzing the tombs of Silwan was made extremely difficult due to the filthy conditions of the village and the hostility
of its inhabitants, long noted for their animosity to outsiders. Nevertheless,
he succeeded in removing the stone surrounding the inscriptions and sending it to the British Museum. Subsequent work by archaeologists was not
immediately forthcoming, no doubt in part because of the difficulty in ac-
cessing the site. Nearly thirty years later (1899), Clermont-Ganneau expressed his belief that the necropolis he had uncovered was one of the most
ancient of all those in Jerusalem and begged future archaeologists to devote
appropriate attention to it.

It would not be until 1968, following the Six-Day War, when Silwan became
accessible to Israeli archaeologists, that Clermont-Ganneau's plea would be
heeded. Two Israeli archaeologists from Tel Aviv University, David Ussishkin
and his colleague, Gabriel Barkay, began work at that time on the Silwan necropolis and the tomb from which the inscriptions had been taken. But their
work was as difficult as that of Clermont-Ganneau; open sewage in the village
polluted the tombs, and the hostility of villagers frequently interrupted or prevented their work. Yet, like their predecessor, they persevered and eventually
succeeded in surveying some fifty tombs. Most of these were arranged in two
parallel rows, one line above the other, cut into the limestone rock face. The
entrances to the tombs were rectangular and originally blocked with single
stones, which have disappeared. The insides of some of the tombs were archi-
tecturally simple and unremarkable. Others had gabled ceilings or flat ceilings
with cornices, similar to the Phoenician-style tombs discovered at the necropolis of Salamis on the eastern coast of Cyprus. At least one had a pyramid on

its roof, and Ussishkin suggested that the tomb with the Shebna inscription originally might also have had a pyramid (which clearly would have identified it as ostentatious).[1]

The inscriptions discovered at the necropolis proved to be historic. The ancient Hebrew script in which these were written had fallen into disuse after the Babylonian destruction of Jerusalem in 587 B.C.E., and therefore this writing provided a verifiable means of dating the tombs. As a result, these tombs are known as the first burial chambers from the First Temple period ever discovered. But just as decades had passed before the full examination of the necropolis could take place, so it would be eighty years before the longer of the two inscriptions could be read. The condition of this inscription was extremely poor, but in 1953 the renowned Hebrew epigrapher, Nahman Avigad of the Hebrew University of Jerusalem, finally was able to decipher its three lines:

1) This is [the sepulchre of . . .]yahu who is over the house. There is no silver and no gold here
2) but [his bones] and the bones of his slave-wife with him. Cursed be the man
3) who will open this![2]

Because of the damaged condition of the inscription, the name of the owner of the tomb was partially obliterated. Who was "yahu, who is over the house"?

Biblical Significance

In 2 Kings 18–19 and Isaiah 22, 36–37, Shebna is identified as an official of the court of Hezekiah. In 2 Kings he is referred to as a scribe or secretary, and in Isaiah 22 as the top official (steward or governor) of the palace. Clermont-Ganneau had guessed that the tomb inscription might indicate the burial place of Shebna, but he had no way of dating the tomb to know for certain. Likewise, Nahman Avigad suggested that the word "yahu" remaining on the inscription represented the final letters of the name Shebnayahu, a variant of the name Shebna, and that the nature of the Hebrew script of the inscription established it as appropriate for the time of Hezekiah and his court.[3]

In Isaiah 22:15-25, the prophet delivers a blistering denunciation of the palace steward, also referred to by scholars as chamberlain, or comptroller, of the

1. David Ussishkin, "The Necropolis from the Time of the Kingdom of Judah at Silwan, Jerusalem," *Biblical Archaeology* 33, no. 2 (1970): 34-36.
2. Nahman Avigad, "The Epitaph of a Royal Steward from Siloam Village," *Israel Exploration Journal* 3, no. 3 (1953): 137-52.
3. Avigad, "The Epitaph," pp. 142-46.

palace. Isaiah's words perhaps were even spoken face-to-face at the site of the tomb itself, where Shebna was overseeing the work. ("Who are your relatives here . . . a tomb here . . . ?"):

> Thus says the Lord GOD of hosts: Come, go to this steward, to Shebna, who is master of the household, and say to him: What right do you have here? Who are your relatives here, that you have cut out a tomb here for yourself, cutting a tomb on the height, and carving a habitation for yourself in the rock? The Lord is about to hurl you away violently, my fellow. He will seize firm hold on you, whirl you round and round, and throw you like a ball into a wide land; there you shall die, and there your splendid chariots shall lie, O you disgrace to your master's house! I will thrust you from your office, and you will be pulled down from your post.
>
> On that day I will call my servant Eliakim son of Hilkiah, and will clothe him with your robe and bind your sash on him. I will commit your authority to his hand, and he shall be a father to the inhabitants of Jerusalem and to the house of Judah. I will place on his shoulder the key of the house of David; he shall open, and no one shall shut; he shall shut, and no one shall open. I will fasten him like a peg in a secure place, and he will become a throne of honor to his ancestral house. And they will hang on him the whole weight of his ancestral house, the offspring and issue, every small vessel, from the cups to all the flagons. On that day, says the LORD of hosts, the peg that was fastened in a secure place will give way; it will be cut down and fall, and the load that was on it will perish, for the LORD has spoken.

Why such a heated rebuke from the prophet? Was the extravagance of his tomb, highly visible above ground, his only fault? Various answers have been given by biblical interpreters. Perhaps Shebna had a long history of extravagant indulgence while supporting measures to oppress the poor. Or, was he also lining his own pockets with funds from the palace treasury? Was Judah's foreign policy also in play here, with Shebna favoring foreign assistance in the looming crisis in opposition to the position of Isaiah, who counseled against looking to a weakened Egypt for support? The text is silent on these matters. Yet it is plain that Isaiah foresees a day in which Shebna will be thrust into a foreign land, never to occupy his splendid tomb, his position also given to another (which seems to be the situation in 2 Kings).

Many questions have been raised by scholars about the date of the writing of these verses in Isaiah. More than likely, they represent a composite of earlier and later writings, so that history and perhaps *ex eventu* (after the fact) prophecy are intermingled. Nevertheless, the majority of biblical scholarship regards the identification of the biblical Shebna with the Silwan tomb owner as likely.

The Taylor Prism

Six-sided baked clay cylinder

▷ Size: 38.5 cm. (15.15 in.) high; 16.5 cm. (6.50 in.) wide; each face, 8.57 cm. (3.37 in.) wide
▷ Writing: Akkadian language in cuneiform script
▷ Provenance: Nineveh, Assyria (modern Nebi Yunus, Iraq)
▷ Date: 690 B.C.E.
▷ Present location: British Museum (room 55)
▷ Identification number: ME 91032

When Sennacherib came to the throne of Assyria in 704 B.C.E. following the death of his father, Sargon II, in battle, his first activity was directed toward relocating the capital city. The death of a monarch in battle was rare, and the Assyrians regarded it as the worst of omens. The body also had been buried on foreign soil. A fragmentary text records an inquiry to the gods by Sennacherib, asking what terrible sin his father had committed to receive such an awful fate. No evidence remains of the answer he received from the gods, if any was forthcoming. Nevertheless, he immediately abandoned the still-unfinished capital of Sargon and began the work of moving it elsewhere. Soon Sennacherib was successful in establishing a magnificent new capital city, Nineveh, which replaced Dur-Sharrukin (modern Khorsabad). His new Southwest Palace in particular became a spectacular example of his desire to lead Assyria to even greater heights of splendor and power. (See the article "Scenes from Sennacherib's Southwest Palace at Nineveh.")

Sennacherib's next concern was pacifying the newly retaken region of Babylonia, a task made even more personal by the Babylonian kidnapping and murder of one of his sons. Rebellions were common within vassal states following a change in monarchs, and Sennacherib's long reign of twenty-four years would be occupied with holding on to the existing Assyrian kingdom. For the next fourteen years, he and his generals would be involved in a difficult campaign to control the southern portions of Mesopotamia. In 689 B.C.E. this goal was finally accomplished with the taking and destroying of the city of Babylon after a siege of fifteen months.

Between 704 and 681 B.C.E., Sennacherib conducted a total of eight campaigns against various rebellious states under his control, a war that he attributed to inspiration from his principal god, Ashur. His third campaign, which involved the siege of Jerusalem, is of particular interest to biblical scholars. This historic siege is clearly described in one of the most significant archaeological discoveries in the history of biblical research, the Taylor Prism. The

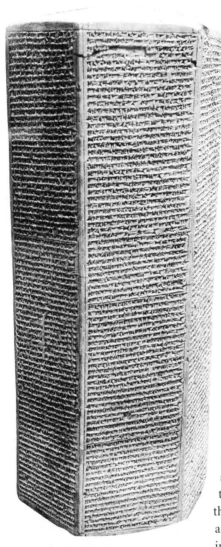

48. The Tayor Prism, which describes Sennacherib's siege of Jerusalem

six-sided prism was a foundational record, discovered at Nineveh, likely buried originally beneath the arsenal at Nebi Yunus. The writing is typical of Assyrian annals, blending fact with ideological propaganda. It was acquired in 1830 by Colonel R. Taylor, British consul general at Baghdad, and was purchased by the British Museum from Taylor's widow in 1855. Even though it is the latest of the annals of Sennacherib — seven other prisms have been discovered with essentially the same information — it has long been regarded as the standard inscription of his campaigns. One of these additional prisms, found at Nineveh (ME 103000) and dated to ca. 694 B.C.E., is on display in room 10b of the British Museum. It contains the standard record of Sennacherib's first five campaigns, including the third campaign which involved the siege of Jerusalem and the destruction of Lachish, although curiously the latter is not mentioned (see the article "Siege of Lachish"). Another important prism with Sennacherib's campaigns (OIM A2793) is in the Assyrian Empire Gallery of the Museum of the Oriental Institute Museum of the University of Chicago. Yet another prism is known as the Israel Museum Cylinder (IMJ 71.72.249), on display in the Bronfman Archeology Wing of the Israel Museum. The Taylor Prism remains today as one of the most celebrated objects in the great collection of antiquities in the British Museum, as well as a vital piece of evidence for the history of the biblical period.

Biblical Significance

In 701 B.C.E., Sennacherib opened his western campaign against rebellious vassals by marching against the cities of Phoenicia, including Sidon and Tyre. Subsequently, Ashkelon, Joppa, and other towns along the coastal plain were subdued. Nine miles south of Joppa, the Assyrians were confronted by Egyptian troops seeking to aid the rebels, along with some fighters from Ashkelon. The result was the conquest of Ashkelon and Timnah, as well as numerous smaller cities.

Sennacherib next turned to the southeast and led his armies against the powerfully defended city of Lachish, second only to Jerusalem as a principal city of Judah. Located on a steep hill to the west of Jerusalem, Lachish was key to guarding Jerusalem against attacks from the southwest. In a dramatic series of events, Sennacherib laid siege to the city and built a ramp for his siege engines to counter the effectiveness of the glacis (a steep, smooth slope, covered with plaster, rising from a ditch or moat) that surrounded the city. After a bitter fight, the city was taken in the usual brutal fashion of the Assyrians, and the entire campaign was documented on alabaster wall reliefs in the Southwest Palace. (Strangely, neither the Assyrian annals nor the Bible contains any mention of the destruction of Lachish, in spite of the lavish treatment accorded the battle on these palace reliefs.)

With no further obstacles of any significance in his path, Sennacherib moved against Jerusalem. After the sacking of Lachish, he sent senior military officers and a large army against the capital city (2 Kings 18:17). The Assyrian army encamped in the area of Mount Scopus — a site that would be chosen some 700 years later by Titus in the Roman siege of Jerusalem — laid siege to the city, and waited.

The events from that point forward are not entirely clear. The chief Assyrian official at the site demanded surrender from King Hezekiah, who himself did not appear on the walls but sent messengers to listen to the Assyrian demands (Shebna, Eliakim, and Joah; 2 Kings 18:18). They reported the Assyrian insistence on total surrender to Hezekiah, who was despondent at the news. But the prophet Isaiah assured him that the Lord had revealed that the Assyrians would withdraw without military action on his part (2 Kings 19:5-7; Isa. 37:5-7).

The biblical account of these events is unusually extensive, appearing in both historical and prophetic books (2 Kings 18:13–19:37; 2 Chron. 32:1-22; Isaiah 36–37). Some differences occur in these accounts, but essentially they follow the outline of the material in 2 Kings 18–19:

> In the fourteenth year of King Hezekiah, King Sennacherib of Assyria came up against all the fortified cities of Judah and captured them. King Hezekiah of Judah sent to the king of Assyria at Lachish, saying, "I have done

wrong; withdraw from me; whatever you impose on me I will bear." The king of Assyria demanded of King Hezekiah of Judah three hundred talents of silver and thirty talents of gold. Hezekiah gave him all the silver that was found in the house of the LORD and in the treasuries of the king's house. At that time Hezekiah stripped the gold from the doors of the temple of the LORD, and from the doorposts that King Hezekiah of Judah had overlaid and gave it to the king of Assyria. (2 Kings 18:13-16)

After additional pressure from Sennacherib to surrender, Hezekiah turned to the prophet Isaiah for advice. Isaiah responded to Hezekiah with the following words:

"Therefore thus says the LORD concerning the king of Assyria: He shall not come into this city, shoot an arrow there, come before it with a shield, or cast up a siege ramp against it. By the way that he came, by the same he shall return; he shall not come into this city, says the LORD. For I will defend this city to save it, for my own sake and for the sake of my servant David."

That very night the angel of the LORD set out and struck down one hundred eighty-five thousand in the camp of the Assyrians; when morning dawned, they were all dead bodies. Then King Sennacherib of Assyria left, went home, and lived at Nineveh. (2 Kings 19:32-36)

Column 3 of the Taylor Prism describes this assault on Judah and Jerusalem from the Assyrian viewpoint:

As for Hezekiah, the Judean,[1] I besieged forty-six of his fortified walled cities and surrounding smaller towns, which were without number. Using packed-down ramps and applying battering rams, infantry attacks by mines, breaches, and siege machines, I conquered (them). I took out 200,150 people, young and old, male and female, horses, mules, donkeys, camels, cattle, and sheep, without number, and counted them as spoil. He himself, I locked up within Jerusalem, his royal city, like a bird in a cage. I surrounded him with earthworks, and made it unthinkable for him to exit by the city gate. His cities which I had despoiled I cut off from his land and gave them to Mitinti, king of Ashdod, Padi, king of Ekron, and Silli-bel, king of Gaza, and thus I diminished his land. I imposed dues and gifts for my lordship upon him, in addition to the former tribute, their yearly payment.

---

1. The Oriental Institute Prism adds at this point, "who had not submitted to my yoke."

He, Hezekiah, was overwhelmed by the awesome splendor of my lordship, and he sent me after my departure to Nineveh, my royal city, his elite troops (and) his best soldiers, which he had brought in as reinforcements to strengthen Jerusalem, with 30 talents of gold, 800 talents of silver, choice antimony, large blocks of carnelian, beds (inlaid) with ivory, elephant hides, ivory, ebony-wood, boxwood, multicolored garments, garments of linen, wool (dyed) red-purple and blue-purple, vessels of copper, iron, bronze and tin, chariots, siege shields, lances, armor, daggers for the belt, bows and arrows, countless trappings and implements of war, together with his daughters, his palace women, his male and female singers. He (also) dispatched his messenger to deliver the tribute and to do obeisance.[2]

As the Taylor Prism confirms, there is no evidence that the Assyrians took the city — nor is there any record of death among the Assyrian troops. The record is clear, however, that the army did withdraw and that Sennacherib only "later" received tribute from Hezekiah. (The amount of this tribute varies somewhat in the biblical account.) Notice also the often-quoted expression concerning King Hezekiah, "He himself, I walled up within Jerusalem, his royal city, like a bird in a cage."[3] This convention of speech was used previously in the annals of Tiglath-pileser III concerning his attempt to capture the city of Damascus and its king, Rezin: "I set up my camp around the city for 45 days; and I confined him like a bird in a cage." One Assyriologist makes an interesting comparison between this comment and the corresponding phrase by Sennacherib that refers to the siege of Jerusalem:

> The true sense of these passages is that of a total blockade, and the hyperbole is employed as a face-saving device to cover for failure to take the enemy's capital and punish the rebellious king. In the case of Rezin, this was accomplished in the following year (732); in the case of Hezekiah, Sennacherib was forced to make do with heavy tribute delivered to Nineveh after his retreat.[4]

(Interestingly, the capture of Damascus and the execution of Rezin are recorded in 2 Kings 16:9, but not in any of the Assyrian annals.)

---

2. "Sennacherib's Siege of Jerusalem," translated by Mordechai Cogan (*COS* 2.119B: 303).

3. "The Calah Annals," translated by K. Lawson Younger Jr. (*COS* 2.117A: 286).

4. H. Tadmor, *The Inscriptions of Tiglath-Pileser III King of Assyria* (Jerusalem: The Israel Academy of Sciences and Humanities, 1994), p. 79, n. to 11'; cited in "The Calah Annals," translated by K. Lawson Younger Jr. (*COS* 2.117A: 286, n. 31).

Sennacherib also claims that he deported 200,150 people to Assyria, a number that might be questioned in light of the fact that Jerusalem itself was not taken. Ancient numbers are notoriously untrustworthy, due to the tendency of royal scribes and chroniclers to inflate, sometimes extravagantly, the actual figures involved. Nevertheless the historical correspondence between the two accounts is in agreement on certain essential points: Sennacherib attacked Judah and laid siege to Jerusalem; for some reason, he withdrew without taking the city, which the Jews regarded as a miracle from God; and, subsequently, Hezekiah was forced to pay heavy tribute to Sennacherib.

In 1815, George Gordon, Lord Byron, wrote a poem destined to be often quoted concerning the fate of Sennacherib's army according to the biblical account:

The Destruction of Sennacherib

The Assyrian came down like the wolf on the fold,
And his cohorts were gleaming in purple and gold;
And the sheen of their spears was like stars on the sea,
When the blue wave rolls nightly on deep Galilee.
Like the leaves of the forest when summer is green,
That host with their banners at sunset were seen;
Like the leaves of the forest when autumn hath blown,
That host on the morrow lay withered and strown.

For the Angel of Death spread his wings on the blast,
And breathed in the face of the foe as he passed,
And the eyes of the sleepers waxed deadly and chill,
And their hearts but once heaved, and forever grew still!
And there lay the steed with his nostrils all wide,
But through it there rolled not the breath of his pride
And the foam of his gasping lay white on the turf,
And cold as the spray of the rock-beating surf.
And there lay the rider distorted and pale,
With the dew on his brow and the rust on his mail;
And the tents were all silent, the banners alone,
The lances unlifted, the trumpet unblown.
And the widows of Ashur are loud in their wail,
And the idols are broke in the temple of Baal;
And the might of the Gentile, unsmote by the sword,
Hath melted like snow in the glance of the Lord.

Bull Inscription of Sennacherib: The Tribute of Hezekiah

Limestone slab with inscription

▷ Size: 2.86 m. (9.38 ft.) wide

▷ Writing: Akkadian language in cuneiform script

▷ Provenance: Nineveh, Assyria (modern Kuyunjik, Iraq)

▷ Date: 694-693 B.C.E.

▷ Present location: British Museum (room 10c)

▷ Identification number: ME 118815

The discovery of this insignificant-appearing slab of limestone was regarded as one of the most sensational finds of its time. It presents the first archaeological evidence ever discovered of Sennacherib's siege of Jerusalem and the subsequent tribute sent to him by King Hezekiah of Judah. Subsequent discoveries would further document these events, but this panel was the first and most detailed record (see the articles "The Taylor Prism" and "Scenes from Sennacherib's Southwest Palace at Nineveh").

In his obsession to build "the palace without rival" at Nineveh, Sennacherib was determined to leave a monument to himself for all time. He made sure that a significant portion of this monument would be devoted to propagandistic accounts of his various achievements at home and abroad. The official annals of the various kings of Mesopotamia were more matter-of-fact, historical records, and they are regarded as the premier, unbiased sources of information into the period — at least as unbiased as any governmental record can be. The so-called public records, those inscriptions placed in palaces and temples for reading by the few who were literate who might see them, were a different matter. Sennacherib chose to place enormous statues of bulls and lions throughout the palace, principally in his throne room and at doorways or principal passages, with inscriptions of his deeds placed below them and between their legs. Even an illiterate who viewed these colossal figures could not fail to be impressed with the power of the monarch who erected them. Their various inscriptions glorified the achievement of the king and generally followed a standard pattern: a titulary at the beginning of the inscription (titles of the king with adjectives describing his magnificence), followed by claims of his military victories and/or building accomplishments, and the promise that subsequent kings who preserved them would be honored by the gods. However, unlike his predecessor, Sargon, who placed the same text on every bull inscription in his palace, no two texts of Sennacherib are exactly the same. Twenty-four pairs of these colossi are known to have existed; four of these

49. Inscription from under a bull statue mentioning Hezekiah's tribute payment to Sennacherib

pairs are human-headed lions, nineteen are human-headed bulls, and one is undesignated in the records. Most of these figures were left *in situ* (in their original position). Many of them are in extremely poor condition. Unfortunately, since the Second Gulf War the chaos in the country has allowed some of the remaining figures to be plundered. Many are known to have been hacked into pieces and sold in the black market antiquities trade.

Fortunately for biblical history, the discoverers of this bull in the nineteenth century recognized the inscription that refers to Hezekiah. Subsequently, the panel was sawn apart from its base and sent to the British Museum. Like many of the others, this inscription is badly weathered and almost illegible. Nevertheless, careful translation has preserved the record of its important contents, a description of Sennacherib's third campaign, which included the Assyrian assault on Jerusalem:

> I drew near to Ekron, — the governors who had rebelled (committed sin) I slew with the sword. The citizens who had rebelled (sinned) I counted as spoil. The rest of them, who had not rebelled, I pardoned. Padî, their king, I brought out of Jerusalem and placed on the throne over them. My royal tribute I imposed upon him. As for Hezekiah, the Jew, who had not submitted to my yoke, 46 of his strong, walled cities and the cities of their environs, which were numberless, I besieged, I captured, I plundered, as booty I counted. Him, like a caged bird in Jerusalem, his royal city, I shut up. Earth works I threw up about it. His cities which I plundered, I cut off from his land and gave to the kings of Ashdod, Ashkelon, Ekron and Gaza — I diminished his land. To the former tribute, I imposed and laid upon him the

giving up of his land as a gift. That Hezekiah, — the terrifying splendor of my royalty overcame him, and the Arabs and his picked troops whom he had brought into Jerusalem, his royal city, ran away. With 30 talents of gold, 800 talents of silver and all kinds of treasure from his palace, he sent his daughters, his palace women, his male and female singers, to Nineveh, and he dispatched his messenger to pay the tribute.[1]

The annalist's account of Sennacherib's first six campaigns, which included the text about Hezekiah, consisted of 146 lines of text inscribed between the legs and under the bellies of two colossal bulls that faced each other on opposite sides of the main entrance to the throne room of the Southwest Palace at Nineveh. The text quoted above is lines 25-32 (out of a total of 46 lines) of column 1 of the inscription, which is located on panel ME 118815 (see fig. 49). This panel (which is in two pieces) came from under the belly of one of the bulls. Panel ME 118821, which contains the second column of text, is also on display in room 10c of the British Museum. It came from between the hind legs of the same bull. (At the time of this writing, the inscribed slabs in the British Museum were mislabeled, with the larger slab mistakenly identified as ME 118821 and the smaller labeled as ME 118815.)

The Taylor Prism also contains an account of this Assyrian invasion of Judah (701 B.C.E.), although in somewhat different form (see the article "The Taylor Prism").

Biblical Significance

Curiously, neither this bull inscription nor the Taylor Prism mentions Sennacherib's lengthy and successful siege of Lachish, the great fortified city standing between the Assyrians and Jerusalem. (For some reason, the biblical account also never mentions the fall of Lachish.) The attack on Lachish was portrayed in extraordinary detail, however, on numerous wall reliefs in Sennacherib's palace (see the article "Scenes from Sennacherib's Southwest Palace at Nineveh"). No doubt Sennacherib preferred this visual medium to portray his dramatic victory over Lachish, rather than merely recounting it in an inscription. Obviously he did not capture Jerusalem, since no account, Assyrian or biblical, says that it fell at that time. Perhaps Sennacherib believed that these scenes of his army destroying the city of Lachish and capturing its inhabitants might divert attention from whatever issues caused him not to pursue the siege and assault on Jerusalem. Thus

1. Daniel David Luckenbill, *The Annals of Sennacherib*, The University of Chicago Oriental Institute Publications, vol. 2 (Chicago: University of Chicago Press, 1924), p. 70.

the emphasis of this inscription, as in the Taylor Prism, was placed on his principal success in the campaign against Jerusalem — the tribute paid to him by Hezekiah.

Although some of the amounts are different, the biblical account agrees for the most part with the Assyrian record of Hezekiah's tribute, but only the Assyrian accounts mention the sending of women and court personnel to Sennacherib's palace:

> In the fourteenth year of King Hezekiah, King Sennacherib of Assyria came up against all the fortified cities of Judah and captured them. King Hezekiah of Judah sent to the king of Assyria at Lachish, saying, "I have done wrong; withdraw from me; whatever you impose on me I will bear." The king of Assyria demanded of King Hezekiah of Judah three hundred talents of silver and thirty talents of gold. Hezekiah gave him all the silver that was found in the house of the LORD and in the treasuries of the king's house. At that time Hezekiah stripped the gold from the doors of the temple of the LORD, and from the doorposts that King Hezekiah of Judah had overlaid and gave it to the king of Assyria. (2 Kings 18:13-16)

The Hebrew Scripture is surprisingly open in its inclusion of Hezekiah's confession of his "wrongdoing" in rebelling against Assyrian power. By sending such an admission to Sennacherib while he was laying siege to Lachish, along with his promise to pay whatever tribute Sennacherib demanded, no doubt Hezekiah hoped to avoid a Syrian attack on Jerusalem. The account in 2 Kings also adds another detail of the event not in any Assyrian record, namely that Hezekiah "stripped the gold from the doors of the temple of LORD, and from the doorposts that King Hezekiah of Judah had overlaid."

Although the bull inscription shown here yields no information that is not now available from other sources, it should be remembered that at the time of its discovery and translation only the biblical account was known. The finding of the bull inscription therefore served as a significant corroboration of the basic historical account of Sennacherib's invasion of Judah as found in the Old Testament, as much by what it does not say as by what it says. That is, even in his own propagandistic account of the invasion of Judah, which he erected in his "palace without rival," Sennacherib does not claim to have conquered Jerusalem.

Scenes from Sennacherib's Southwest Palace at Nineveh

Stone wall reliefs

▷ Size: Panels generally range from ca. 1.75 to 3 m. (ca. 5.75 to 10 ft.) high
▷ Provenance: Nineveh, Assyria (modern Kuyunjik, Iraq)
▷ Date: ca. 700-691 B.C.E.
▷ Present location: British Museum (rooms 9, 10b, and 88a); Museum of the Ancient Orient in Istanbul (Mesopotamia Hall); and Ashmolean Museum in Oxford, England
▷ Identification numbers: See text below

In 1947 the British diplomat-turned-archaeologist, Austin Henry Layard, uncovered the Southwest Palace of Sennacherib (704-681 B.C.E.) — the "Palace without Rival," in Sennacherib's words — and nearly two miles of spectacular wall reliefs, mostly found *in situ* (in place). The discovery created a worldwide sensation (see the article "The Taylor Prism"). In all, Layard uncovered eight royal Assyrian palaces as well as colossal winged bulls, inscriptions, and other treasures of the Assyrian empire that had lain buried and forgotten for more than 2000 years.

Some of the most spectacular of the palace wall panels depict the Assyrian siege of the city of Lachish in Judah (see the article "Siege of Lachish"). Yet many others show aspects of court life, geography, the military, and various campaigns of the Assyrians. Partly because of the location of the panels in underground rooms and partly because of the lack of adequate photographic equipment, Layard was forced to resort to sketches by artists he employed — none proved entirely satisfactory — and some drawings he even made himself. Eventually many of these reliefs were sent abroad, by far the largest number to the British Museum, where they reside today.

Dating the panels proved complicated for archaeologists because of the succession of kings in the palace. Which reliefs were by Sennacherib, and which by Ashurbanipal? Various scholars have attempted to establish criteria for differentiation between the scenes. For one example of their approach, the style of military equipment, uniforms, and other forms of dress is highly diagnostic. Here are a few of those indicators:

Sennacherib's Period	Ashurbanipal's Period
Helmets: pointed; hinged earflaps	Helmets: conical; earflaps, one piece with helmet
King's chariot wheels: smooth	King's chariot wheels: studded with nails

Horse armor: none	Horse armor: large (likely leather) blankets
Beards: mostly bearded	Beards: mostly beardless
Horses' heads: heavy muzzles	Horses' heads: thinner muzzles with underbite

Of course, there are many other important criteria regarding form, arrangement of elements, motifs, and other distinguishing characteristics. Some of these criteria involve the specific themes favored by these kings. For example, a number of Assyrian monarchs, including Ashurbanipal, favored hunting scenes in their wall panels; Sennacherib had none of them. Likewise, Sennacherib did not favor lengthy panels showing long lines of subjects bearing tribute to him. Nor did he regularly utilize inscriptions at the thresholds to the palace rooms, as did others; instead, he favored decorative, rug-like floor patterns. Long texts were put only on the colossal bull figures. The motifs of his wall panels principally emphasized two themes: his accomplishments in war, and pictorial representations of building activities. The latter have been particularly useful and fascinating to scholars due to the uniqueness of some of the techniques portrayed.[1]

To see the most prominent of the wall reliefs of Sennacherib in the British Museum, visit rooms 9, 10b, and 88a. Notable panels on display (with the exception of the wall panels depicting the siege of Lachish, which are covered in a separate article) include:

1. Prisoners, probably from Phoenicia or Palestine, playing lyres (room 10b; ME 124947; see fig. 50). Though the dress of these prisoners is not the same as that of the people of Lachish, it is possible that they were from one of the other forty-six cities Sennacherib claimed to have captured in Judah. Musicians were often taken in captivity, and music, as shown here, was not limited to religious ceremonies and court life. These musicians are playing lyres with the use of a plectrum.

2. Royal guards (ME 124901; formerly in room 88, check with museum personnel for current location). This panel was found somewhere between the palace of Sennacherib and the historic temple of Ishtar, principal goddess of Nineveh. It depicts two figures. One is an archer, whose dress suggests he was from the Aramaic-speaking regions near Nineveh that had been conquered by the Assyrians. Most interesting, however, is the figure on the right. This spear bearer is dressed almost identically to the men of Lachish shown in the

---

1. John Malcolm Russell, *Sennacherib's Palace without Rival at Nineveh* (Chicago: University of Chicago Press, 1991), pp. 119-35.

50. Relief panel showing prisoners from Phoenicia or Palestine playing lyres

several panels depicting the siege of that city. His headband with long earflaps, which fastens a turban wound about his head, and his short kilt that curves above his knees denote a war captive from Judea. The fact that he is part of the royal guard of the palace indicates considerable dependability on his part and trust in a captive on the part of the palace authorities.

3. The movement of a stone sculpture from the quarries (room 9; ME 124820, ME 124821, ME 124822, ME 124823, ME 124824). These panels are not as pristine as others, but they are well worth careful examination. They picture the transport of a winged bull from the quarry to the palace. This human-headed bull, known as a *lamassu,* is destined to stand as a guardian figure at the entrance to the palace. Thus far it has only been roughly formed, to reduce weight for transport; its final carving will be done in place at the palace. (That is also true of the panels themselves.) It is being transported on a sledge pulled by gangs of prisoners — some from Palestine — as trumpeters direct the operation (while standing on the sledge, which could not have been appreciated by the men trying to pull it!). One group of prisoners uses a lever on the back of the sledge so that rollers can be placed under it. King Sennacherib himself is shown in panel ME 124824, personally directing the work, in which he took great pride. One of the panels from this series (ME 124823) shows workmen carrying the great iron saws used to cut large blocks of stone. (Some of these saws were excavated at Nimrud.) This scene was part of a series that originally decorated a courtyard at Sennacherib's palace.

4. Two guardian figures (room 9; ME 118932). One of Sennacherib's innovations was the invention of several new types of guardian figures. This panel

shows two of them. On the left is a creature with the head of a lion and the feet of an eagle, known as an *ugallu* (great lion, or great storm demon); it holds a mace and a dagger. The figure on the right, a man with the horned headdress of a god, may be the "House God" whose duty was preventing the effects of witchcraft. (Figurines of these were regularly buried in the foundation of new buildings.)

5. Assyrian cavalry, slingers, and archers (room 10b; ME 124775–ME 124777). These panels give a good representation of the various divisions within the Assyrian army. Slingers were common to all ancient Mediterranean nations, including Israel. They were the foot soldiers, the "shock troops," generally at the front of an attack. Their weapon is estimated to have had an effectiveness of approximately one hundred meters. Archers were especially chosen by contests designed to test their accuracy at great ranges. Archers generally moved at the rear of foot soldiers, firing over their heads. Most elite of all were the members of the cavalry. These units generally were composed of upper class, wealthier individuals. The tactics of the Assyrian cavalry gave them great advantages in battle against more primitive armies.

6. Other distinctive panels include a picture of a Phoenician galley, with a pointed prow for ramming, and its oarsmen (room 9; ME 124772); and several panels that once lined a corridor in the palace, among the last ever carved at Nineveh, depicting the Assyrians in a military campaign in southern Iraq (room 9, ME 124953–ME 124960; ME 124774). Among the scenes depicted are tribesmen (likely either Chaldeans or Arameans) hiding in the marshlands, escaping in reed boats, and brought as prisoners with their families and possessions to the Assyrian headquarters.

The Museum of the Ancient Orient in Istanbul and the Ashmolean Museum in Oxford, England, each have on display a relief panel from Sennacherib's palace at Nineveh. The panel in Istanbul (inventory number 2; Mesopotamia Hall) shows archers and spear bearers along the top and prisoners working on construction of the palace along the bottom of the panel. In the center between the two scenes is an inscription. The relief in the Ashmolean (AN 1971.994) depicts Assyrian soldiers carrying away captives and loot from a city that can be seen in the background. The entourage is walking beside a river filled with fish.

An interesting stela set up in Nineveh by Sennacherib is in the Museum of the Ancient Orient in Istanbul (inventory number 1; Mesopotamia Hall). In the inscription on the stela, Sennacherib boasts of his enlarging the city of Nineveh and building the royal road through the city. The inscription warns that anyone who builds a new house whose foundation encroaches on the royal road shall be hung on a stake over that house.

Biblical Significance

The name of Nineveh occurs repeatedly in the Bible. It is first mentioned in Genesis 10:11, which attributes its founding to Nimrod. The name reappears in the story of Jonah, where it is described as "an exceedingly large city, a three days' walk across" (Jon. 3:3; exaggeration for effect, since the circumference of the city walls of Nineveh at their greatest was approximately eight miles around. Nevertheless, if Layard's concept is correct that the city was composed of the various mounds of the capital, widely spaced and established over different periods of time, then it composed a parallelogram at least eighteen miles long and twelve miles wide, or some fifty miles in circumference). The city is mentioned also in 2 Kings, but it is especially prominent in the prophets. Nahum directs his prophecy against it, and Zephaniah speaks of its destruction (Zeph. 2:13-15). In the Gospels of Matthew and Luke, Nineveh is used as an example of pride (Matt. 12:41; Luke 11:32).

The image of musicians from the region of Palestine is reminiscent of the later words of the deportees into Babylon (586-587 B.C.E.). There they were encouraged by their captors to play songs from their native land. Their poignant reply speaks of the sorrow of any people who are forced to leave their homeland and live in a foreign country (Ps. 137:1-6):

> By the rivers of Babylon —
> > there we sat down and there we wept
> > when we remembered Zion.
> On the willows there
> > we hung up our harps.
> For there our captors
> > asked us for songs,
> and our tormentors asked for mirth, saying,
> > "Sing us one of the songs of Zion!"
>
> How could we sing the LORD's song
> > in a foreign land?
> If I forget you, O Jerusalem,
> > let my right hand wither!
> Let my tongue cling to the roof of my mouth,
> > if I do not remember you,
> if I do not set Jerusalem above my highest joy.

Siege of Lachish

Alabaster panels with reliefs

▷ Size: Originally, the panels were ca. 2.69 m. (8.83 ft.) high; total width of all panels, ca. 18.9 m. (62 ft.)

▷ Provenance: Southwest Palace of Nineveh, Assyria

▷ Date: ca. 700-691 B.C.E.

▷ Present location: British Museum (room 10b)

▷ Identification number: ME 124904–ME 124915

The best-preserved series of reliefs from the Southwest Palace of Sennacherib, and the most dramatic, depicts the siege of the Judean city of Lachish. This spectacular group of scenes is an almost moving-picture view of the entire siege, from the preparation of the army to the destruction of the city and the deportation of its citizens to Assyria. The correlation of these scenes with the biblical account provides corroboration of the military skill, savagery, and relentless force of the Assyrian army in the time of Sennacherib. One room in the British Museum is wholly devoted to these panels. Visitors never fail to be impressed, and it is impossible to see them without coming away with the impression of having gained a firsthand view of the siege.

Located approximately twenty-five miles southwest of Jerusalem, Lachish (modern Tell al-Hasi) became an important city for Judah during the late tenth or early ninth century B.C.E. when a fortress was established on the site upon a platform approximately 30.5 meters (100 ft.) square (known as Podium A). Subsequently the city was encircled by two walls; the upper wall was made of mud brick resting on a stone foundation, and in places it was 6 meters (20 ft.) thick. A very large double gate system was constructed, the largest four-entry gate thus far found in Israel. Once the wall had been constructed, the fortress was expanded to include a palace, and the subsequent podium (Podium B) reached the size of 76 meters by 30.5 meters (250 ft. by 100 ft.). The prominence of Lachish, however, would condemn it to one of the most savage assaults in the history of Israel.

When Sennacherib came to the throne (704 B.C.E.) following the death of his father, Sargon II, many of the vassal states attempted to use the unsettled times as an excuse to avoid the tribute owed to Assyria or to break away altogether. Sennacherib's third military campaign was directed against the rebellious states in the west, principally Phoenicia and Israel. He therefore marched his army westward to the Mediterranean and proceeded down the coastal plain, subduing Sidon, Tyre, and other Phoenician cities. Next, Sennacherib continued into Philistia and defeated the cities of Ashkelon and Ekron, among others. Along the way, he brushed aside an attack from an Egyptian force and turned inland against Judah, attacking and sacking cities as he went. (Altogether, Sennacherib claims to have taken forty-six cities from the Judeans.) Finally he marched against the strongly fortified city of Lachish, the principal barrier to his main objective — the capital city of Jerusalem.

The result of this siege is vividly depicted on the panels in the British Museum (room 10b). These reliefs were carved in place in room 36 of Sennacherib's palace in Nineveh. They were given a prominent location in a room at the end of a long corridor that had a series of three monumental portals, each flanked by a pair of gigantic, human-headed bulls varying in height from 5.5 meters (18 ft.), at the beginning of the corridor, to 3.7 meters (12 ft.) at the room entrance. The resulting effect gave great perspective to the room, all four walls of which were covered with the Lachish reliefs. One wall of this room was the main focal point visible from the corridor. The prominence given to these panels, and the exclusive use of great bulls to create a focal perspective on the room, emphasize the importance Sennacherib attached to his success at Lachish.[1] (Since clearly Hezekiah and his capital were the object of Sennacherib's Judean invasion, we might wonder if this room would not have been covered with reliefs of the destruction of Jerusalem had he taken it.)

The panels in the museum begin on the viewer's left with the Assyrian army marching to Lachish through the landscape of Judah (ME 124904–ME 124905). Subsequent panels dramatically depict the assault on the walls of Lachish (ME 124905–124907). Burning firebrands and sling stones are hurled from walls and defenders shoot arrows at the attackers, who return the fire and climb scaling ladders. A battering ram ascends the siege ramp to assault the walls, while an Assyrian soldier uses a large ladle to pour water on a burning portion of the siege engine. Bodies fall from the walls, and captives are impaled on stakes (see fig. 51). Next, captives are depicted — men, women, and children — as they exit the city, carrying their meager possessions over their shoulders; camels and wagons are also shown (ME 124907). The panels continue their story with the ongoing march of the deported peoples through a changing landscape (ME 124908). The procession of tribute shows soldiers carrying a scepter, and two men carry large, ceremonial chalices (ME 124907–ME 124908). Leaders of the rebellion are gruesomely portrayed being skinned alive and some soldiers are impaled on stakes outside the city, true to the Assyrian war policy toward resisting cities (ME 124909; see plate 5). One soldier holds a prisoner by his hair and appears to be stabbing him in the shoulder, or perhaps preparing to decapitate him (ME 124910).

---

1. John Malcolm Russell, *Sennacherib's Palace without Rival at Nineveh* (Chicago: University of Chicago Press, 1991), p. 252.

51. Detail of a relief panel depicting Sennacherib's assault on the city of Lachish (ME 124906)

As the line of prisoners and captors winds uphill and approaches the king, some Lachishites prostrate themselves, begging for mercy. Sennacherib sits on a high throne with a footstool beneath his feet, his position made more prominent by a pair of epigraphs that horizontally bracket his head (ME 124911–ME 124912). Eunuchs (identified by their beardless faces) wave ostrich feathers to cool him. Adjacent to the king, his bodyguards and chariot await (ME 124912–ME 124913). The Assyrian camp also is portrayed in a circle lined with towers; a road runs through its midst, a priest offers prayers and sacrifice, and a soldier enjoys food and refreshments in his tent (ME 124914–ME 124915). The high point of the scene — at least from Sennacherib's perspective — comes with this statement written above and to the left of the king's head: "Sennacherib, the king of the world, the king of Assyria, sat on his *nimedu*-throne [portable throne], and the spoil of the city of Lachish passed before him."

In addition to containing the wall reliefs, room 10b of the British Museum displays (in a case) several objects recovered from the site of Lachish, including a collection of stones from Lachish used as projectiles launched with a sling (ME 132127–ME 132140). Also in the case is one of several prisms inscribed with a record of some of Sennacherib's military campaigns (ME 103000), including his campaign against Judah during which Lachish was destroyed and Jerusalem was put under siege. Surprisingly, Lachish is not mentioned in the record of the campaigns (see the article, "The Taylor Prism"). Even more items discovered by archaeologists from the siege and destruction of Lachish — including a bronze helmet crest, flint sling stones, bronze armor scales, iron arrowheads, and an iron chain — are on display in a case in the Bronfman Archaeology Wing of the Israel Museum in Jerusalem.

Biblical Significance

The site of Lachish was first occupied by the Canaanites as early as the fourth millennium B.C.E. Later it became the seat of the Egyptian governor of southern Canaan, as documented in the Amarna letters from Egypt. The Bible attributes the capture of Lachish by the Israelites to Joshua (Josh. 10:1-32). The name of Lachish emerges again in the Bible when King Amaziah of Judah (797-769 B.C.E.) fled to Lachish following a rebellion in Jerusalem, but he was found there by his enemies and killed (2 Kings 14:19). During this time Lachish became the second most important city in Judah. An earthquake around 760 B.C.E. destroyed much of the city, but the principal buildings subsequently were rebuilt and enlarged. The city truly gained lasting fame — although not of the sort it would have preferred — when it was besieged and subsequently destroyed by the Assyrians under Sennacherib in 701 B.C.E.

Archaeological excavations in recent years at Lachish have clearly discovered evidence of a great siege having taken place there. The Assyrian siege ramp was discovered on the northwest corner of the mound (portions of it were removed in 1933, but a part of it still remains). Hundreds of arrow points and sling stones were found about the mound. Evidence of a great conflagration on the site of the fortress and palace indicated a massive assault. An extremely large number of storage jars with the Hebrew *lmlk* stamp ("[belonging] to the king") on their handles also were found in the strata just beneath the destruction layer attributed to Sennacherib, possible evidence that Hezekiah had attempted to prepare the city for a lengthy siege. Finally, a pit containing more than fifteen hundred bodies, strewn about in careless fashion, was also uncovered. Based on archaeology alone, there can be no doubt of an Assyrian attack on Lachish.

Nevertheless, the discovery of the Lachish panels provided information regarding the siege of Lachish that was strangely absent from Sennacherib's written annals, especially given the obvious importance of this battle to the king. Since he did not take Jerusalem, certainly his ultimate objective, perhaps the king decided to make an abbreviated statement on the matter and simply contented himself with these dramatically rendered scenes of his spectacular victory over the heavily fortified city of Lachish. It is also true that the low state of literacy at this time in Assyria meant that likely only the palace scribes, who made the lengthy, complex statements typical of the historical annals, were able to read them. Other visitors to the palace would be duly impressed by these remarkable reliefs, which were clearly understandable to all.[2]

Furthermore, in spite of his failure to take Jerusalem (see the article "The Taylor Prism"), it was only following this western campaign that Sennacherib adopted for himself the title "king of the world," and that titulary inscription first appears on these Lachish reliefs. Previously he had confined himself to the more modest appellation "unrivaled king," but he added the new title after this third campaign. (After his fifth campaign, he would replace "unrivaled

---

2. Russell, *Sennacherib's Palace*, p. 204.

king" with "king of the four quarters [of the earth]."")[3] Nevertheless, regardless of Sennacherib's growing self-esteem after the taking of Lachish, the very presence of these panels in his palace rather than scenes from a siege of Jerusalem demonstrates unmistakably that "the king of the world" never captured the capital of Judah.

Stela of Esarhaddon

Dolerite stela

▷ Size: 3.22 m. (10.56 ft.) high; 1.35 m. (4.43 ft.) wide
▷ Writing: Akkadian language in cuneiform script
▷ Provenance: Sam'al (Zinjirli, in the southeastern part of modern Turkey)
▷ Date: Seventh century B.C.E.
▷ Present location: Museum of the Ancient Near East, Pergamum Museum, Berlin (room 3)
▷ Identification number: VA 2708

Esarhaddon, whose name means "the god Ashur has given a brother," was king of Assyria from 680 to 669 B.C.E. Although the ancient sources are not entirely consistent, a possible scenario is that he succeeded his father, Sennacherib, as king after his brothers assassinated Sennacherib. Even though the brothers were older than Esarhaddon, none of them was the heir apparent because Sennacherib had already designated Esarhaddon as his successor. Jealous and resentful, the brothers eventually conspired to murder their father. After they succeeded in their attempt, they escaped to Urartu (in modern Turkey), and Esarhaddon ascended the throne. (If the suggested identity of two political refugees in the land of Shubria mentioned in

52. Stela showing King Esarhaddon of Assyria with two captives

3. Russell, *Sennacherib's Palace*, p. 242.

177

one of Esarhaddon's writings is correct, then later in his reign he succeeded in capturing the two murderous brothers and dealt fiercely with them, cutting off their hands, noses, and ears, and gouging out their eyes.) Esarhaddon proved to be a powerful and effective ruler. Early in his reign when the king of Sidon in Tyre revolted from Assyrian control, Esarhaddon marched his army against the city and destroyed it. When Esarhaddon captured the king of Sidon, he had the rebel king and another captured king who had been an ally of Sidon decapitated and their heads hung from the necks of their nobles, who were then paraded through the main street of Nineveh to the accompaniment of singers with harps. Esarhaddon had to flex his military muscles against several other peoples as well, including the people of Tyre, the Elamites, the Cimmerians, the Scythians, the Babylonians, and the Egyptians.

The Babylonians created a special problem for Esarhaddon. His father, Sennacherib, had dealt with the unrest caused by the troublesome Babylonians and their allies, the Elamites, on several occasions. At one point Sennacherib placed his eldest son on the Babylonian throne in order to control the area. Within six years, however, his son had been kidnapped by rebellious Babylonians and handed over to the Elamites, who killed him. Furious over these events, Sennacherib attacked the Babylonians and utterly destroyed the city, including its temples and statues of the gods. He carried the statue of Marduk, the main god of Babylon, back to Assyria. The action of Sennacherib was seen as a sacrilege, not only by the Babylonians, but by the Assyrians as well, because Babylon was thought to be a city under the special protection of the gods. To destroy it was unthinkable. When Esarhaddon came to power, he reversed the vengeful treatment of Babylon carried out by his father and rebuilt the city. Three years before his death, Esarhaddon named one of his sons, Ashurbanipal, as the heir to the Assyrian throne and another son, Shamash-shum-ukin, as the heir to the Babylonian throne.

One of the most significant accomplishments of Esarhaddon's reign was his conquest of Egypt, a task that was not easy. Due to anti-Assyrian agitation in Syria-Palestine by the Egyptians, Esarhaddon decided to launch an attack against Egypt. During his first Egyptian campaign, he marched to the borders of Egypt and captured the frontier town of Arza. A setback in his plans occurred during his next campaign five years later when the Assyrian army was defeated by Egypt. In 671, however, Esarhaddon once more marched against Egypt, this time capturing the city of Memphis and defeating Tirhakah (or, Taharqa), the pharaoh. Tirhakah escaped, but his family was captured. Two years later, Esarhaddon mounted a new campaign against Egypt, but this attempt ended when Esarhaddon died on the way.

Esarhaddon erected this stela (fig. 52), now in the Museum of the Ancient Near East in Berlin, in the inner gate room of the citadel of Sam'al (modern

Zinjirli, located in the southeastern part of Turkey). The stela was discovered during excavations of the city in 1888 and is sometimes referred to as the Zinjirli (or, Senjirli) Stela. The large figure is Esarhaddon, with his right hand raised and his left hand holding a mace and two ropes that secure two prisoners. Each of the ropes seems to end in a ring that goes through the lips of one of the prisoners. The first captive, kneeling, is thought to be the Egyptian pharaoh Tirhakah or his son, the Egyptian crown prince who had been captured by Esarhaddon. (He appears to be wearing the uraeus, a stylized cobra that was the symbol of Egyptian kingship.) The second prisoner has Semitic features and is perhaps a Syrian king or maybe Baal I, king of Tyre, who violated his treaty with Esarhaddon and was attacked by the Assyrian king during his campaign against Egypt in 671 B.C.E. At the top right of the stela are symbols of Assyrian gods and figures of four gods riding on their respective animals. The lower half of the front of the stela, as well as the entire back side, is covered in cuneiform writing that details the conquests of Esarhaddon, including his wounding of Tirhakah and the capture of his family. The two figures carved on the sides of the stela are possibly the sons of Esarhaddon, with the crown prince Shamash-shum-ukin on the left and the crown prince Ashurbanipal on the right.

A variety of other objects related to Esarhaddon are on display in several museums, including:

1. A plaster cast of a rock relief depicting Esarhaddon (VAG 31; room 3, Museum of the Ancient Near East, Pergamum Museum, Berlin). The king had this relief carved into the rock at the mouth of the al-Kelb River (Dog River) in the Mediterranean Sea, north of Beirut. This carving is sometimes called the Dog River Stela.

2. A bronze relief, formerly covered with gold, commemorating the rebuilding of Babylon by Esarhaddon (AO 20185; Louvre, room 6, ground floor, Richelieu Wing, section 3). Esarhaddon is shown with his mother, Naqiya, who was an influential and powerful figure during Esarhaddon's reign. She was of Aramean background and behaved like a king in many ways. The inscription on the relief describes the return to Babylon of the statue of the god Ea to the temple of Marduk.

3. A limestone slab probably from Nineveh or the nearby town of Tarbisu that contains the name, titles, and ancestry of Esarhaddon (ME 22465; British Museum; formerly in room 89, check with museum personnel for current location). One of the titles that Esarhaddon claims for himself in the inscription is "king of the kings of Egypt," which indicates that this inscription should be dated sometime after Esarhaddon's defeat of Pharaoh Tirhakah and his conquest of Egypt in 671 B.C.E.

4. A tablet with an inscription that was intended for a royal statue (ME K2801;

British Museum; formerly in room 89, check with museum personnel for current location). In the inscription, Esarhaddon describes how the various gods bestowed favor on him, destined him to become king, and granted him wisdom and vision. The remainder of the inscription contains the king's descriptions of his rebuilding of Babylon and his return of the images of the gods to their restored temples.

5. A black basalt stone (ME 91027; British Museum, room 55). Presented to the museum by the Earl of Aberdeen in 1861, this inscribed stone describes Esarhaddon's restoration of Babylon, including his rebuilding the walls and temples of the city.

6. Three letters to Esarhaddon, one from the crown prince Shamash-shum-ukin to his father, Esarhaddon, reporting on treasonous activities by certain astrologers who have failed to follow orders from the king and are acting on their own (ME 135586); one from an individual requesting that Esarhaddon have the city of Nippur, with its temples to the gods, rebuilt (ME K8681); and one from the king's chief scribe, an authority on astrology, warning the king about a conspiracy (ME K112). These are all located in room 55 of the British Museum.

7. A clay prism telling of Esarhaddon's restoration of the city of Babylon, for which task he claims he was chosen by Marduk (ME 78223; room 55 of the British Museum).

Biblical Significance

During the entire reign of Esarhaddon as king of Assyria, Manasseh ruled as king of Judah (the northern kingdom of Israel had been destroyed by the Assyrians in 722 B.C.E.). Judah at this time was a small vassal state under Assyrian domination. Even though Esarhaddon was the dominant power in the ancient Near East, he received scant mention in the biblical texts. The author of 2 Kings mentioned him only in passing, taking note that upon the death of Sennacherib "his son Esar-haddon succeeded him" (2 Kings 19:37; this part of the 2 Kings text is copied in Isa. 37:38. See also Tobit 1:21; 2:1). The only other mention of Esarhaddon in the Bible occurs in Ezra 4:2 in a passage describing the attempt to rebuild the Jerusalem temple after the exile. A group of non-natives who had been resettled in Israel by the Assyrians offered to help rebuild the temple, saying, "Let us build with you, for we worship your God as you do, and we have been sacrificing to him ever since the days of King Esarhaddon of Assyria who brought us here." The returning exiles refused to allow the "foreigners" to help.

Even though Esarhaddon is barely mentioned in the biblical texts, as one of the most powerful of the Assyrian rulers he certainly impacted Manasseh and the land of Judah. The royal inscriptions of Esarhaddon record that on two separate occasions he ordered the kings of Syria-Palestine and Cyprus to provide building materials for his projects, the first time to build a new port in the vicinity of Sidon, which he named Kar-Esarhaddon ("Port of Esarhaddon"), and the second time to build his palace in Nineveh. In the first instance the inscriptions do not list any specific kings, but Manasseh was almost certainly included. In the second case, "Manasseh, king of Judah" is one of the rulers specifically mentioned who had to contribute to the building effort.[1] Although evidence about the reign of Manasseh is sketchy, the Judean king was apparently a loyal subject to the Assyrians. As powerful as the Assyrians were, Manasseh likely had little choice but to play the role of a faithful vassal king. On several occasions Esarhaddon led military campaigns through Syria-Palestine and Egypt, but there is no evidence that he had any trouble with Judah. The completely negative assessment of Manasseh's reign, and particularly his support and tolerance of non-Yahwistic worship, by the author of 2 Kings perhaps reflects Manasseh's loyalty to the Assyrians and the proliferation of Assyrian religion within Judah. (The Egyptian pharaoh, Tirhakah, who is perhaps depicted on the stela, is mentioned in 2 Kings 19:9 [repeated in Isa. 37:9], where he is called the king of Ethiopia.)

The depiction on this stela of two individuals with what appear to be hooks through their lips is reminiscent of the warning of the prophet Amos to the wealthy people of Israel during the eighth century B.C.E. Because of their oppression of the needy and lack of concern for social and legal justice, Amos declared,

> The Lord GOD has sworn by his holiness:
>   The time is surely coming upon you,
> when they shall take you away with hooks,
>   even the last of you with fishhooks. (4:2)

A similar imagery occurs in Ezekiel 38:4 in an oracle directed against the enigmatic figure "Gog, of the land of Magog": "I will turn you around and put hooks into your jaws, and I will lead you out with all your army, horses and horsemen, all of them clothed in full armor, a great company, all of them with shield and buckler, wielding swords."

---

1. For these inscriptions, see *ANET*, pp. 290-91.

Stela of Ashurbanipal

Red sandstone stela

> ▷ Size: 37 cm. (14.57 in.) high; 22 cm. (8.66 in.) wide; 10 cm. (3.94 in.) deep
> ▷ Writing: Akkadian language in cuneiform script
> ▷ Provenance: Babylon (in modern Iraq)
> ▷ Date: ca. 669-655 B.C.E.
> ▷ Present location: British Museum (room 55)
> ▷ Identification number: ME 90864

The figure on this stela is Ashurbanipal, king of the Neo-Assyrian Empire from 669 to 627 B.C.E. Before Esarhaddon, the previous Assyrian king, died, he had appointed two of his sons, Ashurbanipal and Shamash-shum-ukin, re-spectively, as heirs to the thrones of Assyria and Babylonia. (Babylonia was then under Assyrian control.) Ashurbanipal was the last of the powerful Assyrian kings, for soon after his death, Assyria was conquered by Babylonia. Like his predecessors, Ashurbanipal led his armies on several military campaigns in order to expand and secure the boundaries of his empire. Among the problem states he had to handle during his reign were Egypt, Tyre, Elam, and even Babylonia, led by his brother. The latter two nations, who joined in an anti-Assyrian alliance, were especially troublesome. Yet, neither Elam nor Babylonia was successful in its attempt at rebellion, and Ashurbanipal dealt harshly with them, especially with Elam.

53. Stela depicting King Ashurbanipal carrying a ceremonial basket of earth

In addition to being a skillful military figure, Ashurbanipal was also a lover of literature and education. He amassed a large library of Mesopotamian writings containing thousands of cuneiform tablets, much of which has been recovered by excavators at his palace in Nineveh. This cuneiform library held literary compositions, religious texts, historical and economic inscriptions, scientific treatises, lexical works, legal texts, letters, and contracts. Ashurbanipal himself was literate, which was certainly the exception in his day, even for kings.

(For examples of items found in the library of Ashurbanipal at Nineveh, see the articles on "*Enuma Elish,* the Epic of Creation," "The Epic of Gilgamesh," and "*Ludlul Bēl Nēmeqi,* the 'Babylonian Job.'" Also see the references below to the copy of the law code of Hammurabi, the incantation tablet, and the copy of a Sumerian-Akkadian syllabary now in the Louvre.)

Found in Babylon, this stela depicts Ashurbanipal carrying a load of dirt in a basket above his head. As a Mesopotamian king, he was responsible for the building and maintaining of the temples of the gods. This scene shows him fulfilling that responsibility by carrying a basket of earth for the ceremonial making of the first brick for the temple. In the cuneiform inscription on the stela, Ashurbanipal boasts of completing the construction of Esagila, the temple of Marduk in Babylon, which his father Esarhaddon had begun. He specifically points out that he built Ekarzaginna, the shrine to Ea, the god of fresh water and wisdom, which was located within the temple of Marduk.

Other objects related to Ashurbanipal that are on display in various museums include the following:

1. A stela of Ashurbanipal in the British Museum (ME 90865; located in room 55). Like ME 90864, this small stela shows Ashurbanipal with the ritual basket of earth for the construction of a temple. The wording of the inscription is very similar to that of ME 90864, except that it describes the restoration of a temple in Borsippa named Ezida, the temple of Nabu, the god of writing.

2. An autobiography of Ashurbanipal (ME K2694; located in room 55 of the British Museum). In this interesting clay tablet, Ashurbanipal recounts his early years of schooling and training and his selection and accession to the Assyrian throne. He also tells of the installation of his brother Shamash-shum-ukin as king of Babylonia.

3. Prism F of Ashurbanipal (AO 19939; located in room 6, ground floor, Richelieu Wing, section 3, of the Louvre). This six-sided prism, one of several similar prisms from Ashurbanipal that have been discovered, contains the king's annals, describing his various military expeditions, including his campaigns against Egypt, Tyre, and Elam. The Elamite campaigns, the last of which ended with the sack of Susa, take up a major portion of the text. The text also mentions the incident when Gyges of Lydia sent messengers to Ashurbanipal asking for his help against the invading Cimmerians. (See the article "Tablet Mentioning Gyges of Lydia.")

4. A clay tablet from Ashurbanipal commemorating his rebuilding of the temple of Sin at Haran (ME K2675; room 55). This building text contains selections from the king's annals, including the story of Gyges requesting his assistance. (See the article "Tablet Mentioning Gyges of Lydia.")

5. A fragment of a copy of the Law Code of Hammurabi from Ashurbanipal's

library at Nineveh (AO 7757; located in room 3, ground floor, Richelieu Wing, section 3, of the Louvre).

6. A clay tablet containing incantations, prayers, and ceremonial rites from Ashurbanipal's library at Nineveh (K7593, K2784; located in room 6, ground floor, Richelieu Wing, section 3, of the Louvre).

7. A clay tablet with the text of the legend of Etana from the library of Ashurbanipal (ME K19530; room 55 of the British Museum).

8. A cuneiform tablet from the library of Ashurbanipal containing the legend of the descent of the goddess Ishtar to the underworld (ME K162; room 55 of the British Museum).

9. A clay tablet from the library of Ashurbanipal concerned with omens (ME K2007; room 55 of the British Museum). This cuneiform tablet is one of many that were found that describe the significance of the occurrence of unusual events. This particular tablet interprets the birth of malformed humans and animals as omens.

10. A Sumerian-Akkadian syllabary from Ashurbanipal's library at Nineveh (AO 7092; located in room 6, ground floor, Richelieu Wing, section 3, of the Louvre). This baked clay tablet is an example of a reference tool used by ancient scribes. Such bilingual syllabaries list the cuneiform symbols for Sumerian syllables along with the corresponding Akkadian symbol for that syllable. These texts allowed the scribes to learn the Sumerian language and to translate Sumerian writings into the Akkadian language.

11. A small, barrel-shaped cylinder pertaining to one of the two city walls at Babylon (VA 601; located in room 6, Museum of the Ancient Near East, Pergamum Museum, Berlin). The inner wall of the city's double walls, which was named Nemitti-Ellil (or, Nemet-Enlil), is the one mentioned on this cylinder.

12. Carved relief panels from Ashurbanipal's palace at Nineveh. See the following article, "Wall Reliefs from Ashurbanipal's Palaces at Nineveh."

Biblical Significance

The only mention of Ashurbanipal in the Bible occurs in Ezra 4:10, and even that reference is uncertain. The passage in Ezra reports that a letter was sent to Artaxerxes, king of Persia (i.e., Artaxerxes I, 465-424 B.C.E.), from various peoples who had been deported by "Osnappar" from their homelands and resettled "in the cities of Samaria and in the rest of the province Beyond the River." No king named Osnappar ruled over Assyria. Many scholars have reasonably concluded that "Osnappar" is a corruption of the name Ashurbanipal. (The spellings of the two names are somewhat similar in Aramaic. This portion of Ezra was written in Aramaic instead of Hebrew.) Although neither the Assyrian records nor the biblical accounts provide any evidence of resettlement by Ashurbanipal of conquered peoples into the western province that included Syria and Palestine, such actions by Ashurbanipal are certainly plausible. Furthermore, among the peoples mentioned in Ezra 4:9 as captives who had been resettled in the west are "the people of Susa, that is, the Elamites." Assyrian writings record that Ashurbanipal conducted several successful military campaigns against the Elamites, many of whom likely were forcibly deported to other lands.

Another possible reference to Ashurbanipal occurs in 2 Chronicles 33:11-16, although the name of the Assyrian king is never mentioned. The author of 2 Chronicles claims that when Manasseh was king of Judah (697-642 B.C.E.) "the commanders of the army of the king of Assyria" took Manasseh captive and carried him in chains to Babylon, which the author interprets as God's punishment on Manasseh for his wickedness. Manasseh soon repents and is restored to his throne. The Assyrian king in this story would have been either Esarhaddon or Ashurbanipal, since they were the Assyrian rulers during the time that Manasseh was king of Judah. Many scholars have questioned the authenticity of this account in 2 Chronicles, however, for several reasons. The account of Manasseh's reign in 2 Kings 21:1-18, which the author of Chronicles used as a source, does not tell of any Assyrian capture of Manasseh, nor of his repentance. Furthermore, the Assyrian records do not tell of any revolt by Manasseh or provide any reason to suspect that he would have been taken captive by the Assyrians. In fact, in the Assyrian records of both Esarhaddon and Ashurbanipal, Manasseh appears as a faithful subject of the Assyrians.

Even though Ashurbanipal receives scant mention in the biblical texts, he still affected the history of Palestine. Like most of the other nations and city-states in Syria-Palestine, Judah was a vassal state that was subject to Assyrian control throughout the reign of Ashurbanipal. He led several campaigns against Egypt, marching his army through Palestine. According to Ashurbanipal's records, during one of these campaigns Manasseh, the king of Judah, was forced to pay tribute to Ashurbanipal and provide some military forces to assist the Assyrians.

Wall Reliefs from Ashurbanipal's Palaces at Nineveh

Alabaster wall reliefs

▷ Size: Panels generally ca. 1.5–2 m. (ca. 5–6.5 ft.) high
▷ Provenance: Nineveh (Kuyunjik, in modern Iraq)
▷ Date: ca. 645 B.C.E.

▷ Present location: British Museum (room 10a and formerly room 89, check with museum personnel for current location); the Louvre (room 6, ground floor, Richelieu Wing, section 3); and the Museum of the Ancient Near East, Pergamum Museum, Berlin (room 12)

▷ Identification numbers: See text below

Like many Mesopotamian kings, Ashurbanipal decorated the walls of his palace with carved stone panels depicting military expeditions, royal court scenes, and hunting episodes. In addition to being impressive examples of Assyrian artistry and skill, these pictorial reliefs at Nineveh provide valuable insights into ancient Mesopotamian history, culture, and lifestyles. Viewers will be richly rewarded by a careful scrutiny of these compositions. The best collection of these wall reliefs that can be viewed is in the British Museum. When Ashurbanipal first became king, he used the palace at Nineveh that had been built by Sennacherib, the Southwest Palace. He decorated the palace with new wall reliefs, sometimes having new scenes carved over existing scenes. Later, he built for himself a new palace, the North Palace.

An interesting relief in the British Museum (formerly in room 89, check with museum personnel for current location) consisting of three panels (ME 124801) and found in the Southwest Palace, portrays the capture and beheading of Teumman, the Elamite king. Inscriptions on the reliefs describe some of the events that are portrayed. The scenes on the relief are not simultaneous but sequential. At the top of the middle panel, Teumman and his son lie upside down under their overturned chariot. In the next scene to the right, Teumman's son is helping his father, who has been wounded by an arrow, get to his feet. Farther along on the right, the son pauses to shoot an arrow at their pursuers, who soon overtake them and kill them. An Assyrian hits Teumman over the head and then decapitates him. At the top of the left panel, an Assyr-

54. Relief of King Ashurbanipal and his queen in his garden, sometimes called the "Garden Party" (ME 124920)

55. Ashurbanipal in his chariot on a lion hunt (ME 124866-ME 124868)

ian soldier races away in a chariot, holding aloft in his hand the severed head of Teumman.

One of the wall reliefs in the British Museum (ME 124920; see fig. 54; formerly in room 89, check with museum personnel for current location), also from the Southwest Palace, shows Ashurbanipal reclining on a couch in his garden, drinking from a dish. Sitting in a chair opposite him is his queen, who is also drinking from a dish in her hand. Behind the royal couple are servants attending to their needs, some bearing trays of food, others waving fans to cool the king and queen. The garden setting is indicated by the presence of trees and other plants in the scene. Hanging in a tree behind the queen, at the left side of the panel, is a macabre detail — the severed head of Teumman, the Elamite king. The faces of the king and queen have been damaged, likely by an enemy soldier after the capture of Nineveh by the Babylonians in 612 B.C.E.

Panel ME 124802 (formerly in room 89, check with museum personnel for current location), also from the Southwest Palace, shows Assyrian soldiers executing Chaldean rebels. Note the violent methods of execution — some of the Chaldeans are being beheaded, while others are tied to stakes in the ground and are being flayed alive. The ancient Assyrians had a notorious reputation for cruel and barbaric treatment of their enemies, a reputation supported by ancient inscriptions and grisly scenes carved on wall panels, stelae, and monuments. Captives were sometimes impaled on stakes, beheaded, dismembered, or staked to the ground and flayed alive. Although this reputation for brutal treatment was likely deserved, the Assyrians were probably no more atrocious in their treatment of captives than were most peoples of the ancient world. The boastful claims of the Assyrian kings in their annals and other inscriptions about the torture and annihilation of their enemies, along with the pictorial representations of these acts, functioned not only as self-congratulatory bravado but also as official propaganda. They were intended, at least in part, to produce fear and awe. The message was plain — this treatment is what happens to anyone who revolts against or resists the Assyrians.

Other reliefs (formerly in room 89, check with museum personnel for current location), show scenes from various military expeditions by Ashurbanipal. Among the scenes depicted are the capture of a fortress in Egypt (ME 124928), captured goods being hauled away from a sacked Elamite city (possibly Susa) and Ashurbanipal reviewing booty from the capture of Babylon (ME 124945–ME 124946), and the king reviewing prisoners from the Elamite city of Hamanu (ME 124930). All of these reliefs came from the North Palace at Nineveh. Also from the North Palace are several reliefs in the Louvre (room 6, ground floor, Richelieu Wing, section 3), among which are ones that show Ashurbanipal in his chariot (AO 19904), Ashurbanipal defeating a lion (AO 19903), deportations of Chaldeans (AO 19910, AO 19911) and Elamites (AO 19913), and soldiers and musicians (AO 19908, AO 19909).

Room 10a in the British Museum contains an impressive series of reliefs (all from various rooms of the North Palace) depicting a variety of hunting scenes, including deer being driven into a net to be killed (ME 124871), massive hunting dogs heading out for a hunt (ME 118915), and gazelle being hunted by the king (ME 124872–ME 124875). The most dramatic hunting scenes are the numerous panels in room 10a that depict several royal lion hunts (ME 124781, ME 124850–ME 124870, ME 124874–ME 124878, ME 124883–ME 124887, ME 124921). Lion hunts were popular pastimes of Assyrian kings, and their portrayal in ancient art was a way of emphasizing the king's bravery and skill. The lion hunts were often done, however, with lions that had been previously captured or raised in captivity. The lions were released from cages into restricted areas where the king, with the help of several individuals armed with spears, swords, and bows, would successfully kill or gravely injure the lions. One series of lion hunt scenes is depicted in panels ME 124886–ME 124887. The action of the scenes in the reliefs flows from right to left. In the top row, a lion is released from a cage, and then springs toward the king who shoots it with an arrow. The animal is wounded but not killed by the arrow. In the middle row a horseman distracts a lion as the king comes from behind and grabs the lion by the tail and kills it with the mace in his upraised right arm. (The king's arm cannot be seen because of damage. The inscription over the lion's head, however, reads, "I seized a lion of the plain(?) by its tail, and at the command of Ninurta and Nergal, the gods in whom I trust, I smashed its skull with my own mace."[1] Notice that the lion's tail has been chiseled off, thus setting the lion free. It has been suggested that this defacement was an attempt at humor by an enemy soldier when the palace was ransacked in 612 B.C.E.) In the middle of the bottom row of the relief, the king pours a libation of wine over the bodies of four dead lions.

Panels ME 124866–ME 124868 show the king in his chariot shooting arrows at lions in front of him (see fig. 55). Behind the king, two men thrust spears into an attacking lion that has already been wounded by arrows. Underneath the horse and behind the chariot lie several dead and wounded lions. The top row of panels ME 124874–ME 124877 feature the king on foot, engaged in a lion hunt. The scenes show the lion being released from its cage (ME 124877) and the king shooting an arrow at the lion (ME 124876). In ME 124875 (see plate 6), a wounded lion stands on its hind legs facing the king. The king is grabbing the lion's mane with one hand, while stabbing him with the sword in his other hand. A particularly powerful scene from a royal lion hunt is a small panel on display in room 55 showing a dying lion (ME 1992-4-4, 1). Like the other lion hunt reliefs, this one came from the Nineveh North Palace. The lion, with a fatal wound from an arrow, sits hunched over, with blood gushing from its mouth. The sculptor has skillfully captured not only the strength of the lion but also its defeat. The realism and detail of the work render it a masterpiece of Assyrian art.

Another scene of a royal lion hunt from one of Ashurbanipal's Nineveh palaces is on display in room 12 of the Museum of the Ancient Near East, Pergamum Museum, in Berlin. The scene (on panels VA 960 and VA 963) shows Ashurbanipal (or perhaps the crown prince) thrusting a spear into an attacking lion while two attendants stand by holding weapons and his horse. To the right of this scene is another scene depicting the king standing in a ceremonial pose, accompanied by two attendants.

Biblical Significance

In addition to the significance of Ashurbanipal for biblical studies as described in the previous article, these wall reliefs also have another connection to the Bible. Some of these reliefs portray the Assyrian conquest of Elam, a country in southern Mesopotamia east of the Tigris River, whose capital was located at Susa. Elam is mentioned in Genesis 14 where Chedorlaomer, king of Elam, and a coalition of other eastern kings attacked the kings of the Dead Sea area, including the kings of Sodom and Gomorrah. During the fighting, Lot, the nephew of Abraham, was captured. Subsequently, Abraham gathered a group of fighters and defeated the eastern kings, thus rescuing Lot. Later in the Bible, the book of

1. P. R. S. Moorey, "Assyria," in *The Cambridge Ancient History,* Plates to Volume 3, ed. John Boardman, new ed. (Cambridge: Cambridge University Press, 1984), p. 40.

Ezra includes "the people of Susa, that is, the Elamites" as among those "whom the great and noble Osnappar deported and settled in the cities of Samaria and in the rest of the province Beyond the River" (Ezra 4:9-10; Osnappar is generally identified with Ashurbanipal). This deportation of the Elamites to Samaria (that is, the former northern kingdom of Israel) apparently took place as a result of the wars between Assyria and Elam, which ended with the destruction of the Elamite capital of Susa by the armies of Ashurbanipal in 646 B.C.E.

In a message of hope, Isaiah 11:11 lists Elam as one of the places from which God will eventually gather the scattered "remnant that is left of his people" for their return to the land of Palestine, implying that residents of Israel or Judah had previously been deported to Elam. Two oracles in Isaiah depict Elam as involved in military attacks, once against Babylon (Isa. 21:2) and once against Judah (Isa 22:6). In Jeremiah 49:35-38, as a part of the oracles against the nations who were the traditional enemies of Israel, Elam is among the countries whose destruction God will cause to occur. (Verse 39, which is likely a later editorial addition, foretells the eventual restoration of Elam.) The prophet Ezekiel gives a picture of Elam, who had "spread terror in the land of the living," as now residing in the Underworld after its people had been killed by the sword, likely a reference to the defeat of Elam by the Assyrians (Ezek. 32:24-25). Furthermore, one of the visions of Daniel is set in Elam. Daniel 8:2 states, "In the vision I was looking and saw myself in Susa the capital, in the province of Elam, and I was by the river Ulai." (The river Ulai, near Susa, is the river that appears at the right edge of the wall relief ME 124801 described above.)

Elam is mentioned once in the New Testament. The book of Acts includes Elamites as among the pious Jews who were present in Jerusalem for the feast of Pentecost on the occasion when Peter preached to the crowds gathered there (Acts 2:9).

Tablet Naming Gyges of Lydia

Clay tablet

- ▷ Size: 26.37 cm. (10.38 in.) high; 11.13 cm. (4.38 in.) wide
- ▷ Writing: Akkadian language in cuneiform script
- ▷ Provenance: Nineveh (Kuyunjik, in modern Iraq)
- ▷ Date: ca. 660 B.C.E.
- ▷ Present location: British Museum (room 54)
- ▷ Identification number: ME K2675

Ashurbanipal, king of Assyria from 669 to 627 B.C.E., had this tablet inscribed to commemorate his rebuilding at Haran of the temple of the god Sin. Included in the building text is a recounting of several events of Ashurbanipal's reign, among them his defeat of Tirhakah of Egypt, who tried to retake control of Memphis after the death of Esarhaddon, Ashurbanipal's father. The tablet contains seventy-seven lines of text on the front side and seventy-four lines of text on the reverse. This clay tablet has been included primarily because it mentions Gyges, who was king of Lydia in Asia Minor during the middle of the seventh century B.C.E. Herodotus, the fifth-century B.C.E. Greek historian, recounts an entertaining story of how Gyges became king, and thus the founder of the Mermnad dynasty of Lydia (Herodotus, *Histories* 1.8-12). Gyges had been a bodyguard for King Candaules. The king was so proud of his wife's beauty that he invited Gyges to hide in her bedroom and see for himself the queen's beauty when she disrobed. Afraid to anger the king by refusing, Gyges did as the king suggested. As he fled the bedroom, however, the queen saw him. She then gave him a choice — either kill Candaules and marry her or be killed himself. He understandably chose the former option and thus became the new king. Several variations of this tale, which may or may not have any historical basis, appear in ancient writers.

56. Clay tablet from Nineveh that mentions King Gyges of Lydia

As the ruler of the Lydian kingdom, whose capital was at Sardis, Gyges was initially loyal to the Assyrians. In this tablet in the British Museum, Ashurbanipal records that Gyges had a dream in which the god Ashur instructed him to seek the favor of Ashurbanipal. That very day, Gyges dispatched a delegation to the Assyrian king, sending along a large tribute and some Cimmerian invaders who had been captured in battle. (The Cimmerians were a nomadic tribe from the Ukraine who invaded Asia Minor in the seventh century B.C.E.) Later, Gyges shifted his allegiance and sided with the Egyptians when they went against the Assyrians. Gyges established a rather powerful kingdom in western Asia Minor, but he eventually met his death at the hands of the Cimmerians.

Biblical Significance

The book of Ezekiel warned of a ruler, "Gog, of the land of Magog, the chief prince of Meshech and Tubal" who would lead an invading army from the north to attack Israel (38:2). This invader and his forces, however, would be utterly destroyed by God, which would be a sign to all nations that the people of Judah had been carried away in exile to Babylon because of their sinfulness and not because of God's weakness or lack of concern. God would then restore the people to their own land (Ezekiel 38–39). Almost seven hundred years later, the author of the book of Revelation adapted this Gog and Magog imagery to describe the last assault of the forces of evil against the people of God. In Revelation, however, Gog has been changed from the name of a person to the name of a place, so that in Revelation 20:8 both Gog and Magog are the names of evil nations.

The source of the name Gog in Ezekiel is uncertain. Many scholars, however, have suggested that the name is derived from the name of the Lydian king, Gyges, who was known to the Assyrians as *Gugu*. If this suggestion is correct, Ezekiel borrowed the name of Gyges of Lydia, who indeed had been the powerful ruler of a kingdom to the north of Israel, to represent this enigmatic enemy of God and God's people. Although the name Gog may have its origin with the historical figure of the Lydian king, in both Ezekiel and Revelation the figure of Gog has assumed mythical proportions.

Cylinder of Nabopolassar

Clay cylinder

- ▷ Size: 9.8 cm. (3.86 in.) long; 5.2 cm. (2.05 in.) wide
- ▷ Writing: Akkadian language in cuneiform script
- ▷ Provenance: Babylon (in modern Iraq)
- ▷ Date: Late seventh century B.C.E.
- ▷ Present location: Carlos Museum of Emory University, Atlanta, Georgia (Ancient Near Eastern Gallery)
- ▷ Identification number: 1921.131

Nabopolassar is considered the founder and first king of the Neo-Babylonian Empire. Prior to his reign (625-605 B.C.E.), Babylonia had been under Assyrian control. The last years of the powerful Assyrian king Ashurbanipal (who died ca. 627 B.C.E.), as well as the time immediately following his death, were a pe-

57. Clay cylinder commemorating Nabopolassar's rebuilding of the inner wall of Babylon

riod of chaos and turmoil in Assyria. Nabopolassar, who described himself in this cylinder inscription as "the son of a nobody," meaning he was not of the proper descent to become king, took advantage of the tumultuous situation to establish himself as king of Babylonia and to wrest Babylonia from Assyrian control. (For additional details of his reign see the following article, "Babylonian Chronicle, 616-609 B.C.E. — The Fall of Nineveh.")

This barrel-shaped, clay cylinder was found in 1921 in Babylon. The cuneiform inscription on the cylinder commemorates Nabopolassar's rebuilding of the wall Imgur-Enlil, which was the inner defensive wall in the city of Babylon. Foundation cylinders such as these were commonly placed in the foundations or in special niches of buildings or walls when they were constructed or renovated. In the inscription, Nabopolassar states that during the rebuilding of the wall he found a similar object from one of his predecessors and was replacing it, along with this cylinder, in the foundations of the wall. He left specific instructions for the person who would find his cylinder when the wall would need rebuilding in the future: "When that wall becomes dilapidated and you relieve its disrepair, in the same manner as I found the inscription of a king who preceded me and did not alter its location, find my own inscription and place it with your inscription."[1]

Nabopolassar extols the wall in glowing praise, describing it as "the great fortification wall of Babylon, . . . the solid border as ancient as time immemorial, . . . the mighty shield which locks the entrance to the hostile lands."[2] The wall had collapsed due to heavy rains and its foundation was reduced to a

---

1. "Nabopolassar's Restoration of Imgur-Enlil, the Inner Defensive Wall of Babylon," translated by Paul-Alain Beaulieu (*COS* 2.121:308).

2. "Nabopolassar's Restoration" (*COS* 2.121:307).

mound of ruins. The king had the rubble removed, the foundation resurveyed, and the wall rebuilt.

Before describing his restoration of the city wall, Nabopolassar recounted how with the help of the gods Nabu and Marduk, he, who was "the son of a nobody ... the servant who was anonymous among the people, ... the weak one, the powerless one," was able to become king and free Babylonia from Assyrian control.[3]

Biblical Significance

Most readers of the Bible are likely not familiar with Nabopolassar. He is never mentioned in the biblical writings, but his actions affected the history of the nation of Judah. During the last half of the seventh century B.C.E. (ca. 640-609 B.C.E.), Josiah was king of Judah. According to 2 Kings 22-23, during the eighteenth year of Josiah's reign a copy of "the book of the law" was found in the Jerusalem temple when it was being repaired. The discovery of this book, likely an early form of the book of Deuteronomy, led Josiah to instigate a major religious reform in Judah. His reform efforts included purging the Jerusalem temple and its precincts of non-Yahwistic elements, the removal of the "high places" for worship throughout Judah (which Josiah considered illegitimate), and the destruction of the cultic sanctuaries and shrines in the former northern kingdom of Israel.

The list of foreign cults that Josiah purged does not specifically mention Assyrian religious practices, but since Judah had been under Assyrian control for over a hundred years, Assyrian worship had likely been introduced into Judah and would have been among those practices attacked by Josiah. If so, an attack on Assyrian religion would have had political implications for Josiah, interpreted as an attempt to throw off Assyrian domination. Furthermore, his inclusion of the northern territory in his reform efforts certainly would have been seen as a political act, because this area was technically the Assyrian province of Samaria. When Josiah's grandfather, Hezekiah (726-697 B.C.E.), had led a religious reform movement and rebelled against Assyria, Sennacherib, the Assyrian king, mounted a retaliatory attack against Judah. Josiah's revolt, however, received no such response from Assyria because at this time Assyria was in steep decline as a nation, faced with internal problems and external challenges. Among those external challenges was Nabopolassar, who had taken control over Babylonia. Partially due to Nabopolassar's revolt against Assyria, Josiah was able to assert more independence from Assyria, at least religiously if not politically, and avoid Assyrian retaliation.

---

3. "Nabopolassar's Restoration" (*COS* 2.121:307).

Babylonian Chronicle, 616-609 B.C.E. — The Fall of Nineveh

Clay tablet

▷ Size: 13.65 cm. (5.37 in.) high; 7.14 cm. (2.81 in.) wide
▷ Writing: Akkadian language in cuneiform script
▷ Provenance: Babylon (in modern Iraq)
▷ Date: ca. 550-400 B.C.E.
▷ Present location: British Museum (room 55)
▷ Identification number: ME 21901

As discussed in the previous article, Nabopolassar was the founder of the Neo-Babylonian Empire. After taking over the throne in Babylon, Nabopolassar began asserting his independence from Assyria. By means of an alliance with Cyaxares, the king of Media, Nabopolassar brought about the downfall of Nineveh (capital of Assyria during the seventh century) in 612 B.C.E. and the eventual demise of the Assyrian Empire. Egypt, concerned by the growing strength of Babylon, had allied itself with Assyria at least as early as 616 B.C.E. and had sent troops to assist Assyria. After Nineveh fell and a new Assyrian king, Ashuruballit II, set up his government at Haran, a contingent of Egyptian soldiers was stationed there to assist the Assyrians. Nabopolassar soon marched against the city of Haran. Ashuruballit quickly abandoned the city, which was plundered by the Babylonians. In 609 B.C.E., Pharaoh Neco II marched through Palestine, crossed the Euphrates River, and arrived at Haran with a larger contingent of his army to support Assyria. Neco and Ashuruballit proceeded to put the city under siege and defeated the garrison of Babylonian soldiers at Haran. The Assyrian king fades from view after this; his fate is unknown. Although the Egyptians remained in the area and established their headquarters at Carchemish for the next few years, even the aid of the Egyptians was not enough to salvage the remnants of the weakened Assyrian Empire, whose last hopes came to an end when the Babylonians defeated the Egyptians at Carchemish in 605 B.C.E. (See the article "Babylonian Chronicle, 605-595 B.C.E. — The Capture of Jerusalem" for more information about the battle at Carchemish.)

This clay tablet is a part of the Babylonian Chronicle, a series of tablets which told the history of ancient Babylonia. This tablet, Chronicle 3, begins with the tenth year of the reign of Nabopolassar (616 B.C.E.) and ends with his seventeenth year (609 B.C.E.). Unfortunately part of the tablet is missing, including the portion dealing with the events of 612 B.C.E. The text on the tablet describes the conflicts between Nabopolassar and the Assyrians. During the twelfth year of Nabopolassar's reign, the Medes successfully assaulted and captured the city of Ashur. Nabopolassar had gone with his army to help the Medes, but did not arrive in time. According to this chronicle, Nabopolassar and the Median king, Cyaxares, became acquainted and cemented an alliance against the Assyrians outside the defeated city of Ashur. Two years later, in 612 B.C.E., Nabopolassar and Cyaxares (with the assistance of others) attacked the city of Nineveh, the Assyrian capital, eventually capturing it. The chronicle claims that this was "a great defeat inflicted on the people and (their) chiefs. . . . They carried off much spoil from the city and temple-area and turned the city into a ruin-mound and heap of debris."[1]

After the capture of Nineveh, the Medes returned to their own land. Assyria continued to hang on, though greatly crippled. The fate of the Assyrian king, Sin-shar-ishkun, is unknown; he may have fled, although a later tradition possibly claims that he died in the flames of his palace.

58. Babylonian Chronicle 3, which covers the years 616-609 B.C.E. and tells of the fall of Nineveh

Part of the Assyrian army had escaped from Nineveh and fled westward to the city of Haran, where a new king, Ashuruballit II, established an exiled government with the support of Egypt as his ally. Nabopolassar was now firmly in control in Babylon and portions of Assyria. In 610 he marched against the city of Haran, easily plundering the city when Ashuruballit and the small Egyptian force that was with him abandoned the city. By 609 B.C.E., the larger force of Pharaoh Neco II's army arrived to provide assistance to the Assyrians, and they were successful in defeating the Babylonian soldiers who were stationed in the city. This chronicle ends shortly after this episode, and Ashuruballit is not mentioned again. The Egyptians, however, set up headquarters about fifty miles east of Haran at Carchemish,

---

1. "The Babylonian Chronicle," translated by D. J. Wiseman (*DOTT*, p. 76).

where four years later the decisive battle between the Babylonians and the Egyptians took place.

Also on display in room 55 is a tablet (ME 22047; labeled "Chronicle of Nabopolassar") containing the continuation of the Babylonian Chronicle, describing the years 608-606 B.C.E. of the reign of Nabopolassar. This tablet gives an account of the military activities of Nabopolassar and his son, the crown prince Nebuchadnezzar, particularly describing the increased problems with the Egyptians.

Biblical Significance

To many people in the ancient Near Eastern world, Assyria was a nation to be feared. At the apex of its power it dominated an area that included parts of Egypt, Syria-Palestine, and most of the Mesopotamian region. Assyrian kings dealt decisively and ruthlessly with any nation that resisted their advances or that tried to foment a rebellion. Those who dared to offer armed resistance against Assyrian armies frequently found themselves the victims of beheadings, impalements, flayings, dismemberments, and other atrocities. Assyrian rulers routinely deported large segments of the population of defeated territories and resettled the captives in distant lands. Such resettlements served not only a punitive purpose, but also helped to prevent future rebellions.

The people of Palestine had experienced firsthand the Assyrian might. When the northern kingdom of Israel had attempted to resist control at the end of the eighth century B.C.E., Assyrian armies destroyed its capital of Samaria and deported the citizens of the area. Judah, reduced to the status of a vassal nation subservient to Assyria since the time of Ahaz (end of the eighth century), attempted revolt on more than one occasion. Its most notable attempt to throw off the yoke of the Assyrians was led by King Hezekiah, whose effort ended in failure and an increase in tribute payment. It is no wonder, then, that for the biblical writers Nineveh, the sometime capital of the Assyrian Empire, epitomized evil and wickedness.

Assyria's strongly negative reputation provided the setting for the book of Jonah in the Hebrew Bible. In the book, Nineveh represents the embodiment of wickedness, the last city that a Jewish audience would expect to repent. Although the book is supposedly based on a relatively unknown prophet who lived during the first half of the eighth century B.C.E. prior to Assyrian control of Palestine, the book was likely written much later, perhaps in the fifth or fourth century B.C.E. Such a late dating allows for the unexplained wicked reputation of Nineveh that is assumed in the story, while also making acceptable the unexpected repentance of the city and the humor that appears in the book (such as all animals in the city being required to fast and wear sackcloth; 3:7-8).

Enough time has elapsed that the horrible reputation of Assyria and the pain it had inflicted have dulled, and the city can be used in conjunction with humor. (The story of Nineveh and Jonah is also referred to in the New Testament at Matt. 12:39-41 and Luke 11:29-32.)

This mild tone toward Nineveh is in stark contrast to the mood of the book of Nahum, in which the author speaks in exultant tones about the fall of Nineveh. At the end of the seventh century, Assyria was no longer the strong force it once had been. It was weak and vulnerable, a situation that offered hope to many people who had suffered under its former iron grip. The book of Nahum, written shortly before or just after the demise of Nineveh in 612 B.C.E. mentioned in the Babylonian Chronicle, is filled with taunts and celebrations of the deserved destruction of this symbol of Assyrian cruelty. In 3:1-3, the grim aftermath of the city's fall is portrayed in triumphal language:

> Ah! City of bloodshed,
>   utterly deceitful, full of booty —
>   no end to the plunder!
> The crack of whip and rumble of wheel,
>   galloping horse and bounding chariot!
> Horsemen charging,
>   flashing sword and glittering spear,
> piles of dead,
>   heaps of corpses,
> dead bodies without end —
>   they stumble over the bodies!

For the prophet Nahum, Nineveh's destruction came as the result of God's judgment against the nation of Assyria for its history of atrocities, wickedness, and subjugation of Israel and Judah. No mourners would be found for the fallen city: "Then all who see you will shrink from you and say, 'Nineveh is devastated; who will bemoan her?'" (3:7). The prophet Zephaniah, who lived in the latter half of the seventh century B.C.E., likewise included an oracle about the desolation of Nineveh (2:13-15).

Another event mentioned in this tablet of the Babylonian Chronicle, in addition to the fall of Nineveh, that intersects with the biblical narrative is Pharaoh Neco's expedition to assist Assyria in 609 B.C.E. On his way to Haran to help the Assyrian king, Neco passed through northern Palestine. Josiah, king of Judah, went to meet Neco, likely in an effort to prevent him from offering assistance to the Assyrians. For Josiah, a weakened or destroyed Assyria offered the possibility of freedom from foreign domination. The Babylonian Chronicle describes the arrival of the Egyptians at Haran, but does not mention

Josiah's encounter with Neco. Information about that event is provided by 2 Kings 23:29-35 and 2 Chronicles 35:20–36:4. Josiah met Neco with his army at Megiddo. The result for Josiah was disastrous, for Josiah was wounded by an arrow in the fighting and was taken back in his chariot to Jerusalem, where he died and was buried. The people of Judah then named Josiah's son Jehoahaz as king. His reign was short-lived, however, for Neco intervened three months later, deporting Jehoahaz to Egypt and placing Jehoahaz's half brother, Eliakim (whose name was changed to Jehoiakim), on the throne. The Egyptians apparently retained control over Judah as a vassal state for the next few years until they were driven from Syria and Palestine by Nebuchadnezzar after his defeat of the Egyptians at Carchemish in 605 B.C.E.

Ishtar Gate and Processional Way of Babylon

Walls of baked mud brick, overlaid with polychrome glazed tiles

- ▷ Size: ca. 14.73 m. (48.33 ft.) high; ca. 15.70 m. (51.51 ft.) wide (reconstruction)
- ▷ Provenance: Babylon (modern Al Hillah, Iraq; ca. 55 mi. south of Baghdad)
- ▷ Date: ca. 575 B.C.E.
- ▷ Present location: Museum of the Ancient Near East, Pergamum Museum, Berlin (rooms 8 and 9)

The reconstruction of the Ishtar Gate and Processional Way of Babylon in the Berlin Museum of the Ancient Near East is one of the largest and most spectacular displays of any archaeological objects in the world and certainly the most colorful. Covered with polychrome glazed tiles of yellow, white, brown, and blue, they continue to amaze modern viewers, just as they did visitors to ancient Babylon during the days of King Nebuchadnezzar II (or, Nebuchadrezzar). Portions of the decorated façades may also be seen in other museums: The Museum of Fine Arts, Boston; the Detroit Institute of Arts; the Metropolitan Museum of Art, New York; the Oriental Institute Museum, Chicago; the Rhode Island School of Design Museum; the Louvre, Paris; the Museum of the Ancient Orient, Istanbul; and the Röhsska Museum of Design and Decorative Arts, Gothenburg, Sweden.

A team of German excavators, sponsored by the Berlin Museums and the German Oriental Society and led by the archaeologist and architect, Robert Johann Koldewey, began work on the site of the ancient capital of Babylon in 1899. The spectacular remains of this capital of the Neo-Babylonian Empire first appeared to the excavators as nothing more than scattered mounds of earth and heaps of rubble. Nevertheless, they patiently worked for the next fourteen years at the site and made numerous discoveries that attracted world-wide attention. Still, in 1913 Koldewey estimated that only half of the work needed had been accomplished. After the outbreak of World War I, virtually nothing more was done.

Babylon (*babil*, "the gate of the god") flourished under kings Nabopolassar (625-605 B.C.E.) and Nebuchadnezzar (604-562 B.C.E.). It was during this period that the city was restored to its former glory, as it enjoyed great wealth from its agricultural income as well as revenue from the peoples it had conquered. Babylon stood on both sides of the Euphrates River and was protected by two encircling walls, the larger of which was more than twenty feet thick. The outer wall was surrounded by a moat that varied in width between 65 and 250 feet. The city was one of the largest of the ancient world. The old town alone, on the east side of the river, comprised an area almost fifteen miles square. Two of the most spectacular and gigantic structures of antiquity stood in the center of the city, the temple of the god Marduk, Esagila, and the great ziggurat (or step-temple), Etemenanki, possibly the image for the "tower of Babel" (*babel*, Heb., "confusion") of the Bible. The palace buildings of the king were equally colossal in size.

59. Nebuchadnezzar's Ishtar Gate at Babylon

At least eight double gates, four of which have been excavated, allowed entrance into the city. The most spectacular of these gates was one commissioned by Nebuchadnezzar himself, the Ishtar Gate on the north side of the city (see fig. 59). According to inscriptions found at the site, the king gave instructions that this gate should have bronze-plated doors of cedar (of which nothing remains), and walls decorated with enameled reliefs of bulls, symbolic of the weather god, Adad, and dragons symbolic of Marduk, the god of the city. These dragons are portrayed as having the head of a serpent, the body and forelegs of a lion, the hind claws of an eagle, and the sting of a scorpion in their tails. Although these are the symbols of Marduk and Adad, Nebuchadnezzar ordered that the gate should be named for Ishtar, goddess of war and sexuality, whose temple was nearby. The Ishtar gate was a double gate originally; the reconstruction in the Berlin museum is of the smaller of the two gates. The main gate that stood behind this one, and connected to it, was much taller (approximately 65 ft.), as is visible in the model in the museum. Altogether, the two gates together extended approximately 90 feet in width and 150 feet in depth, so that anyone entering the city had to pass through 150 feet of the gatehouse before actually entering the city. As a result, the gate provided security for Babylon in addition to its beauty.

The street that led into the city from the Ishtar Gate was known as the Processional Way, or Procession Street (see plate 7). After leaving the gate, the street continued to the Marduk sanctuary and finally ended at a bridge that crossed the Euphrates. At the time of the New Year's Festival, priests carried statues of the gods of the city southward along this street beside the eastern wall of the palace. When the procession reached the ziggurat enclosure, it turned westward toward the Euphrates, passing the temple of Marduk, and then crossed the bridge to enter the western sector of the city. Procession Street was as spectacular as the Ishtar Gate. The only portion of the street excavated by the German team was that which passed between the walls of the palace and the inner wall of the city, a section approximately 250 meters long (ca. 760 ft.). These walls were decorated with the same glazed tiles as the Ishtar Gate, but the figures on them were those of roaring lions in full stride. It is estimated that some 120 lions once decorated the sides of the walls. The technique by which these figures were produced is fascinating:

The figures of lions which decorate walls of the Processional Way were mass-produced. Each is made of many bricks formed in special moulds; one stretcher side of each standard-sized brick ($33 \times 33 \times 8$ cm.) bore a small segment of a relief figure of a lion. First the bricks were composed into sections of eleven courses and these in turn then assembled to create each figure. Two complete sets of moulds were required, one for the lions walking to the right and another for the left-facing figures. The same technique was used to produce the relief figures of bulls and dragons that adorn the gate.[1]

The pavement of the street also was decorative, composed of red breccia blocks and white limestone. The replica of Procession Street in the Berlin museum is 8 meters wide (ca. 26 feet), only one-third of the original width of the street, and 30 meters long (ca. 98 feet); the original decorated section of the street was established at approximately 180 meters long, nearly 600 feet. Portions of the reconstruction consist of the original tiles; the remainder is modern.

Nebuchadnezzar took great pride in his building accomplishments, particularly his work in enlarging and beautifying the city of Babylon. Numerous monuments were created to perpetuate the memory of these achievements. A striking example of these monuments is the handsome inscribed stone known as the East India House Inscription (ME 129397; room 55, the British Museum), so named because it was presented to the representative of the East India Company in Baghdad in 1801. The inscription declares the devotion of the king to the god Marduk and asks that the god would lead him "in a straight path." Nebuchadnezzar also asks for heavy tribute from humankind and the continued future rule of his descendants. He speaks of his various building works in the capital and in Borsippa, particularly the building of temples.

It was also the custom of Mesopotamian kings to bury inscribed cylinders beneath temples and other monumental buildings (usually at the corners or the entrance) as historical records of their achievements, and several such cylinders have been found that describe the work of Nebuchadnezzar. The British Museum has four of these terracotta cylinders, one from Sippar and three from Babylon. The Sippar Cylinder (ME 91091; room 55) tells of the king's restoration of the Shamash temple in Sippar. After consulting omens to learn whether the gods favored such a rebuilding project, Nebuchadnezzar restored the temple, which had fallen into total disrepair. The Babylonian cylinders all speak of various building projects of the king: the first gives a general account of work done in Babylon but also describes the reconstruction of shrines, gates, harbors, and processional boats used in the New Year Festival (ME 85975; room 55); a second cylinder commemorates repairs to the temple of a healing goddess at Babylon (ME 91137; room 55); a third describes repairs to the ziggurats of Babylon and Borsippa, as well as repairs to his father's palace that had been damaged by flooding (ME 91142; room 55). Another cylinder displayed in the Museum of the Ancient Orient, Istanbul, likewise speaks of temple repairs but includes the renewal of city walls in Babylon (ES 6259; Mes-

---

1. Liane Jakob-Rost et al., *Pergamon and Bode Museum: The Ancient World on Museum Island, Berlin* (Mainz: Verlag Philipp von Zabern, 1990), p. 54.

opotamia Hall). A building inscription for the temple of the city god of Marad in the form of a truncated cone, honoring Nebuchadnezzar, is located in the Museum of the Ancient Near East, Pergamum Museum, Berlin (VA 3862; room 6). Some bricks stamped with the name and titles of Nebuchadnezzar also have been found; they are shown in the British Museum (ME 90081; room 55) and the Oriental Institute Museum of the University of Chicago (OIM A2502; Mesopotamian Gallery).

Biblical Significance

One of the truly determinative events in all of Jewish history was the capture and destruction of Jerusalem by the Babylonians under Nebuchadnezzar and the subsequent deportation of thousands of citizens of Judah to Babylon. Under guard by the Babylonian army, these people were forced to travel the hundreds of miles to that capital city. If they were brought into the city as part of the spoils and trophies of Nebuchadnezzar's victory, they may well have been marched through the principal entrance to the city, the Ishtar Gate. Whether they viewed with awe the spectacular sight of the gleaming tiles of the great gate and Processional Way on that occasion, it is certain they would have seen it over the following five decades of their captivity in Babylon.

According to the biblical record (2 Kings 24, 25 and Jeremiah 52), Babylonia conducted three deportations of citizens from Judah between 597 B.C.E. and 582 B.C.E. The first, and largest, of these occurred when Nebuchadnezzar attacked Judah for the rebellion of King Jehoiachin (597 B.C.E.), who was taken into exile in Babylon:

> At that time the servants of King Nebuchadnezzar of Babylon came up to Jerusalem, and the city was besieged. King Nebuchadnezzar of Babylon came to the city, while his servants were besieging it; King Jehoiachin of Judah gave himself up to the king of Babylon, himself, his mother, his servants, his officers, and his palace officials. The king of Babylon took him prisoner in the eighth year of his reign. . . . He carried away all Jerusalem, all the officials, all the warriors, 10,000 captives, all the artisans and the smiths; no one remained, except the poorest people of the land. (2 Kings 24:10-12, 14)

The second deportation followed a subsequent rebellion by Zedekiah, who had been appointed king by the Babylonians following the taking of Jehoiachin. Considered a traitor by the Babylonians, the fate of Zedekiah was much worse, as was the fate of Jerusalem. Zedekiah was forced to watch the execution of his sons, and afterwards he was blinded and taken in chains to Babylon. Then the temple was burned, temple officials, military leaders, and noblemen were executed, and the city was destroyed (587 B.C.E.). The fate of the survivors among the people is described in 2 Kings 25:11-12:

> Nebuzaradan the captain of the guard carried into exile the rest of the people who were left in the city and the deserters who had defected to the king of Babylon — all the rest of the population. But the captain of the guard left some of the poorest people of the land to be vinedressers and tillers of the soil.

Nebuchadnezzar subsequently appointed Gedaliah to serve as governor over the remnants of Judah at a new administrative center at Mizpah, seven miles north of Jerusalem. But two months later, Gedaliah was assassinated. That prompted the Babylonians to deport still more Jews to Babylon (582 B.C.E.), a third and final deportation. Thus occurred the Babylonian captivity of the Jews, which was to last fifty years, ending with the capture of Babylon by Cyrus the Great of Persia in 539 B.C.E.

Much remains unknown about the experiences and living conditions of the Jews in Babylon. Nevertheless, certain facts are known, both from the Bible and from cuneiform documents discovered in excavations at Nippur. The prophet Jeremiah gave this advice in a letter he sent to the exiles:

> These are the words of the letter that the prophet Jeremiah sent from Jerusalem to the remaining elders among the exiles, and to the priests, the prophets, and all the people, whom Nebuchadnezzar had taken into exile from Jerusalem to Babylon. . . . It said: Thus says the Lord of hosts, the God of Israel, to all the exiles whom I have sent into exile from Jerusalem to Babylon: Build houses and live in them; plant gardens and eat what they produce. Take wives and have sons and daughters; take wives for your sons, and give your daughters in marriage, that they may bear sons and daughters; multiply there, and do not decrease. But seek the welfare of the city where I have sent you into exile, and pray to the Lord on its behalf, for in its welfare you will find your welfare. (Jer. 29:1-7)

This seems to be the course of action followed by the exiles (only the royal family and high officials were truly prisoners). They were settled in several communities in the vicinity of the city of Babylon, including one settlement by the river Chebar (an irrigation canal of the Euphrates) called Tel-abib (Ezek. 3:15). Cuneiform texts from the Persian period indicate that some among the exiled Jewish community who had remained in Babylon were able to do very well in business and agriculture. Therefore, while Babylon was no substitute for Jerusalem, enough of the Jewish people were well settled there to constitute the nucleus of what would become one of the largest Jewish settlements outside of Israel.

Strangely, the Jewish opinion of Babylon did not give the city its reputation of evil and wantonness; that came from Christian sources. To call someplace "a modern Babylon" is to imply moral laxity. The New Testament book of Revelation, particularly in chapters 17 and 18, portrays Babylon as the world epicenter of corruption and blasphemy, the antithesis of the kingdom of God. The best known, and most damning, statement to the memory of the city occurs in Revelation 17:3-5:

> I saw a woman sitting on a scarlet beast that was full of blasphemous names . . . holding in her hand a golden cup full of abominations and the impurities of her fornication; and on her forehead was written a name, a mystery: "Babylon the great, mother of whores and of earth's abominations."

These words, however, do not refer to ancient Babylon, but to first-century Rome and its threat to the young Christian movement.

Arad Ostracon Mentioning "House of Yahweh"

Clay ostracon

▷ Size: 6.2 cm. (2.44 in.) high; 4.3 cm. (1.69 in.) wide
▷ Writing: Hebrew language
▷ Provenance: Arad, Israel
▷ Date: Early sixth century B.C.E.
▷ Present location: Israel Museum (Bronfman Archaeology Wing)
▷ Identification number: IAA 1967-669 (Arad letter 18)

During excavations at Arad from 1962-1967, archaeologists discovered more than two hundred inscribed objects, most of them ostraca. (An ostracon is a pottery fragment used for writing material.) Of the ostraca, eighty-seven were written in Hebrew, eighty-five in Aramaic, five in Arabic, and two in Greek. Later, four more Hebrew ostraca were found, one in 1974 and three in 1976. Of the Hebrew ostraca, over twenty of them can be identified as letters, dated to the tenth to sixth centuries B.C.E. (The Aramaic ostraca are from the mid-fourth century B.C.E. during the Persian period.) Some of these letters are addressed to military commanders, dealing with matters of military intelligence and administration. Others deal with the storage of wine, wheat, oil, and food or with the disbursement of these items to different military units and other people. Many of these letters either are addressed to or make reference to an individual named Elyashib, whose exact office at Arad is not clear. Some scholars have referred to him as the military commander at Arad; however, he may not have had such an authoritative position. Instead, he may have been the chief supply officer in charge of the supply depot at Arad.

The town of Arad, located in the south of Judah in the Negeb region, was the site of an Israelite fortress as early as the tenth century B.C.E. (The site was occupied prior to this period, but not as an Israelite fortress. See the article "Sanctuary of Arad," for additional information on Arad.) Arad seems to have been

60. Ostracon found at Arad (letter 18) addressed to Elyashib that mentions the "house of Yahweh"

destroyed as a part of Sennacherib's invasion of Judah in 701 B.C.E. Sometime during the last half of the seventh century, the fortress at Arad was rebuilt, only to be destroyed again, this time either by the Egyptians in 609 B.C.E. or by the Babylonian king, Nebuchadnezzar, during his campaign against Judah in 597 B.C.E. Very soon after its destruction, the site was refortified by Judah. Once more the site was destroyed, this time likely in 587 B.C.E. by Nebuchadnezzar.

Letter 18 (IAA 1967-669) is one of the letters addressed to Elyashib dated to ca. 597 B.C.E. It was found in the ruins of the office of Elyashib at Arad. In the letter, a subordinate requests that Elyashib dispense supplies to a certain Shemaryahu and informs Elyashib that the person he had asked about was in the temple (literally, "house of Yahweh"). It reads:

To my lord Elyashib. May Yahweh concern himself with your well-being. And now, give Shemaryahu a *letek*-measure (?) (of flour?) and to the Qerosite give a *homer*-measure (?) (of flour ?). As regards the matter concerning which you gave me orders: everything is fine now: he is staying in the temple of Yahweh.[1]

1. "Arad Ostraca," translated by Dennis Pardee (*COS* 3.43I:84).

(The amounts of a *letek*-measure and a *ḥomer*-measure are unknown.)

Five other Arad letters are on display in the Israel Museum (Bronfman Archaeology Wing). Letter 2 (IAA 1967-625), letter 3 (IAA 1967-623), letter 7 (IAA 1972-165), and letter 16 (IAA 1967-990) were also found in the ruins of Elyashib's office. These letters are from commanders requesting Elyashib to send various food supplies (wine, wheat, bread, flour, dough, oil, and vinegar). Letter 40 (IAA 1967-631), dated variously to the last third of the eighth century or to the second half of the seventh century B.C.E., is a poorly preserved letter written by Gemaryahu to his father Malkiyahu. This letter refers to a problem situation with the Edomites and an intelligence report about the situation that Gemaryahu had sent to his father. The identity of the Judean king who is mentioned is unknown. Gemaryahu writes:

> Your son Gemar[yahu], as well as Neḥemyahu, (hereby) send [greetings to] (you) Malkiyahu. I bless [you to Yahweh]. And now, your servant has applied himself to what you ordered. [I (hereby) write] to my lord [everything that the man] wanted. [Eshyahu has come] from you but [he has not given] them any men. You know [the reports from] Edom. I sent them to [my] lord [before] evening. Eshyahu is staying [in my house.] He tried to obtain the report [but I would not give (it to him).] The king of Judah should know [that] we are unable to send the [X. This is] the evil which (the) Edom(ites) [have done].[2]

Biblical Significance

In addition to providing insights about the political, military, and economic situation of Judah during the tenth to six centuries, the Arad letters have other connections with the Bible. Letter 18 is of special interest because of its mention of "the temple of Yahweh." The Hebrew actually reads, "the house of Yahweh." This phrase is almost certainly a reference to the Jerusalem temple. Even though a religious sanctuary did exist in Arad from the tenth to the eight centuries B.C.E. which could be the "house of Yahweh" mentioned in this letter, if the dating for this letter (early sixth century B.C.E.) is correct, the Arad sanctuary could not be the referent because it had already been destroyed. The letter likely is describing a situation in which an individual has taken up residence, or perhaps asylum, in the Jerusalem temple. The situation is intriguing, but unfortunately nothing more is known about the enigmatic circumstances hinted at in the letter. This letter provides one of the earliest, if not the earliest, epigraphic references to the temple in Jerusalem. One of the individuals mentioned in the

---

2. "Arad Ostraca," translated by Dennis Pardee (*COS* 3.43L:85).

letter to whom supplies were to be given is "the Qerosite." A passage in Ezra 2:44 and Nehemiah 7:47 lists the temple servants who returned to Jerusalem after the Babylonian exile. Among those listed are the descendants of a person named "Keros" (or, "Qeros"). The "Qerosite" of this Arad letter could be a reference to one of the temple personnel in Jerusalem prior to the exile.

Several of the letters mention "the Kittim," including letters 2 and 7 in which the Kittim are people to whom supplies are to be given. Literally, the word "Kittim" means a person from Kition (or, Citium), a town on Cyprus. The term was used in several ancient writings to describe not only inhabitants of Kition, or even of Cyprus, but also Greeks, Romans, or others who came from the islands or maritime countries. In Numbers 24:24, Jeremiah 2:10, and Ezekiel 27:6, the term apparently refers to Cyprus, or more generally, some distant land. Daniel 11:30 uses the term to refer to the Romans. The writer of 1 Maccabees describes Alexander the Great as being from Kittim (1:1). Various writings among the Dead Sea Scrolls use the term to refer to the Romans. The identity of the Kittim in the Arad correspondence is never clarified. Since they were to receive supplies from the Arad storehouse, they were apparently either mercenaries in the service of Judah or persons helping to deliver supplies to the Judean army. To call them "Kittim" may mean they were from Cyprus or Greece, or were Greek-speaking persons in general.

Babylonian Chronicle, 605-595 B.C.E. — The Capture of Jerusalem

Clay tablet

▷ Size: 8.25 cm. (3.25 in.) high; 6.19 cm. (2.44 in.) wide
▷ Writing: Akkadian language in cuneiform script
▷ Provenance: Babylon (in modern Iraq)
▷ Date: ca. 595-539 B.C.E.
▷ Present location: British Museum (room 55)
▷ Identification number: ME 21946

In 1884 Theophilus G. Pinches, an Assyriologist with the British Museum, published an abstract of his translation of the Babylonian Chronicle, a series of historical accounts of the kings of Babylon from Nabopolassar (625 B.C.E.) to the capture of the city by the Persian king Cyrus (539 B.C.E.). Pinches found these records among numerous clay tablets previously discovered at Babylon by Hormuzd

61. Babylonian Chronicle 5, covering the years 605-595 B.C.E., which mentions the capture of Jerusalem in 597 B.C.E.

Rassam, an early explorer, and brought back to London by his overseer. Unlike the propagandistic boasting and self-aggrandizement by the Mesopotamian monarchs on their public inscriptions, these chronicles are as close to modern historiography as the ancient world ever came. Who produced these tablets remains uncertain. Rather than documents from the scribes of the imperial court, these chronicles appear to have originated from an independent source, or rather, sources, over a very long period of time. Whoever the scribes were, it is clear that they referred to other sources for information, or at least depended on historical traditions handed down to them. The tablets cover Babylonian history down to the reign of Seleucus II (246-225 B.C.E.). Altogether, thirteen texts are now known to exist, but they have notable gaps in certain periods of the history. Some of the tablets are in poor condition as well. Nevertheless, the Babylonian Chronicles represent a rare treasure trove of information for our knowledge of the ancient Near East.

In many respects, these documents are unlike any other from that period of time. They do not present a year-by-year history, nor do they delve into extensive details in any particular year. Most of the tablets cover one year out of every three, and even that record is spare. The subject matter of the tablets seems limited to only such events as affect the future of the empire. Usually the chronicler will report battles, both of Babylonia and its neighbors; surprisingly, for ancient documents, these texts tell of Babylonian defeats as well as victories. Other topics include significant events affecting the king or his rule and any problems in the cult (issues in the Babylonian clergy, the capture of statues of gods, etc.). Familiar terms are used repeatedly in the narration, as if to establish order and continuity of tradition. Overall, the chronicles more resemble a dry, sparse list of facts rather than an interesting narration of history.

One small tablet in the group proved to be the most significant of these accounts from a biblical point of view. Known as Babylonian Chronicle 5, and sometimes referred to as "the Jerusalem Chronicle," it covers the years 605-595 B.C.E. The narrative begins with the defeat of the Egyptian stronghold of Carchemish by the Babylonians. Located today on the Turkish-Syrian border, ancient Carchemish commanded a vital stretch of the Euphrates River and was Egypt's dominant outpost in the north. According to this account, the Babylonian defeat was so complete that "not one man [returned] to his country."[1] The conquest of Carchemish by Nebuchadnezzar gave the Babylonians unfettered access to all Syria and Palestine. From the standpoint of biblical history, the crucial section of this chronicle tells of the capture of Jerusalem by the armies of Nebuchadnezzar:

> The seventh year, in the month of Kislev, the king of Akkad mustered his troops, marched on Hatti, and set up his quarters facing the city of Yehud. In the month of Adar, the second day, he took the city and captured the king. He installed there a king of his choice. He colle[cted] its massive tribute and went back to Babylon.[2]

The "seventh year" is the seventh year of the reign of Nebuchadnezzar. He set out from Babylonia in the month of Kislev, November/December. "Akkad" is Babylonia; "Hatti" refers to Palestine; and the "city of Yehud" is Jerusalem, the capital of Judah. The chronicle, therefore, says that Nebuchadnezzar captured Jerusalem on the second day of Adar, which is the 16th of March, 597 B.C.E. Jerusalem was besieged again in 587 B.C.E. and destroyed, but unfortunately the tablets between 594 and 556 B.C.E. are missing and therefore there is no Babylonian account of the final destruction of Jerusalem. What we do have of the history, however, agrees with the account in the biblical record. That would suggest that the missing Babylonian account of the last days of Judah would also agree with the biblical record, the only information on that period that exists.

Biblical Significance

Though the Babylonian Chronicle of the attack on Jerusalem is typically brief, it does provide the specific date of the event and corroboration of the parallel narrative in the Bible. Following the assault and capture of the city, Nebuchadnezzar deposed Jehoiachin as king and installed "a king of his own choice." From the biblical account we know this puppet king to be Zedekiah. King Jehoiachin was subsequently deported to Babylon, along with a large number of the leaders, educated people, and skilled laborers of the city. This was the first of three waves of deportations. The second deportation occurred following a rebellion led by Zedekiah that resulted in the destruction of Jeru-

1. Jean-Jacques Glassner, *Mesopotamian Chronicles*, ed. Benjamin R. Foster, Society of Biblical Literature Writings from the Ancient World, no. 19 (Atlanta: Society of Biblical Literature, 2004), p. 229.

2. Glassner, *Mesopotamian Chronicles*, p. 231.

salem in 587 B.C.E., and the third was caused by the assassination of Gedaliah, the governor appointed to take the place of Zedekiah.

The books of Kings and Jeremiah graphically recount the brutality of the reprisal of the Babylonians against Judah's rebellion. For eighteen months Nebuchadnezzar and his army laid siege to Jerusalem until the people were starving. Then the wall of the city was breached. Zedekiah and his leaders escaped by night and fled, but they were caught on the plain of Jericho. For his rebellion, Zedekiah was forced to watch his sons executed, and then he was blinded so that the last thing he saw would be the death of his children. Jerusalem subsequently was destroyed, the temple was burned, and the religious and political leaders of the city were executed (2 Kings 25:7-21; Jer. 39:1-10; 40-43). The summary of these events in 2 Kings is brief, but vivid:

> In the fifth month, on the seventh day of the month — which was the nineteenth year of King Nebuchadnezzar, king of Babylon — Nebuzaradan, the captain of the bodyguard, a servant of the king of Babylon, came to Jerusalem. He burned the house of the LORD, the king's house, and all the houses of Jerusalem; every great house he burned down. All the army of the Chaldeans who were with the captain of the guard broke down the walls around Jerusalem. Nebuzaradan the captain of the guard carried into exile the rest of the people who were left in the city and the deserters who had defected to the king of Babylon — all the rest of the population. But the captain of the guard left some of the poorest people of the land to be vinedressers and tillers of the soil. (2 Kings 25:8-12)

After Gedaliah, the successor to Zedekiah, was assassinated in 582 B.C.E., his supporters fled to Egypt. In reprisal, the Babylonians once again deported many citizens of Judah to Babylon. How many of the Jewish people were sent into exile? That question is impossible to answer, as is often the case in any question regarding ancient numbers, because of contradictions in the sources. According to Jeremiah, 3,023 people were taken in the first deportation (597 B.C.E.), 832 others in 587 B.C.E., and a final group of 745 people in 582 B.C.E. (Jer. 52:28-30). But those numbers differ from the figures given in 2 Kings. There the writer has no figures at all for the second and third deportations, but gives 10,000 as the number of people taken in the first deportation (2 Kings 24:14). The Babylonian Chronicle is of no help here because it has no account of any deportation — though that was certainly a practice of the Babylonians — saying only that Nebuchadnezzar "collected its [Jerusalem's] massive tribute and returned to Babylon." Whatever the case, these deportations marked the end of the kingdom of Judah and the beginning of fifty years of Jewish exile, the Babylonian captivity.

Lachish Letters

Clay ostraca

▷ Size: See text below
▷ Writing: Hebrew language
▷ Provenance: Lachish (modern Tell ed-Duweir), Israel
▷ Date: Early sixth century B.C.E.
▷ Present location: Israel Museum (Bronfman Archaeology Wing) and British Museum (room 57)
▷ Identification numbers:
▷ Israel Museum: IAA 1938.127 (ostracon 3), IAA 1938.128 (ostracon 4)
▷ British Museum: ME 125701 (ostracon 1), ME 125702 (ostracon 2), ME 125703 (ostracon 5), ME 125704 (ostracon 8), ME 125705 (ostracon 9), ME 125706 (ostracon 16), ME 125707 (ostracon 17), ME 125715a (ostracon 7)

During the tenth or ninth century B.C.E. a large fortified city was constructed on the site of Lachish, which earlier had been the location of a Canaanite city. With its well-built defensive structures, Lachish became the most important and best-fortified city in Judah after Jerusalem. When Sennacherib, king of Assyria, invaded Judah in 701 B.C.E., he destroyed the city of Lachish, an event graphically portrayed on the wall reliefs in his palace at Nineveh, now on display in the British Museum. (See the article "Siege of Lachish.") The city was not rebuilt until sometime during the last third of the seventh century B.C.E., this time on a much smaller scale than before. A new defensive city wall was built, but the palace-fortress in the center of the city remained in ruins. The rebuilt city was destroyed by fire when the Babylonians under Nebuchadnezzar invaded Judah in 587 B.C.E.

When the ruins of Lachish were excavated during the 1930s, the objects found in the destruction layer from 587 B.C.E. included a large number of items with Hebrew inscriptions. Among these inscribed objects were twenty-one texts written in black ink on broken pieces of pottery (called ostraca), most of which were found in a guard room inside the main entry gate of the city. (An additional ostracon was found in 1966.) At least twelve of these ostraca were letters, all of which seem to have been written shortly before the destruction of the city in 587 B.C.E. The pottery sherds on which five of the letters were written all came from the same piece of pottery. The letters, some of which were written on both sides of the ostraca, vary in size from 3.4 cm. by 3.4 cm. (1.34 in. by 1.34 in.) to 20 cm. by 17.3 cm. (7.87 in. by 6.81 in.). Three of the letters are specifically addressed to a person named Yaush. The other letters do not include an addressee, but may have been addressed to Yaush as well. Ostracon 3 (IAA 1938.127) is the only letter to mention the name of the sender, Hoshayahu. Some scholars assume that he was the sender of all the letters. The sender of the letters, perhaps an officer in charge of communications or intelligence, was a subordinate to the recipient of the letters to whom he sent reports or asked for instructions. Where he was located is not stated.

Several questions surrounding the Lachish ostraca yield different answers by scholars, including the question of whether the letters were written to Lachish or from Lachish. Some scholars understand Yaush to have been an officer stationed at Lachish; others suggest he was located elsewhere, perhaps in Jerusalem. In the latter case, the letters are understood as drafts or copies of the letters that were sent to him by Hoshayahu or other individuals at Lachish.

Two of the most important of the Lachish letters are ostraca 3 and 4, on display in the Israel Museum. Ostracon 3 reads:

> Your servant Hoshayahu (hereby) reports to my lord Yaush. May Yahweh give you the very best possible news. And now, please explain to your servant the meaning of the letter which you sent to your servant yesterday evening. For your servant has been sick at heart ever since you sent (that letter) to your servant. In it my lord said: "Don't you know how to read a letter?" As Yahweh lives, no one has ever tried to read *me* a letter! Moreover, whenever any letter comes to me and I have read it, I can repeat it down to the smallest detail. Now your servant has received the following information: General Konyahu son of Elnatan has moved south in order to enter Egypt. He has sent (messengers) to fetch Hodavyahu son of Aḥiyahu and his men from here. (Herewith) I am also sending to my lord the letter of Ṭobyahu, servant of the king, which came to Shallum son of Yada from the prophet and which says "Beware."[1]

This letter is the only one that names Hoshayahu as the sender. His manner of address to Yaush, "my lord," indicates that Yaush is his superior. Interestingly, Hoshayahu is indignant that Yaush would imply that he could not read. The literacy rate in ancient Palestine would have been low, so Hoshayahu is justly proud of his reading ability. Hoshayahu passes on the information that one of the Judean army commanders had made plans to go to Egypt, perhaps to try to persuade the Egyptians to help them against the Babylonians. (None of the individuals named here or elsewhere in the letter can be otherwise identified.) Along with this letter, Hoshayahu is sending another letter. The translation and interpretation of this final part of the ostracon are debated. One

---

1. "Lachish Ostraca," translated by Dennis Pardee (*COS* 3.42B:79).

view is that the letter was written by Ṭobyahu to an unnamed prophet warning him to be careful. Somehow Shallum gained possession of the letter, which he then sent to Hoshayahu. An alternative view is that the prophet wrote the letter and sent it to Shallum. Ṭobyahu then somehow confiscated the letter as subversive material and sent it to Hoshayahu.

The text of ostracon 4 (IAA 1938.128; see fig. 62) also is intriguing:

> May Yahweh give you good news at this time. And now, your servant has done everything my lord sent (me word to do). I have written down everything you sent me (word to do). As regards what my lord said about Bet-HRPD, there is no one there. As for Semakyahu, Shemayahu has seized him and taken him up to the city. Your servant cannot send the witness there [today]; rather, it is during the morning tour that [he will come (to you)]. Then it will be known that we are watching the (fire)-signals of Lachish according to the code which my lord gave us, for we cannot see Azeqah.[2]

Nothing is known about the situation involving Semakyahu and Shemayahu that is alluded to in the letter. One possibility is that Semakyahu had accused the writer (or his military unit) of dereliction of duty in not watching the signal fires closely. The writer assured the letter's recipient that such was not the case. The city that is mentioned may be Jerusalem, since the letter describes taking him "up to the city," a typical way of talking about going to Jerusalem since Jerusalem was located in the Central Highlands on a mountain ridge. The signal fire that is mentioned was apparently part of a communication system between cities or military installations to warn of the approach of the enemy. Unfortunately the meaning of this letter is not clear. One proposed interpretation understands the letter as being written during the final phase of the Babylonian invasion of Judah. The unknown city Bet-HRPD (Beth-harapid?) has already been abandoned or destroyed, as has apparently the city of Azeqah as well, since it (or its signal fires) can no longer be seen. If this is a correct interpretation, this ostracon is a poignant letter written just prior to the destruction of the city of Lachish. (Depending upon whether the letter is understood as having been sent from Lachish or sent to Lachish, the signal fire at Lachish is being "tended" or "watched.") Another way of interpreting the letter is to view it as being written when the Babylonian invasion was near but had not yet begun. (The letters indicate that travel to various places was still possible.) The communication system of signal fires was being tested; the one at Azeqah could not be seen during the test run. The city of Beth-HRPD had perhaps participated in a trial evacuation.

---

2. "Lachish Ostraca" (*COS* 3.42C:80).

62. Front and back sides of ostracon 4 found at Lachish

One of the letters on display in the British Museum (ME 125705; ostracon 9) authorizes the release of bread and wine to the bearer of the letter and requests instructions for the following day. In another letter (ME 125703; ostracon 5) the writer extends wishes for a good grain harvest and humbly thanks the recipient for having sent him letters: "Who is your servant (but) a dog that you should have sent to your servant these letters? Your servant (herewith) returns the letters to my lord."[3] This same expression of humility — a courteous way for a subordinate to address a superior — occurs in ostracon 2 (ME 125702), which is simply a brief note expressing good wishes to the recipient. Ostracon 16 (ME 125706) is a letter fragment. Like ostracon 3, it mentions a prophet. Only the last part of his name is present ("-yahu") — not enough to identify this prophet. Unfortunately, not much else is legible on the fragment.

3. "Lachish Ostraca" (*COS* 3.42D:80).

Ostracon 1 (ME 125701) is not a letter, but a list of five Hebrew names (in the form of "X, son of Y"), likely for some administrative use. The individuals named have no connection to biblical persons, although the names are the same as that of persons mentioned in the Bible (such as Gemaryahu [Gemariah in Jer. 36:10] and Yirmeyahu [Jeremiah]). Ostracon 8 contains writing on both sides, but portions of it are illegible, rendering a translation of this fragmentary letter impossible (other than its opening greeting). The small fragment known as ostracon 17 contains only three complete words: "(thy or his) slave . . . my lord" and what may be the name Yirmeyahu (Jeremiah).[4] Ostracon 7, of which only a fragment is on display (ME 125715a), is almost entirely illegible. The text was written on both sides of the ostracon, but only a few letters here and there (including one word) can be discerned. No translation or interpretation is possible. The arrangement of the ostraca in the display case in the British Museum is as follows: (left to right) top row — ostraca 1 and 2; middle row — ostraca 16 and 8; bottom row — ostraca 17, 7, 9, and 5.

Biblical Significance

In addition to the information these letters provide about the Hebrew language and Hebrew writing during the sixth century B.C.E., these letters are important also for the glimpses they provide of the situation in Judah prior to its conquest by the Babylonians and the beginning of the exile. The letters contain some tantalizing connections, or at least possible connections, to biblical texts. Letter 4 mentions Lachish and Azeqah in the context of signal fires that would have served as a warning system for an invasion. These are the same two cities mentioned in Jeremiah 34:7 as being the last two fortified cities left during Nebuchadnezzar's attack against Jerusalem in 587 B.C.E. The inscription on ostracon 3 reports that an army commander named Konyahu (or, "Coniah") son of Elnatan had prepared to enter Egypt. Could this be connected to the activity recounted by Ezekiel in which Zedekiah, king of Judah, rebelled against Nebuchadnezzar "by sending ambassadors to Egypt, in order that they might give him horses and a large army" (Ezek. 17:15; cf. Jer. 37:3-10)? Was this Elnatan of letter 3 related to the Elnathan son of Achbor who was sent by King Jehoiakim to Egypt to capture and return the prophet Uriah so that he could be executed (Jer. 26:22-23)? Were the prophets mentioned in letters 3 and 16 among the prophets named in the Hebrew Bible, such as Jeremiah who was

---

4. Harry Torczyner, *Lachish I: The Lachish Letters* (London: Oxford University Press, 1938), p. 177. Olga Tufnell in *Lachish III: The Iron Age* (London: Oxford University Press, 1953), p. 337, offers a different suggestion for the letters that Torczyner read as possibly the name Jeremiah. She suggests it may be the words "my lord."

at odds with the political authorities of Judah? What was the situation mentioned in ostracon 3 about a letter connected to a prophet and to Ṭobyahu, a royal servant, which involved a warning? Was this a situation similar to the conflict between royal authorities and prophetic figures associated with the Babylonian crisis depicted in the stories of the prophet Jeremiah or the earlier prophet Uriah?

As intriguing as these questions are, we must admit that the texts do not offer any definite answers. Although the Lachish texts may not provide the specific details that a modern reader would like, they do offer hints of political turmoil, military preparations, and heightened anxiety in the weeks or months leading up to the Babylonian destruction of Jerusalem and Lachish.

Babylonian Rations: The Judean Royal House as Prisoners

Clay tablet

- ▷ Size: 9.2 cm. (3.62 in.) high; 10.5 cm. (4.13 in.) wide
- ▷ Writing: Akkadian language in cuneiform script
- ▷ Provenance: Babylon (in modern Iraq)
- ▷ Date: Neo-Babylonian (ca. 595-570 B.C.E.)
- ▷ Present location: Museum of the Ancient Near East, Pergamum Museum, Berlin (room 6)
- ▷ Identification number: VAT 16378

In the excavations at Babylon conducted between 1899 and 1917 by Robert Koldewey, large numbers of cuneiform tablets were discovered in a barrel-vaulted underground building not far from the famous Ishtar Gate. A stairway from the palace led down to this room, which was probably the records room of the official in charge of rations for prisoners and certain skilled laborers of the royal employ in Babylon. The tablets document monthly rations of oil and barley, and occasionally of dates and spices, that were allotted to these people. Many nationalities were named in the various tablets: Egyptians, Persians, Phoenicians, Elamites, and others from the Mediterranean coasts. Some of these were exiles; others were palace employees, or both. Among the names were those of persons from Judah that bore the same names as some people in the Bible: Gaddiel (Num. 13:10), Semachiah (1 Chron. 26:7), and Shelemiah (Ezra 10:39).

A few broken lines in one of these records immediately attracted the attention of biblical scholars. In the right-hand column of the tablet pictured, lines 38-40, reference is made to rations given to Jehoiachin, king of Judah, and his five sons; Jehoiachin was ruler at the time Jerusalem was captured by Nebuchadnezzar II (597 B.C.E.) and then deported to Babylon as a prisoner:

> 32 pints (15 liters) (of sesame oil) for Jehoiachin king of Judah
> 5 pints (2.5 liters) (of sesame oil) for [the 5] sons of the king of Judah
> 8 pints (4 liters) (of sesame oil) for 8 men of Judah: 1 pint (½ liter) each[1]

For the first time in documents external to the Hebrew Scriptures, these cuneiform tablets provided evidence pertaining to the Judean royal house during the Babylonian captivity. Archaeology had previously uncovered evidence from the Persian period, contemporary with the books of Ezra and Nehemiah, of banking and business transactions of Jews in various areas of Mesopotamia (the Murashu tablets, from the business house at Nippur by that name; fifth century B.C.E.). These people were presumed to be descendants of the earlier captives, but no data contemporaneous with the exile itself was known to exist. As meager as the information on the ration tablets might seem, it has been regarded by scholars as anything but insignificant. Why is it valuable to an understanding of the biblical record?

Biblical Significance

Jehoiachin came to the throne (598 B.C.E.) at the age of eighteen following the death of his father, Jehoiakim (2 Kings 24:8), who may have been assassinated. But the Babylonians under Nebuchadnezzar II invaded Judah and laid siege to Jerusalem, shortly before or after Jehoiakim's death, in reprisal for his violation of the vassal-treaty provisions concerning tribute. The young king therefore was on the throne for only three months before he was forced to surrender the city, no doubt seeking favorable terms from the invaders. Nebuchadnezzar deposed him nevertheless and took him and his household prisoner (2 Kings 24:12). In his place, Nebuchadnezzar installed Jehoiachin's uncle, Mattaniah, to whom he gave the name Zedekiah. Such renaming was done by ancient monarchs to indicate the subservience of the official to their new lord. (This tradition may be part of the significance of the stories of God's giving of a new name to various persons in the Old Testament: Jacob/Israel, etc.) When Zedekiah subsequently rebelled, his punishment was one frequently given to

1. Benjamin Studevant-Hickman, Sarah C. Melville, and Scott Noegel, "Neo-Babylonian Period Texts from Babylonia and Syro-Palestine," in *The Ancient Near East: Historical Sources in Translation,* ed. Mark W. Chavalas (Malden, Mass.: Blackwell, 2006), p. 386.

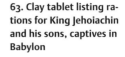

63. Clay tablet listing rations for King Jehoiachin and his sons, captives in Babylon

disobedient slaves; he was blinded — but not until he had witnessed his sons being put to death. Other members of the royal family, including the Queen Mother, and the leading court officials, went into exile with Jehoiachin.

Beyond that point, Jehoiachin is mentioned next in the Bible by the prophet Jeremiah, who prophesied that the king would never return to the land of Judah (Jer. 22:27). But the opponent of Jeremiah, the false prophet Hananiah, declared that Jehoiachin would return to Judah within two years (Jer. 28:2-4). Jeremiah ultimately would be proved right, as Jehoiachin lived out his days in Babylonia. The final word on the king in the Bible is given in the last few verses of 2 Kings:

> In the thirty-seventh year of the exile of King Jehoiachin of Judah, in the twelfth month, on the twenty-seventh day of the month, King Evil-merodach of Babylon, in the year that he began to reign, released King Jehoiachin of Judah from prison; he spoke kindly to him, and gave him a seat above the other seats of the kings who were with him in Babylon. So Jehoiachin put aside his prison clothes. Every day of his life he dined regularly in the king's presence. For his allowance, a regular allowance was given him by the king, a portion every day, as long as he lived. (2 Kings 25:27-30)

This account shows that Jehoiachin had indeed been a prisoner, though perhaps only under house arrest, and that eventually, at the age of fifty-six (561-560 B.C.E.), he was released and treated well by the incoming king, Evil-merodach. (This treatment may have resulted from some type of amnesty policy in the new king's inaugural year.)

The four Babylonian ration tablets that refer to Jehoiachin and his sons (identified as tablets a, b, c, and d) date to a considerably earlier period (ca. 595-570 B.C.E.), yet they indicate favorable treatment even then. Jehoiachin was given many times the amount of oil given to the other Judeans. It is probable that he and his family lived in the South Citadel in Babylon under house arrest, and that Jehoiachin administered his own household, perhaps even with its own kitchen. Thus, these inscriptions both corroborate the overall historical information given in the book of 2 Kings and add additional information to the silence of the Bible regarding the years of captivity and imprisonment of the Judean royal house in Babylon.

The Period of the Babylonian Exile

Lamentation over the Destruction of Ur

Clay tablet

▷ Size: 24.5 cm. (9.65 in.) high; 13.6 cm. (5.35 in.) wide

▷ Writing: Sumerian language in cuneiform script

▷ Provenance: Nippur (Niffar, or Nuffar, in modern Iraq)

▷ Date: ca. 1800 B.C.E.

▷ Present location: Louvre (room 2, ground floor, Richelieu Wing, section 3)

▷ Identification number: AO 6446

In 1889 the University of Pennsylvania sponsored an archaeological expedition to ancient Nippur, approximately ninety miles southeast of the modern city of Baghdad in Iraq. Their work, and that of subsequent excavators (including archaeologists from the Oriental Institute of the University of Chicago and from the American Schools of Oriental Research), yielded over fifty thousand documents on clay tablets. The discoveries at Nippur have produced about eighty percent of all known Sumerian literature. Nippur, though not a political capital, was an important religious center for the various empires of the Mesopotamian region. The city contained the temple of Enlil, the main god of the Sumerians. The documents

discovered at Nippur are a rich collection of administrative, legal, commercial, medical, and religious texts.

Among this collection of cuneiform documents is a group of twenty-two fragmentary tablets that contains multiple copies of a lengthy lamentation over the destruction of Ur, an important city on the Euphrates River that served at times as the capital of the ancient land of Sumer. The text, comprising four hundred thirty-six lines, is divided into eleven cantos or stanzas and is written in Sumerian language using cuneiform script. Com-

64. Tablet containing a portion of the Sumerian Lamentation over the Destruction of Ur

posed between 2000 and 1500 B.C.E., the laments mourn the fall of Ur to the
Elamites in 2004 B.C.E. The tablet pictured above is in the Louvre. Most of the
remaining tablets of this lamentation are in the University Museum of Archaeology and Anthropology at the University of Pennsylvania in Philadelphia.

The Lamentation over the Destruction of Ur opens with a litany of the various gods of Sumer, describing how they have abandoned their cities and temples (the latter referred to metaphorically as stables or sheepfolds). The poet
then calls upon Ur to raise a lament over its own destruction. Ningal, who is the
wife of Nanna, the Sumerian moon-god and the city god of Ur, pleads with her
husband and then with the gods Enlil and An (or Anu) to save Ur. She cries,

> Truly I shed my tears before An,
> Truly, I myself uttered supplication
> > before Enlil:
> "May the city not be destroyed!"
> > I said indeed to them.
> "May Ur not be destroyed!"
> > I said indeed to them,
> "May an end not be put to its people!"
> > I said indeed to them.
> But An never changed that word,
> Enlil never soothed my heart with that
> > "It is good; so be it!" . . .
> Verily they gave instructions
> > that my city be utterly destroyed,
> Verily they gave instructions
> > that Ur be utterly destroyed,
> Verily they decreed its destiny
> > that its people be killed.[1]

Ningal's petitions cannot save the city, whose destruction is described as a
mighty storm sent by the god Enlil. The devastating effects of the "storm"
(metaphorical language for military destruction of the city) are described in
detail, followed by Ningal's lament over the ruined city:

> My ox no more crouches in its stable,
> > gone is its oxherd,
> My sheep no more crouches in its sheepfold,

---

1. "Lamentation over the Destruction of Sumer and Ur," translated by Jacob Klein (*COS*
1.166:536).

gone is its herdsman.
In the river of my city dust has gathered,
    it has verily been made into foxholes,
In its midst no flowing water is carried,
    its tax-collector is gone.
In the fields of my city there is no grain,
    their farmer is gone,
My fields, like fields devastated(?) by the hoe,
    have verily grown tangled(?) weed,
My orchards and gardens, full of honey and wine,
    have verily grown mountain thorn.
. . . .
My birds and fowl have verily flown away
  — let me cry: "Alas, my city!"
    My daughters and sons have verily been
    carried off as captives in ships
      — let me cry: "Alas, my city!" . . .
    [Woe is me! My city] which ceased to exist
      — I am no longer its queen,
    [Nanna], Ur which ceased to exist
      — I am no longer its queen![2]

The lamentation ends with both a prayer to Nanna, urging him to keep the destructive storm away from the city and to restore the city, and a supplication that Nanna accept the offerings of the people and that the people's hearts might become pure.

In addition to the Lamentation over the Destruction of Ur, four other ancient Sumerian city laments are known: laments over Sumer and Ur, Nippur, Eridu, and Uruk. It is thought that these laments were composed when the temple for the patron deity of the city was being rebuilt, probably intended as an effort to appease the gods so that they would not be angered over the temple being rebuilt (since the god was the one responsible for its destruction in the first place), or so that the gods would not be upset that the remains of the former temple had to be demolished before a new one could be constructed. The laments also functioned to persuade the gods not to allow the city to be destroyed again. If this is a correct understanding of the original purpose of the city laments, then their purpose would have been served once the reconstruction of the city and temple was completed. The laments continued to survive, however, as copies were made for instruction of scribes during the Old

2. "Lamentation over the Destruction of Sumer and Ur" (*COS* 1.166:537-38).

Babylonian period (2017-1595 B.C.E.), after which time their usage ceased. The influence of these older city laments persisted if, as some scholars suggest, they were adapted during the Old Babylonian period and served as the basis for congregational laments that were used in the temples to ward off divine anger.

Biblical Significance

In 587 B.C.E. the Babylonian king Nebuchadnezzar captured and destroyed the city of Jerusalem and deported many of the citizens of Jerusalem and the surrounding area of Judah to Babylon. The destruction of Jerusalem and its temple was a crushing blow to the people of Judah. Not only did they suffer from the physical devastation of their city and land, but they also struggled with theological questions raised by this devastation, including such questions as "Why has God allowed us to be captured and Jerusalem to be destroyed?" "Has God abandoned us?" "Are the Babylonian gods more powerful than our God?" One of the literary responses to this predicament was the book of Lamentations. As the title indicates, this writing is a collection of poetic laments in which its unknown author(s) cries out in grief and pain over the loss of the city of Jerusalem. Likely written shortly after the destruction of the city in 587 B.C.E., the poetic compositions of the book eloquently express the feelings of grief, shock, bewilderment, and loss felt by the people of Judah. The opening words of the first lament describe the plight of the city:

> How lonely sits the city
>   that once was full of people!
> How like a widow she has become,
>   she that was great among the nations!
> She that was a princess among the provinces
>   has become a vassal.
>
> She weeps bitterly in the night,
>   with tears on her cheeks;
> among all her lovers
>   she has no one to comfort her;
> all her friends have dealt treacherously with her,
>   they have become her enemies.
>
> Judah has gone into exile with suffering
>   and hard servitude;
> she lives now among the nations,
>   and finds no resting place;

her pursuers have all overtaken her
    in the midst of her distress. (1:1-3)

The poet understands the destruction as punishment from God, who allowed the Babylonians to wreak havoc on the land. He writes,

The Lord has destroyed without mercy
    all the dwellings of Jacob;
in his wrath he has broken down
    the strongholds of daughter Judah;
he has brought down to the ground in dishonor
    the kingdom and its rulers.

He has cut down in fierce anger
    all the might of Israel;
he has withdrawn his right hand from them
    in the face of the enemy;
he has burned like a flaming fire in Jacob,
    consuming all around. (2:2-3)

Rather than blaming God for what has happened, the poet acknowledges that the people have sinned and rebelled against God, while God has acted rightly. The final lament in the book is a communal lament in which the people cry to God to remember them once again and to "restore us to yourself, O LORD, that we may be restored; renew our days as of old" (5:21).

Similarities between the biblical book of Lamentations and the various Mesopotamian city laments, such as the Lamentation over the Destruction of Ur, have often been noted, including such elements as: expressions of grief over the fall of the city that has occurred due to conquest by an invading army; the destruction of the city attributed ultimately to divine action; abandonment of the city by the protective god of the city; extensive descriptions of the destroyed city; the loss of the temple and activities associated with it; an appeal to the god for restoration of the city/people. Scholars disagree over whether or not the similarities between Lamentations and the Sumerian/Babylonian laments are strong enough to warrant claims that the book of Lamentations is directly dependent upon these compositions (or related laments). Even if the biblical text is not dependent upon the ancient Mesopotamian laments, the latter serve as examples of a similar type of literature that existed in the ancient world. (In addition to the book of Lamentations, several psalms in the Hebrew Bible, such as Psalms 74, 79, and 137, function as laments over the fall of Jerusalem and its temple.)

The Nabonidus Chronicle

Clay tablet

▷ Size: 13.97 cm. (5.5 in.) long; 14.6 cm. (5.75 in.) wide
▷ Writing: Akkadian language in cuneiform script
▷ Provenance: Babylon (in southern Iraq)
▷ Date: End of the fourth century to the middle of the first century B.C.E.
▷ Present location: British Museum (room 55)
▷ Identification number: ME 35382

The Nabonidus Chronicle is a clay tablet with cuneiform writing in two columns on both sides of the tablet. Unfortunately the tablet is badly damaged, with the bottom portion and most of the left-hand side of the tablet broken off. As a result, most of column one and four is missing, and the bottom of column two and the top of column three are missing. This tablet is part of a series of ancient tablets known as the Babylonian Chronicle Series that describe the major events during the reigns of the various rulers over Babylonia. This particular tablet, also referred to as Chronicle 7, describes events of Nabonidus's rule (555-539 B.C.E.), including Nabonidus's residing at Tema and the fall of Babylon and capture of Nabonidus by Cyrus of Persia. Based on the script of the text, this particular tablet was likely copied by a scribe during the Seleucid period (end of the fourth century to the middle of the first century B.C.E.). The original version of Chronicle 7, however, was probably written during the late sixth or the fifth century B.C.E.

After Nebuchadnezzar died in 562 B.C.E., his son Amel-marduk was named king. (This is the king called Evil-merodach in 2 Kings 25:27 who released the Judean king, Jehoiachin, from prison in Babylon.) He only lasted two years, however, before he was killed in a conspiracy possibly led by his brother-in-law and successor, Neriglissar (called Nergal-sharezer in Jer. 39:3, 13). This king's reign was relatively brief as well, lasting just over three and a half years. Even briefer was the rule of his son who followed him to the throne, Labashi-marduk, who occupied the throne for only three months before he fell victim to a murderous conspiracy and was killed in 556 B.C.E. His successor was Nabonidus, who ruled Babylon for seventeen years and was the last king of the Neo-Babylonian Empire. Nabonidus was not a member of the royal family but apparently a Babylonian military commander of Aramean background. (Some scholars have suggested that Nabonidus or his son Bel-shar-usur, the biblical Belshazzar, may have been involved in the death of Labashi-marduk.)

1. One of the two figures of a "Ram Caught in a Thicket" found at Ur, now in the British Museum (ME 122200). See p. 32.

2. Small figurine of the Canaanite god El in the Oriental Institute Museum of the University of Chicago. See p. 86.

3. Carved ivory found at Nimrud with a scene of a lion attacking a Nubian boy. See p. 114.

4. Relief panel from Sargon II's palace at Khorsabad showing a hero figure, possibly Gilgamesh, holding a lion. Adjacent to this panel is a winged, human-headed bull figure. See p. 136.

5. A scene from one of the panels in Sennacherib's Southwest Palace at Nineveh showing the assault on Lachish. This detail from panel ME 12909 shows a gruesome scene of Assyrian soldiers flaying prisoners. See p. 174.

6. A scene from the top band of a relief panel (ME 124875) from Ashurbanipal's North Palace at Nineveh showing the king holding a lion by its mane while stabbing it with his sword. See p. 189.

7. A portion of the Processional Way in Babylon with scenes of striding lions made of glazed bricks. See p. 201.

8. A frieze, made of glazed bricks, from the palace of Darius I at Susa showing two sphinxes sitting beneath a winged solar disk, the symbol for the god Ahura Mazda (Sb 3325). See p. 273.

9. A limestone column capital in the form of two bulls back to back (AOD 1), from the palace of Darius I at Susa. See p. 273.

10. Mosaic from Pompeii of the battle of Issus showing Alexander the Great (bareheaded figure on the left) defeating Darius III of Persia (the figure in the chariot, near the center of the scene). See p. 292.

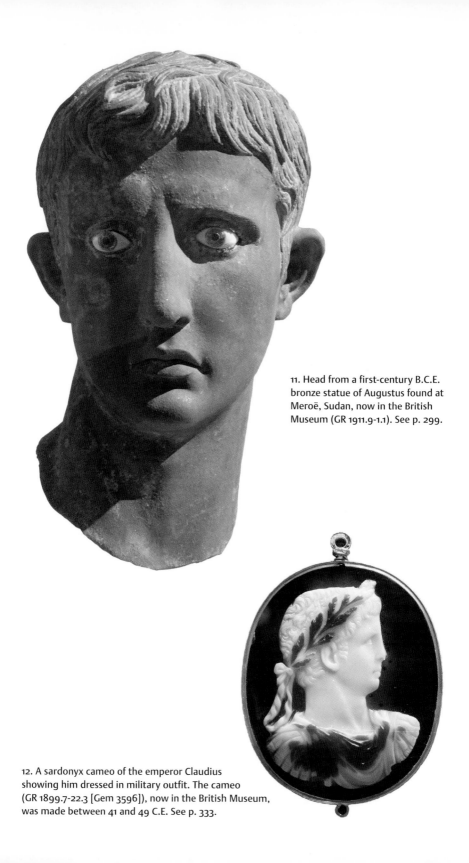

11. Head from a first-century B.C.E. bronze statue of Augustus found at Meroë, Sudan, now in the British Museum (GR 1911.9-1.1). See p. 299.

12. A sardonyx cameo of the emperor Claudius showing him dressed in military outfit. The cameo (GR 1899.7-22.3 [Gem 3596]), now in the British Museum, was made between 41 and 49 C.E. See p. 333.

13. Statue known as "the Beautiful Artemis," now in the Ephesus Museum. See p. 355.

14. Statue of Titus outfitted in military dress (inventory number 6059), owned by the National Archaeological Museum of Naples, Italy. See p. 380.

15. A bronze sestertius stamped with the image of Emperor Domitian. The coin was struck to commemorate the emperor's success against some of the Germanic tribes during his campaigns from 85 to 89 C.E. See p. 392.

16. Bronze sculpture of the head of the emperor Trajan (inventory number 10345), now in the Museum of Anatolian Civilizations in Ankara, Turkey. See p. 397.

65. Babylonian Chronicle 7, known as the Nabonidus Chronicle

During his reign Nabonidus was a major supporter and worshipper of the moon-god Sin, of whom his mother had been a devoted follower and possibly a priestess. Although like other Mesopotamian kings he repaired temples and maintained worship of a variety of gods, including the god Marduk, his major devotion was to the cult of Sin at Haran. (Haran was likely the city of his birth.) This support of Sin created ill-will between Nabonidus and the priests of Marduk in Babylon. In 553 B.C.E. Nabonidus left Babylon for a military campaign in Syria, Edom, and Arabia. For most of the next ten years, the king was away from the capital city of Babylon, residing in the north Arabian town of Tema (or, Tayma). During his absence from Babylon, his son, the crown prince Belshazzar, ruled in his place as co-regent. For this ten-year period, Nabonidus made the oasis town of Tema his major residence, enhancing the town, increasing its defenses, and stationing troops in the city. During those ten years, the New Year Festival in Babylon had to be cancelled because the king's presence was required for the festival to be celebrated. The description of the king's activities for each of those years is the same:

The king stayed <in> Tayma. The prince, the officers, and the army were in Akkad. In the month of Nisan, the king did not go to Babylon. Nabû did

not go to Babylon. Bēl did not go out. The New Year's festival was not celebrated. The sacrifices to the gods of Babylon and Borsippa were offered in
the Esagila and the Ezida as in normal times.[1]

The reason for his abandonment of Babylon for such a long period is not clear.
Some scholars have suggested he went to Tema to gain better control of the lu-
crative trade routes from Arabia to Mesopotamia. Others have pointed to the
conflict between Nabonidus due to his support of Sin and the powerful priests
of Marduk as a major reason for his leaving the city. Nabonidus, himself,
claimed that he was following divine orders — Sin had commanded his absence.

Soon after his return to Babylon in 543 B.C.E., Nabonidus demonstrated his
religious devotion by rebuilding Ehulhul, the temple to Sin in Haran, which
had been destroyed by the Medes and Babylonians in 609 B.C.E. Unfortunately
for Nabonidus, however, even his patron god was not enough to save his monarchy. A new power was gaining strength — Cyrus of Persia. Cyrus had already
conquered Media and portions of Asia Minor, including Lydia, by the time
Nabonidus returned from Tema to Babylon. He soon turned his attention toward Babylonia, and by 539 B.C.E., the Persian army had taken the city of Babylon. Nabonidus fled the city before it was captured but soon returned and
surrendered.

A basalt stela of Nabonidus in the British Museum (ME 90837; room 55; see
fig. 66) shows the king in traditional dress, holding a standard in his left hand. At
the top of the stela are the symbols of three Mesopotamian deities. Closest to the
figure of Nabonidus is a crescent moon, the symbol for the moon-god Sin. Next
are the symbols of the sun-god Shamash and the goddess Ishtar. The British Museum also displays in room 55 three cylinders from Nabonidus. One of the cylinders (ME 91109), found in the temple of Shamash at Sippar, describes his rebuilding of this temple, as well as the temple of the goddess Anunitum at Sippar
and the temple of Sin at Haran. In the inscription, Nabonidus claimed that the
god Marduk directed him to rebuild Sin's temple in Haran. Nabonidus expressed concern, since the Medes had control of the area around Haran. Marduk
replied, "The Mede whom you mentioned, he, his country and the kings who
march at his side will be no more."[2] The inscription also describes how Cyrus of
Persia then defeated Astyages, king of Media, and took control of Media. Another cylinder (ME 91143) includes a description of the king's restoration of the

---

1. "Chronicle of Nabonidus (556-539)" in Jean-Jacques Glassner, *Mesopotamian Chronicles*, ed. Benjamin R. Foster, Society of Biblical Literature Writings from the Ancient World,
no. 19 (Atlanta: Society of Biblical Literature, 2004), pp. 235-37.
2. "The Sippar Cylinder of Nabonidus," translated by Paul-Alain Beaulieu (*COS*
2.123:311).

66. Basalt stela of Nabonidus in the British Museum (ME 90837)

temple of Shamash at Larsa; a third cylinder (ME 91128) describes his restoration of the ziggurat at Ur, which was a part of the temple complex of Sin (see the following article, "Nabonidus Cylinder Mentioning Belshazzar"). An additional Nabonidus cylinder, mentioning dedications to various gods by the king, is on display in the Museum of the Ancient Orient in Istanbul (A.H. 4-28, 1; Mesopotamia Hall). Exhibited there also is a stela (1327) from Babylon erected by Nabonidus. The lengthy text on the stela, written in twelve columns (four on the front, eight on the back), begins by recounting the history of Babylon from the time of Sennacherib to the beginning of the reign of Nabonidus. The text focuses on the destruction and eventual restoration of various cult centers in Assyria and Babylonia. The next part of the inscription describes the deeds of Nabonidus during the early part of his reign, culminating in a lengthy statement of Nabonidus's plan to restore the temple of Sin in the city of Haran.[3]

Biblical Significance

Nabonidus is never mentioned in the Bible, but the story of his abandonment of Babylon and residence at Tema for ten years may have shaped the story of Nebuchadnezzar in the book of Daniel. The stories in the book of Daniel jump from Nebuchadnezzar to Belshazzar, with no mention of Nabonidus. Chapter 4 of Daniel contains the story of Nebuchadnezzar being afflicted with a form of insanity or mental illness in which he believed he was an animal and acted accordingly (zoanthropy). During this time, "he was driven away from human society, ate grass like oxen, and his body was bathed with the dew of heaven, until his hair grew as long as eagles' feathers and his nails became like birds'

---

3. For a translation of the inscription on the Istanbul stela, see "Nabonidus' Rise to Power," translated by A. Leo Oppenheim (*ANET*, 308-11).

claws" (Dan. 4:33). This illness came upon the king as punishment from God because of the king's arrogance and pride. After an unspecified period, Nebuchadnezzar came to his senses, recognized the sovereignty of God, and was restored to his kingdom.

Both this account in Daniel and the story of Nabonidus's stay at Tema have strong similarities to a text from the Dead Sea Scrolls. A work called the *Prayer of Nabonidus* tells how Nabonidus was afflicted by God for seven years with an evil ulcer while living in Tema. After his prayers for seven years to other gods failed, Nabonidus was finally helped by a Jewish "exorcist" who pardoned his sins, thus healing him. The *Prayer of Nabonidus* is a revised account from a Jewish perspective of the tradition of Nabonidus at Tema. This Dead Sea Scrolls version of the story portrays Nabonidus as a foreigner who ultimately acknowledged the Jewish God as the only true God, the one who was able to heal him. Most scholars have concluded that the story in Daniel 4 is also a reworking of the Nabonidus tradition; in Daniel the account of a king who was absent from Babylon for a period of time has been transferred to Nebuchadnezzar. Both the story in Daniel and the account in the *Prayer of Nabonidus* were possibly elaborations of a common tradition which had already attributed Nabonidus's absence to an illness sent by God, who ultimately healed him.

Nabonidus Cylinder Mentioning Belshazzar

Clay cylinder

- ▷ Size: 10.4 cm. (4.1 in.) long
- ▷ Writing: Akkadian language in cuneiform script
- ▷ Provenance: Ur (Tell Muqqayyar, in modern Iraq)
- ▷ Date: Sixth century B.C.E.
- ▷ Present location: British Museum (room 55)
- ▷ Identification number: ME 91128

This tiny clay cylinder is one of four cylinders with the same inscription that were found in 1854 in the ruins of the ziggurat at Ur in southern Iraq by J. E. Taylor, who found the cylinders in each of the four corners of the top stage of the ziggurat. Known as "Ur of the Chaldeans" in the Bible (Gen. 11:28, 31; 15:7; Neh. 9:7), this location was the site of a major temple complex to the moon god Sin, first built by Ur-nammu and his son, Shulgi, who ruled over Ur from

67. Clay foundation cylinder belonging to Nabonidus of Babylon

2112 to 2095 B.C.E. The ziggurat, in whose remains the cylinder was found, was a part of this temple complex. The temple complex was restored at various times by later rulers, including Nabonidus, who was responsible for depositing these clay cylinders with their building inscriptions. Kings commonly placed foundation cylinders such as these in buildings or walls as messages to the gods and as a record of their building accomplishments. After describing his rebuilding of the damaged temple, Nabonidus concludes his inscription with a prayer to Sin. The ending of the prayer entreats: "As for me, Nabonidus, king of Babylon, save me from sinning against your great godhead and grant me as a present a life of long days, and as for Belshazzar, the eldest son my offspring, instill reverence for your great godhead (in) his heart and may he not commit any cultic mistake, may he be sated with a life of plenitude."[1]

Belshazzar, the son of Nabonidus, served as the ruling authority in Babylon during the ten-year period when Nabonidus was absent from the city and lived in the oasis town of Tema in Arabia (see the previous article, "The Nabonidus Chronicle"). Although he was the authority figure in Babylon during his father's absence, Belshazzar was technically not the king during this period, as evidenced by the cancellation of the New Year Festival in Babylon during Nabonidus's residence in Tema. Observance of the New Year Festival required the presence of the king. When Nabonidus returned to Babylon in 543 B.C.E., Belshazzar is not mentioned in further records, so his status after 543 B.C.E. is unknown.

---

1. "Nabonidus' Rebuilding of E-lugal-galga-sisa, the Ziggurat of Ur," translated by Paul-Alain Beaulieu (COS 2.123B:314).

Biblical Significance

Belshazzar makes his only biblical appearance in the book of Daniel, where he is presented as the king of Babylon following Nebuchadnezzar. In several verses in chapter 5 of Daniel, Nebuchadnezzar is called the father of Belshazzar. Belshazzar, in fact, was the son of Nabonidus, not the son of Nebuchadnezzar. Some readers have proposed that these statements should be understood to mean that Nebuchadnezzar was his ancestor, specifically his grandfather, claiming that Nabonidus may have married one of the daughters of Nebuchadnezzar, who became the mother of Belshazzar. While such a situation is possible, no evidence exists that would support this claim. The book of Daniel is well-known for its historical inaccuracies; the identification of Belshazzar as the son of Nebuchadnezzar is one example. (Although the book of Daniel is written as if it comes from the sixth century B.C.E., most scholars are convinced that it was actually composed around 165 B.C.E. during the time of the persecution of the Jews in Palestine by Antiochus IV. Many of the historical errors, then, may be attributed to the chronological distance between the events and the time of writing.)

The episode in Daniel 5 describes Belshazzar hosting a feast in his palace, during which he brazenly sent for the vessels of gold and silver that Nebuchadnezzar had taken from the temple in Jerusalem when the city was captured in 587 B.C.E. In an act of arrogance and sacrilege, he and his guests drank their wine from these sacred vessels. As a result, he saw a human hand appear and write a mysterious message on the wall that was interpreted to him by Daniel as a warning that the days of his kingdom were numbered. Subsequently, "that very night Belshazzar, the Chaldean king, was killed. And Darius the Mede received the kingdom" (Dan. 5:30-31).

Nothing is known of the actual manner or time of Belshazzar's death, other than this statement in Daniel, which cannot be corroborated. The claim that the conqueror of Babylon was Darius the Mede is inaccurate on several accounts, among them being that no Darius the Mede is known to historians and that Cyrus of Persia was the individual who captured Babylon. Later in the book of Daniel, two of Daniel's visions are supposed to have occurred during the reign of Belshazzar (7:1; 8:1).

The Legend of Aqhat

Baked clay tablet (the third in a series of three tablets)

▷ Size: 17.5 cm. (6.89 in.) high; 11.6 cm. (4.57 in.) wide
▷ Writing: Ugaritic language in cuneiform script
▷ Provenance: Ugarit (Ras Shamra, in modern Syria)
▷ Date: Fourteenth century B.C.E.
▷ Present location: Louvre (room B, ground floor, Sully Wing, section 4)
▷ Identification number: AO 17323

This tablet is part of the rich collection of writings, artifacts, and structural remains discovered near the Mediterranean coast of Syria at Ras Shamra. After a farmer plowing nearby (at Minet el-Beida) in 1928 accidentally discovered a slab from an ancient tomb, French archaeologists, led by Claude F. A. Schaeffer, began excavating the area in the spring of the following year, finding a large necropolis (cemetery) and harbor area at Minet el-Beida. Near the necropolis was the tell of Ras Shamra, which Schaefer also began to explore. With the exception of a few brief interludes, excavations have continued at the site ever since. The abundant finds at Ras Shamra indicate that the site was the location of the ancient city of Ugarit, the capital of the Ugaritic kingdom. Although the site was occupied as early as ca. 6500 B.C.E., the city's major development was during the second millennium B.C.E., from approximately 1900 to around 1180 B.C.E., when the city was apparently destroyed by raids from the "Sea Peoples." The strength and prosperity of Ugarit fluctuated during the second millennium, as it at various times came under the control or influence of the Egyptians and the Hittites. Excavations at the site have uncovered the remains of the royal palace, several temples, private homes, walls, and streets. Among the most important finds at Ras Shamra are numerous clay tablets written primarily in the Ugaritic and Akkadian languages in cuneiform style. The contents of the tablets include letters, royal documents, commercial transactions, and religious texts.

Among the earliest clay tablets discovered (in 1930 and 1931) were large portions of three tablets found in the House of the High Priest that contain the story of Aqhat and his father, Danel. Unfortunately the beginning and the ending of the story are lost. (One or more missing tablets likely contained the remainder of the tale.) Danel, whose name means "God judges" or "judge of God," is described as one sitting at the city gates, rendering judgments on behalf of the widows and the orphans. Since this task was normally that of ancient kings who were responsible for protecting the powerless, Danel was perhaps a king. In the story, Danel has a daughter but no son. Yearning for a son, Danel spends seven days in the temple making offerings to the gods. On the seventh day, the god Baal intercedes with El, the chief god, on Danel's behalf, and as a result, Danel's wife conceives and gives birth to a son named Aqhat. As he grows, the child becomes a hunter and is presented an exquisite bow by the craftsman god Kothar-wa-Hasis. The goddess Anath covets the bow and when Aqhat will not give it to her even when promised immortality, Anath has him killed. Danel recovers Aqhat's remains (from inside a hawk or vulture) and buries them. Paghat, Aqhat's sister, then seeks revenge on the man hired by Anath to kill her brother. The third tablet ends at this point and the remainder of the story is unknown.

The tablet pictured here, written in Ugaritic cuneiform in two columns of text on each side of the tablet, records the last part of the story existing on the three tablets. Danel is mentioned also on three other fragments discovered at Ras Shamra, but the relationship of these fragments to the three tablets is unclear.

Biblical Significance

In Ezekiel 14:12-20, the prophet Ezekiel warns against the coming destruction of the city of Jerusalem due to its sinfulness. As an indication of how serious the situation is, Ezekiel claims that when a country sins against God, even if Noah, Daniel, and Job were present in the land, their righteousness could not forestall God's judgment, although they themselves would be spared. Daniel is mentioned again in Ezekiel 28:3, where he is known for his wisdom. Who is this Daniel that Ezekiel holds up as a model of righteousness? Although often assumed to be a reference to the title character of the book of Daniel, that identification is unlikely since the book of Daniel was not written until over four hundred years

68. Clay tablet from Ras Shamra containing part of the Legend of Aqhat

after the time of Ezekiel (although the tales about Daniel, supposedly a contemporary of Ezekiel, are probably much older). Since Noah and Job are ancient exemplars of righteousness for the author of Ezekiel, then the Daniel figure is likely a figure from antiquity as well. The Daniel mentioned in the book of Ezekiel is more likely a reference to the Danel figure in the Aqhat story, known for his righteousness and his judging cases of the widows and the fatherless.

This legendary figure, apparently well-known to the people of the ancient Near East, may even have been the source for the name of the central character in the book of Daniel. The tales in the first half of the book of Daniel likely arose in the third or early second century B.C.E. among Jews living in the area of ancient Babylon or Persia. They may not have necessarily known the details of the story of Aqhat, but they may have been familiar with the tradition of a wise and righteous hero named Danel. They thus borrowed the name for the central character of their stories, who is presented as one of the heroic Judean figures carried away into the Babylonian exile. Later in the second century, the author of the book of Daniel expanded the role of Daniel, presenting him as the recipient of apocalyptic visions. (The name in the Ugaritic texts has been variously transliterated as Danel, Dan'el, Daniil, or Daniel. The Hebrew name in Ezekiel 14:14, 20 and 28:3 is spelled slightly differently than it is in the book of Daniel. The spelling in Ezekiel is closer to the Ugaritic spelling and should perhaps be transliterated as Danel.)

Poetry and Wisdom Literature

Sumerian Proverbs Tablet

Clay tablet

▷ Size: 22 cm. (8.66 in.) high; 17 cm. (6.69 in.) wide
▷ Writing: Sumerian language in cuneiform script
▷ Provenance: Nippur, in lower Mesopotamia (in modern Iraq)
▷ Date: ca. 1900-1800 B.C.E.
▷ Present location: Museum of the Ancient Orient, Istanbul
▷ Identification number: Ni 4085 + Ni 4432 + Ni 9804

Wisdom traditions are a part of every culture. Wisdom is the advice that one generation passes on to the next generation, advice about how to be successful and happy, advice about the meaning of life, instructions on the proper code of conduct, and practical knowledge about the ways that society and the world operate. One of the major forms of wisdom traditions was the proverb. Proverb collections are known from both Mesopotamia and Egypt from as early as the third millennium B.C.E. At least twenty-eight collections of Sumerian proverbs have survived, some dating from ca. 2600 to 2550 B.C.E. during the Early Dynastic Period. The tablet pictured here, on display in the Mesopotamia Hall of the Museum of the Ancient Orient in Istanbul, is from the Isin-

Larsa period, ca. 1900-1800 B.C.E. The proverbs on this tablet comprise what is known as Collection 1 (or SP 1). Collection 1 consists of a total of 202 proverbs, of which nearly 120 are completely or almost completely preserved. Approximately eighty tablets with portions of this collection are known to exist. Even though the tablet shown

69. Fragments of a clay tablet containing a collection of Sumerian proverbs

here dates to the beginning of the second millennium, many of the proverbs are likely much older, having circulated earlier in oral form, if not also in previous written collections. This tablet originally contained the entire Collection 1. It is now incomplete, however, with several portions of the tablet missing, as well as some of the lines on the extant tablet obliterated. Three major pieces of the tablet have survived, which have been joined (Ni 9804, Ni 4085, and Ni 4432; at the time of this writing, the sign in the Museum of the Ancient Orient mistakenly labels one of the fragments Ni 8804, instead of the correct Ni 9804). These pieces of the tablet were discovered at Nippur by the Babylonian Excavation of the University of Pennsylvania during the years 1889 to 1900. The tablet contains eight columns of writing, four on the obverse and four on the reverse. The ancient scribes drew a set of double lines across each column to separate each proverb.

Proverbs were frequently used for writing exercises in the scribal schools. Consequently, archaeologists have found numerous copies of tablets written by pupils as a part of their scribal education. Many of these contain proverbs, sometimes with a proverb written by the teacher, followed by the more clumsily written version of the student. Collection 1 was one of the most popular collections for scribal exercises. The tablet in the Museum of the Ancient Orient in Istanbul is not one of the school tablets. Rather, it is one of a smaller number of tablets containing an entire collection of proverbs. These collections were likely master copies written by well-trained, skilled scribes.

Because of the damaged nature of the tablet, the following proverbs from Collection 1 are missing: proverbs 21-36, 58-66, 73-76, 89-93, 96, 119-139, 152, 154, 156-161, 178-183, 187-189, and 197-198. Following are some of the proverbs from Collection 1 (the numbers refer to the number assigned to the proverb):

1.3 Don't cut the neck of that which has had its neck cut.

1.7 To destroy something is in the power of God. There is no escape.

1.8 "Let my bread be left over, let me eat your bread!" Will this endear a man to the household of his friend?

1.9 If bread is left over, the mongoose eats it. If I have bread left over, a stranger consumes it.

1.11 You don't speak of that which you have found. You speak of that which you have lost.

1.12 Something which has never occurred since time immemorial: Didn't the young girl fart in her husband's lap?

1.14 Don't talk about what hurts you!

1.15 Wealth is far away, poverty is near.

1.16 He who possesses many things is constantly on guard.

1.18 Wealth (like) migratory birds never finds a place to settle.

1.28 When a purchase is settled, it is soon out of mind.

1.47 Although the pea-flour of the home-born slaves is mixed with honey and fine oil, there is no end to their lamentations.

1.48 (Coarse) barley-flour in the fields is meat and fat.

1.52 There is no baked cake in the middle of the dough.

1.65 In the city of no-dog, the fox is overseer.

1.66 In the city of the lame, the halt are couriers.

1.74 Things are traded in the city, but (it was) the fishermen (that) caught the food supply.

1.76 Like a clod thrown into the water, may he perish as he slowly disintegrates.

1.81 To accept a verdict is possible. To accept a curse is impossible.

1.82 What has been spoken in secret will be revealed in the women's quarters.

1.85 (If) the oars of a boat [slip into the water(?)], one must handle it like a raft.

1.89 Like a boat, he always comes up in the water.

1.91 My girlfriend's heart is a heart made for me.

1.103 He who eats too much cannot sleep.

1.105 A heart never created hatred, speech created hatred.

1.146 Marry a wife according to your choice! Have children to your heart's desire.

1.151 In marrying a thriftless wife, in begetting a thriftless son, an unhappy heart was assigned to me.

1.154 A thriftless wife living in a house is worse than all diseases.

1.157 A disorderly son, his mother should not have given birth to him. His god should not have created him.

1.159 An unfaithful penis matches an unfaithful vulva.

1.160 Marrying is human. Getting children is divine.[1]

Another collection of Sumerian proverbs is a work known as The Instructions of Shuruppak. Authorship of this text was attributed to Shuruppak, the legendary last pre-flood king of the ancient city of Shuruppak (Tell Fara). More than eighty fragmentary copies of this collection of Sumerian instructions are known, representing different versions: A Sumerian version from ca. 2500-2400 B.C.E., a "classical" or standard Sumerian version from the Old Babylonian period (ca. 1800 B.C.E.), and two Akkadian translations (ca. 1500 B.C.E. and ca. 1100 B.C.E.) of the Old Babylonian version. The fragmentary

---

1. Bendt Alster, *Proverbs of Ancient Sumer: The World's Earliest Proverb Collection*, vol. 1 (Bethesda, Md.: CDL Press, 1997), pp. 7-33.

tablet (OIM A645) shown in figure 70 dates to ca. 2500-2400 B.C.E. It is on display in the Mesopotamian Gallery of the Oriental Institute Museum in Chicago.

The complete text of The Instructions of Shuruppak is thought to have contained around 282 lines. The work is organized around three lists of instructions, each prefaced by the words,

> Suruppak, son of Ubartutu, gave instructions to his son Ziusudra:
> My son, let me give you instructions, may you take my instructions!
> Ziusudra, let me speak a word to you, may you pay attention to it!
> Do not neglect my instructions!
> Do not transgress the word I speak![2]

The instructions which Shuruppak conveys to his son consist of negative commands or prohibitions, positive commands, and conventional proverbs. The individual instructions often have little discernible connection between them. Rather, they seem to be randomly arranged in the work. The following examples of some of the instructions are from the standard version (ca. 1800 B.C.E.). The numbers refer to the line numbers in the text.

17. Do not dig a well in your field; the people will cause you to suffer damage.
18. Do not place your house close to a public square; the heaviest traffic(?) is there.
19. Do not vouch for someone; that man will have a hold on you.
20. And you, let nobody vouch for you; the man will despise you.
21. Do not spy upon a man; the town will make you pay back.
22. Do not loiter about where there is a dispute.
23. Do not appear as a witness in a dispute.
33. Do not laugh with a girl who is married; the slander is strong.
34. My son, do not sit (alone) in a chamber with a woman who is married.
35. Do not pick a quarrel; do not humiliate yourself.
36. Do not spit out lies; it causes disrespect.
37. Do not boast; your word stands (forever).
42-43. Do not utter nonsense; in the end it will reach out for you like a trap.

---

2. Bendt Alster, *The Instructions of Suruppak: A Sumerian Proverb Collection*, Mesopotamia. Copenhagen Studies in Assyriology, vol. 2 (Copenhagen: Akademisk Forlag, 1974), p. 35.

49. Do not have sexual intercourse with your slave girl; she will name you with disrespect.

153. Do not beat a peasant's son; he will "beat" your irrigation canal.

154. Do not buy a prostitute; she is the sharp edge of a sickle.

156. Do not buy a free-born man; he will lean against a wall.

157. Do not buy a palace-slave-girl; the house will be on a bad track.[3]

Biblical Significance

Like other ancient cultures, the people of ancient Israel developed and passed on to succeeding generations their own wisdom traditions. The major wisdom writings in the Hebrew Bible are the books of Job, Proverbs, and Ecclesiastes. In many ways these wisdom traditions were similar to, and even indebted to, the wisdom literature of their surrounding neighbors. Parallels can be seen between Israel's wisdom literature and that of the people of Egypt and Mesopotamia. For example, one of the collections of Egyptian proverbs is known as The Instruction of Amenemope. The material in this writing is so similar to Proverbs 22:17–24:22 that borrowing from the Egyptian literature by the biblical writers is highly likely. The complete text of The Instruction of Amenemope is found on a papyrus manuscript (EA 10474/2) in the British Museum, consisting of twenty-seven pages of text written on the recto (inner side of the scroll) and one line of text on the verso. Unfortunately, this papyrus is in a study collection and not normally on display. Small portions of the text are also known from another papyrus, three writing tablets, and an ostracon. Examples of passages similar to the biblical book of Proverbs would include the following (selections from The Instruction of Amenemope are cited by page and line number):

Do not move the markers on the borders of fields. (7:12; cf. Prov. 22:28)

Do not strain to seek increase,
What you have, let it suffice you.
If riches come to you by theft,
They will not stay the night with you.
Comes day they are not in your house;
Their place is seen but they're not there;
. . . .
They made themselves wings like geese,
And flew away to the sky. (9:14–10:5; cf. Prov. 23:4-5)

3. "Shuruppak," translated by Bendt Alster (COS 1.176:569).

Do not befriend the heated man,
Nor approach him for conversation. (11:13-14; cf. Prov. 22:24)

Do not covet a poor man's goods,
Nor hunger for his bread;
A poor man's goods are a block in the throat,
It makes the gullet vomit.[4] (14:5-8; cf. Prov. 23:6-8)

70. Fragmentary tablet with a portion of the text of The Instructions of Shuruppak

The two Sumerian collections discussed here also exhibit affinities with biblical wisdom literature, particularly with the book of Proverbs. In this case, however, one should be more cautious about assuming any direct dependence of the biblical works upon the Sumerian traditions. Rather, the Sumerian proverb collections, when compared with the biblical wisdom literature, demonstrate the extent to which Israel was a part of the ancient Near Eastern world, sharing the form and general contents of much of its traditions. Furthermore, the similarity between many of the topics found in Mesopotamian and biblical wisdom traditions should not be surprising. The ancient sages in each of the cultures were dealing with the same questions and concerns that arise in almost all cultures. Certain similarities in form deserve special mention. Both the Sumerians and the biblical writers preserved collections of proverbial sayings. Furthermore, these collections were often loosely strung together, with little or not thematic unity to the collections. Both traditions crafted some of the proverbs in a two-part form. The first part presented the advice; the second part provided the reason or motivation for following the advice. Another literary form used by both biblical and Sumer-

---

4. "The Instruction of Amenemope," in Miriam Lichtheim, *Ancient Egyptian Literature: A Book of Readings*, vol. 2, *The New Kingdom* (Berkeley and Los Angeles: University of California Press, 1976), pp. 151-55.

ian sages (as well as by Egyptian writers) was the instruction, often cast as a father giving advice to his son (compare, for example, Proverbs 1–9 with The Instructions of Shuruppak).

Sumerian Love Poem

Clay tablet

▷ Size: 10.7 cm. (4.21 in.) high; 6 cm. (2.36 in.) wide; 3.1 cm. (1.22 in.) thick
▷ Writing: Sumerian language in cuneiform script
▷ Provenance: Nippur, in lower Mesopotamia (in modern Iraq)
▷ Date: ca. 2025 B.C.E.
▷ Present location: Museum of the Ancient Orient, Istanbul (Mesopotamia Hall)
▷ Identification number: Ni 2461

This tablet in the Museum of the Ancient Orient in Istanbul has been called the world's oldest love poem. Discovered at Nippur (modern Niffar in Iraq), the tablet was one of several thousand Sumerian tablets found by archaeologists at the mound of Nippur during excavations between 1889 and 1900. The poem on this tablet has been given the title "Bridegroom, Spend the Night in Our House till Dawn." Composed of twenty-nine lines, the poem is a monologue directed to King Shu-sin, the fourth ruler of the Third Dynasty of Ur (ruled 2037-2029 B.C.E.). In erotic language, the speaker in the poem expresses her ardent desires and longings for Shu-sin. The last three lines of the poem seem to be a euphemistic invitation to a sexual encounter between the speaker and Shu-sin. The poem is usually understood to be re-

71. Tablet containing the Sumerian love poem "Bridegroom, Spend the Night in Our House till Dawn."

lated to the Dumuzi-Inanna love songs that celebrated the courtship and sacred marriage between Inanna (the Sumerian name for Ishtar, the goddess of love and fertility) and Dumuzi (the Sumerian name for Tammuz, the Akkadian deified shepherd king). More specifically, this song belongs to the category known as royal love songs, which apparently would have been sung during the ritual ceremony celebrating the divine marriage. In the ritual, perhaps celebrated annually at the New Year festival, the king, representing Dumuzi, engaged in sexual intercourse with a priestess, representing Inanna. The ritual "marriage" and sexual intercourse were thought to insure the fertility of the earth and the fecundity of people and livestock, thus guaranteeing prosperity for the king and his people. The poem, therefore, is not simply a personal, individual expression of sensual love between a man and a woman, but is also a ritualized celebration of love and sexuality. (Other scholars have argued that the royal love songs were not cultic in nature, but were secular songs celebrating human love and physical desire.) The final line of the text, line 30, is not a part of the poem but is a subscript: "It is a BALBALE-song of Inanna." The meaning of this subscript, which occurs at the end of several Sumerian love songs, is unclear, but the suggestion has been made that this is an indication of the type of ceremony or function during which the song was to be sung or recited (or perhaps the manner in which it was to be performed).

Translated, the poem states:

Bridegroom of my heart, [my beloved] one,
Your allure is a sweet thing, [is as sweet as] honey;
Dear(?) of my heart, my beloved one,
Your allure is a sweet thing, is as sweet as honey.

You have captivated(?) me, of my own will(?) I will come to you,
Bridegroom, let me run after you to the couch;
You have captivated(?) me, of my own will(?) I will come to you,
Dear(?), let me run after you to the couch.

Bridegroom, I will do to you all the sweet things,
My precious sweet, honey I will bring(?) to you,
In the bedchamber dripping with honey —
Let us enjoy your sweet allure, the sweet things!

Dear(?), I will do to you all the sweet things,
My precious sweet, honey I will bring(?) to you.
Bridegroom, you who have fallen in love with me,

Speak to my mother, (and) I shall offer myself to you,
(Speak) to my father, he will give (me to you) as a gift.

Soothing the reins, the place which soothes the reins, I know,
Bridegroom, spend the night in our house till dawn.

Of your heart, its place which gladdens the heart, I know,
Dear(?), spend the night in our house till dawn.
You, since you have fallen in love with me,
Dear(?), if only you would do to me your sweet things!

The lord my god, the lord my guardian-angel,
My Shu-sin, who cheers Enlil's heart,
If only you would do to me your sweet things!
Your "place" (is) sweet as honey — if only you would lay hand on it!

Lay (your) hand upon it for me like a cap(?) on a measuring cup,
Spread(?) (your) hand over it for me like a cap(?) on an old
      measuring cup.

(It is a BALBALE-song of Inanna)[1]

Biblical Significance

The Dumuzi-Inanna love songs are part of an assortment of love poems that were popular in the ancient Near Eastern world. Examples of love poetry exist in Sumerian, Akkadian, Egyptian, and possibly Ugaritic texts. One ancient Mesopotamian tablet originally contained a list of approximately 400 hundred songs. Of the 275 titles that are legible, fifty-five are love songs. Whereas some of the ancient Near Eastern love poems are cultic in nature, such as the Dumuzi-Inanna songs, others are secular songs, perhaps performed for entertainment at ordinary weddings, parties, private banquets, public festivals, and other functions.

The biblical text that has the closest affinities with the Near Eastern love poems is Song of Songs (Song of Solomon, or Canticles). This text, with its frank expressions of sexual desires by the male and female speakers in the work and its erotic imagery, has generated a variety of interpretations through the years. Some commentators (ancient and modern) who were uncomfort-

---

1. "Bridegroom, Spend the Night in Our House till Dawn," translated by Yitschak Sefati (*COS* 1.169B:541-42).

able with the sexuality and eroticism of the text solved the problem by "neutering" the text, claiming that the subject matter was actually not human sexual desires but divine love expressed in metaphorical language. According to this approach, the text is expressing either God's love for Israel or Christ's love for the church. While such readings may make the text more comfortable for some readers, they surely fail to capture the power and the sensuality of the love songs. The view of most scholars today is that the Song of Songs should be taken at face value as erotic love poetry celebrating human love and sexuality, rather than as a divine allegory.

Even if consensus is reached that the text is an expression of human love and sexuality, disagreements persist over the setting and function of the work. Some scholars have argued that the work has a cultic origin and purpose, somewhat akin to the Mesopotamian sacred marriage songs. According to this view, the song was used in a sacred rite celebrating an Israelite king's "sacred marriage" with Astarte, the Canaanite goddess of love and fertility. Several problems, however, with this view (such as the absence in the Song of Songs of any descriptions of cultic rituals, divine blessings, or prayers for fertility, all of which are a part of the Sumerian cultic love poems) suggest that the Song of Songs is best understood as secular love poetry. The Sumerian royal love songs, such as the one that is the subject of this article, do contain some interesting parallels to the Song of Songs. Both extol the pleasure of human love and sexuality; both express frank sexual yearnings; in both, the woman's sexuality and sexual desires are freely and unabashedly proclaimed; and both talk of the sweetness of love.

Whereas significant chronological, cultural, and functional distances separate the Sumerian love songs and the biblical Song of Songs, it is possible that some of the language or forms of the Mesopotamian love poetry could have indirectly influenced the biblical text. The value of the Mesopotamian and Egyptian love songs for the reader of the Song of Songs, however, is not that they demonstrate possible (if only remote) dependence of the Song of Songs on this ancient literature. Rather, their value is that they demonstrate that the Song of Songs, like other ancient love poetry, shared in the universal celebration and exaltation of human love and sexual desire.

The Great Hymn to Osiris

Limestone stela

▷ Size: 1.06 m. (3.48 ft.) high; 62 cm. (2.03 ft.) wide

▷ Writing: Hieroglyphics

▷ Provenance: Egypt (exact provenance unknown)

▷ Date: Eighteenth Dynasty (ca. 1539-1292 B.C.E.)

▷ Present location: Louvre (room 13, entresol [lower ground floor], Sully Wing, section 6)

▷ Identification number: C 286

Hymns to various gods and goddesses are found among the extant literature of almost all the civilizations of the ancient Near Eastern world — Babylonian, Assyrian, Hittite, Sumerian, Egyptian, Aramean, Phoenician, and Israelite. Through these poetic compositions, the peoples of the ancient world sang the praises of their deities, extolled their virtues, recounted their deeds and actions, and expressed thanksgiving for their benefi-cence. Examples of these ancient hymns — written on clay tablets, cylinders, or papyri; carved or painted on the walls of tombs; or inscribed on stelae and statues — can be found in numerous museums through-out the world today. The selection described here, known as The Great Hymn to Osiris, is inscribed on a stela (C 286) now in the Louvre. The stela belonged to Amenmose, described at the be-ginning of the inscription as "the overseer of the cattle of Amun" (Amon or Amen; god of Thebes and chief deity of Egypt from the Middle Kingdom period on). Amenmose, who lived during the period of the Eighteenth Dynasty (ca. 1539-1292 B.C.E.), is the one who offers the hymn to Osiris. At the top of this stela are two scenes, perhaps depicting a funerary ban-

72. Stela of Amenmose with the text of The Great Hymn to Osiris

quet reuniting Amenmose and his family. On the left are pictured Amenmose and his wife Nefertari, who are seated in front of a table. A son stands on the other side of the table, while another son stands behind the couple. Six seated sons and daughters are pictured below the scene. On the right, a woman named Baket sits before an offering table while a priest making offerings stands across the table from her.

The inscription consists of twenty-eight lines of hieroglyphics written horizontally. The hymn is a hymn of praise to Osiris, whose virtues and attributes are extolled. The latter part of the hymn provides the fullest account in any Egyptian text of the myth of Osiris, although even this account does not include the entirety of the myth. Osiris was one of the greatest and most popular of the Egyptian gods. He was the king of Egypt, but was murdered by the god Seth, his brother, who dismembered Osiris's body and scattered the pieces throughout Egypt. Isis, the sister and wife of Osiris, eventually gathered all the pieces, reunited them, and breathed life back into Osiris. Osiris impregnated Isis, who gave birth to Horus, who later became the king of Egypt. Osiris then ruled as the king of the underworld. Although earlier in Egyptian history, life in the next world was basically reserved for the pharaohs, the living manifestations of Horus, by the time of the New Kingdom period (ca. 1539-1075 B.C.E.), this Osiris myth of death and resurrection to life in the next world was applied to all persons. The myth provided hope for all people to experience resurrection and eternal life in the next world. The following lines present a sampling of the words of praise offered by Amenmose to Osiris.

Hail to you, Osiris,
Lord of eternity, king of gods,
Of many names, of holy forms,
Of secret rites in temples!

. . . .

Oldest in the joined Two Lands,
Nourisher before the Nine Gods,
Potent spirit among spirits.
Nun has given him his waters,
Northwind journeys south to him,
Sky makes wind before his nose,
That his heart be satisfied.
Plants sprout by his wish,
Earth grows its food for him,

Sky and its stars obey him,
The great portals open for him.
Lord of acclaim in the southern sky,
Sanctified in the northern sky,
The imperishable stars are under his rule,
The unwearying stars are his abode.
One offers to him by Geb's command,
The Nine Gods adore him,
Those in *dat* kiss the ground,
Those on high bow down.
The ancestors rejoice to see him,
Those yonder are in awe of him.

The joined Two Lands adore him,
When His Majesty approaches,
Mightiest noble among nobles,
Firm of rank, of lasting rule.
Good Leader of the Nine Gods,
Gracious, lovely to behold,
Awe inspiring to all lands,
That his name be foremost.
All make offering to him,
The lord of remembrance in heaven and earth,
Rich in acclaim at the *wag*-feast,
Hailed in unison by the Two Lands.
The foremost of his brothers,
The eldest of the Nine Gods,
Who set Maat throughout the Two Shores,
Placed the son on his father's seat.
Lauded by his father Geb,
Beloved of his mother Nut,
Mighty when he fells the rebel,
Strong-armed when he slays his foe.
Who casts fear of him on his enemy,
Who vanquishes the evil-plotters,
Whose heart is firm when he crushes the rebels.

Geb's heir (in) the kingship of the Two Lands,
Seeing his worth he gave (it) to him,
To lead the lands to good fortune.
He placed this land into his hand,

Its water, its wind,
Its plants, all its cattle.[1]

Biblical Significance

Hymns and songs are found throughout the Hebrew Bible (including Exod. 15:1-18, 21; Deut. 32:1-43; Judg. 5:1-31; 1 Sam. 2:1-10; 2 Sam. 22:2-51; Isa. 12:4-6; 38:10-20; 42:10-13; and Hab. 3:2-19), with the book of Psalms being the most well-known collection of such material. Some of the biblical songs are laments in which the writer cries out in anguish and pain to God and are similar to other ancient Near Eastern laments (see the articles "Lamentation over the Destruction of Ur," "Dialogue between a Man and His God," and "*Ludlul Bēl Nēmeqi,* 'The Babylonian Job'"). Many of the biblical songs, however, are hymns of praise or songs of thanksgiving. In these songs, the biblical writers express their awe and admiration of God, or offer thanks to God for God's compassion and concern. Hymns of praise are some of the best-known psalms in the Psalter, although they actually do not comprise the largest genre of psalms. (There are more psalms of lament than any other type of psalm in the book of Psalms.) Ancient Near Eastern hymns bear resemblances to the biblical hymns of praise, both in their form and in their contents.

Two specific psalms that are often cited by scholars as examples of biblical psalms that have similarities with ancient Near Eastern hymns are Psalm 29 and Psalm 104. Psalm 29, which describes Yahweh in thunderstorm imagery and as king over the flood (the waters of chaos), has perhaps borrowed this language and imagery from Canaanite/Ugaritic hymns to Baal (or Hadad), the god of the storm (see the article "Myths of the Baal Cycle"). Scholars have long noted the similarities between the creation hymn, Psalm 104, and The Great Hymn to the Aten that was found on the wall of the tomb of the Egyptian courtier Ay at Amarna. This Egyptian hymn from the fourteenth century B.C.E. praises Aten as the only god and as the one responsible for all creation. The writer exclaims:

How many are your deeds.
Though hidden from sight,
O Sole God beside whom there is none!
You made the earth as you wished, you alone,
All peoples, herds, and flocks;

---

1. "The Great Hymn to Osiris," in Miriam Lichtheim, *Ancient Egyptian Literature: A Book of Readings,* vol. 2, *The New Kingdom* (Berkeley and Los Angeles: University of California Press, 1976), pp. 81-83.

All upon the earth that walk on legs,
All on high that fly on wings,
The lands of Khor and Kush,
The land of Egypt.
You set every man in his place,
You supply their needs;
Everyone has his food,
His lifetime is counted.
Their tongues differ in speech,
Their characters likewise;
Their skins are distinct,
For you distinguished the peoples.[2]

Whether or not the author of Psalm 104 was indebted to this hymn to Aten is disputed. Some scholars have claimed that this hymn had become known in Israel and was adapted by the biblical writer for the worship of Yahweh. Others have argued that literary dependence is improbable due to chronological and cultural gaps. They would explain the similarities as being due to independent reflection on a common subject matter — the role of the divine in creation.

The hymn to Osiris that is featured here is another example of an Egyptian hymn that resonates with some of the biblical psalms. Here the similarity is as much in the form and tone of the hymn as in its details or imagery. In both the Osiris hymn and biblical hymns of praise, the writers express their praise and admiration for the divine in effusive language, unabashedly lavishing praise and compliments. As Yahweh was extolled by the biblical writers as king over the earth (cf. Pss. 96:10; 97:1), Osiris is lauded in this hymn as the god-king who rules over Egypt. He is "Lord of eternity, king of gods." Furthermore, nature obeys and tends to Osiris: "Plants sprout by his wish,/Earth grows its food for him,/Sky and its stars obey him,/The great portals open for him."

As the various hymns and songs from the ancient Near East attest, ancient Israel worshipped and celebrated the God of Israel in language and genres that were similar to the language and genres of their neighbors. While one should not overlook the important differences and the distinctiveness of the Israelite psalms, neither should one fail to appreciate what they shared with the praise literature of neighboring cultures.

2. "The Great Hymn to the Aten," in Miriam Lichtheim, *Ancient Egyptian Literature: A Book of Readings*, vol. 2, *The New Kingdom* (Berkeley and Los Angeles: University of California Press, 1976), p. 98.

Dialogue between a Man and His God

Clay tablet

▷ Size: 18.1 cm. (7.13 in.) high; 9.4 cm. (3.7 in.) wide
▷ Writing: Akkadian language in cuneiform script
▷ Provenance: Babylonia
▷ Date: Seventeenth century B.C.E.
▷ Present location: Louvre (room 3, ground floor, Richelieu Wing, section 3)
▷ Identification number: AO 4462

This tablet was purchased by the Louvre in 1906 from an antiquities dealer, thus its exact provenance is unknown. Because of certain characteristics of the writing on the tablet, as well as similarities to other tablets, this clay tablet has been dated to the seventeenth century B.C.E. The text, written in cuneiform script, is divided into nine strophes of ten verses each. Each strophe is separated by a horizontal line etched in the clay tablet. Unfortunately, the tablet is badly mutilated so that some portions of the text are missing or illegible. This tablet is the only known copy of this text.

The Dialogue between a Man and His God is one of the earliest Akkadian examples of literature that deals with theodicy, that is, a struggle with the problem of evil or suffering. The text presents a man suffering from undisclosed illness and misery who calls upon his unnamed god for assistance. The man does not seem to be an innocent or righteous sufferer, but rather is an individual who admits his guilt, even if he is not certain about what he has done wrong. (The reading of several of the lines is questionable, so there is room for debate about whether the man protests or admits his guilt.) Even though he may not be an innocent victim, he still places

73. Clay tablet with part of the text of the Dialogue between a Man and His God

blame for his condition on his god, who was responsible for bringing evil upon him.

> A young man was imploring his god as a friend,
> He was constantly supplicating, he was [praying to(?)] him.
> His heart was seared, he was sickened with his burden,
> His feelings were sombre from misery.
> He weakened, fell to the ground, prostrated himself.
> His burden had grown too heavy for him, he drew near to weep.
> He was moaning like a donkey foal separated (from its mother),
> He cried out before his god, his master.
> . . . .
> He recounts the burdens he suffered to his lord,
> The young man expounds the misery he is suffering:
> "My Lord, I have debated with myself, and in my feelings
> [. . .] of heart: the wrong I did I do not know!
> Have I [. . .] a vile forbidden act?"
> . . . .
> "How much you have been kind to me, how much I have
>   blasphemed you, I have not forgotten.
> In[stead(?)] of good you revealed evil, O my lord, you made glow . . .
> My bad repute is grown excessive, it . . . to (my) feet.
> It [rains] blows on my skull(?).
> Its [. . .] turned my mouth . . . to gall."[1]

After the man has voiced his complaints, his god responds, restoring him to health and assuring him of long life and good fortune. The god states:

> Your disease is under control, let your heart not be despondent!
> The years and days you were filled with misery are over.
> . . . .
> The path is straight for you, mercy is granted you.
> You must never, till the end of time, forget [your] god,
> Your creator, now that you are favored.[2]

The god instructs the man that he must act with charity toward those who

---

1. "Dialogue between a Man and His God," translated by Benjamin R. Foster (*COS* 1.151:485). (The *COS* text is a slightly altered reprint of the text in Benjamin R. Foster, *Before the Muses: An Anthology of Akkadian Literature*, vol. 1 [Bethesda, Md.: CDL Press, 1993], pp. 75-76.)

2. "Dialogue between a Man and His God" (*COS* 1.151:485).

are in need — feed the hungry, give water to the thirsty, and anoint the parched. The text ends with words that may be either a supplication from the sufferer or a liturgical formula, "Make straight his way, open his path: May your servant's supplication reach your heart!"[3]

Biblical Significance

The problem of suffering, particularly the suffering of the righteous, receives its most elaborate and sophisticated treatment in the Bible in the book of Job. The title character in the book is a man who "was blameless and upright, one who feared God and turned away from evil" (Job 1:1). In spite of his righteousness, however, Job suffers extensively, including the loss of his livestock, his health, and his children. Job rails against God, demanding to know why God has abandoned him and why God allows the just to suffer and the wicked to prosper. Although the book of Job provides no satisfactory answer to the problem of theodicy (other than the idea that the ways of God are beyond human understanding), the work does grapple seriously and honestly with the issue.

Other works in the Bible also struggle with the issue of human suffering, including the book of Ecclesiastes and several of the works in the book of Psalms. The book of Psalms contains both communal and individual laments in which the psalmists call upon God for assistance in their time of trouble (such as Psalms 6, 7, 13, 22, 25, 26, 31, 38, 60, 71, 80, and 88). In some of the psalms that are classified as individual laments, the psalmist admits his or her guilt, repents, and seeks God's forgiveness and help, either for healing or rescue from persecution. In other individual laments, the psalmist does not claim to be an innocent sufferer. This latter type of individual lament, in fact, provides a closer parallel to the Dialogue between a Man and His God than does the book of Job because, like this Akkadian tablet, the psalmists do not claim to be innocent sufferers. (The use of a dialogue between the sufferer and his god, however, is similar to parts of Job. This literary technique is not typical of biblical psalms of lament.) The words of Psalm 38:1-4 serve as a good example:

O LORD, do not rebuke me in your anger,
  or discipline me in your wrath.
For your arrows have sunk into me,
  and your hand has come down on me.

There is no soundness in my flesh
  because of your indignation;

---

3. "Dialogue between a Man and His God" (*COS* 1.151:485).

There is no health in my bones
    because of my sin.
For my iniquities have gone over my head;
    they weigh like a burden too heavy for me.

The Dialogue between a Man and His God, which predates the written material in the Hebrew Bible by more than a millennium, illustrates one of the ways in which the people of the ancient Near East confronted the problem of human suffering. Like the biblical psalms of lament, the author of this text saw his god as having ultimate control over his life and his well-being. Whether his illness was caused by his own transgressions or not, his god was the one who could relieve him of his distress. Thus, as in the psalms of lament, the sufferer called upon his god to hear his entreaty and restore his health.

Ludlul Bēl Nēmeqi, the "Babylonian Job"

Clay tablet

▷ Size: 16.3 cm. (6.42 in.) high; 8.2 cm. (3.23 in.) wide; 2.9 cm. (1.14 in.) thick
▷ Writing: Akkadian language in cuneiform script
▷ Provenance: Nineveh (Kuyunjik, in modern Iraq)
▷ Date: Seventh century B.C.E.
▷ Present location: Louvre (room 3, ground floor, Richelieu Wing, section 3)
▷ Identification number: K 2518 + DT 358

Several works from ancient Mesopotamia have been discovered that deal in some way with the universal human problem of suffering or evil, including A Man and His God (the "Sumerian Job"), The Babylonian Theodicy, Dialogue between a Master and His Slave (The Dialogue of Pessimism), Dialogue between a Man and His God (see the previous article), and the present text, *Ludlul Bēl Nēmeqi* (the "Babylonian Job"). In some of these works the focus is simply on the problem of an individual's suffering or misfortune. In other works, the problem is heightened by the seeming innocence of the sufferer, and thus the question of unjust suffering comes to the fore.

As is the case with other ancient Mesopotamian texts, the title by which this work was known in antiquity was derived from the opening words of the Akkadian text: *ludlul bēl nēmeqi* ("I will praise the lord of wisdom"). The work originally consisted of four tablets, each containing approximately one hundred twenty lines of text. Multiple copies of portions of the text (more than twenty-five tablets and fragments) have been found at Ashur, Nineveh, Babylon, Sippar, and Sultantepe. Almost all the text is preserved among these various tablets and fragments, allowing scholars to reconstruct nearly the entire text. Questions still exist about the rearrangement and wording of fragments thought to belong to tablet four of the work.

The clay tablet on display in the Louvre (K 2518 + DT 358) was discovered in Nineveh in the remains of the palace library of Ashurbanipal, king of Assyria. This particular copy of the text dates to the seventh century B.C.E., although the story itself has been dated as early as the fourteenth to the twelfth century B.C.E. This tablet is tablet two of the four-tablet work. The text is written

74. Clay tablet from Nineveh containing a portion of "the Babylonian Job"

on both sides of the tablet and consists of a total of one hundred twenty lines. Most of the obverse (front side) of the tablet (at least through line 36) is in good condition. The majority of the remaining portion of the obverse, as well as almost all the reverse, is badly damaged.

Written in the form of a monologue from an individual named Shubshi-meshre-Shakkan (who may have been the actual author), the text begins and ends with words of praise to the Babylonian god Marduk, the "lord of wisdom" of the opening line of the text. Even though the sufferer blames Marduk for his misery, he still praises Marduk and encourages others to do so as well because Marduk does eventually respond to his complaints and heals him. In tablet one, the author, who previously was a man of importance, prestige, and wealth, has lost his status and become a social outcast to his friends and his family, and even to his own god and goddess. Weeping, moaning, terror, and anxiety fill his life, and his prayers and entreaties yield no results. Tablet two is an extensive catalog of ills that Shubshi-meshre-Shakkan suffers. He writes:

Debilitating disease is let loose upon me:
An evil vapor has blown against me [from the] ends of the earth,
Head pain has surged up upon me from the breast of hell,

. . . .

My eyes stare, they cannot see,
My ears prick up, they cannot hear.
Numbness has spread over my whole body,
Paralysis has fallen upon my flesh.
Stiffness has seized my arms,
Debility has fallen upon my loins,
My feet forgot how to move.
[A stroke] has overcome me, I choke like one fallen,
Signs of death have shrouded my face!

. . . .

For lack of food my features are unrecognizable,
My flesh is waste, my blood has run dry,
My bones are loose, covered (only) with skin,
My tissues are inflamed, afflicted with gangrene(?).
I took to bed, confined, going out was exhaustion,
My house turned into my prison.

. . . .

From writhing, my joints were separated,
My limbs were splayed and thrust apart.
I spent the night in my dung like an ox,
I wallowed in my excrement like a sheep.

. . . .

No god came to the rescue, nor lent me a hand,
No goddess took pity on me, nor went at my side.[1]

His physical pain is made even worse by his confusion over why such suffering is happening to him. He complains that he is being treated like someone who had failed to perform his pious duties or had ignored his god and goddess. Yet, such was not his situation, he points out, for he was always faithful in his supplication and prayers, in offering praise and sacrifices.

The sufferer never explicitly names Marduk as the cause of his suffering, but that seems to be the implication of the opening words of tablet three:

Heavy was his hand upon me, I could not bear it!
Dread of him was oppressive, it [me].
His fierce [pun]ishment [ ], the deluge. . . .[2]

1. "The Poem of the Righteous Sufferer," in Benjamin R. Foster, *Before the Muses: An Anthology of Akkadian Literature,* vol. 1 (Bethesda, Md.: CDL Press, 1993), pp. 315-17.
2. "The Poem of the Righteous Sufferer," p. 317.

The remainder of the third tablet describes how the sufferer is finally healed, a process that is explicitly attributed to the "merciful Marduk." The fourth tablet concludes the work with praise for Marduk, who has restored and healed him.

Biblical Significance

Like the biblical Job, Shubshi-meshre-Shakkan suffers loss of property and health. Except for the death of Job's children, the sufferings of Shubshi-meshre-Shakkan seem even more extensive than those of Job. Compared to the book of Job, the text of *Ludlul Bēl Nēmeqi* does not spend much time dealing with the question of why its protagonist suffers. Yet, that issue is still at the heart of the work. Shubshi-meshre-Shakkan is a pious man who faithfully performs his acts of devotion. Why, then, does Marduk allow, or even cause, him to suffer? The text does not dwell on this question. About all the speaker says on the subject is that divine standards may be different from human standards and perhaps are beyond human understanding. After describing the acts of piety he has performed, he proclaims:

> I wish I knew that these things were pleasing to a god!
> What seems good to one's self could be an offense to a god,
> What in one's own heart seems abominable could be good to one's god!
> Who could learn the reasoning of the gods in heaven?
> Who could grasp the intentions of the gods of the depths?
> Where might human beings have learned the way of a god?[3]

One of the striking differences between this Akkadian poem and the book of Job is the praise that the sufferer ultimately offers to his god. At the end of Job is a brief statement where Job claims, "I despise myself, and repent in dust and ashes" (42:6). Shubshi-meshre-Shakkan, on the other hand, offers effusive praise to Marduk and calls on others to do so as well. In this regard, *Ludlul Bēl Nēmeqi* is similar to the psalms of lament in the Hebrew Bible in which the writers typically cry out to God, declare their afflictions, call on God to act on their behalf, and then conclude with words of affirmation and praise to God. An even closer parallel in form exists between this work and individual songs of thanksgiving in the book of Psalms. Songs of thanksgiving (such as Psalms 30, 34, 116, and 118) usually follow a typical pattern of praise, description of suffering and cry for help, recounting of God's healing or deliverance, and praise of God.

Like the biblical writers, the author of *Ludlul Bēl Nēmeqi* struggled with the

---

3. "The Poem of the Righteous Sufferer," pp. 314-15.

question of human suffering. Even though he may have held Marduk ultimately responsible for causing his problems, he was still able to offer praise to Marduk for restoring him to health.

The Persian Period

The Cyrus Cylinder

Clay tablet

▷ Size: 22.86 cm. (9 in.) long
▷ Writing: Akkadian language in cuneiform script
▷ Provenance: Babylon (in modern Iraq)
▷ Date: ca. 539-530 B.C.E.
▷ Present location: British Museum (room 52)
▷ Identification number: ME 1880, 0617.1941/90920

The Cyrus Cylinder was discovered in Babylon in 1879 by Hormuzd Rassam, working under the auspices of the British Museum. Although the exact details of his discovery of this object are not certain, it is thought that Rassam found the damaged cylinder in the remains of the temple of Marduk in Babylon. Thirty-six lines of text were still present on the barrel-shaped, clay cylinder (some lines were damaged, while additional lines were missing). In 1970, P.-R. Berger recognized that a clay fragment (BIN II, 32) in the Yale Babylonian Collection at Yale University was a part of the missing section of the Cyrus Cylinder. This fragment, containing lines 37-45 of the text, has since been joined to the larger portion now in the British Museum. Even with this additional fragment, the text remains incomplete. The purpose of the cylinder, similar in style and content to Mesopotamian building texts, likely was to commemorate Cyrus's restoration of the temple and other parts of the city of Babylon.

Cyrus, the founder of the Achaemenid Empire, became king of Persia in 559

75. The Cyrus Cylinder, which contains a description of Cyrus returning captives to their homelands

B.C.E. Hostilities soon erupted between Cyrus and Astyages, king of Media. (Astyages was the successor to, and possibly son of, Cyaxares who, in 612 B.C.E., had joined with the Babylonian king Nabopolassar to conquer Nineveh, the Assyrian capital. The evidence is not clear, but Cyrus may have been a vassal of Astyages.) In 550 B.C.E., Cyrus defeated Astyages and gained control over Media, which was only the first step in the expansion of his territory. Soon thereafter he defeated Croesus, king of Lydia, and took over much of Asia Minor. In 539 B.C.E., Cyrus conquered Babylon, then under the control of Nabonidus. With the acquisition of the territory of the Babylonian Empire, Cyrus now controlled almost the entire ancient Near East, with the exception of Egypt. His conquest of Babylon and the restoration of the city was the occasion for the production of the Cyrus Cylinder.

The inscription on the cylinder begins by describing the misdeeds of Nabonidus, king of Babylon. He was "an incompetent person" who "did away with the worship of Marduk, the king of the gods; he continually did evil against his (Marduk's) city. Daily, [without interruption . . .], he [imposed] the corvée upon its inhabitants unrelentingly, ruining them all."[1] (Corvée was a type of forced labor.) Marduk heard the cries of the people of his city and looked for someone to deliver them. "He surveyed and looked throughout all the lands, searching for a righteous king whom he would support. He called out his name: Cyrus, king of Anshan."[2] Obeying Marduk's command, Cyrus marched on Babylon and captured the city without a fight. Not only does Cyrus attribute his conquest of Babylon to Marduk, but he also states that Marduk delivered Nabonidus into his hands and then rejoiced at the good deeds that Cyrus performed when he took over the throne of Babylon. Specifically the good deeds he performed included freeing the people from the corvée service that had been imposed upon them. Furthermore, Cyrus returned the captured statues of various gods to their homelands, along with the inhabitants of those lands. Cyrus boasts:

> From [Ninev]eh (?), Ashur and Susa, Agade, Eshnunna, Zamban, Meturnu, Der, as far as the region of Gutium, I returned the (images of) the gods to the sacred centers [on the other side of] the Tigris whose sanctuaries had been abandoned for a long time, and I let them dwell in eternal abodes. I gathered all their inhabitants and returned (to them) their dwellings. In addition, at the command of Marduk, the great lord, I settled in their habitations, in pleasing abodes, the gods of Sumer and Akkad, whom Nabonidus, to the anger of the lord of the gods, had brought into Babylon.[3]

---

1. "Cyrus Cylinder," translated by Mordechai Cogan (*COS* 2.124:315).
2. "Cyrus Cylinder" (*COS* 2.124:315).
3. "Cyrus Cylinder" (*COS* 2.124:315).

In the last portion of the text, Cyrus describes his reconstruction of Imgur-Enlil, the wall of the city of Babylon, stating that during the work on the wall an inscription with the name of Ashurbanipal, the Assyrian king, was discovered.

Biblical Significance

With the conquest of Judea and the destruction of Jerusalem in 587 B.C.E. by the Babylonians, a significant portion of the inhabitants of Jerusalem and the surrounding area was carried away to Babylon as exiles. The expansion and growing strength of the Persian kingdom under Cyrus during the sixth century B.C.E. was interpreted by the anonymous writer of Isaiah 40-55 (referred to by scholars as Second Isaiah) as a hopeful sign. Second Isaiah, writing shortly before the fall of Babylon, believed that Cyrus was God's instrument to bring about the eventual release of the Judean exiles from captivity. In Isaiah 44:28, the writer portrays God as describing Cyrus with the words, "He is my shepherd, and he shall carry out all my purpose." The writer even designates the Persian king as God's "anointed" (i.e., "messiah") when he writes:

> Thus says the Lord to his anointed, to Cyrus,
> > whose right hand I have grasped
> to subdue nations before him
> > and strip kings of their robes,
> to open doors before him —
> > and the gates shall not be closed:
> I will go before you
> > and level the mountains,
> I will break in pieces the doors of bronze
> > and cut through the bars of iron,
> I will give you the treasures of darkness
> > and riches hidden in secret places,
> so that you may know that it is I, the Lord,
> > the God of Israel, who call you by your name
> . . . .
> I have aroused Cyrus in righteousness,
> > and I will make all his paths straight;
> he shall build my city
> > and set my exiles free,
> not for price or reward,
> > says the Lord of hosts. (Isa. 45:1-3, 13)

In 539 B.C.E. Cyrus conquered Babylon and brought the Babylonian Empire under his control. This newly acquired territory, along with the lands previously conquered by Cyrus, expanded the Persian Empire to include all of the Near East except for Egypt. The hope expressed by Second Isaiah that Cyrus's rise to power would result in the conquest of Babylon and the end of the Babylonian exile for the people of Judah who had been carried away by Nebuchadnezzar became a reality. In 538 B.C.E., Cyrus allowed the exiles from Judah to return home and rebuild their temple in Jerusalem. The book of Ezra in the Hebrew Bible describes this event, claiming that in the first year of his reign (meaning the first year after his capture of Babylon), Cyrus issued a decree allowing the Jews to return home. The contents of the decree are given in two places in Ezra, once in 1:2-4 and again in 6:2-5. (The wording of the decree in 1:2-4 is almost identical to a reporting of it in 2 Chron. 36:23.) The wording and language of the two passages are different: the first version is in Hebrew and emphasizes the return of the exiles; the second version is in Aramaic and focuses on the rebuilding of the temple. Scholars disagree over whether these represent two separate decrees or variants of one decree, the degree of authenticity of the decrees, and whether one or the other is more authentic. In general, most scholars concur that the passages in Ezra (and 2 Chronicles) do reflect the contents (but not always the wording) of an authentic Persian document or documents granting permission for the Jewish exiles to return home and rebuild the Jerusalem temple.

The statement in the Cyrus Cylinder that the Persian king allowed the inhabitants from various locations to return to their homelands does not mention the return of the people of Judah. Neither is this return a generalized repatriation of all conquered peoples. The return described in the inscription is limited to places in or near Babylonia. Thus, contrary to some popular claims, the Cyrus Cylinder does not prove the historical accuracy of the biblical texts. On the other hand, what the inscription on the cylinder does provide is general support for the specific event of the Jewish return from exile; that is, the granting of permission for the Jews to return to Judah is not inconsistent with the practice sometimes followed by Cyrus (and other Mesopotamian kings).

In keeping with the general biblical perspective that the events of ancient history occurred at the direction or permission of Yahweh, biblical writers attributed the rise of Cyrus and his conquest of Babylon to the work of Yahweh (Isa. 45:1-8; cf. Dan. 5:31 and 9:1 where, strangely, the writer claims an otherwise unknown "Darius the Mede" was the one who conquered Babylon). In the Cyrus Cylinder inscription, Cyrus acknowledges Marduk as the one responsible for his success.

Frieze of Archers

Polychrome, glazed siliceous brick

▷ Size: 4.75 m. (15.58 ft.) high; 3.75 m. (12.30 ft.) wide

▷ Provenance: Susa, in modern Iran

▷ Date: ca. 510 B.C.E.

▷ Present location: Louvre (room 12b, ground floor, Sully Wing, section 4)

▷ Identification number: AOD 488

When Cambyses, king of Persia, died following his campaign to Egypt, the throne was briefly taken by his brother, Bardiya. But shortly thereafter Bardiya was assassinated, and a military commander named Darius seized the throne (521 B.C.E.). The truth about what took place in the succession can never be known, because the only record of these events is that of Darius himself which he had carved on the Behistun rock. For the next several years, the new king — Darius I, as he would be known — busied himself with consolidating his power over the empire. Eventually he turned his attention to the construction of new capitals for his kingdom. The Persian monarchs had a tradition of employing several royal capitals at the same time, between which they moved according to the seasons. For example, in the hot summer months the court convened at Ecbatana, high on the Iranian Plateau, while the cold winter season would find the kings at Susa, a milder climate on the Mesopotamian plains. In addition to an improved climate, this movement of the court got the kings in proximity to their widely diverse geographical and ethnic groups.

Darius seems to have picked Susa, long-time site of a local capital in the region known as Elam, for his first major building project. Here the new king would show himself to be a restorer of order and glory to the Persian kingdom. On a terraced platform nearly fifty feet high, Darius erected a magnificent audience hall, or *apadana,* 109 meters (358 feet) square, with thirty-six columns on square bases, each column over sixty feet tall. The three exterior porticos of the building featured twelve columns on bell-shaped bases. Enormous bull's head capitals crowned several of the columns, and the massive cedar beams of the roof rested on their backs. Four monumental staircases, elaborately decorated, provided entrance to the site. Darius boasted that many peoples and nations contributed to the construction. Cedar timbers were brought from Lebanon; gold came from Sardis and Bactria; ivory came from Ethiopia and India. The stonecutters who worked on the building were Ionians and Sardians; the woodworkers were Egyptians; Babylonians made the baked bricks; the wall reliefs were created by Medes and Egyptians. By these assertions Darius sought to show the universal power and unifying nature of his rule.

As grand as these structures must have been, it is the glazed brick reliefs of the walls that have elicited admiration over the succeeding centuries. The inspiration for their construction, particularly in the motifs — bulls and striding lions — clearly comes from the Processional Way of Babylon (see the article "Ishtar Gate and Processional Way of Babylon"), but the glazed bricks reflect different techniques. Whereas the Babylonian bricks were of baked clay, these bricks were of siliceous earth (containing silica, a crystalline compound) and powdered flint, with a calcareous binder; therefore they were harder and glossier, even in the unglazed portions. The colored glazes on the surfaces also were applied in repeated coats, which resulted in the vivid depth of color visible today. This technique was adapted from the jewelry-making methodology of the region (Elam), and shows similarity with Elamite cloisonné, a technique of inlaying jewelry with colored stones.

A spectacular example of this art is the decorative scene known as the Frieze of Archers. (See fig. 76. The Marcel Dieulafoy expedition of 1884-86 found enough bricks to make possible this relief.) These panels contain two rows of archers, who have been interpreted as slowly marching toward one another in parade fashion, bows and quivers slung over their shoulders. The ends of the bows are shaped like a duck's head. Each archer has both hands clasped around the shaft of a spear held vertically. The butts of the spears are finished in a knob that rests on the front foot of a soldier, and the soldiers are shod with laced ankle-boots. The long robes they wear indicate a formal dress "uniform" rather than a field costume for war. The posture of the archers, however, particu-

76. Frieze made of glazed bricks from the palace at Susa showing a group of archers (AOD 488)

larly with the spear being held atop the front foot, seems to militate against a depiction of marching soldiers. Rather, the pose appears to reflect stationary figures who may be the court bodyguard of the king, as some have suggested; perhaps these are the crack troops who formed part of the royal guard of Darius, called "the Immortals" by Herodotus. Exactly where in the palace these figures once stood is unknown, since portions of the relief were found scattered over a wide area. However, the number of bricks found in the vicinity of the western entrance to the palace suggests that area as a likely possibility for their original location.

Various museums in the world have examples of these magnificent reliefs, as well as colossal bull figures and other objects pertaining to Darius I: the Museum of the Ancient Orient in Istanbul, the British Museum, the Oriental Institute Museum (University of Chicago), and an extensive collection at the Louvre, among others. For example, in addition to other friezes of archers, the Louvre (in rooms 12a to 15, ground floor, Sully Wing, section 4) also contains friezes of lions (AOD 489a, AOD 489b, and AOD 489c); a frieze of two sphinxes, with winged lion bodies and human faces (Sb 3324 and Sb 3325; see plate 8); two friezes of a griffin (Sb 3326 and Sb 3327); a colossal capital from a column of the palace (AOD 1; see plate 9); a column base with an inscription of Darius (Sb 2715); two foundation bricks with the name of Darius (Sb 14084, Sb 15567); three bricks with foundation inscriptions of Darius in three languages, Babylonian, Elamite, and Old Persian (Sb 3342, Sb 3341, Sb 3340); two foundation documents of Darius (Sb 2789, Sb 9722); a small administrative tablet that reports the distribution of rations of oil and contains an imprint of the seal of Darius (Sb 13078); and a fragment of a stela commemorating the opening of a canal between the Nile and the Red Sea by the king (AO 2251). The British Museum has a relief panel of a guard with a spear (ME 132525; room 52) and a cylinder seal of Darius shooting lions (ME 89132; room 52); and the New York Metropolitan Museum of Art has a gold bowl inscribed with the name and titles of Darius (54.3.1; Ancient Near Eastern Art Gallery, second floor), though it is uncertain whether the name refers to Darius I or Darius II. The Oriental Institute Museum in Chicago has a stone weight, inscribed in Old Persian, Elamite, and Babylonian with the words, "I am Darius, Great King, King of Kings, King of Countries, King in this earth, son of Hystaspes, an Achaemenian." The stone was likely used as an official standard weight against which other weights were measured. The stone (OIM A23316; Persian Gallery) weighs ca. 10 lbs., 13 oz. and is made of diorite.

Biblical Significance

Darius was not the Persian king who released the Jews from Babylonian captivity — that remarkable event occurred under King Cyrus — but he nevertheless holds a place in Jewish memory for an important act related to the earlier act of deliverance. According to the Hebrew Scriptures, when the returning Jews began the process of rebuilding the temple of Jerusalem, they were challenged as to their authority to do so. It was only by the further authorization of Darius that they were able to continue and thus construct the second temple:

> Then Zerubbabel son of Shealtiel and Jeshua son of Jozadak set out to rebuild the house of God in Jerusalem; and with them were the prophets of God, helping them. . . .
>
> The copy of the letter that Tattenai the governor of the province Beyond the River . . . sent to King Darius; they sent him a report, in which was written as follows: "To Darius the king, all peace! May it be known to the king that we went to the province of Judah, to the house of the great God. It is being built of hewn stone, and timber is laid in the walls; this work is being done diligently and prospers in their hands. Then we spoke to those elders and asked them, 'Who gave you a decree to build this house and finish this structure?' We also asked them their names, for your information, so that we might write down the names of the men at their head. This was their reply to us: 'We are the servants of the God of heaven and earth, and we are rebuilding the house that was built many years ago, which a great king of Israel built and finished. But because our ancestors had angered the God of heaven, he gave them into the hand of King Nebuchadnezzar of Babylon, the Chaldean, who destroyed this house and carried away the people to Babylonia. However, King Cyrus of Babylon, in the first year of his reign, made a decree that this house of God should be rebuilt. Moreover, the gold and silver vessels of the house of God, which Nebuchadnezzar had taken out of the temple in Jerusalem and had brought into the temple of Babylon, these King Cyrus took out of the temple of Babylon, and they were delivered to a man named Sheshbazzar, whom he had made governor. He said to him, "Take these vessels; go and put them in the temple in Jerusalem, and let the house of God be rebuilt on its site." . . .' And now, if it seems good to the king, have a search made in the royal archives there in Babylon, to see whether a decree was issued by King Cyrus for the rebuilding of this house of God in Jerusalem. Let the king send us his pleasure in this matter."
>
> Then King Darius made a decree, and they searched the archives where the documents were stored in Babylon. But it was in Ecbatana, the capital in the province of Media [one of the four palaces of Cyrus], that a scroll was found on which this was written: "A record. In the first year of his reign, King Cyrus issued a decree: Concerning the house of God at Jerusalem, let the house be rebuilt, the place where sacrifices are offered and burnt offerings are brought; . . . let the cost be paid from the royal treasury. . . ."

"Now you, Tattenai . . . keep away; let the work on this house of God alone; let the governor of the Jews and the elders of the Jews rebuild this house of God on its site. . . . The cost is to be paid to these people, in full and without delay, from the royal revenue. . . . Whatever is needed — young bulls, rams, or sheep for burnt offerings to the God of heaven, wheat, salt, wine, or oil, as the priests in Jerusalem require — let that be given to them day by day without fail, so that they may offer pleasing sacrifices to the God of heaven, and pray for the life of the king and his children. . . . I, Darius, make a decree; let it be done with all diligence." (Ezra 5:2–6:12)

Unfortunately for biblical history, neither the original decree of Cyrus nor the record of the verification of Darius has ever been found. However, the names and places and the biblical record do correspond with external data in other Persian inscriptions (Ecbatana as a capital, Tattenai as governor in the west, "Beyond the River," etc.). At least the magnificent artifacts from the palaces of Darius allow us to view the power and wealth of this foreign ruler who is credited not only with giving permission to the Jews to rebuild their temple, but also with providing funds both for its rebuilding and for the sacrifices of the people. Darius may well have pursued such a policy of generosity toward the religious practices of the former captive peoples of Babylon, just as did Cyrus, not only that they would "pray for the life of the king and his children," but that they might live quietly on the borders of his empire.

Column Capital from Persepolis

Limestone column capital

▷ Size: 1.75 m. (5.74 ft.) high; 80 cm. (31.5 in.) wide; length of portion on display is approximately 80 cm. (31.5 in.)
▷ Provenance: Persepolis (in modern Iran)
▷ Date: Fifth century B.C.E.
▷ Present location: Oriental Institute Museum of the University of Chicago (Persian Gallery)
▷ Identification number: OIM A24066

Xerxes I, the son of Darius I, ascended the Persian throne in November 486 B.C.E. following the death of his father. The first task confronting the new king was the suppression of a revolt in Egypt that had begun a few months before his father's death. Soon after quelling this uprising in January 484 B.C.E., a revolt erupted in Babylon, which Xerxes' forces decisively crushed after putting Babylon under siege. The city's fortifications were destroyed, the temple of Marduk (called the Esagila) and the great ziggurat were severely damaged, and the great golden statue of Marduk, the supreme Babylonian god, was reportedly carried to Persepolis and melted down. The most significant, as well as most disastrous, military campaign of the Persians during the reign of Xerxes was the invasion of Greece in 480 B.C.E. The Persians achieved initial success with their famous victory at Thermopylae and advanced toward Athens, capturing and burning down the city, including the Acropolis. The Persians did not have long to savor their victory, however, for the following month the Persian navy suffered defeat by the Greeks in the Gulf of Salamis. In 479, the Greeks delivered a decisive defeat of the Persian army at the battle of Salamis, and the Persians withdrew from Greece.

During his reign, Xerxes embarked on several building programs, including construction of several buildings at Persepolis and Susa. Little information is known about the last fourteen years of Xerxes' reign. He was murdered in August of 465 B.C.E., although the circumstances surrounding his death are cloudy. Apparently he was killed in his bedroom by Artabanus, the commander of the palace guard. The question is whether one of Xerxes' sons was also involved. Some ancient writers say that Artaxerxes I, the youngest son of Xerxes, instigated the death of his father (Xerxes had at least three sons). Other ancient sources place the blame on Darius, the oldest son. Regardless of who was to blame, Artaxerxes emerged the winner, for he took over the throne, killed his brother Darius, and eventually killed Artabanus (who was also plotting to kill Artaxerxes).

The column capital pictured here (fig. 77) was discovered at Persepolis by the Oriental Institute of Chicago during its Persepolis Expedition from 1931 to 1939. The capital and column were part of the roof supports for the Central Building (also known as the Tripylon or the Council Hall), located on the terrace of Persepolis. The Central Building was begun by Xerxes and finished during the reign of Artaxerxes I. The capital originally consisted of matching double figures, arranged back to back. (Only half of the double figure is on display.) The figure has the legs, body, and ears of a bull, and the bearded face of a man. Its chest appears to be covered with feathers, and it wears a crown and large, dangling, pendant earrings. A wooden roof beam would have rested on the creatures' backs.

A similar double-figure column capital is in the same room in the Oriental Institute Museum. As is the case with the other capital, the figures on this capital (OIM A26070) are bulls, except these have bull faces instead of hu-

77. Part a column capital shaped like a human-headed bull, from Persepolis

man faces. The horns and ears are missing (they were made separately), and part of the capital has been restored. The capital, which was discovered in the west portico of the *apadana* (audience hall) at Persepolis, has been placed on top of a reconstruction of a column (OIM A24069) similar to those used at Persepolis and other Persian centers. Also in the Persian Gallery at the Oriental Institute Museum is a colossal bull's head made of dark grey limestone (OIM A24065) that originally belonged to one of two colossal bull statues that guarded the portico of the Hall of a Hundred Columns at the palace complex at Persepolis. Construction of the Hall of a Hundred Columns was started by Xerxes, but completed after his death by his son Artaxerxes I. The colossal bull's head weighs approximately ten tons.

An astrological tablet now in the British Museum (ME 1876-11-17, 1961/ 32234; room 52) provides the most exact known evidence for the date of the death of Xerxes. Written in cuneiform script, this clay tablet, whose contents are yet to be published, provides reports of lunar eclipses, arranged in eighteen-year groups. On the reverse side of the tablet, the beginning of column four describes an eclipse that took place on June 5-6, 465 B.C.E. The text also mentions that in that year, between the fourteenth and eighteenth day of the Babylonian month of Abu (which would be between August 4 and 8; the number of the day of the month is not well-preserved and could be any number between fourteen and eighteen), "Xerxes' son killed him."[1] Unfortunately the text does not specify which son killed the king.

Additional items related to Xerxes can be seen in the British Museum, the Louvre, and the Oriental Institute Museum in Chicago. Among these items are the following:

1. Matthew W. Stolper, "Some Ghost Facts from Achaemenid Babylonian Texts," *The Journal of Hellenic Studies* 108 (1988): 196.

1. A vase fragment on display in room 52 of the British Museum (ME 91459). The fragment contains a portion of a trilingual inscription in Old Persian, Elamite, and Babylonian cuneiform. The complete inscription would have read, "Xerxes, the great king." This same trilingual inscription, along with an Egyptian hieroglyphic version of the inscription, is on a complete alabaster vase that was restored from various fragments (ME 1857.20-20.1/ 132114). It can be seen in room 15 of the British Museum.

2. Inscribed vases and fragments in the Louvre. On display in room 14, ground floor, Sully Wing, section 4, is an alabaster vase (AO 2634) inscribed with the name of Xerxes in Old Persian, Elamite, and Babylonian cuneiform, as well as in Egyptian hieroglyphs. Another vase (Sb 561) has been reconstructed from fragments (some of which are missing), with an inscription in Old Persian, Elamite, and Babylonian cuneiform that reads, "Xerxes, the great king." It also contains an Egyptian inscription that reads, "King of Upper and Lower Egypt, lord of the double country, Xerxes, who lives eternally, Year 2." The same room also contains a fragment from an alabaster vase with the name of Xerxes (Sb 564; see fig. 78) and a fragment of a green stone dish bearing the royal title of Xerxes I (Sb 548).

3. Inscribed column bases. Room 15 of the Louvre (ground floor, Sully Wing, section 4) displays two limestone column bases from Susa (Sb 10056, Sb 131), each with a trilingual inscription in Old Persian, Elamite, and Babylonian that reads, "Xerxes, the king, says: by the grace of Ahura Mazda, this residence Darius, the king, has constructed, he who was my father." The columns were likely a part of the palace built by Darius at Susa.

4. Inscribed fragments from dishes. A display case in the Persian Gallery of the Oriental Institute Museum contains several pieces from stone plates, each originally inscribed around its outer rim in Old Persian, Elamite, Babylonian, and Egyptian with the words, "Xerxes, the great king." (The Egyptian text reads, "Xerxes, pharaoh, the great.") An adjacent case contains a variety of other fragments and small items found at Persepolis.

5. A limestone foundation document (OIM A24120). Located in the Persian Gallery of the Oriental Institute Museum, this large stone was inscribed on both sides and proclaims the titles and attributes of Xerxes, describes the countries that were under his rule, and tells of his restoration of the proper worship of Ahuramazda.

6. Architectural pieces. These pieces, which are also displayed in the Persian Gallery of the Oriental Institute Museum, both came from Persepolis. The carved limestone window lintel (OIM A24074) was discovered in the harem of King Xerxes. The carved stone canopy (OIM A24068) was found near one of the residential palaces of Darius, where it had been reused in the balustrade for a stairway. The carving on the canopy depicts a row of striding lions.

Biblical Significance

Xerxes I is one of the major characters in the story of Esther in the Hebrew Bible, although in the story he is known as King Ahasuerus, "who ruled over one hundred twenty-seven provinces from India to Ethiopia" (1:1). The story of Esther is set within the court of Xerxes in the city of Susa. After Queen Vashti is banished and stripped of her royal status for refusing to obey the king's order that she appear at his banquet "in order to show the peoples and the officials her beauty" (1:11), a contest is held to choose a new queen. Esther (whose Hebrew name was Hadassah), a young girl whose Jewish identity is kept secret, is chosen to be the next queen. Haman, one of the king's officials and the villain of the story, becomes furious when Esther's cousin (and adopted father) Mordecai refuses to bow down before him in respect. As an act of revenge, Haman plots to have all the Jews in the kingdom killed. Risking her own life to save her people, Esther goes before the king and ultimately saves her people from the planned pogrom. In a delightful ironic twist in the story's plot, the evil Haman ends up being hanged on the very gallows he had ordered constructed for the execution of Mordecai.

78. Fragment of a vase with the name of Xerxes I in hieroglyphics, now in the Louvre (Sb 54)

Because the story of Esther is filled with so many historical difficulties and improbabilities (for example, Xerxes' queen throughout his reign was Amestris; no record exists of Vashti or Esther as queen), most scholars understand the book to be a work of fiction. Its purpose was likely to establish a historical basis for the Jewish festival of Purim, a popular carnival-like festival that celebrates Esther's saving of her people through her courage and initiative. Although the origin of the festival is uncertain, Purim may be an adaptation of a Persian spring New Year festival. The book of Esther was one of the Jewish writings whose place in the Jewish canon was questioned, in part because the book never mentions God. Its place in the canon was likely secured because of its close connection with the festival of Purim.

Silver Bowl of Artaxerxes I

Inscribed silver bowl

▷ Size: 4.8 cm. (1.89 in.) high; 29.5 cm. (11.61 in.) diameter
▷ Writing: Old Persian language in cuneiform script
▷ Provenance: Persia (modern Iran); exact provenance unknown
▷ Date: Fifth century B.C.E.
▷ Present location: Freer Gallery of Art of the Smithsonian Institution in Washington, D.C. (in a wall-mounted case outside gallery 9)
▷ Identification number: F1974.30

This silver bowl in the Freer Gallery of Art is one of four very similar silver bowls found before 1935 with identical inscriptions, although with slight variations in size and weight. This type of bowl or saucer, known by its Greek name *phialē*, was used as a wine-drinking vessel. Such bowls are particularly interesting because the Bible mentions that Nehemiah was a "cup-bearer" to King Artaxerxes (Neh. 1:11; 2:1). The role of the cup-bearer was to serve the wine to the king, after having tasted it to make sure it was safe. Nothing is known about the discovery or original owners of the bowls. Of the other three bowls, one was purchased by the Metropolitan Museum of Art in New York, one is in the British Museum (ME 1994,0127.1; room 52), and one is in the Resa Abbasi Collection in Tehran. The bowl in the Freer Gallery is composed of very high quality silver (approximately 96 to 97 percent pure silver) and was crafted from a single sheet of silver. The embossed decoration on the bowl features a stylized lotus flower design with fourteen petals and oval-shaped buds. The authenticity of the bowl is supported by its similarity in design and size to several other Persian bowls from this time period. Engraved on the flared rim of the bowl is an inscription in Old Persian cuneiform that reads, "Artaxerxes the Great King, King of Kings, King of Countries, son of Xerxes the King, of Xerxes [who was] son of Darius the King; in whose house this silver saucer was made."[1] Although earlier

---

1. Translation by Roland Kent, cited in Ann C. Gunter and Paul Jett, *Ancient Iranian Metalwork in the Arthur M. Sackler Gallery and the Freer Gallery of Art* (Washington, D.C.: Smithsonian Institution, 1992), p. 69.

doubts were raised about the authenticity of the inscription due to grammatical errors and unattested vocabulary, its authenticity is now generally accepted.

The Artaxerxes who is named in the inscription is Artaxerxes I Longimanus, Persian king of the Achaemenid Dynasty who ruled from 465 to 424 B.C.E. ("Longimanus," meaning "long arm," is the nickname given to him by the Greeks because his right arm was longer than his left.) Artaxerxes came to the throne after his father, Xerxes, had been assassinated by Artabanus, the commander of the palace guard. In the ensuing struggles for control of Persia, Artaxerxes, son of Xerxes, claimed the throne and killed his older brother Darius and eventually the conspirator Artabanus, who was planning to kill Artaxerxes. (Some ancient writers implicate Darius in his father's murder and say that is why Artaxerxes killed him. Others blame Artaxerxes for being the instigator behind the plot to kill his father.) These struggles for the Persian throne created an opportunity for Egypt to revolt against Persian control, an uprising that was encouraged and supported by Athens, but eventually suppressed by Artaxerxes. The Persian king encountered additional troubles from Athens, including an attack on Cyprus, which was under Persian control. Finally in 449 B.C.E., in a treaty known as the Peace of Callias, Persia and Athens reached an agreement: Athens would not intervene in affairs in Egypt or Cyprus, and Persia would not meddle with the Greek cities along the southern and western coasts of Asia Minor that were in league with Athens. Artaxerxes

79. A silver bowl inscribed with the name of Artaxerxes I, now in the Freer Gallery of Art

died in 424 B.C.E. in Susa. After his death, his son Xerxes II assumed power, but he was assassinated after reigning for only a few weeks.

Biblical Significance

Artaxerxes is mentioned several times in the books of Ezra and Nehemiah (Ezra 4:7, 8, 11, 23; 6:14; 7:1, 7, 11, 12, 21; 8:1; Neh. 2:1; 5:14; 13:6). Unfortunately, the texts do not specify which of at least three Persian kings with the name of Artaxerxes is meant. The question is whether the references are to Artaxerxes I or to Artaxerxes II, who ruled from 404 to 359 B.C.E. Ezra and Nehemiah both were individuals who returned to Jerusalem after the end of the exile, leading groups of returnees and helping to restructure and govern Judean society. Although there are some apparent discrepancies in the arrangement of the materials in Ezra and Nehemiah and in some of the historical references, the Ezra-Nehemiah texts present Ezra's return and work in Jerusalem as preceding the return of Nehemiah. Almost all scholars are agreed that Nehemiah's activities occurred during the reign of Artaxerxes I (from 445 B.C.E. to ca. 432 B.C.E.). If the traditional arrangement is correct, then Ezra also was active during the time of Artaxerxes I (beginning in 458 B.C.E.), which is the view held by most scholars today. Thus Artaxerxes I was the Persian ruler during the time of Nehemiah and likely during the time of Ezra as well. (Some scholars, however, have proposed that Ezra's return to Jerusalem actually occurred after the time of Nehemiah and place his activity during the time of Artaxerxes II [beginning in 398 B.C.E.]).

Ezra 4:7-24, which is out of order chronologically, contains a letter sent by some of Jerusalem's neighbors (Persian officials and foreign settlers in the satrapy of Samaria) to Artaxerxes, warning him not to allow the city of Jerusalem to be rebuilt because it had a history of being a rebellious city. Artaxerxes then responded with a letter to the Samaritan officials, authorizing them to order the cessation of the rebuilding efforts. Ezra 6:14 gives Artaxerxes partial credit, along with Cyrus and Darius, for completing the rebuilding of the Jerusalem temple. In reality, the temple was completed in 516/515 B.C.E., several decades before the time of Artaxerxes.

Ezra 7 reports on a letter that Artaxerxes gave to Ezra authorizing the return to Jerusalem of exiles, granting Ezra religious and judicial duties, and requiring the officials of the satrapy of Samaria to provide financial assistance. Upon his return, Ezra instituted measures to ensure the preservation of the Jewish religious and ethnic identity, including forbidding intermarriage with foreigners. Most importantly, he brought back with him from Babylonia a copy of "the law of your God," which he used as the basis for a covenant renewal ceremony for the people of Jerusalem.

Nehemiah had been serving as a cup-bearer to King Artaxerxes (Neh. 1:11; 2:1) when the king sent him to Jerusalem as governor. In spite of opposition from Sanballat, the governor of Samaria, Nehemiah succeeded in rebuilding the wall of Jerusalem, improving the economic situation in the city, and initiating religious reforms such as proper observance of the Sabbath. Nehemiah remained in Jerusalem for approximately twelve years (Neh. 5:14) and then apparently returned to Persia. Shortly afterwards, he went once more to Jerusalem with the permission of Artaxerxes (13:6-31), again carrying out religious reforms.

Column Base with Inscription of Artaxerxes II

Limestone column base

▷ Size: 58 cm. (22.83 in.) high; 89 cm. (35.04 in.) diameter
▷ Writing: Old Persian, Elamite, and Babylonian languages
▷ Provenance: Susa in Persia (modern Iran)
▷ Date: 404-359 B.C.E.
▷ Present location: Louvre (room 15, ground floor, Sully Wing, section 4)
▷ Identification number: AOD 14

This bell-shaped column base in the Louvre was found in the ruins at Susa, one of the capital cities of ancient Persia. The base contains an inscription carved around its edge, written in cuneiform script in three languages — Old Persian, Elamite, and Babylonian. The inscription reads, "I, Artaxerxes, the Great King, King of Kings, son of Darius, the King." The column base was discovered by Marcel Dieulafoy at Susa during his archaeological expedition from 1885 to 1886. Dieulafoy found the base in the ruins of the so-called "donjon" palace, a late (Hellenistic, Parthian, or Sasanian) building at the southernmost tip of the site. The Achaemenid architectural ruins found here are thought to have been reused pieces from earlier buildings. (The Achaemenid period refers to the Persian dynasty of Cyrus and his successors, 559-330 B.C.E.) The king who is the subject of the inscription is Artaxerxes II, king of Persia from 404 to 359 B.C.E. Artaxerxes II, son of Darius II and grandson of Artaxerxes I, was faced with troubles throughout much of his reign, starting with his brother Cyrus, who tried to seize the throne for himself. Cyrus raised an army, composed partially of Greek mercenaries, and marched against Artaxerxes. Cyrus not only lost the battle, but he also lost his life. The Persian king soon was faced with troubles from Egypt, Sparta, Athens, and Asia Minor. Artaxerxes lost control over Egypt in 401 B.C.E., but reached an agreement called the "King's Peace" (or, the "Peace of Antalcidas") with Sparta and Athens in 386 that recognized Persian authority over the Greek cities of Asia Minor and over Cyprus. During his long reign of forty-six years, Artaxerxes completed several building projects, including restoring the palace built by Darius I at Susa, which had been destroyed by a fire

80. Base of a column from Susa containing the name of Artaxerxes II

during the closing days of the reign of Artaxerxes I. It was at this time that the column bases inscribed with his name were put in place. He also rebuilt part of the palace at Ecbatana.

The British Museum displays two fragments from other column bases inscribed with the name of Artaxerxes II. These fragments, ME 90854 and ME 90855, are located in room 52. Both of the fragments were discovered before 1885 at Hamadan (Ecbatana in ancient Persia). The inscription, written in Old Persian, Elamite, and Babylonian, was the same on both columns. One fragment preserves part of the inscription in the Elamite and Babylonian languages; the other fragment preserves a portion of the inscription in Old Persian and Babylonian. The complete inscription would have read:

> Saith Artaxerxes the Great King, King of Kings, King of Countries, King in this earth, son of Darius the King, of Darius [who was] son of Artaxerxes the king, of Artaxerxes [who was] son of Xerxes the King, of Xerxes who was son of Darius the King, of Darius who was son of Hystaspes, an Achaemenian. By the favour of Ahuramazda, Anahita and Mithra, this palace [*apadana*] I built. May Ahuramazda, Anahita and Mithra protect me from all evil, and that which I have built may they not shatter or harm.[1]

1. John Curtis and Shahrokh Razmjou, "The Palace," in *Forgotten Empire: The World of Ancient Persia,* ed. John Curtis and Nigel Tallis (London: The British Museum Press, 2005), p. 61.

Biblical Significance

The Bible contains no unambiguous reference to Artaxerxes II. Several passages in Ezra and Nehemiah mention a Persian king named Artaxerxes, but fail to specify which Artaxerxes is meant. (See the article "Silver Bowl of Artaxerxes I.") Whereas the Artaxerxes who was king during the time of Nehemiah was almost certainly Artaxerxes I, some scholars have argued that the Artaxerxes during the time of Ezra was Artaxerxes II. If this identification is correct (which is not accepted by most scholars), then Artaxerxes II was the king who authorized the return of Ezra, along with other exiles, gave orders to provincial treasurers to provide financial assistance to Ezra, and decreed to Ezra that "all who will not obey the law of your God and the law of the king, let judgment be strictly executed on them" (Ezra 7:26).

The Hellenistic Period

Statue and Head of Alexander the Great

Marble statue and head

▷ Size: Statue — 1.9 m. (6.23 ft.) high; head — 42 cm. (16.54 in.) high
▷ Provenance: Statue — Magnesia on the Sipylum (modern Manisa, Turkey); head — Pergamum (modern Bergama, Turkey)
▷ Date: Statue — mid-third century B.C.E.; head — first half of the second century B.C.E.
▷ Present location: Archaeological Museum, Istanbul (ground floor, hall 16)
▷ Identification number: Statue — 709; head — 1138.

These two striking images of Alexander the Great are representative of the many sculptures of him to be found in numerous world museums. (Another well-known bust of the youthful Alexander, often pictured, is in the British Museum [GR 1872.5-15.1; sculpture 1857, room 22].) This statue of Alexander (fig. 81) shows him poised, as if ready for action, his left leg advanced, with the knee bent slightly forward. His left hand rests on the hilt of his sword, the scabbard of which is concealed beneath his robe. Originally his right arm likely was raised and held a bronze spear. His shock of wavy hair, his prominent eyebrows, and his head tilted to one side and slightly upward, all are typical characteristics of portraits of Alexander. The sculpture of his head (fig. 82) likewise shows the same features, with the hair parting in the middle to either side, another recognizable characteristic of portrayals of him.

This larger than life-size statue was found with an inscription attributing the work to a sculptor of Pergamum: "Menas of Pergamum, son of Aias, made [it]." The rendering of the work overall strongly resembles similar statues of Apollo and is clearly in the style of Pergamene art in the Hellenistic age. The sculpture of Alexander's head was found during excavations on the lower agora of Pergamum and might have fallen there from the upper terrace, perhaps even from the Great Altar of Pergamum, where perhaps it was part of the many reliefs of its decoration. The style of this image reflects a fourth-century B.C.E. portrait of Alexander by the sculptor Lysippos and is typical of Pergamene art during the reign of King Eumenes II.

A recent traveling exhibition of museum objects entitled "Treasures of Alexander the Great" did not contain a single item that once belonged to Alexander; all of the objects were related to Philip II, his father. Unfortunately, except for coins and statues, nothing at all remains of the possessions of Alexander the Great. To experience the atmosphere of his world, one must travel to the tombs of the Macedonian kings in Vergina, Greece (some fifty miles west of Thessaloniki), preserved in a magnificent modern, below-ground museum.

There the spectacular marble doors to the tombs of his father and his brother (Alexander IV) may be seen, as well as the golden ossuary, oak leaf diadem, and magnificent shield of Philip II. The tomb of Alexander himself, along with his mummified remains — which originally rested in Memphis, Egypt, then moved to Alexandria, and finally (by Ptolemy Philopater, 221-204 B.C.E.) to a communal mausoleum in Alexandria — has long since disappeared. It was visited by a lengthy succession of Roman emperors and generals, including Augustus (30 B.C.E.), who placed a golden diadem on the mummified head of Alexander, and Caracalla (215 C.E.), but it disappeared sometime in the third century C.E. and by the fourth century its location was no longer known.

Though the life of Alexander was brief (356-323 B.C.E.), it was filled with incredible complexity and almost immeasurable influence. Born to Philip II of Macedon and his fourth wife, Olympias, Alexander had a remarkable upbringing. His ability to ride the great stallion, Bucephalus, which had never been ridden, became legendary. (That accomplishment was a matter of some reassurance to his father, who been concerned that the boy showed some effeminate characteristics.) Alexander was tutored by the famous philosopher, Aristotle, and he retained an interest in history and natural science throughout his life. Nevertheless, he was intensely superstitious and fascinated by oracles of any sort, never passing a chance to visit the site of any famous oracle. Although he stood only five feet, five inches tall, he was noted for his incredible, often foolhardy daring. Alexander quickly had proved himself a skilled cavalry officer as he fought in his father's army. He also had a reputation as a

81. Marble statue of Alexander the Great in the Archaeological Museum in Istanbul

swift runner, and once raced against an Olympic champion in Athens. (When Alexander perceived that the runner had allowed him to win, he chided him severely and told him never to do such a thing again.)

His troubles with his family, particularly with his father, were as legendary as his skill on the battlefield. Philip had taken another wife who, unlike Olympias, was a pure-blooded Macedonian princess. (Olympias was from Epirus, a province to the southwest.) During the wedding feast, Philip defended one of his noblemen, Attalus, uncle of the bride, who had given a toast implying that Philip could at last have a legitimate son. Enraged, Alexander hurled his goblet at Attalus. Instead of defending Alexander, Philip attempted to draw his sword and attack his son. But he tripped and fell to the floor, which prompted Alexander to say sarcastically, "That, gentlemen, is the man who has been preparing to cross from Europe into Asia — and he can't even make it from one couch to the next!"[1] Olympias and Alexander then fled to her home in Epirus, thus becoming bitter enemies of Philip.

Subsequently, at the wedding of his daughter at the small theater beside the old ancestral palace of Aegae (on the hill above modern Vergina), Philip was assassinated by one of his own bodyguards, a former lover, who was killed trying to escape. Philip and most of his Macedonian nobles practiced homosexuality, particularly with boys and young men, and this bodyguard had been gang-raped during a drunken party. Philip had nothing to do with it, but he also had ignored the young man's pleas for justice. Although it is impossible to establish historically, it is generally believed that Olympias and Alexander, or one of them alone, arranged the murder. The subsequent events, however, are not in question. Olympias put a golden crown on the head of the dead assassin, and every year thereafter she poured libations on his grave on the anniversary of the event. Alexander immediately seized power, and in a series of rapid events solidified his hold on Macedonia, and from there to Athens and all of Greece with the exception of the Peloponnesus.

Motivated by a desire to exceed his famous father, and an equally burning desire to exact vengeance against the Persians for their attacks on Greece more than one hundred years before, Alexander mobilized an army of ten thousand and proceeded to return the cities of Asia (the coastal district of western Turkey) to Greek control. His many battles against the Persians, his defeat of King Darius and his implacable search for the remaining Persian leaders, his incredible tactics that led to the subjugation of the island city of Tyre, his experiences in taking Egypt and visiting the oracle at the Silwan oasis, and his incredible incursion into India that (to his frustration) terminated at the Indus river after

---

1. Peter Green, *Alexander of Macedon* (Los Angeles: University of California Press, 1991), p. 89.

an eight-year campaign — these and many other exploits are too complex to explore in this context. (It is often claimed that Alexander "wept because he had no more worlds to conquer" — actually, he pouted because his exhausted Macedonians would follow him no farther.) Nevertheless, in each of these adventures Alexander showed himself to be an unmatched field general, devising unique tactics as each challenge presented itself. His personal courage at the head of his troops was never questioned, and he was often wounded. Also, however, he frequently displayed paranoia and rashness in his personal decisions, often following repeated bouts of drunkenness. At the last, Alexander insisted on leading his men back to Babylon from India by the southern desert route and lost the majority of his troops in doing so. By the time he died of fever shortly after reaching Babylon, there could have been few who re-

82. A sculpture of the head of Alexander the Great found at Pergamum

gretted his death. Typically, he was already planning to attack and conquer the entire Arabian Peninsula, and had further dreams of a later invasion of Spain.

The famous mosaic of the battle of Issus (as this scene is usually interpreted), which depicts Alexander's defeat of the army of Darius III of Persia in 333 B.C.E., was found at Pompeii in a large private residence referred to as the House of the Faun (see plate 10). Even though Alexander won this battle and forced Darius to retreat, the Persian king and his forces continued to be a problem for Alexander until 331 B.C.E. when Darius was seized and murdered by rebel Persian satraps (governors), who were themselves killed by Alexander. The scene portrays the turning point at Issus when Darius fled the battle. Originally a floor mosaic, the object is now on display on a wall in room 61 of the National Archaeological Museum in Naples, Italy. The mosaic (museum inventory number 10020), dated to ca. 100 B.C.E., measures 3.13 m. (10.27 ft.) by 5.82 m. (19.09 ft.). It is thought to be a copy of an earlier Greek painting or fresco.

Biblical Significance

The process of Hellenization — the spreading of Greek culture — had begun long before the time of Alexander. Merchants and travelers, as well as the ruling Persians themselves, had already transmitted many elements of Greek culture to the Near East before the invasions of Alexander, but there can be no doubt that he solidified its hold on the region. The ten cities known as the Decapolis, established in the territories of Israel, Jordan, and Syria, became centers for Greek trade and culture. Whereas the Greek language previously had been an option for a few intellectuals, after Alexander it became the essential language of the ancient world. As such, it had the effect of tying cultures together and facilitating communication across national lines. Without the prevalence of the Greek language, the Hebrew Scriptures would have remained in a little-known, obscure dialect, but their translation into Greek in the edition of the scriptures known as the Septuagint made the history and tradition of the Jews accessible to the world. The New Testament, of course, was written in Greek, which was responsible in no little part for its availability to the Roman world and facilitated the unifying, egalitarian nature of the organization known as the Christian church.

Nevertheless, the Jews could hardly have been happy when Alexander invaded Palestine in 332 B.C.E., since their life under the Persians had been considerably more independent than they had known previously. Once Alexander died, the division of his kingdom among his four generals — most notably, for Israel, among Seleucus in Syria and Ptolemy in Egypt — resulted in almost continual warfare between the two factions over Israel. The triumph of the Seleucids led to the reign of Antiochus IV, who desecrated the temple in Jerusalem and banned the practice of the Jewish religion and whose brutality is chronicled in the books of Maccabees. The Maccabean rebellion eventually succeeded in throwing off the yoke of the Syrian Greeks, but it was one of the darkest days of Jewish history. Perhaps it should not be surprising, given the complex mixture of genius and brutality in Alexander, that his legacy in the land of the Bible should be equally mixed.

Head and Coin of Antiochus IV

Marble head and silver tetradrachma

- ▷ Size: Head — 24.3 cm. (9.57 in.) high; coin — 30 mm. (1.18 in.) diameter
- ▷ Provenance: Head — unknown; coin — unknown
- ▷ Date: Head — ca. 170 B.C.E.; coin — ca. 175-164 B.C.E.
- ▷ Present location: Head — Altes Museum, Berlin; coin — Oriental Institute Museum of the University of Chicago (Mesopotamian Gallery)
- ▷ Identification number: Head — 1975.5; coin — OIM A24016

Antiochus IV Epiphanes, one of the most infamous figures in Jewish history, is depicted in this marble portrait head in the Altes Museum in Berlin. Dated to around 170 B.C.E., the sculpture depicts Antiochus wearing a simple diadem, a symbol of royalty, around his hair. A likeness of the Seleucid king is presented also on the silver tetradrachma shown in figure 84. The obverse (front) of the coin contains an image of the head of Antiochus with his hair bound by a diadem, at the end of which are two stars. The reverse of the coin (not shown) pictures Zeus seated on a throne and holding Nike (Victory) in his hand.

After Alexander the Great died in 323 B.C.E., his kingdom was fought over and ultimately divided up by his generals. Among those men were Ptolemy, who gained control of Egypt, and Seleucus, who took possession of Syria, much of Asia Minor, and the northern Mesopotamian region. The Ptolemaic rulers controlled Palestine for approximately one hundred years. Then after the battle of Panias in 198 B.C.E., Palestine came under the Seleucid ruler Antiochus III the Great, whose capital was in Syria. In 175 B.C.E., his son Antiochus IV became the Seleucid king and adopted the surname Epiphanes, an abbreviation of "Theos Epiphanes," which means "god manifest." Antiochus was such an eccentric and unpredictable ruler — sometimes cruel and despotic, other times pleasant and generous — that certain ancient writers, with a play on words in Greek, called him *epimanes* (madman) instead of *epiphanes.*

Antiochus attempted to promote Greek culture throughout his kingdom, including in Palestine. Some of the Jews cooperated with these efforts of Antiochus and were rewarded with leadership roles in the government. When others, however, resisted these Hellenistic influences, Antiochus looted the treasury of the Jewish temple and eventually attempted to outlaw the practice of Judaism. He turned the temple in Jerusalem into a temple to Olympian Zeus and issued a decree that anyone found with a copy of the book of the Law or with a circumcised child was to be put to death. Jews who resisted were massacred or sold into slavery. Several stories of faithful Jews who died gruesome deaths as martyrs for their faith come from this period, including the popular story of the seven brothers and their mother (2 Maccabees 6–7; 4 Maccabees 5–18). Open defiance of Antiochus's efforts led to a revolt

83. Marble head of Antiochus IV Epiphanes

under the initial direction of the priest Mattathias. At his death, leadership was assumed by his son Judas Maccabeus, who succeeded in regaining control of the temple, which was rededicated to the worship of the Jewish god on the twenty-fifth day of the month of Kislev in 164 B.C.E. That event, which was a regaining of religious freedom for the Jews in Jerusalem, is commemorated each year by the celebration of Hanukkah. After the practice of Judaism and worship in the temple was established once more, Judas and some of his supporters continued the struggle, hoping to gain political independence as well. Although this goal was not achieved in the lifetime of Judas, it was accomplished by one of his successors (and brothers) — Simon, who was the first to rule over an independent or semi-independent Jewish nation since the destruction of Jerusalem by the Babylonians in 587 B.C.E.

Biblical Significance

The events surrounding Antiochus IV's attempt to eradicate the practice of Judaism in Palestine, including the martyr stories and the Maccabean Revolt, are recounted in the books of 1 and 2 Maccabees. These writings, part of what is usually known as the deuterocanonical writings or the Apocrypha, provide valuable historical information about the revolt led by Judas Maccabeus and his brothers against the Seleucid rulers and their success in gaining independence for Judea.

Antiochus IV also appears in the book of Daniel in the Hebrew Bible, although he is never mentioned by name. The book of Daniel is written as if it were a product of the period of the Babylonian exile of the Jewish people (sixth

84. Silver tetradrachma containing a likeness of Antiochus IV

century B.C.E.); however, most scholars today would date the actual writing of the book to around 165 B.C.E. — that is, during the time of Antiochus IV and his persecution of the Jews. The stories in the first half of the book that tell of the courage and faithfulness of Daniel and his friends during the exile served as models for the book's readers for how they should respond to the persecutions by Antiochus IV. Thus the book was a literary response to Antiochus IV, just as the Maccabean Revolt led by Judas was a military response to the same crisis. The last half of the book of Daniel contains four visions that present a review of history from the time of the Babylonian Empire to the Hellenistic rulers, culminating in a prediction of God's ultimate victory over the world powers. (The review of history is cast in future tense since it is presented in the form of a vision received by Daniel in the sixth century, prior to the events recounted.) Antiochus appears in chapters 7 and 8 as the "little horn" who arises from among the "ten horns" (i.e., the Hellenistic kings) and as "the prince who is to come" in 9:26-27. The fullest and clearest depiction of Antiochus is in 11:21-45, which gives a resume of his political and military activities. Verses 31-33 recount his taking over the Jerusalem temple and turning it into a temple to Zeus, along with the resistance by some of the faithful Jews and their persecution:

> Forces sent by him shall occupy and profane the temple and fortress. They shall abolish the regular burnt offering and set up the abomination that makes desolate. He shall seduce with intrigue those who violate the covenant; but the people who are loyal to their God shall stand firm and take action. The wise among the people shall give understanding to many; for some days, however, they shall fall by sword and flame, and suffer captivity and plunder.

Although he was initially successful, Antiochus would eventually be destroyed, the author assured his readers, for "he shall come to his end, with none to help him" (11:45). Antiochus may have thought he was a mighty ruler, but in reality he was only an upstart "little horn" who would soon be broken. Thus the readers of the book of Daniel were encouraged to remain faithful to God and not yield to the demands of Antiochus.

The Roman Period

Equestrian Statue of Augustus

Bronze statue

- ▷ Size: Life-size statue
- ▷ Provenance: Found in the Aegean Sea (near Euboea, modern Greece)
- ▷ Date: End of the first century B.C.E. (ca. 10-1 B.C.E.)
- ▷ Present location: National Archaeological Museum, Athens, Greece (room 31)
- ▷ Identification number: 23322

Divers discovered this remarkable bronze statue in the Aegean Sea between the islands of Euboea and Agios Efstratios. It is the only known life-size equestrian statue of Augustus. (Only the top part of the statue has survived.) He is portrayed as sitting on a horse, the reins once held in his left hand, his right hand raised in greeting. The emperor is dressed in a chiton (tunic) with a vertical purple stripe and a fringed cloak with a meander pattern. (The purple stripe is the mark of a senator; the fringed cloak is emblematic of a general.) The museums of the world contain numerous busts and statues of Augustus, some life size, but this representation is unique. Other notable images of the emperor, among many, include: a bronze head of Augustus in room 70 of the British Museum (GR 1911.9–1.1), found at Meroë, Sudan (see plate 11); a larger-than-life-size statue (ca. 2 m. [80 in.] high; "Augustus of Prima Porta") in the Vatican Museums (the Braccio Nuovo) in the Vatican City; a statue in the Louvre (MR 99, also numbered Ma 1278; room 23, ground floor, Denon Wing, section 8); and one head (4026 T) and two busts (385 T and 2165 T) in the Archaeological Museum in Istanbul (ground floor). (One study of busts and statues of Augustus in world museums lists over 120 examples.)

Augustus was born as Gaius Octavius on September 23, 63 B.C.E. His father, Octavius, who died when he was only four years of age, was a senator. His mother, Atia, was the niece of Julius Caesar; young Octavian (as he later was called), therefore, was the great nephew of Julius Caesar. Caesar saw in the boy a future leader, and at the age of seventeen Octavian followed Caesar on his campaign to Spain (45 B.C.E.), where he earned the admiration of the emperor. Subsequently, Caesar named him as his Master of Horse (an official named to be his representative either on the field of battle or in Rome). At the time of the assassination of Caesar, Octavian had been sent ahead to Apollonia in advance of Caesar's planned campaign against the Parthians. Fearful that Octavian might suffer the same fate as the emperor, his friends advised him to take refuge with the army in Macedonia, but on the advice of his family he chose to slip into southern Italy as a common citizen. When he learned that he

85. Upper portion of a bronze statue of Augustus on a horse

had been adopted by Caesar and named in his will, he promptly began calling himself C. Julius Caesar Octavianus, or most simply, Caesar, as Julius Caesar was now his legal father. Octavian used the power of that name to raise an army among those legions still loyal to the memory of Julius Caesar.

The next years were a complicated series of political, and sometimes military, duels with Mark Antony, who was frustrated because Julius Caesar had passed his name and wealth to Octavian instead of to himself. After a series of initial conflicts, Octavian succeeded in persuading Antony, along with another general, Lepidus, to join forces with him. These three formed the Second Triumvirate (the first being Caesar, Pompey, and Crassus) and proceeded to move against Caesar's assassins, Brutus and Cassius. First, however, they eliminated enemies at home by instituting proscriptions against anyone who had opposed them. The orator Cicero, a longtime political enemy of Antony, was one of the first to go. Antony and Octavian then moved east and attacked Cassius and Brutus in October of 42 B.C.E. at Philippi, soundly defeating them. Both of the plotters committed suicide, and the Roman world was divided between Antony and Octavian. Antony took the east; Octavian took most of the west. (Lepidus was relegated to North Africa. His final bid for power against Octavian resulted in his being confined to lifelong house arrest in Sicily.)

The uneasy alliance between Octavian and Antony could not endure long, although military necessities for each forced them to a series of compromises in cooperation against mutual threats. Their massed armies finally met near the promontory of Actium (Greece), but the battle was settled by a naval engagement in which the ships of Antony and Cleopatra were trapped in the harbor, and the two of them barely escaped with their lives to Egypt. Most of Antony's infantry promptly defected to the side of Octavian. Subsequently, Octavian pursued the pair to Alexandria, where Antony's forces were defeated — his navy and cavalry deserted in battle before his very eyes, and his remaining infantry was overwhelmed — and the two lovers committed suicide. Octavian — the new Caesar — was at last master of the Roman world.

In spite of his power, Augustus could not rule without the senate. Their cooperation was required to carry out his orders and provide leadership for the day-to-day functioning of the state. Consequently Augustus became known for his ability to negotiate compromises, and though no one could be crueler when disposing of enemies, his reputation in general was that of a shrewd leader. With the enormous wealth of the empire at his disposal, Augustus was responsible for numerous spectacular building projects, the grandest of which was the forum that bore his name. Of those activities, Augustus reportedly said that he had found Rome a city of brick and left it a city of marble (Suetonius, *Augustus* 28.3). He also made extensive repairs to the road system of the empire, essential both militarily and for commerce; notably, the Via Egnatia, which led to the east. His greatest accomplishment, however, was the Pax Augustus, "the peace of Augustus" — which also inaugurated the Pax Romana, "the peace of Rome" — though it was obtained and maintained at the point of the sword.

Concerning his person, Octavian was not imposing in stature; he stood only five feet, six inches tall, but he was well proportioned and handsome, with a particularly penetrating gaze. At times he had difficulties with his health, but likely no more so than any other person of that age who lived such a long life. He was noted for his insistence on public morality, and he banished his only child, Julia, and her daughter for their profligate behavior with notable men, including certain senators, of Rome. He was frugal in his personal habits, both with regard to food and drink as well as money, and he was never ostentatious in his garb. Augustus would not allow temples to be erected with his name alone on them, insisting that Rome should also be named (such as the Temple of Augustus and Roma at Athens). At times he could be treacherous to allies, but he managed to rule for forty years, longer than any other emperor, by his maneuverings. In 2 B.C.E. the senate named him "Father of the Country." He died peacefully on August 19, 14 C.E. — in the month named for him — and subsequently Augustus was declared to be divine.

Biblical Significance

Among all of the Roman emperors, none exercised more influence over the New Testament world than Caesar Augustus. The words of Luke concerning the birth of Jesus, "In those days a decree went out from Emperor Augustus that all the world should be registered" (Luke 2:1), indicate the sway the emperor had over the various provinces of the Roman Empire. When he spoke, the world — including the world of the New Testament — obeyed. At the time Jesus was born, Augustus would have been about fifty-eight years of age, approximately the age of the mature Augustus portrayed in the equestrian statue. When Augustus died at the age of seventy-six, Jesus would have been in his later teen years.

Though the world of Galilee lay far from the court scenes of imperial Rome, the images of the emperor were everywhere, especially on coins; the face of Augustus would have been known to Jesus, even as a boy. The puppet king of the Jews, Herod the Great, ruled at the pleasure of Augustus. The emperor had reaffirmed Herod's rule in order to maintain the stability of the province of Judea, in spite of the fact that Herod had supported the cause of Mark Antony against him. During the lifetime of Jesus, Roman culture was rapidly expanding in Judea, largely due to the unified nature of the empire under Augustus. Herod did everything in his power to transform Jerusalem into a city that even the Romans would admire; and while the orthodox decried his Romanizing tendencies, and those of his sons, the relative stability of Judea during the lifetime of Jesus and his apostles was due in no small measure to the stability of that empire established by Caesar Augustus. Nevertheless, the death of Jesus and the later persecutions of both Christians and Jews because of the emperor cult are at least partly to be laid at the feet of the inheritance of the Augustan age.

Bust and Silver Denarius of Tiberius

Marble and red breccia bust; silver denarius coin

▷ Size: Bust — 76 cm. (29.92 in.) high; coin — 18 mm. (0.71 in.) diameter
▷ Provenance: Bust — Athens; coin — Rome (place of minting)
▷ Date: Bust — first quarter of the first century C.E.; coin — ca. 36-37 C.E.
▷ Present location: Bust — State Hermitage Museum, St. Petersburg, Russia; coin — Nu-

mismatic Collection, Collection of Classical Antiquities, Pergamum Museum, Berlin (room 17)

▷ Identification number: Bust — A54; coin — 18202610

Images of the emperor Tiberius (14-37 C.E.), while not as numerous as those of Augustus, nonetheless may be found in many of the world's museums: the British Museum, the Louvre, the Vatican Museum, the Ephesus Museum (Seljuk), and the Istanbul Archaeological Museum, among others. This particular bust in the Hermitage Museum (fig. 86) has much to commend it. Composed of marble and spectacular red breccia, it dates to the first quarter of the first century C.E. and therefore is contemporaneous with its subject. Tiberius is portrayed as a young man — apparently obligatory in any representation of Tiberius, who was fifty-six years old when he became emperor. Though the image has certain similarities with that of Tiberius's predecessor, the great Augustus, the features are clearly as described of Tiberius in ancient sources: a sharp, hooked nose, a prominent, pointed chin (characteristics shared in common with his mother, Livia, whose portraits in museums are also numerous), and long hair on the back of his head, which even covered his neck (according to the biography of Suetonius). The wavy locks of hair on this bust extend in back to the edge of his toga. The style of the portrait overall is consistent with Augustan classicism. This portrait head originally was intended for a large statue that was to stand in ancient Athens. It was acquired by John Lyde Brown of London and later purchased by Catherine II of Russia for the imperial collection.

Due to the paucity of objective sources, modern historians find it difficult to analyze the careers and personalities of the Roman emperors. The ancient sources most quoted — Suetonius, Tacitus, Dio Cassius, and Josephus — certainly all had agendas other than objective reporting. Perhaps no emperor is more difficult to assess in these regards than

86. Marble bust of Emperor Tiberius

87. Silver denarius bearing the image of Tiberius

Tiberius. Until recent times, his regime uniformly was regarded as brutal, repressive, and marked by excessive paranoia. As to his personal characteristics, it was agreed that Tiberius was a brilliant military commander, one of the best in Roman history, but greedy, selfish, vindictive, and, in his latter years, guilty of incredible perversions and deviant practices including children and even infants. Modern scholars have called into question some of these negative conclusions, based on the political views of the writers, most particularly with regard to his administration of the empire.

Certain facts of the life and career of Tiberius, however, seem reliable. He was born Tiberius Claudius Nero on November 16, 42 B.C.E.; his mother was Livia Drusilla, his father, Tiberius Nero. His father had supported Mark Antony, and when Octavian (later, Caesar Augustus) demanded that he divorce Livia, even though she was pregnant with her second child, he was forced to agree. Octavian's subsequent marriage to Livia, the mother of Tiberius, caused Tiberius to become the stepson, and eventual heir, to the future ruler of the Roman Empire. When Octavian, now Augustus, triumphed over Antony and Cleopatra at the Battle of Actium, he was given a triumph in Rome in 29 B.C.E. and Tiberius rode on his left in the chariot.

No one questions the brilliance of the military career of Tiberius. In 20 B.C.E. he was sent by Augustus to the east against the Parthians, where he regained the standards of the legions that had been lost by Mark Antony and Marcus Crassus. Subsequently, after fighting against the tribes in Gaul, Tiberius became consul of Rome in 13 B.C.E. In a surprising turn of events, in 6 B.C.E., with no warning, Tiberius renounced public life and withdrew to the island of Rhodes. Augustus regarded this action as a snub, frustrating his plans of succession, and refused to allow Tiberius to return to Rome in spite of the insistence of his mother, Livia. Later Tiberius would let it be known that he was afraid of becoming a victim of assassination, since he was seen as a rival to Gaius Caesar and Lucius Caesar, sons of Octavian. Nevertheless, after Lucius

Caesar died of an illness in 2 C.E., Augustus finally agreed to allow his return. When Gaius Caesar died of a wound received during a siege in Armenia, Augustus, heartbroken, was forced to turn to Tiberius as his successor and adopted him as his son. By 13 C.E. the senate extended his proconsular power equal to that of Augustus, so that he served as virtual co-emperor. When Augustus died on August 19, 14 C.E., it was a foregone conclusion that Tiberius, at the age of fifty-six, would be his successor.

But Tiberius proved to be as clumsy in his dealings with the senate as Augustus was clever. First he refused to accept the office until he had thoroughly frustrated the senators. Then he was accused of the death of Germanicus, the popular son of his brother Drusus, whom he had been forced to adopt by Augustus. On his deathbed, Germanicus had accused Piso, the governor of Syria, of murdering him, and at his trial before the senate Piso claimed he had documents that would implicate the emperor. But Piso committed suicide without producing any incriminating records. The affair caused great turmoil among the nobility of Rome. For protection, Tiberius relied upon the prefect of the Praetorian Guard, Lucius Aelius Sejanus. Sejanus had powerful connections in the senate, and shortly thereafter became the closest friend and adviser of Tiberius. He deliberately increased the paranoia of Tiberius, who was not lacking in it to begin with. Soon no one in Rome felt safe, as Sejanus used informers to accuse many wealthy noblemen of treason in order to seize their wealth. In 23 B.C.E., Sejanus actually had Drusus, son of Tiberius and his likely heir, secretly poisoned, though his involvement was unknown to Tiberius. (He only learned the truth after the death of Sejanus.) Now in his old age, Tiberius once again withdrew from Rome, convinced that he would be assassinated. This time he retreated to the island of Capri, where he built several luxury villas and spent the last eleven years of his life. It was here that his reputation for extreme debauchery developed, although how much it was true cannot be established.

Sejanus had steadily moved himself into position to become the next emperor. He had become betrothed to Tiberius's granddaughter, thereby preparing to become part of the imperial family, and in 31 C.E. he was granted a share of the emperor's proconsular power. When Sejanus was summoned to the senate on October 18, he was told that he was about to receive additional honors. The letter from Tiberius to the senate began innocently enough, but then it denounced Sejanus and called for his condemnation. He was arrested and taken to prison, and the next day the senate ordered his execution. Again, the emperor's motivations behind this action are not clear, though he himself later attributed it to learning of Sejanus's violent hatred of the family of Germanicus, and fear for the life of his own grandson.

When Tiberius died at the age of seventy-eight after a reign of twenty-three years, there were rumors that he had been murdered. But he was in poor health anyway, and there is no evidence of murder. His general unpopularity, however, is evidenced by the fact that he was never granted divine honors by the senate, and, at least according to Suetonius, upon his death the people celebrated.

Biblical Significance

Tiberius is mentioned only once in the New Testament, where it is said that John the Baptist began his public ministry in the fifteenth year of the reign of Tiberius (Luke 3:1-2):

> In the fifteenth year of the reign of Emperor Tiberius, when Pontius Pilate was governor of Judea, and Herod was ruler of Galilee, and his brother Philip ruler of the region of Ituraea and Trachonitis, and Lysanias ruler of Abilene, during the high priesthood of Annas and Caiaphas, the word of God came to John son of Zechariah in the wilderness.

That piece of historical information should be eminently helpful in establishing the beginning of the ministries of both John the Baptist and Jesus. Unfortunately, the matter is complicated because we do not know which calendar — Julian, Jewish, Egyptian, or Syrian-Macedonian — Luke was using. Nor is "the fifteenth year of the reign of Emperor Tiberius" as cut and dried as one might think. Does Luke see the reign of Tiberius beginning at the time of his co-regency with Augustus (11-12 C.E.) or only at the death of Augustus (14 C.E.)? If 14 C.E. is taken as the beginning date intended, then the fifteenth year of the reign of Tiberius would be approximately 28-29 C.E. (The time spans of the rule of the other individuals mentioned are too broad to give us a more specific indication of the date.) In spite of these complications, this extensive historical reference does provide us with a clear framework for the period in which both John the Baptist and Jesus lived and worked.

Although Tiberius is mentioned only once by name, he is the "Caesar" referred to in every citation in the Gospels, with the exception of the Lukan birth narrative (Luke 2:1). When the Gospel writers speak of the question put to Jesus concerning the payment of taxes, the coin he called for and received was a silver denarius that bore the image of Tiberius (Mark 12:13-17; Matt. 22:15-22; Luke 20:20-26):

> So they watched him and sent spies who pretended to be honest, in order to trap him by what he said, so as to hand him over to the jurisdiction and authority of the governor. So they asked him, "Teacher, we know that you are right in what you say and teach, and you show deference to no one, but teach the way of God in accordance with truth. Is it lawful for us to pay

taxes to the emperor, or not?" But he perceived their craftiness and said to them, "Show me a denarius. Whose head and whose title does it bear?" They said, "The emperor's." He said to them, "Then give to the emperor the things that are the emperor's, and to God the things that are God's." And they were not able in the presence of the people to trap him by what he said; and being amazed by his answer, they became silent. (Luke 20:20-26)

The inscriptions on the coin (fig. 87) are also interesting. About the head of Tiberius are the words, TI[berius] CAESAR DIVI[ni] AUG[usti] F[ilius] AU-GUSTI; "Tiberius Caesar, of the divine Augustus, son of Augustus." The obverse of the coin displays a female image of Pax ("Peace") — some have identified the woman as Livia (though without any evidence), the mother of Tiberius, in costume representing Pax — surrounded by the words, PONTIF[ex] MAXIM[us], "Supreme Priest"; literally, "Supreme Bridge-builder" (that is, between humans and the gods).

The influence of Tiberius — and, most likely, also of Sejanus — is evident through the notorious prefect of Judea at that time, Pontius Pilate. Pilate was appointed to the post in 26 C.E. and ruled until 36 C.E. (Some authorities suggest his rule may have begun as early as 19 C.E. See the article "Pontius Pilate Inscription.") His administration began on a sour note when he insisted on his soldiers carrying the Roman standards into Jerusalem — idolatrous images, according to orthodox Jews — and protests erupted. Similar blunders affected his career, until finally Vitellius, legate of Syria, ordered him recalled to Rome to face Tiberius. (The emperor died shortly before Pilate reached Rome, and future events of Pilate's life are unknown.) Whether or not Sejanus, who had developed a reputation for hostility toward the Jews, appointed Pilate, as many authorities believe possible, he was certainly appointed under the administration of Tiberius. The emperor himself was suspicious of foreign cults, including the Jews, whom he briefly expelled from Rome in 19 C.E. for reasons that are not known. Furthermore, both Tacitus and Josephus say he ordered four thousand young Jewish men to military service in Sardinia, noted for the unhealthy climate of its marshes. (Later, however, Tiberius did allow the Jews to return to Rome.) As Tiberius aged and became more paranoid, and as Sejanus increasingly carried out treason trials against Roman citizens, the atmosphere of Rome became more poisonous. It is not difficult to imagine that such sensibilities during the age of Tiberius lay behind Rome's willingness to arrest, and eventually crucify, a peasant from Galilee who was alleged to be plotting to create a kingdom above that of the Roman Empire — Jesus of Nazareth.

The Galilee Boat

Wooden fishing boat

▷ Size: 8.2 m. (26.90 ft.) long; 2.3 m. (7.55 ft.) wide; 1.2 m. (3.94 ft.) deep
▷ Provenance: Sea of Galilee, Israel
▷ Date: ca. 120 B.C.E.–40 C.E.
▷ Present location: Yigal Allon Museum, Kibbutz Ginosar (Migdal), Israel

A severe drought in Israel in 1985-86 resulted in an unusual amount of water being pumped from the Sea of Galilee, or the Kinneret ("harp," because of the shape of the lake), as the lake is called in Hebrew. As the lake shrank to levels not seen in modern times, more and more of the shoreline was exposed. Two brothers, Moshe and Yuval Lufan, who lived in the Kibbutz Ginosar near Migdal on the northwestern shore of the lake, often went walking along the muddy shore looking for coins and possible archaeological objects. In January of 1986 they had found a few ancient iron nails and some ancient bronze coins, when suddenly they saw the oval outline of a boat buried in the mud. Not knowing whether the boat was modern or ancient, they contacted the local inspector for the Department of Antiquities, who in turn contacted Shelley Wachsmann, Inspector of Underwater Antiquities for Israel. Wachsmann, knowing that ancient boats were constructed with mortise-and-tenon joints, and fastened with wooden pegs, only had to clear the mud from the top rail of one side of the boat to discover that the boat was indeed ancient. Subsequent carbon-14 dating determined that it could be dated between 120 B.C.E. and 40 C.E., or eighty years either side of 40 B.C.E.

Marine specialists who examined the boat suggested that it was built by a master craftsman who either learned his trade in the Mediterranean or had been apprenticed to someone who had. The boat's builder, however, did not have at his disposal the quality of materials normally found in a Mediterranean vessel due to the scarcity of wood in the area. Cedar planking and oak frames were used over most of the boat, but five other woods were discovered as well: sidar, Aleppo pine, hawthorn, willow, and redbud. The boat had been repaired many times, and some of its timbers were in secondary use. Obviously the boat at some point had outlived its usefulness, and its mast and much of its usable materials had been stripped away. Finally, it was pushed out into the lake where it sank just off shore.

The immediate problem for the discoverers of the boat was how to raise the hull without destroying it. Lifting it was impossible. The excavators said that after so many centuries its consistency was like cheese, or wet cardboard, and it would have crumbled instantly had they attempted to lift it. Every day that they waited, the boat was drying out, and in spite of constantly spraying it with water, hairline cracks continued to appear. An expert in preservation, Oma Cohen, decided to try a new technique. The entire boat was encased in a fiberglass and polyurethane cocoon. A shallow canal was dug in the mud, and the intact boat was floated back into the lake. From there it was lifted onto the shore by a giant crane and placed into a reinforced concrete pool that would serve as the boat's conservation tank. The tank was filled with a solution of water and polyethylene glycol, the amount of which was gradually increased in the mixture each year, in order to penetrate the wood and replace the water that was saturating the cells. The excavator of the boat, Shelley Wachsman, originally estimated that the process would take five to seven years for completion. Actually, eleven years were required to safely stabilize the vessel so that it could be put on display.

Such boats as this one were common on the lake known as the Sea of Galilee. It is estimated by marine specialists that approximately two thousand of these vessels would have been in use on the Sea of Galilee during the time span of this boat's life. Evidence of a mast block, to which a ship's mast would have been fastened, was discovered, so that the boat could have been sailed when there was wind, or rowed when there was not. It probably also had a stern platform, or deck, with possibly another platform in the bow, though these are missing. Normally these boats would carry four oarsmen and one man at the helm. Yet various historical documents speak of such boats on occasion carrying as many as ten to fifteen men. The average size of a Galilean male in the first century has been estimated by a physical anthropologist at the Depart-

88. The remains of the "Galilee Boat"

ment of Antiquities as being five feet, five inches in height and one hundred forty pounds in weight. This boat was judged large enough to accommodate at least ten men of this size.

Thanks to the diligence and skill of the excavators, and the incredible luck of the drought and its revelations, visitors to Galilee today can view this boat in a beautiful, modern museum beside the lake — the only ancient boat ever found from the Sea of Galilee.

Biblical Significance

Galilee was the home of Jesus and all of his apostles. The Sea of Galilee figures prominently in many of the stories of the New Testament, and fishing was the profession of some of Jesus' closest followers. Naturally, boats are featured repeatedly as Jesus and the disciples cross the lake, or fish, and on one occasion Jesus even steps into a boat beside the shore to address a great throng crowding around him. The following quotations are from some of the most familiar of the biblical references to such boats in the New Testament.

When Jesus called two pairs of brothers, Simon and Andrew, and James and John, the sons of Zebedee, they were fishermen pursuing their business:

> As Jesus passed along the Sea of Galilee, he saw Simon and his brother Andrew casting a net into the sea — for they were fishermen. And Jesus said to them, "Follow me and I will make you fish for people." And immediately they left their nets and followed him. As he went a little farther, he saw James son of Zebedee and his brother John, who were in their boat mending the nets. Immediately he called them; and they left their father Zebedee in the boat with the hired men, and followed him. (Mark 1:16-20)

At times, great crowds seem to have attended the teaching of Jesus, so much so that on one occasion he found it necessary to use a boat at the shore as a platform for his teaching: "Again he began to teach beside the sea. Such a very large crowd gathered around him that he got into a boat on the sea and sat there, while the whole crowd was beside the sea on the land" (Mark 4:1).

Once when Jesus was crossing the lake with some of his disciples, a fierce storm arose that terrified the disciples; but Jesus was said to be sleeping in the stern:

> On that day, when evening had come, he said to them, "Let us go across to the other side." And leaving the crowd behind, they took him with them in the boat, just as he was. Other boats were with him. A great windstorm arose, and the waves beat into the boat, so that the boat was already being

swamped. But he was in the stern, asleep on the cushion; and they woke him up and said to him, "Teacher, do you not care that we are perishing?" He woke up and rebuked the wind, and said to the sea, "Peace! Be still!" Then the wind ceased, and there was a dead calm. (Mark 4:35-39)

The "cushion" upon which Jesus was said to be sleeping was probably the sandbag kept for ballast under the platform in the stern, and Jesus likely was sleeping under the platform, as was common, both for shelter and to be out of the way of the others in the boat.

A final example of boats in the life of Jesus is the famous story of Jesus walking on the water:

Immediately he made his disciples get into the boat and go on ahead to the other side, to Bethsaida, while he dismissed the crowd. After saying farewell to them, he went up on the mountain to pray.

When evening came, the boat was out on the sea, and he was alone on the land. When he saw that they were straining at the oars against an adverse wind, he came towards them early in the morning, walking on the sea. He intended to pass them by. But when they saw him walking on the sea, they thought it was a ghost and cried out; for they all saw him and were terrified. But immediately he spoke to them and said, "Take heart, it is I; do not be afraid." (Mark 6:45-50)

Naturally, it is tempting for Christian pilgrims to imagine that this very boat may be one in which Jesus or his disciples once traveled the lake. Of course, there is no evidence of that and the odds against it are very large. Nonetheless, those who view the boat popularly called the "Jesus boat" are correct in thinking that this was exactly the kind of boat mentioned in the stories so familiar to them in the New Testament.

Pontius Pilate Inscription

Inscribed limestone slab

- ▷ Size: 82 cm. (32.28 in.) high; 68 cm. (26.77 in.) wide; 21 cm. (8.27 in.) thick
- ▷ Writing: Latin language
- ▷ Provenance: Caesarea, Israel
- ▷ Date: 26-36 C.E.

▷ Present location: Israel Museum, Jerusalem (Bronfman Archaeology Wing)
▷ Identification number: IAA 1961-529

In 1961 during excavations at Caesarea Maritima in Israel, Italian archaeologists working on the theater at the site discovered a stone bearing an inscription with the name Pontius Pilate. The stone, only partially intact, had been turned upside down and reused as part of a flight of steps during one of the renovations of the theater, perhaps in the fourth century C.E. Unfortunately, since the stone had been reused, its original location and usage are not known. The inscription on the stone consists of four lines of text, only part of which is legible. The generally agreed upon reconstruction (with translation) of the text reads:

```
[    ]S TIBERIÉVM          [     ]s Tiberieum
[PON]TIVS PILATVS          [Pon]tius Pilate
[PRAEF]ECTVS IVDA[EA]E     [Pref]ect of Juda[ea]
[        ]É[ ]             [        ]e[ ]
```

The proposed restoration of lines two and three of the text is widely accepted. Line two provides the name (Pontius Pilate), while line three gives the title (prefect of Judea). These two lines are important for two reasons. First, although the name of Pontius Pilate appears in several ancient literary sources, including Josephus, Philo, Tacitus, and the New Testament, this stone slab provides the only inscriptional evidence of the name Pontius Pilate. Second, prior to the discovery of this Pilate inscription, uncertainty existed concerning the title and rank of Pontius Pilate. Ancient writers used different terms to describe Pilate's office, including the terms translated as "procurator," "prefect," and "governor," the last of which could refer to either a procurator or a prefect. Some scholars had already argued that the title procurator was not used for provincial governors in the empire until after the time of Pilate. The presence of the title prefect in the third line of the inscription provides reliable evidence that "prefect" was indeed the title for Pontius Pilate. A prefect was a governor of equestrian rank in one of the lesser provinces of the Roman Empire. From the time of the emperor Claudius (41-54 C.E.) onwards, the title "procurator," instead of prefect, came to be used for the governors of these lesser provinces.

Whereas the reconstruction of the second and third lines of the text is virtually undisputed, the same is not true for lines one and four. In line four, only one letter can be ascertained, the letter E. Based on similar type inscriptions, scholars have proposed that the single word in this line was *refecit* ("has restored"), *dedicavit* ("has dedicated"), or *dedit* ("has given"), suggesting that this was a dedicatory inscription or building plaque placed on a building when it was first

89. Limestone slab from Caesarea mentioning Pontius Pilate

built or later renovated. Even more problematic is the proposed reconstruction of line one. Antonio Frova, who first published the inscription in 1961, suggested that the first line originally read CAESARIENS TIBERIEVM (Caesareans' Tiberieum), indicating that Pilate had dedicated a "Tiberieum" to the inhabitants of Caesarea. Since then, various other reconstructions have been proposed, including that it read "the Tiberium of the Jews," "the Tiberium of the Divine Augusti," or "the Tiberium Building." Most recently one scholar has proposed the reading "the Seamen's Tiberium," referring to a building built for the seamen of Caesarea Maritima. Even the type of building meant by a "Tiberium" is not clear. Perhaps it was a temple built to honor the emperor Tiberius (14-37 C.E.); or perhaps it was a building for some other purpose (an administrative or municipal building) that Tiberius himself had constructed or for which he had provided the funding. Because of his role in its construction, it was thus known as "the Tiberium," which is how Pilate referred to it in the building inscription when he restored the building.

Pontius Pilate served as prefect of Judea apparently from 26 to 36 C.E., although some scholars have suggested that his term of office may have begun as early as 19 C.E. The official residence of the Roman prefect, and the capital of the province, was in Caesarea Maritima (Caesarea-by-the-sea), a city located on the Mediterranean coast approximately fifty-five miles northwest of Jerusalem. Caesarea had been constructed by Herod the Great, who built a major international port city on the site, including an impressive artificial harbor complex, a theater, temples, a palace, a hippodrome, paved streets, and an elaborate water and sewer system. The city was named in honor of Caesar Augustus and contained a grand temple dedicated to Augustus and Roma, which towered over the city.

Biblical Significance

Pontius Pilate earned his place in history as the prefect of Judea who oversaw the trial of Jesus and then sentenced him to death by crucifixion. The New Testament Gospels depict Pilate as being unconvinced of Jesus' guilt and wanting to set him free. However, yielding to the demands of the mob, Pilate eventually went against his better judgment and ordered Jesus to be beaten and then publicly executed. This characterization of Pilate as being weak and indecisive is at odds with the portrayal of him in the writings of Philo and Josephus, both of whom present the Roman governor as being rather ruthless and arrogant. For example, Josephus describes an incident when Pilate ordered the Roman soldiers to enter Jerusalem at night, carrying their standards that bore the image of the emperor. Due to Jewish concerns over the use of images in the city, previous governors had instructed Roman troops not to carry their standards into the city. Pilate's lack of concern for Jewish sensibilities in this instance led to a massive Jewish protest in the city that lasted for five days. Pilate ordered his soldiers to surround the people with their swords drawn. The people refused to disperse and instead bared their necks, daring Pilate to slaughter them. Apparently realizing that going forward with his threat could jeopardize his standing with the emperor, Pilate eventually relented and ordered the Roman standards removed from the city.

On another occasion, Pilate confiscated some of the funds from the Jerusalem treasury and used them to build an aqueduct for the city. Although the use of the money was for a good cause, his actions met with resistance from the Jewish population. Later when he visited Jerusalem, a mob surrounded him. Having been warned in advance of impending trouble, Pilate had instructed some of his soldiers to mingle with the crowd, dressed in civilian clothing. When the crowd became unruly and threatening, Pilate gave the signal and his soldiers pulled out clubs hidden under their clothing and attacked the unarmed protesters, killing several of them.

Both the New Testament writers and the Jewish authors (Philo and Josephus) were perhaps guilty of exaggerating certain aspects of the character of Pilate. The authors of the Gospels portrayed Pilate as being forced into condemning Jesus, perhaps partially because of their desire to present Christianity as not being a threat to the Roman Empire. Philo and Josephus, on the other hand, may have exaggerated his cruelty in order to cast him in a negative light. In reality, Pilate likely was a generally effective governor (he lasted at least ten years), who at times was guilty of using unnecessary force and demonstrating insensitivity toward the beliefs and concerns of the people of Judea.

Ossuary of the High Priest Caiaphas

Limestone burial box

▷ Size: 74 cm. (29.13 in.) long; 37 cm. (14.57 in.) high; 29 cm. (11.42 in.) wide
▷ Writing: Aramaic language
▷ Provenance: North Talpiot, Jerusalem, Israel
▷ Date: First century C.E.
▷ Present location: Israel Museum, Jerusalem (Bronfman Archaeology Wing)
▷ Identification number: IAA 1991-468

Sometimes archaeological treasures are found after years of patient searching; sometimes they are found completely by accident. The discovery of the ossuary (bone box used in burial) of Caiaphas, the high priest who presided at one of the trials of Jesus, was one of those lucky accidents. In November of 1990, Zvi Greenhut, an archeologist with the Israel Antiquities Authority, received news that a cave had been found in the Peace Forest, a park approximately two miles south of the Zion Gate of the Old City of Jerusalem. Construction was under way on a water park in the area when a bulldozer broke through the roof of a cave, revealing the site of an ancient burial place. Six ossuaries were found *in situ* (in their original locations) in four rectangular recesses within the cave, each about one and a half feet wide and six feet deep, carved in the rock walls (two of the boxes were wedged into one recess). The remains of six other ossuaries were scattered about on the floor of the cave where they had been plundered long ago by grave robbers, who possibly were interrupted in their work. Five of the boxes were marked with names. Two of these ossuaries were inscribed with forms of the name "Caiaphas," known to history from both the New Testament and the writings of the first-century Jewish historian Josephus. Generally identified only by his last name, the full name of the high priest was Joseph bar Caiaphas ("Yehosef bar Qayafa," the Aramaic form of the name), "Joseph, son of Caiaphas." In other words, the man's name was Joseph, and his clan bore the name of Caiaphas, a name adopted generations before by someone whose trade was related either to basket making or the vineyard business. (The commonality between the two possibilities comes from the root word which means either basket or wooden pole, such as used for the support of vines.)

The words on the more ornate box were inscribed twice, once on its back and once on one end. (The cave served as the burial place for a small family, used over many years, but nothing is known about the occupants of the other ossuary marked with the family name.) The front of this ossuary was beautifully decorated with rosettes in an elaborate manner rarely seen. In contrast, however, the engraving of the person's name was scratched into the surface of the box in an obviously amateur fashion, probably with a large nail that was found nearby. None of this is unusual. Ossuaries were commercially produced in this period of their use, accounting for the quality of the decoration. (Ossuaries in Israel were used exclusively by Jews, from approximately 100 B.C.E. to 70 C.E.) Some of them might be left completely plain, while the wealthy would be able to purchase such elaborate boxes as this one. Once a box had been placed in a tomb, a member of the family — generally, the eldest son — had the duty of inscribing the name of the person buried in it.

Inside the ossuary were found the bones of six persons — burial places were at a premium in late Second Temple Jerusalem — two infants, a young child, a teenage boy, an adult woman, and a man approximately sixty years of age. Biblical scholars are convinced that this was the man who presided over the trial of Jesus, Joseph bar Caiaphas. (One further item of interest: once the ossuary had been examined, Israeli authorities removed the bones and buried them, as is their custom in all such cases, on the Mount of Olives.)

In a curious side note, a coin was found in the skull of a woman buried in one of the boxes. According to the inscription, her name was Miriam, daughter of Simon (Miryam berat Shimon). The placing of a coin in the mouth of a dead person was a pagan custom carried over from the Greek practice of providing a coin for the dead to pay the god Charon to ferry the deceased across the River Styx. Other evidence of the persistence of polytheistic customs during this period in Israel, including those of Canaanite Baal worship as well as Greco-Roman practices, has been found elsewhere, although these practices were the exceptions. But it is ironic that such evidence should be found in the same tomb where Caiaphas, high priest of Jewish orthodoxy in the time of Christ, was buried.

Biblical Significance

According to Josephus, Joseph Caiaphas was appointed high priest in 18 C.E. by Valerius Gratus, the fourth Roman procurator over Judea, who preceded Pontius Pilate. Caiaphas served an unusually long period of time, from 18 C.E.

to 36 C.E., when Vitellius, Roman governor of the region of Syria (which included Palestine), deposed both him and the current procurator of Judea, Pontius Pilate. According to the Gospel of John, Caiaphas was the son-in-law of the former high priest, Annas, who served from 6 to 15 C.E. (John 18:13). The relationship between the two, however, with reference to the high priestly office is unclear, since the Gospels at points refer to both of them as high priests. John also has Annas active in the various interrogations of Jesus (John 18:19-23). Scholarly consensus favors the view that Caiaphas officially held the office, while Annas may have continued to be referred to as "high priest" (perhaps much as governors of states today are called "governor" even after their term of office).

By the time of the first century, the priesthood had undergone significant changes in its structure as the country continued under the rule of conqueror nations. The only authority vested in the Jews by the Romans lay in the Sanhedrin, the high court of the Jews. Its only authority seemed to lie in religious matters, specifically pertaining to Judea and the temple, but the extent of that authority varied according to the rulers at the time. (Historical information at this point is scarce and frequently contradictory.) This body consisted of seventy-one members, presided over by the high priest. This leader was drawn from a few aristocratic families, and they were associated with the group known as the Sadducees.

The portrayal in the Gospels of the involvement and motivation of Caiaphas

90. Limestone ossuary of Caiaphas

in the events surrounding the trial is unclear. In Matthew, a meeting of elders and "chief priests" to seize Jesus and have him killed is located in the house of Caiaphas (Matt. 26:3-4). (This reference to "chief priests," plural, which is common in the Gospels, seems to refer to the so-called upper priesthood, the aristocratic priests who participated in the Sanhedrin and the governance of the temple, as opposed to the many priests of the villages who only rarely were called upon to render temple service.) According to Matthew, once Jesus has been taken and questioned by Caiaphas, he is judged guilty of blasphemy and found worthy of death (Matt. 26:63-66). Mark and Luke do not provide any information about the location of such a meeting, and Luke particularly seems to focus on the "chief priests" as the active agents in the arrest and trial rather than Caiaphas as the principal actor. John's account of events leading up to the arrest differs significantly from the synoptic Gospels. It is in John that Caiaphas utters the famous words, "You do not understand that it is better for you to have one man die for the people than have the whole nation destroyed" (John 11:50). John understood that to be a prophecy of events yet to come, and he places it early in the ministry of Jesus. In another difference from the accounts in the synoptic Gospels, in John's account, Jesus is taken after his arrest to Annas (John 18:13), where he is interrogated, and then Annas sends him to Caiaphas.

In spite of the Gospels' differences in the details of the trial of Jesus, there is consensus on the two major points regarding Caiaphas: first, that he was the high priest at the time of the trial and execution of Jesus, and second, that he had an active role in the events as they unfolded. As such, the discovery of his burial place and ossuary constitutes one of the most remarkable finds in the history of biblical archaeology.

Heel Bone of a Crucifixion Victim

Nail-pierced heel bone

- ▷ Size: Nail — 11.5 cm. (4.5 in.) long; heel bone — 11 cm. (4.33 in.) long
- ▷ Provenance: Giv'at ha-Mivtar in Jerusalem, Israel
- ▷ Date: First century c.e.
- ▷ Present location: Israel Museum (Bronfman Archaeology Wing)
- ▷ Identification number: IAA 1995-2067/5

In 1968 a crew from the Israel Ministry of Housing, working in an area called Giv'at ha-Mivtar in the northeast part of the city of Jerusalem, accidentally broke into some burial chambers. Subsequent exploration revealed the presence of several tombs in the area that were part of a large Jewish cemetery dating from the second century B.C.E. to the first century C.E. Four of these tombs were excavated by archaeologists, who found numerous ossuaries (bone boxes) and skeletons. Of particular interest was one of the ossuaries found in Tomb I. When opened, this ossuary was found to contain the bones of two individuals, an adult male (twenty-four to twenty-eight years old) and a child (three to four years old). (One bone from an additional adult was also found in the ossuary.) The adult skeleton generated considerable scholarly interest when its right heel was found to be pierced by a rusty iron nail that was 11.5 cm. (4.5 in.) long. The nail had pierced a piece of olive wood before entering the heel bone, a portion of which was still attached to the nail. Another piece of wood of undetermined species, from the vertical beam of the cross, was attached at the pointed end of the nail. The nail was bent at its pointed end, as well as near the nail's head.

The two-centimeter-thick (.79 in.) wooden plaque was placed against the heel, and then the nail was driven through the plaque, the heel, and into the upright. The purpose of the wooden plaque was to prevent the foot from being torn loose from the nail. In this particular case, when the nail was driven into the upright beam, it apparently hit a knot, causing the end of the nail to bend. The bent nail likely caused much difficulty in removing the dead victim

91. Heel bone, pierced by a large nail, from a victim of crucifixion

from the cross. Also, the nail, with a small part of the wood from the upright beam still attached, could not be removed from the victim by his family without doing damage to his foot. Thus, if the nail had not struck a knot and bent, the nail would not have remained with the victim, and he likely never would have been identified as a crucifixion victim.

The nail and wood pieces attached to the bone indicate that the individual buried in the ossuary had been crucified. From the name inscribed several times on the ossuary, the crucified man can be identified as "Yehohanan, son of HGQWL." (The name of Yehohanan's father cannot be clearly translated. It may have been "Hagkol.") Although several literary texts from the ancient world mention the practice of crucifixion, the discovery of this skeleton was the first archaeological evidence of this gruesome method of execution. Because the bones of neither the hands nor feet showed any evidence of damage from nails, Yehohanan's arms were likely tied to the crossbeam with ropes, rather than having been nailed to it. The victim's feet were apparently nailed to the upright with one foot on each side, rather than being nailed together with one nail. The result is that his legs were straddling the cross. This conjecture is supported by the lack of any bones from the left heel and by the length of the nail. It was not long enough to pierce the wooden plaque, both heels, and the upright beam. (Originally, the examiners of the bones thought portions of the heels from both feet were attached to the nail. This later proved inaccurate. Additionally, the earlier examiners claimed that the victim's legs had been broken and that a scratch mark on the bone of the right forearm indicated that the victim's arms had been nailed to the cross. These claims also were disputed by later examiners.)

From an examination of the skeletal remains, scholars determined that Yehohanan had been between twenty-four and twenty-eight years old and was approximately five feet, five inches tall. He apparently came from a fairly well-to-do family, considering the interment of his bones in an ossuary, since ossuaries were an expensive luxury. Jewish burial practice was to place the body in a burial chamber, often a cave-like room carved from the rock. After the body had decomposed, the family gathered the bones and placed them in a family bone pile in the burial chamber. This practice likely was still followed by the poor. (Sometimes the poor either buried their dead in shallow graves, where they were left to decompose, or the bodies were placed in special niches carved in caves or underground.) By the first century, some wealthier Jewish families around Jerusalem began to place the bones in stone boxes called ossuaries, whose lids and sides sometimes had elaborate decorative carvings. Frequently the name or names of the deceased were carved or scratched on the sides of the ossuary.

Crucifixion was such a terrible form of execution that the Romans normally used it only for slaves, foreigners, and the lower class. Even then, crucifixion seems to have been primarily reserved for the most serious crimes of treason, rebellion, or banditry. Unfortunately, we have no clue as to the circumstances that led to the crucifixion of Yehohanan. The Romans frequently left crucified bodies on the crosses for days to bring further shame to the victims' families and also to serve as a public warning to other would-be violators. Victims of crucifixion were normally denied a regular burial. That Yehohanan was permitted a burial in the family tomb perhaps indicates that his family had political or social connections.

A replica of the heel bone and nail is on display in the Israel Museum in Jerusalem. The actual bone and nail are not displayed because Israeli law requires that bones found in archaeological excavations must be reburied. Furthermore, Jewish religious law forbids people from priestly families being near skeletal remains, which are considered ritually impure. Thus, displaying the actual heel bone could prevent religious individuals from priestly families from visiting the museum. The ossuary (IAA 1968-679) also is in the museum.

Biblical Significance

The discovery of the skeletal remains of a first-century victim of crucifixion generated scholarly and popular excitement because of the crucifixion of Jesus of Nazareth. The skeleton of Yehohanan is the only extant skeleton of someone who died in the same way as Jesus did. A comparison of the skeleton with information about the death of Jesus in the New Testament reveals both similarities and differences. With both Jesus and Yehohanan, they were at least partially nailed to the cross. Whereas the feet of Yehohanan were nailed to the vertical beam, the hands of Jesus were nailed to the cross-beam. The Gospel of John reports that the disciple Thomas, doubting the other disciples' story of the appearance of the resurrected Jesus, asserted that he would not believe their claim unless he saw "the mark of the nails in his hands" (John 20:25). Nothing is said, however, about how Jesus' feet were attached to the cross. Presumably they too were attached by nails, but they could have been bound to the cross by ropes. The use of nails to affix Jesus' hands to the cross differs from the method of Yehohanan's crucifixion. The skeletal evidence seems to indicate that Yehohanan's hands were tied to the cross instead of being nailed. Furthermore, neither Jesus nor Yehohanan apparently suffered the pain of having their legs broken. Breaking a victim's legs prevented him from lifting himself up to assist in breathing, thus hastening death by asphyxiation. The Gospel of John specifically reports that Jesus' legs were not broken, while those of the two individuals crucified with him were broken (19:31-37). Initial reports of the skeleton of Yehohanan claimed that his legs had been broken. Later examination of the bones, however, suggests that the bones were broken after the death of the individual and not as a part of the crucifixion.

The differences between the details of Jesus' crucifixion and the crucifixion of Yehohanan are not unusual. Ancient literary sources describe several variations in the way in which persons were crucified. On some occasions only a vertical stake was used, whereas on other occasions a crossbeam was also used. Sometimes the victims were nailed to the cross; sometimes they were tied. At times they were crucified upside down. Regardless of the variations, crucifixion was an excruciating, degrading, and horrendous method of execution.

Ossuary of Simon, "Builder of the Temple"

Inscribed limestone ossuary (burial box)

▷ Size: 58 cm. (22.8 in.) long; 33 cm. (13 in.) high; 28 cm. (11 in.) wide
▷ Writing: Aramaic language
▷ Provenance: Giv'at ha-Mivtar, Israel (northern suburb of Jerusalem)
▷ Date: First century B.C.E.
▷ Present location: Israel Museum, Jerusalem (Bronfman Archaeology Wing)
▷ Identification number: IAA 1968-441

In the summer of 1968, an archaeological team led by Vassilios Tzaferis of the Israel Antiquities Authority excavated four burial caves at Giv'at ha-Mivtar, just north of the Old City of Jerusalem, on the way to Mount Scopus. Inscribed os-

92. Ossuary belonging to Simon, "builder of the temple"

suaries were found in two of the caves. The sensational find of the skeleton of a young man who had been crucified overshadowed a second find of importance. (See the article "Heel Bone of a Crucifixion Victim.") One of the ossuaries was inscribed twice in Palestinian Aramaic with the words "Simon, builder of the temple," once on one side and once on the end of the box. According to J. Naveh of the Department of Antiquities and Museums, translator of the inscriptions, the two engravings were done by the same person. The letters themselves were large and easily read. However, because the words had neither final letters nor spaces between them, the translation became somewhat problematic. The name "Simon" was clear from the first four letters. Naveh then translated the remaining words as "builder of the temple," and he takes the word "temple" to mean the sanctuary as a whole, not specifically the holy place, the central portion of the sanctuary. Simon may have been a priest, since Josephus suggests that priests were trained to work in the building of this sacred structure. In any case, it seems more likely that Simon was not the principal architect of the building, but rather one of the master builders who worked in its construction. This is suggested by the fact that neither the burial cave nor the ossuary was elaborate, as is the case of the nearby family tomb of Nicanor of Alexandria who made the doors for the temple. Nevertheless, Simon was sufficiently proud of his role in the building of the magnificent temple of Herod that he wished to be remembered for his part in the work.

Biblical Significance

The most historic structure in Jewish history is also the one about which we have the least archaeological evidence. The first temple built by Solomon was destroyed by the Babylonians in 587 B.C.E. A second temple was built by the returning exiles from Babylon, but it was nowhere near the grandeur of the original. Herod the Great, ever anxious to impress his Roman masters and glorify his own name at the same time, rebuilt this temple into a magnificent structure admired around the Mediterranean world. According to Josephus, Herod announced plans in the eighteenth year of his reign (20-19 B.C.E.) to renovate the temple. The religious authorities of Jerusalem were suspicious that Herod might tear down the existing temple and not rebuild it, but he reassured them that he merely wished to return the temple to its former splendor and size. (According to Josephus [*Jewish Antiquities* 15.385], Zerubbabel's temple was not nearly as tall as Solomon's temple, and Herod promised to restore it to its original height.) To show his good faith, Herod accumulated all the materials for the new temple before beginning the work of reconstruction. Thousands of skilled workmen were hired to do the work, and because only priests were allowed to build the temple proper, one thousand priests also were trained as masons and carpenters. "Simon, builder of the temple" may have been one of these priest-builders.

Herod's temple plays a role in several incidents in the life of Jesus. According to the Gospels (Mark 13:1; Matt. 24:1; Luke 21:5), on a visit to Jerusalem one of the disciples of Jesus called his attention to the impressive size of the temple and of the stones used to erect it: "As he came out of the temple, one of his disciples said to him, 'Look, Teacher, what large stones and what large buildings!'" (Mark 13:1). Enormous stones indeed were used in the construction of the temple. The largest stone discovered to date measures approximately 12.2 m. (40 ft.) long, 4.3 m. (14 ft.) high, and 3 m. (10 ft.) deep, and it weighs approximately four hundred tons.

In the Gospel of John, Jesus declares, "Destroy this temple, and in three days I will raise it up." His Jewish hearers scoff, "This temple has been under construction for forty-six years, and will you raise it up in three days?" (John 2:19-20). John says Jesus was speaking of the temple of his body, which they did not understand. Since Herod began building the temple in approximately 20 B.C.E., that would place the date of this conversation around 26-27 C.E. The principal part of the work (the sanctuary itself) was done in the first eighteen months, but the entire complex was not completed until 63 C.E., some eighty years later. Only seven years later, in 70 C.E., the Romans burned the city of Jerusalem and utterly destroyed the great temple. It has never been rebuilt.

"Place of Trumpeting" Inscription

Inscribed marble stone

- ▷ Size: 31 cm. (12.2 in.) high; 84 cm. (33.07 in.) long
- ▷ Writing: Hebrew language
- ▷ Provenance: Temple Mount, Jerusalem, Israel
- ▷ Date: First century C.E.
- ▷ Present location: Israel Museum (Bronfman Archaeology Wing)
- ▷ Identification number: IAA 1978-1439

In 70 C.E., Roman legions under Titus stormed the walls of Jerusalem, burning the city and totally destroying the spectacular temple built by Herod the Great (see the article "Head of Vespasian and Statue of Titus"). Their destruction of the temple was absolute; nothing whatsoever remained of it except masses of rubble from the Temple Mount. (Later the Romans would even build a temple to Jupiter on top of the site where the Jewish temple once stood.) Buried beneath this rubble was a stone block almost three feet long that had fallen from the southwest corner of the Temple Mount. The Israeli archaeologist Benjamin Mazar discovered it at the base of the Herodian wall during his excavations that began in 1968 and continued for ten years. Unfortunately, part of the stone had broken off, leaving the Hebrew inscription on it incomplete. The remaining two words read, "To the place of trumpeting." A portion of a third word also exists. Various possibilities for the ending of the expression have been suggested: "to declare [the Sabbath]," or, "to distinguish [between the sacred and the profane]." In any case, the function of the inscription was to direct the priests to the proper place where they were to sound the trumpet to declare the beginning of the Sabbath and its ending. Presumably from that location these trumpet calls could be heard throughout the city of Jerusalem. This was vital to the Jews because of the strict prohibitions of the traditions against certain activities on the Sabbath, as well as to remind them of their sacred obligations. (Since traces of white plaster were found on parts of the stone, it also has been suggested that the directions were not to the priests, but were merely working instructions to those who installed the stone; in that case, the inscription would not have been visible at all. The quality of the inscription, however, militates against that possibility. While not elegant, it is clearly superior to such inscriptions that have been found previously. Even inscriptions on many ossuaries are inferior to this one.)

93. Inscribed stone from the Jerusalem temple indicating the "place of trumpeting"

The shape of the stone suggests that it was part of a parapet on the top of the outer wall of the Temple Mount. The fact that it was lying beneath other stones from the corner above, which stood approximately fifteen meters (ca. 50 ft.) above the level of the temple court, gives evidence that it had not been moved there from another location. The stone had fallen into a broad street, ten meters (ca. 30 ft.) wide, built by Herod along the western wall of the temple, and lined with shops on its eastern side. Today a replica of the original stone with its inscription lies in the place of its discovery.

Biblical Significance

Certainly one of the great losses of ancient history was the destruction of the magnificent temple of Jerusalem, comparable to the senseless destruction of the temple of Artemis at Ephesus or the Parthenon of Athens. Built by Herod as part of his vast renovation projects in Jerusalem, designed both to impress the Romans and to place his name alongside that of King Solomon, the temple had gained a reputation as a lavish architectural achievement. Its loss deprived later generations of both a cultural and spiritual treasure. So complete was this loss that even fragments from the temple are considered priceless treasures today. From the standpoint of the Jewish tradition, the inscription harkens back to the words of the historian Josephus:

> It was the custom for one of the priests to stand and to give notice, by sound of trumpet, in the afternoon of the approach, and on the following evening of the close, of every seventh day, announcing to the people the respective hours for ceasing work and for resuming their labors. (Josephus, *Jewish War* 4.582 [Thackeray, Loeb Classical Library])

According to the Babylonian Talmud, this tradition continued among Jewish communities for the next four hundred years. Since nothing remains of the temple itself, even this fragmentary inscription calls forth deep emotions among the devout. From the perspective of Christians, any evidence of the temple and its environs, in which occurred so many of the events in the life of Jesus and the experiences of the early church as told in the book of Acts, is a treasured reminder of the origins of the faith.

Temple Warning Inscription

Inscribed limestone block

▷ Size: 90 cm. (35.43 in.) long; 60 cm. (23.62 in.) high; 39 cm. (15.35 in.) deep
▷ Writing: Greek language
▷ Provenance: Jerusalem
▷ Date: First century c.e.
▷ Present location: Archaeological Museum, Istanbul (third floor)
▷ Identification number: 2196 T

The Jewish temple in Jerusalem, rebuilt at the end of the sixth century b.c.e. by Zerubbabel after it had been destroyed by the Babylonians in 587 b.c.e., was later completely rebuilt and expanded by Herod the Great during the first century b.c.e. (Most of the work was completed in a few years, but part of the construction may still have been unfinished when the temple was destroyed by the Romans in 70 c.e.) The temple consisted of a large open courtyard surrounded on three sides by covered porticos. Within this courtyard, known as the outer court or the court of the Gentiles, were the inner courts, first the court of the women, then the court of Israel (the men's court), and finally the court of the priests. Inside the court of the priests was the sanctuary itself, containing the holy place and the holy of holies. No non-Jew was allowed to go beyond the court of the Gentiles. A low stone wall or balustrade separated the inner courts from the court of the Gentiles. At various points on this wall were inscriptions written in Latin and Greek warning non-Jews not to go beyond that point upon threat of death. Josephus, the first-century Jewish historian, provides a description of this area of the temple:

Proceeding across this toward the second court of the temple, one found it surrounded by a stone balustrade, three cubits high and of exquisite workmanship; in this at regu-

94. Limestone block from the Jerusalem temple warning non-Jews against trespassing

327

lar intervals stood slabs giving warning, some in Greek, others in Latin characters, of the law of purification, to wit that no foreigner was permitted to enter the holy place, for so the second enclosure of the temple was called. (Josephus, *Jewish War* 5.193-194 [Thackeray, Loeb Classical Library])

Elsewhere he mentions that the inscription prohibited "the entrance of a foreigner under threat of the penalty of death" (Josephus, *Jewish Antiquities* 15.417 [Thackeray, Loeb Classical Library]).

In 1871, the French archaeologist Charles Clermont-Ganneau (who also played a major role in the discovery and reconstruction of the Mesha Stela) discovered in the area of the temple ruins a limestone block bearing a seven-line inscription in Greek that reads: "No foreigner is to enter within the railing and enclosure around the temple. And whoever is caught will be responsible to himself for his subsequent death."[1] This inscribed block was almost certainly one of the temple warning blocks described by Josephus. Today, this limestone block is displayed on the third floor of the Archaeological Museum of Istanbul (see fig. 94). In 1935 a fragment of a second temple warning block was found by J. H. Iliffe outside the wall of the Old City of Jerusalem near the Lion's Gate. This fragment (IAA 1936.989), containing a portion of the center section of six lines of the inscription, is now housed in the Israel Museum in Jerusalem (Bronfman Archaeology Wing).

Biblical Significance

Two passages in the New Testament — Acts 21:27-36 and Ephesians 2:14-15 — possibly refer to the segregated nature of the temple reflected in its warning inscriptions. The Acts passage tells of the apostle Paul's return to Jerusalem at the end of his third missionary journey. When Paul went to the temple, some of the people in the temple mistakenly believed that he had defiled the temple by taking Trophimus the Ephesian into an area obviously off-limits to Gentiles. As a result, a riot broke out and Paul's life was endangered. Paul was saved from the violence of the mob only by the intervention of Roman soldiers. The inscription warning of the death penalty for any Gentile who entered the restricted area of the temple helps explain the violent reaction of the temple crowd.

In chapter 2 of Ephesians, the author proclaimed the unity that exists in the church between Jewish and Gentile believers, a unity made possible by Christ, who "has made both groups into one and has broken down the dividing wall, that is, the hostility between us" (2:14). Many interpreters have suggested that

---

1. Translation by author (Reddish).

the low wall in the temple with its warning inscriptions may have suggested to the author this imagery of a wall separating Jew and Gentile.

Head of Caligula

Marble sculpture

▷ Size: 47 cm. (18.50 in.) high
▷ Provenance: Thrace (Greece)
▷ Date: ca. 39-40 C.E.
▷ Present location: Louvre (room 24, ground floor, Denon Wing, section 8)
▷ Identification number: MNC 1276 (also numbered Ma 1234)

This portrait head of the emperor Caligula (37-41 C.E.) was sculpted sometime around 39-40 C.E. following the death of his favorite sister, Drusilla, in 38 C.E. (subsequently, he declared her to be a god). The youthful emperor is shown with the stubble of a beard as a sign of mourning. His eyes are downcast, and the expression is melancholy. The style of the sculpture, with such human and expressive qualities, is in sharp contrast to the strict academic, more formal approach demanded during the age of the previous emperor, Tiberius. Nonetheless, the image is flattering to Caligula, who was known to be completely bald on the crown of his head. (Realism in sculpture did not extend to the risk of offending the notorious Caligula.)

In no other Roman emperor are fact and legend so intermingled as in the life of Caligula. His reign was short, as was his life. He was enormously unpopular and almost universally hated, and the accounts we have of him come exclusively from his enemies (Suetonius; Dio Cassius; Philo; Josephus) — although it would be difficult to imagine who might write favorably of him. He was born

95. Marble portrait head of Caligula

Gaius Caesar on August 31, 12 C.E., the son of Agrippina the Elder, grand-daughter of Augustus, and Germanicus, adopted grandson of Augustus. His father, Germanicus, was immensely popular with the common people and the nobility alike, and his death caused riots across the empire. (See the article "Bust and Silver Denarius of Tiberius.") Gaius gained the nickname "Caligula" ("Little Boots"; the common soldier's leather, laced sandal), because as a child he dressed in a little soldier outfit when accompanying his father in the army camps. Throughout his life, and even at death, he would remain popular among those troops who knew him as a child.

Following the death of Germanicus, Caligula lived with a succession of relatives until the year 31 C.E., when he was sent to Capri and the care of the emperor Tiberius. In many respects, association with the aged Tiberius in his private lair on Capri was probably the last thing Caligula needed, but he soon gained the confidence of the emperor. Even his enemies said he was highly intelligent and articulate, and especially knew how to survive in the viper pit of the imperial family. He ingratiated himself with the emperor, who would leave his estate to him. Upon the death of Tiberius in 37 C.E., Caligula moved quickly to gain control. With the help of Macro, prefect of the Praetorian Guard, Caligula eliminated Tiberius Gemellus, Tiberius's own grandson, who had been named in Tiberius's will as joint regent. He accepted the ruling power conferred on him by the senate, which was delighted — at first — that he had become emperor.

By all accounts, the first seven months of his reign were universally admired, and many of his acts, particularly toward potential enemies, seemed exceptionally magnanimous. For example, Caligula abolished treason trials, revived free elections, recalled many exiles, and banished notorious sex offenders from the empire. He also completed a few public works that had been begun by Tiberius. But most of his wildly extravagant goals — rebuilding Polycrates' palace on Samos, completing the temple to the Apollo of Didyma at Miletus, and digging a canal through the Isthmus of Corinth — were never begun. What happened to change Caligula's behavior has never been determined. He fell seriously ill in October of 37 C.E., and he was said to suffer from epilepsy. But whether he was truly insane, as his enemies insisted, is impossible to determine from this distance. In any case, by 39 C.E., when the senate refused him a triumph (following trivial, and mostly contrived, military adventures), he became a hated tyrant and megalomaniac. Though the Roman imperial cult had been established in the time of Augustus, his emperor predecessors had been careful to locate worship not on their own personal divinity, as humans, but on their spirit and that of their ancestors. Yet it suited Caligula to be regarded as a god and to have his capricious nature seen as typical of the acts of the gods. Gods could strike anyone down without reason, and they were above conventional social and sexual mores.

His sexual misadventures and vicious exploits were emphasized by the ancient chroniclers (Suetonius in particular), as were his seeming acts of madness. Most notable among the latter was his devotion to his horse, Incitatus, to whom he gave a house of his own with servants and who often dined at the emperor's own table. Caligula, it was said, even wished to give the horse the highest office in the senate, but the emperor's early death cut short the promising political career of Incitatus. As for his sexual excesses, he was accused of incest with all of his sisters, particularly Drusilla, and sexual liaisons with many notable men as well as an endless variety of women. He had a reputation for a sadistic delight in cruelty and torture, and for causing the wanton murders of anyone whose estate he wished to seize. These crimes were occasioned by his profligate spending and virtual bankrupting for an empire that Tiberius, whatever his other faults, had left in prosperous condition. When the rumor got out in Rome that he was planning to commit even more extensive executions and then move out of the city entirely, his many enemies decided to unite against him.

His assassination came as no surprise to anyone. Caligula loved gladiatorial contests, chariot races in the hippodrome — he was a patron of the "Green Faction," so-called because of the racing colors of a particular team — and, especially, the theater. On the day of his death he had gone to attend a performance by some young men from Asia. He was speaking with them in a private corridor when the assassins, including several members of the Praetorian Guard, attacked him with swords and daggers. Some of the attackers were killed by his German bodyguards who rushed to his assistance, but Caligula died in the passageway of multiple stab wounds; shortly thereafter, his wife and infant daughter both were brutally killed. As Dio Cassius dryly remarked, on that day Gaius learned that he was not a god (Dio Cassius, *Roman History* 59.30.1). He had ruled less than four years and died in his twenty-ninth year.

Biblical Significance

Caligula does not appear in the New Testament, but he was involved in several incidents that affected Jews. Through a strange series of circumstances, he appointed Herod Agrippa I as king over the territory previously held by Agrippa's uncle, Philip. As a child of six, Agrippa had been sent by his parents to Rome for education, and there he was befriended by the younger Drusus, son of the emperor Tiberius. After the death of Drusus (23 C.E.), Agrippa lost his influence in Rome, and after excessive spending left him with a mountain of debts, he returned to Palestine. Things went no better there, and he and his brother-in-law, Herod Antipas, tetrarch of Galilee and Perea, soon clashed. Agrippa returned to Rome, and this time he managed to obtain loans that temporarily assuaged his problems. In the spring of 36 C.E., Agrippa traveled to the island of Capri and again met Tiberius. There he became a close friend of the young Gaius Caligula, who had been sent to live with the emperor for his safety. But when word reached the ears of Tiberius that Agrippa wished Caligula to become emperor, Tiberius promptly put him into prison. Upon the death of Tiberius, Caligula became emperor and Agrippa once again found favor with the court. Caligula presented him with a gold chain, said to be equal in weight to the iron chains that had bound him in prison. Subsequently Caligula named him king over Philip's territory, and then steadily added to his territories until at last his kingdom was as large as that of his grandfather, Herod the Great. (Caligula exiled Antipas in doing so.) Due to his influence with the emperor, Agrippa was able to dissuade Caligula from his plan of installing an image of himself in the temple in Jerusalem. After the assassination of Caligula, Agrippa supported Claudius in his bid to become emperor, and Claudius responded by reaffirming his kingship. The death of Agrippa after a reign of only three years (44 C.E.) is told in Acts 12:19-23, and while the Jews had come to regard him as a great supporter of Pharisaic Judaism, the Acts account shows that Christians did not share their enthusiasm.

Caligula also encountered the Jewish community following anti-Jewish riots that occurred in Alexandria, Egypt, when images of the emperor were set up in all the synagogues of the city and the Jews demanded their removal. Rioting ensued, and some members of the Jewish council were arrested and whipped, others were crucified, and hundreds died. Agrippa, who was visiting in the city, immediately sent a report to Caligula. Flaccus, the Roman governor of Alexandria, was arrested on orders of the emperor, deported, and eventually executed. The citizens of Alexandria sent a delegation to Caligula in 40 C.E. to plead their case concerning their rights. Philo, the Jewish philosopher, was present among those representing the case of the Jews and later gave a full account of the actions of the emperor. After months of waiting, Caligula humiliated the Jews by wandering throughout the palace as they trailed him, talking endlessly about irrelevant matters, and in various ways embarrassing them before his court. Caligula finally dismissed them and declared them unfortunate rather than evil in not being able to discern that he was a god.

Head of Claudius

Bronze head from a life-size statue

▷ Size: 30 cm. (11.81 in.) high

▷ Provenance: River Alde, Rendham (Suffolk), England

▷ Date: First century c.e.

▷ Present location: British Museum (room 49)

▷ Identification number: P&E 1965 12-1.1

This rare bronze head of the emperor Claudius (41-54 c.e.) was found in 1907 at the River Alde, at Rendham, near Saxmundham, in Suffolk, England. (Some scholars have suggested the scupture may represent the emperor Nero, rather than Claudius.) Following the conquest of southern and central England by Claudius (43 c.e.), settlements were expanded in the region, and it is possible that the life-size statue from which this head came once stood in an important public place at Colchester, where a temple had been erected to Claudius, or another such colony. The body of the statue may have been destroyed during the tribal rebellion under Boudicca against the Romans that destroyed the temple (61 c.e.), though that is impossible to determine at this point. Several other representations of Claudius can be seen in various museums, including a sardonyx cameo portrait of the emperor in military dress in room 70 of the British Museum (inventory number GR 1899.7–22.3 [Gem 3596]; see plate 12).

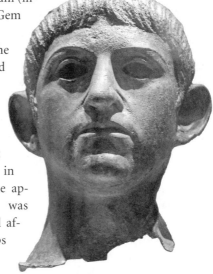

Claudius was born in 10 b.c.e., the younger son of the elder Drusus and Antonia. His full name was Tiberius Claudius Nero Germanicus. Suetonius describes Claudius in maturity as a tall, handsome, well-built man with white hair (he does not mention the large ears, prominent in all of the statues of Claudius). The appearance of Claudius, however, was marred by some unknown physical affliction from childhood, perhaps some form of paralysis or birth defect, which caused him to stumble when he walked. He also had some

96. Bronze head of Emperor Claudius

kind of speech impediment, and his head twitched continually. He was regarded as slow-witted as a child and was treated cruelly by everyone in the imperial family, who regarded him as an embarrassment. His mother spoke of him as a monstrous specimen of humanity, and his grandmother, Livia, wife of Augustus, treated him with profound contempt. When he attended the gladiatorial games, he was obliged to wear a Greek cloak, the garb of invalids. Claudius was the butt of all practical jokes and generally regarded as unfit for public life. The one area in which he showed great ability, even as a boy, was scholarship. He was a master of Greek, an accomplished historian — as a youth he was encouraged by the historian Livy — and a prolific writer. Later in life, he was said to be elegant in oratory.

Yet his defects may have been responsible for Claudius's survival during the reign of his nephew Caligula. Since he was regarded as no threat, he was allowed to continue his obscure life. When Caligula was assassinated, the conspirators missed Claudius, who later was discovered hiding behind a curtain by a soldier. Since Caligula was favored by the army, they literally compelled Claudius, as the uncle of Caligula and the sole remaining male of the family, to become emperor in 41 C.E. Throughout his reign, Claudius would depend upon the army for support, as he was scorned by the nobility and the senate. But he seemed to be popular with the plebs, the common people, whose support he avidly sought by the giving of games and money.

The administration of Claudius was marked by both cruelty and compassion. He was no friend of the nobility, nor they of him, and he saw conspiracies everywhere. According to Suetonius, during his reign he executed more than three hundred of the equestrian class and thirty-five senators. Yet when he learned that some slave owners were depositing their sick slaves on an island rather than paying for their care, he ordered that all such slaves would be given their freedom and have no responsibilities to their former owners. The primary accomplishments of his reign were his successful invasion of Great Britain, his expansion of senate membership to include more members from the provinces, his stabilization of the nation's finances, the improvement of the port at Ostia, and the completion of two aqueducts.

His family and his marriages continued to be a problem throughout his life and eventually resulted in his death. His fourth wife, Agrippina, who was also his niece, had a son who was adopted by Claudius. He was given the name Nero Claudius Drusus Germanicus Caesar and became known as Nero. Agrippa was determined that he should become the next emperor, but Claudius began giving signs that he might favor his own child, Britannicus. Before Britannicus could come of age, however, Agrippa murdered Claudius by giving him poisoned mushrooms. He died October 13, 54 C.E., at the age of sixty-four, after a rule of fourteen years.

Biblical Significance

Overall, Claudius seems to have had a more tolerant policy toward the Jews than did his predecessors. According to Josephus, he was responsible for an edict guaranteeing Jews the right to practice their religion anywhere in the empire without interference. Following the serious rioting that occurred in Alexandria, Egypt, under the policies of Caligula, Claudius issued an order in 41 C.E. that rebuked both Greeks and Jews for their actions, but he ordered the Greeks to act kindly toward the Jews. Nevertheless, at some point Claudius ordered Jews expelled from Rome due to claims of continuous disturbances among them because of "Chrestus." Yet, there are many questions connected with this statement by Suetonius. There is no evidence that the entire city was emptied of Jews, certainly not for any meaningful period of time. Dio Cassius, to the contrary, says Claudius did not order Jews expelled from Rome, but rather insisted that they not resume assembling themselves. Assuming that the statement is factual, such an order certainly would have had the effect of causing many Jews to leave the city rather than give up their worship practices.

Furthermore, what does it mean that there was trouble because of "Chrestus"? A few scholars are of the opinion that it is a reference to some specific person, a Jew, who was a troublemaker in the community. The majority of authorities, however, have held the view that the statement refers to conflicts occasioned by Christian influences impinging upon the synagogues, because the separation of church and synagogue was not yet absolute as it would be toward the end of the century. At this point in history there would have been no reason for the Romans to distinguish Christians, particularly Jewish Christians, as a separate group.

Another question concerns the date of such an event. Most commentators favor the years 48-50 C.E., although a date as early as 41 C.E. has also been suggested. Some historical boundaries are set by the reference in the book of Acts to the two Christian companions of Paul, Aquila and Priscilla (or Prisca), who had left Rome because of the edict of Claudius: "After this Paul left Athens and went to Corinth. There he found a Jew named Aquila, a native of Pontus, who had recently come from Italy with his wife Priscilla, because Claudius had ordered all Jews to leave Rome" (Acts 18:1-2). The critical piece of information pertaining to this text comes from a letter from Claudius known as the Gallio inscription (see the article "The Gallio Inscription at Delphi"). Based on the limited period of administration of Gallio as governor of the region, the date of his encounter with Paul in Corinth generally is estimated to have been 50-51 C.E. This would mean that any order from Claudius that caused Aquila and Priscilla to leave Rome would have been shortly prior to that date.

In summary, the actions of Claudius in this case do not seem to have been specifically anti-Semitic, and certainly not part of any campaign against Christians. Rather, his decree was in reaction to a specific, limited disturbance, which caused some Jews, and obviously some Jewish Christians such as Aquila and his wife, to move away from Rome.

The Gallio Inscription at Delphi

Fragments of a copy of a letter inscribed in stone

- ▷ Writing: Greek language
- ▷ Provenance: Delphi, Greece
- ▷ Date: Middle of the first century c.e.
- ▷ Present location: Delphi Archaeological Museum, Greece (room 14)
- ▷ Identification number: MD 3383 + 2271 + 4001 + 833 + 728 + 500 + 2311 + 2246

Delphi, located below the southern slopes of Mt. Parnassos on the northern side of the Corinthian Gulf, is one of the most incredibly beautiful sites in Greece. Famous in antiquity for being the site of the sanctuary of Apollo, Delphi drew people from all over the Mediterranean world to consult the oracle of Apollo. In 1905 Emile Bourguet was part of a French excavation team working at Delphi when he discovered four fragments of a Greek inscription. The inscription, probably once attached to one of the walls of the temple of Apollo at Delphi, was a copy of a letter from the Roman emperor Claudius. In 1910 Bourguet found three additional fragments that belonged to this inscription. These seven fragments, plus two more that were found, were pieced together and published in 1967 by André Plassart. The letter that was preserved in this inscription was sent by Claudius to the city of Delphi to address the problem of the sparse population of the city. In the letter, Claudius gave instructions to invite people from other cities to move to Delphi and to grant them equal status as citizens. The translation of the first eleven lines of the reconstructed text is as follows:

> Tiber[ius Claudius Caes]ar Au[gust]us Ge[rmanicus, invested with tribunician po]wer [for the 12th time, acclaimed Imperator for t]he 26th time, F[ather of the Fa]ther[land . . . sends greetings . . .]. For a l[ong time I have been not onl]y [well disposed toward t]he ci[ty] of Delph[i, but also solicitous for its pro]sperity, and I have always guar[ded th]e cul[t of t]he [Pythian] Apol[lo. But] now [since] it is said to be desti[tu]te of [citi]zens,

as [L. Jun]ius Gallio, my fri[end] an[d procon]sul, [recently reported to me, and being desirous that Delphi] should continue to retain [inta]ct its for[mer rank, I] ord[er you (pl.) to in]vite [well born people also from ot]her cities [to Delphi as new inhabitants and to] all[ow] them [and their children to have all the] privi[leges of Del]phi as being citi[zens on equal and like (basis)]. For i[f] so[me . . .] were to trans[fer as citi]zens [to these regions . . .][1]

For historians, the importance of this inscription is that it mentions L. Junius Gallio, older brother of the philosopher Seneca and the proconsul of Achaia ("Gallio" [ΓΑΛΛΙΩ] is in line 4 of the fragment pictured in figure 97), and provides information that makes it possible to ascertain with relative certainty the dates of his proconsulship. Achaia was a Roman senatorial province in Greece that included the southern part of the mainland of Greece and the Peloponnesus. Athens, Corinth, and Delphi were all located in Achaia. The proconsul (governor) of the province was appointed by the Roman senate and usually held the office for a year, beginning in June or July. The letter from Emperor Claudius was sent during his twenty-sixth public acclamation as emperor, which would have been between January and August of the year 52 C.E., probably in the spring or early summer of 52 C.E. (Public acclamations occurred after some major military success during the reign of an emperor.)

Gallio likely was not appointed proconsul until after his younger brother Seneca

97. The portion of the inscription at Delphi mentioning the proconsul Gallio

1. Joseph A. Fitzmyer, "Paul," *The New Jerome Biblical Commentary,* ed. Raymond E. Brown, Joseph Fitzmyer, and Roland E. Murphy (New York: Prentice Hall, 1990), p. 1330. Reprinted by permission of Pearson Education, Inc., Upper Saddle River, N.J.

returned from exile in 49 C.E. Probably the earliest year, then, for the start of his proconsulship would have been 50 C.E. Since Claudius received his twenty-seventh acclamation in August of 52 C.E., the latest date for the beginning of his term as proconsul would have been the summer of 52 C.E., which is the date preferred by some scholars. However, if Gallio started as proconsul in June or July of 52 (or even if he arrived a month or two early, as was often the case), that does not leave much time for him to become aware of the situation in Delphi, inform Claudius of the problem, and then for Claudius to send the letter dealing with the problem. More likely Gallio began his term as proconsul in the summer of 51 or even the summer of 50. Thus, either 50-51 C.E. or 51-52 C.E. was the year in which Gallio served as proconsul. For various reasons, most scholars opt for 51-52 C.E. as the year for Gallio's proconsulship. Gallio apparently did not complete his term as proconsul due to an illness and departed Corinth by ship. Thus he may have served only during the summer and early fall of 51 C.E., leaving Corinth before November, after which time the sailing season ended because of bad weather.

Biblical Significance

According to Acts 18, when Paul was in Corinth a group of Jews became upset with him and brought him before Gallio at the tribunal, claiming, "This man is persuading people to worship God in ways that are contrary to the law" (18:13). Gallio refused to get involved, however, claiming that he was not interested in matters of religious law. The case against Paul was dismissed. This incident recounted in Acts is significant because it provides one of the few reliable clues for constructing a chronology of Paul's life and travels. If Gallio was proconsul in Corinth in 51-52 C.E., then obviously this account in Acts must be placed within that time frame. Furthermore, if the suggestion is correct that Gallio was in Corinth for only a few months, then the incident with Paul could be dated more precisely to sometime between July and October of 51 C.E. The book of Acts claims that Paul was in Corinth for eighteen months (18:11). At what point during that eighteen-month stay Paul appeared before Gallio is not stated.

Letter from Apion

Papyrus letter

▷ Size: 22.5 cm. (8.86 in.) high; 14 cm. (5.51 in.) wide
▷ Writing: Greek language
▷ Provenance: Egypt
▷ Date: Second century c.e.
▷ Present location: Papyrus Collection of the Egyptian Museum, Berlin
▷ Identification number: Papyrus 7950

Frequently the material remains of a society unearthed by archaeologists are items that belonged to the rulers, the powerful, and the wealthy — such things as treasures, palaces, and tombs of the kings. Objects that reveal the everyday life of ordinary people of antiquity are not found as frequently (and usually are not as spectacular). Such is especially true of excavated written materials, which are usually limited to official documents, annals of the kings, or literary productions. Seldom do archaeologists find the more mundane records of the life of average citizens. In the late nineteenth and early twentieth centuries, however, large quantities of papyrus documents were discovered in Egypt, where the arid climate preserved the materials from decay. Much of the material was found in ancient rubbish heaps on the outskirts of old Egyptian towns and villages. The piles of papyri had been covered over by the desert sand, which helped preserve them until their modern discovery. Several thousand documents, much of them fragmentary, were found, including thousands of letters pertaining to business deals, family matters, legal concerns, and friendships.

These ancient letters provide a fascinating and at times intimate glimpse into the personal lives of ordinary citizens in the Greco-Roman world. The writings cover a wide range of subject matter: a letter from a soldier writing home to his family; a letter expressing condolences over the death of a mutual friend; a letter of recommendation; a letter from an absentee husband to his pregnant wife; a letter to a schoolboy from his mother; a love letter from a young man to his beloved; a letter dealing with the sale of agricultural products; a letter describing travel plans; and a letter dealing with arrangements for the transportation of a body for burial.

One of the papyrus letters found in Egypt is a letter from a young man named Apion who wrote home to his father, Epimachus (see fig. 98). Apion is apparently a new military recruit. Already feeling homesick, he writes to tell his family he has arrived at his destination of Misenum and to ask his father to write him to keep him informed about his family and friends. Translated, this second century C.E. letter reads:

> Apion to Epimachus, his father and lord, very many greetings. Before all else I pray for your health and that you may always be well and prosperous, together with my sister and her daughter and my brother. I thank the lord Serapis that when I was in danger at sea he straightway saved me. On arriving at Misenum I received from Caesar three gold pieces for travelling expenses. And it is well with me. Now I ask you, my lord and father, write me a letter, telling me first of your welfare, secondly of my brother's and sister's, and enabling me thirdly to make obeisance before your handwriting, because you educated me well and I hope thereby to have quick advancement, if the gods so will. Give many salutations to Capiton and my brother and sister and Serenilla and my friends. I have sent you by Euctemon a portrait of myself. My name is Antonius Maximus, my company the Athenonica. I pray for your health. (Postcript) Serenus son of Agathodaemon salutes you, and . . . , and Turbo son of Gallonius, and . . . (Addressed) To Philadelphia, to Epimachus from Apion his son. (Additional address) Deliver at the camp of the first cohort of the Apameni to Julianus, vice-secretary, this letter from Apion to be forwarded to his father Epimachus.[1]

In addition to providing information about the details of ordinary lives in the ancient world, these papyrus texts also reveal the style and shape of letters from antiquity. This letter follows the typical format found in other Greco-Roman letters. It begins with an identification of the sender and the recipient, followed by a greeting. Next is a short prayer for the recipients and a thanksgiving to the gods (letters usually had one or the other of these elements). Then, in the body of the letter, the sender discloses the main purpose for writing. The closing of the letter consists of a final greeting, a wish for good health, and a farewell. (The material identified in the translation above as "Addressed" and "Additional address" was written on the back side [verso] of the sheet of papyrus, where it would have been visible after the letter was folded.)

Biblical Significance

Letters constitute the largest genre of writings in the New Testament. Included in this category would be Romans; 1 and 2 Corinthians; Galatians; Ephesians; Philippians; Colossians; 1 and 2 Thessalonians; 1 and 2 Timothy; Titus;

---

1. *Select Papyri*, vol. 1, trans. A. S. Hunt and C. C. Edgar. Loeb Classical Library (Cambridge: Harvard University Press, 1932), pp. 305-7.

98. A letter on papyrus from a soldier named Apion

Philemon; James; 1, 2, and 3 John; and 1 and 2 Peter. Some of these should perhaps be considered "quasi-letters," since they seem to be blends of different literary genres. They are all, however, adaptations to various degrees of Greco-Roman letters, containing some or all of the elements of ancient letters. The "letters" to the seven churches in Revelation could be included here as well. However, they are in many ways more similar to royal edicts than to personal letters. The letters of the apostle Paul are among the best examples in the New Testament of early Christian letters. Paul's writings, which for the most part are addressed to churches that he had founded, are the earliest known Christian letters. Although Paul followed the basic format of Greco-Roman letters of his day, he also made significant modifications to the letter genre. By comparing Paul's letters to other ancient letters, such as the letter presented above, a careful reader can appreciate the creative literary and pastoral skills of Paul as he crafted letters to suit the individual needs of his readers.

In the opening section of his letters, Paul frequently expanded the normally curt identification of the sender, describing himself sometimes briefly ("Paul and Timothy, servants of Christ Jesus"; Phil. 1:1), and at other times at great length, depending upon the situation. His longest self-identification, for example, occurs at the beginning of his letter to the Romans, which is understandable since he had never visited this community before. Paul modified the typically cursory and formal word "greetings" (similar to our "Dear So-and-So"), using an expression much richer in theological content: "Grace to you and peace from God our Father and the Lord Jesus Christ" (Rom. 1:7). Likewise the thanksgiving or prayer that follows the salutation in Greco-Roman letters is more robust in Paul's correspondence. In fact, the thanksgiving section of Paul's letters often provides a preview of the major concerns of the body of the letter. His letter to the churches of Galatia exhibits a different modification of the thanksgiving section: it omits the thanksgiving. This omission was likely not accidental. Paul was so upset over the situation in Galatia that he did not pause to express thanks for the believers in the churches there, but launched immediately into a defense of his authority and the correctness of the message that he had been preaching.

The body of Paul's letters contains many of the elements often found in Greco-Roman letters: details of his life and work, instructions for the recipients, concern for their well-being, advice and exhortations, and travel plans. Likewise, Paul concluded his letters in the typical style of his day, sending further greetings from himself and perhaps others with him, final instructions, and a closing farewell, which Paul usually expanded to a benediction such as "The grace of the Lord Jesus Christ be with your spirit" (Phil. 4:23).

In addition to shedding light on the structure of ancient letters, the papyrus discoveries have also been of major importance in helping New Testament (and Septuagint) translators understand the meaning and nuance of certain Greek words that had rarely or, in some cases never, been found outside the New Testament before or that were now used in a different context. In 1914, not long after much of this material was made available, the first section of a groundbreaking work that made use of the papyri was published by J. H. Moulton and George Milligan entitled, *The Vocabulary of the Greek Testament Illustrated from the Papyri and Other Non-Literary Sources*. In that same year, another scholar of New Testament Greek commented admiringly on the benefit of reading these papyri: "One's mind lingers with fascination over the words of the New Testament as they meet him in unexpected contexts in the papyri."[2] Furthermore, these ancient letters often provided scholars with new insights on Greek syntax, word formation, and writing style. For example, A. T. Robertson, one of the major scholars of the Greek New Testament at the beginning of the twentieth century, when writing his massive work *A Grammar of the Greek New Testament in the Light of Historical Research*, frequently cited various passages from these "new" discoveries as examples of grammatical and syntactical constructions. In fact, this same papyrus letter from Apion was cited nearly a dozen times by Robertson to illustrate the Greek of the New Testament.

---

2. A. T. Robertson, *A Grammar of the Greek New Testament in the Light of Historical Research*, 4th ed. (Nashville: Broadman, 1934), p. xii. The comment, written in 1914, is from the preface to the first edition of the work.

Diploma Granting Roman Citizenship

Bronze diptych

- ▷ Size: 16 cm. (6.30 in.) high; 19 cm. (7.48 in.) wide
- ▷ Writing: Latin language
- ▷ Provenance: Egypt
- ▷ Date: Awarded September 8, 79 C.E.
- ▷ Present location: British Museum (room 70)
- ▷ Identification number: GR 1923.1–16.1

This diploma, inscribed on two bronze plaques, was awarded to Marcus Papirius of Arsinoe (Philadelphia), in the Fayum area of Egypt, upon the occasion of his discharge from the Roman navy after twenty-five years of service. It also granted him the privileges of Roman citizenship for the completion of his term of service with the Egyptian fleet. Those rights likewise were extended to his wife, Tapaia, and their marriage was recognized under Roman law. Their son, Carpinius, and any future children, also received such privileges. These privileges included the reduction in certain taxes, the right to vote, and protection under Roman law from some forms of punishment. (Crucifixion, for example, was forbidden as a form of execution for Roman citizens.) Another bronze diploma (P&EE 1813.12-11.1-2), in room 49 of the British Museum, was issued by Emperor Trajan to Reburrus, a Spanish decurion (junior officer) in the 1st Pannonian cavalry regiment. A similar item in the Bronfman Archaeology Wing of the Israel Museum, Jerusalem (IMJ 2002.42.18), was awarded to a member of the Roman Auxiliary Forces (non-Romans) also after twenty-five years of service, whose unit was stationed in Judea (90 C.E.) under Titus Pomponius Bassus, governor of the province.

In the early days of the republic, only inhabitants of the city of Rome itself were recognized as Roman citizens. This limitation gradually weakened as people in other areas were awarded citizenship for various reasons. Sometimes officials in other provinces were given citizenship, sometimes citizenship was awarded for meritorious service to the emperor or the nation, and sometimes citizenship was awarded to artists or others for notable achievements. Social standing generally was involved in the decision, but not invariably. As the empire expanded and Rome won victories over other countries, it became imperative for the Roman army to expand far beyond the ability of Rome or even Italy to provide the necessary troops. Conquered armies were forced into the auxiliary legions and other individuals were recruited, all with the promise of citizenship as a reward for their service. This had the added benefit to Rome of encouraging faithful fulfillment of military obligations, while discouraging desertion. The first documentation of a grant of citizenship to provincial soldiers dates to 89 B.C.E., when a proconsul enfranchised a unit of Spanish cavalrymen and presented them with a bronze tablet recording his decree. Under the emperor Claudius these military diplomas *(diplomata civitatis)* became standardized into the bronze diptych form seen here. Both sides of the diptych contained writing. The names of seven witnesses generally were required on the document. Though it is missing from this pictured diploma, a thin, arched strip of bronze usually covered the seals.

As long as Roman citizenship was limited to Rome or another municipality within Italy, proof of citizenship could be easily established by recourse to the local records. Originally only paternal recognition of a newborn child as legitimate, by the simple act of the father picking him/her up, was necessary for

99. A soldier's bronze diploma granting him Roman citizenship

proof of citizenship. In the Republican period, magistrates within the cities were required to register all citizens every five years for census and tax purposes. With the expansion of the empire and the corresponding migration of Romans to other provinces in the imperial age, the five-year interval proved inefficient and a more comprehensive method of registration was necessary. Under Augustus (4 C.E.), compulsory birth registration became mandatory. The children of Roman citizens received a wooden diploma in the same diptych form as the military diploma.

Usually individuals displayed these birth records in the home, but they were small enough to be carried on a journey, or in relocating to a new area, since they were written on two wooden boards that measured ca. 180 mm. (7 in.) high, 135 mm. (5.25 in.) wide, and only 3 to 4 mm. (ca. .19 in.) thick. (It is possible that persons who traveled a great deal may have obtained a bronze diploma, as it would have been more durable, but there is no record of such documents having been issued.) The inside surfaces of these wooden leaves were carefully cut away with a sharp instrument to a depth of 1 mm. or more, leaving a raised rim around the edges of approximately 1.9 cm. (.75 in.). This depression was then filled with wax, and the essential data written on the surface with a stylus. The same information was written on the outside of the leaves with a brush and ink. (In the provinces where Greek remained the common language, sometimes the outside copy was a Greek summary of the official Latin text inside.) The seals of the witnesses were placed in a row on the back with their signatures beside them, and the document was bound shut with cords through two or three holes in the rim. In ordinary use the outside would be shown, but the inside copy preserved a more permanent record. Parents themselves likely had to purchase these diptychs for their children, since the writing on them was done by professional scribes.

Biblical Significance

The claim of the apostle Paul that he was a Roman citizen is made more than once in the New Testament (though only in the book of Acts). He was a citizen of Tarsus, a notable city near the southern coast of Asia Minor, which was the provincial capital of the area that included the island of Cyprus. Paul says that he was a zealous, faithful Jew, of Jewish parentage:

> If anyone else has reason to be confident in the flesh, I have more: circumcised on the eighth day, a member of the people of Israel, of the tribe of Benjamin, a Hebrew born of Hebrews; as to the law, a Pharisee; as to zeal, a persecutor of the church; as to righteousness under the law, blameless. (Phil. 3:4-6)

345

Similar claims are repeated in Acts 23:6: "When Paul noticed that some were Sadducees and others were Pharisees, he called out in the council, 'Brothers, I am a Pharisee, a son of Pharisees.'" Yet Paul claimed to hold Roman citizenship. When he was being taken to the tower of Antonia in Jerusalem by Roman soldiers, after a mob had begun beating him because they thought he had taken a non-Jew into the temple area, the following exchange occurred:

> And while they were shouting, throwing off their cloaks, and tossing dust into the air, the tribune directed that he was to be brought into the barracks, and ordered him to be examined by flogging, to find out the reason for this outcry against him. But when they had tied him up with thongs, Paul said to the centurion who was standing by, "Is it legal for you to flog a Roman citizen who is uncondemned?" When the centurion heard that, he went to the tribune and said to him, "What are you about to do? This man is a Roman citizen." The tribune came and asked Paul, "Tell me, are you a Roman citizen?" And he said, "Yes." The tribune answered, "It cost me a large sum of money to get my citizenship." Paul said, "But I was born a citizen." Immediately those who were about to examine him drew back from him; and the tribune also was afraid, for he realized that Paul was a Roman citizen and that he had bound him. (Acts 22:23-29)

As a Roman citizen, Paul could not be punished by flogging, or even by binding, without a legal hearing and judgment against him. The tribune was understandably skeptical that this person could be a Roman citizen, since he himself had purchased his citizenship at a great price. (Under Roman law, citizenship could not be bought, but individuals did bribe officials in the bureaucratic system to advance them, and perhaps endorse them, as they sought the granting of citizenship.) Paul's answer was even more startling: he was born a Roman citizen. How Paul's family might have obtained citizenship is unknown. In the absence of additional information, speculation on the possibilities has proved fruitless, if interesting (e.g., perhaps it was gained through meritorious service to the empire, such as making tents for Pompey or Mark Antony when they were campaigning in Cilicia; or, perhaps Paul was a descendant of Antipater, father of Herod the Great, who, along with all of his descendants, was granted citizenship by Julius Caesar; etc.). Nevertheless, there were many Jews in Asia Minor at the time who were Roman citizens, however their citizenship might have been attained.

Another reference to Paul's Roman citizenship occurs in Acts when Paul and Silas are beaten with rods, arrested, and thrown into prison in Philippi. When the magistrates sent word the next day to release Paul and his party, Paul responds: "They have beaten us in public, uncondemned, men who are Roman citizens, and have thrown us into prison; and now are they going to discharge us in secret? Certainly not! Let them come and take us out themselves" (Acts 16:37).

A final incident referring to citizenship details the trial of Paul and his appeal to the emperor as a Roman citizen:

> Paul said, "I am appealing to the emperor's tribunal; this is where I should be tried. I have no done wrong to the Jews, as you very well know. Now if I am in the wrong and have committed something for which I deserve to die, I am not trying to escape death; but if there is nothing to their charges against me, no one can turn me over to them. I appeal to the emperor." Then Festus, after he had conferred with his counsel, replied, "You have appealed to the emperor; to the emperor you will go." (Acts 25:10-12)

Some scholars have challenged these accounts in Acts on the grounds that the requirements of the Jewish law for one as scrupulous as Saul, the Pharisee, would preclude him from being able to observe the responsibilities of a Roman citizen, particularly with reference to the gods. (Of course, it would have been Paul's father who obtained the citizenship initially, and the decision to accept those responsibilities would have been his as head of the family.) Others have speculated that Luke is merely using Roman citizenship in the Acts account to further establish his rhetorical theme that Paul was a person of honor and stature who represented the cause of Christ to the Gentiles. Others note the fact that Paul never mentions it in any of his epistles. In general, however, biblical scholarship regards Paul's Roman citizenship and his Jewish background as dual facets of his life.

Did Paul possess evidence of his Roman citizenship? Did he perhaps carry with him a birth diploma, similar to the military grant of citizenship pictured here, in his long journeys across the eastern Roman Empire? Was it necessary for him at any point to prove his citizenship, more than simply asserting it? What else would prevent anyone in a distant province from falsely claiming such rights? The text gives us no answer to any of these questions; at no point, however, does Acts say that Paul produced such a document in his defense. Nevertheless, some biblical scholars believe it is possible, and even likely, that in his traveling pack Paul had made sure to carry the small wooden version of this soldier's diptych, the document that showed he was born a free Roman citizen.

Market Gate of Miletus

Monumental marble gateway

▷ Size: ca. 30 m. (98.32 ft.) long; 16.68 m. (54.72 ft.) high; 5 m. (16.40 ft.) deep
▷ Provenance: Miletus, Asia Minor (modern Turkey)
▷ Date: 120-130 C.E.
▷ Present location: Collection of Classical Antiquities, Pergamum Museum, Berlin (room 6)

The market gate of Miletus, completely rebuilt in the Pergamum Museum in Berlin, is considered one of the greatest architectural monuments of the ancient world. It was constructed between 120 and 130 C.E. during the reign of the emperor Hadrian and served as the northern entrance to the South Market, or agora, of Miletus. The gate was modified several times over the centuries, including once when Emperor Justinian incorporated it into the city wall in 538 C.E., before it was destroyed and buried by an earthquake in the eleventh century.

Archaeological excavations conducted in Miletus between 1903 and 1905 by

100. The market gate of Miletus, now in the Pergamum Museum

the German archaeologists, Theodor Wiegand and Hubert Knackfuss, uncovered virtually the entire gate intact. In 1907-1908 it was transported to Germany by ship. In the first years after it reached Germany, the gate was placed in storage until a large enough room could be arranged to accommodate its monumental size. During 1928-1929 it was completely rebuilt within the new Pergamum Museum of Berlin, and only a relatively small amount of other materials was necessary for its reconstruction. During its installation in the museum, iron girders were affixed to the rear of the gate and attached to the museum wall for stability. Over the years, deterioration resulted in considerable sagging of the girders and caused cracks to the back of gate, which necessitated extensive restoration of the gate for stability.

This two-story gateway is one of the finest examples of Roman façade architecture in existence. It stood in front of an equally classic square that was surrounded on two sides by the Hellenistic city hall and the three-story façade of a nymphaeum (monumental fountain), 17 meters high (55.77 ft.) — virtually the same height as the gate — and 20 meters wide (65.62 ft.), with a large reflecting pool in front. Three arched openings in the lower level of the gateway, separated by paired columns of composite design, allowed passage to the so-called Ceremonial Street beyond. On its upper level, rounded niches, again separated by smaller, paired Corinthian columns, provided ideal spaces for statues of the gods or the emperors. Two short wings of similar design projected from the outer sides of the gateway, which caused an interplay of light and shadow across the structure. The entire work was richly decorated with motifs of garlands joined by bulls' heads, acanthus, and rosettes. The coffered ceiling of the structure was decorated with geometric designs.

Biblical Significance

The city of Miletus had become famed in antiquity for its philosophers of nature, such as Thales, and its architect and city planner, Hippodamus, who laid out its streets in right angles to one another on a grid plan. Originally allied with Athens and later the Lydian kingdom, the city came under Persian rule in 546 B.C.E. After Alexander the Great drove the Persian conquerors out of the city in 334 B.C.E., Miletus revived as a great center of commerce and culture.

When Paul visited the city at the end of his third missionary journey (likely late 56 or early 57 C.E.), many of its great civic and religious buildings had been constructed: the theater, the temple of Athena, the sanctuary of Apollo, and the newly constructed harbor gate with its sixteen columns, among others. The monumental gateway to the South Market, however, was not yet built; it would not be constructed for another sixty or so years. The South Market itself was there, the largest market known to have existed in the Greek world, and this gate in the Pergamum Museum gives a good idea of the classical beauty of the city in the apostle's era.

When Paul came to Miletus, he was hurrying to arrive in Jerusalem in time for Pentecost (Acts 20:16). He had spent considerable time visiting the various churches in Greece and western Asia Minor in order to raise money for the poor Christians in Jerusalem who were suffering because of a famine. For some reason, he had bypassed Ephesus and come directly to Miletus, perhaps not wishing to be delayed longer by his many acquaintances in Ephesus. In any event, this journey would mark the last time he would set foot in Greece or Asia Minor. Once in Miletus, he summoned the elders of the church in Ephesus and delivered a poignant farewell speech to them:

> "And now, as a captive to the Spirit, I am on my way to Jerusalem, not knowing what will happen to me there, except that the Holy Spirit testifies to me in every city that imprisonment and persecutions are waiting for me. But I do not count my life of any value to myself, if only I may finish my course and the ministry that I received from the Lord Jesus, to testify to the good news of God's grace.
>
> "And now I know that none of you, among whom I have gone about proclaiming the kingdom, will ever see my face again. . . ."
>
> When he had finished speaking, he knelt down with them all and prayed. There was much weeping among them all; they embraced Paul and kissed him, grieving especially because of what he had said, that they would not see him again. Then they brought him to the ship. (Acts 20:22-25, 36-38)

This speech is also important because it contains the only quotation from Jesus in the New Testament that is not found in the Gospels: "It is more blessed to give than to receive" (Acts 20:35).

There is a suggestion of another visit to the city in 2 Timothy 4:20, where Paul is described as leaving Trophimus in Miletus because of illness, but neither Acts nor any of the other letters of Paul provide any further information.

Winged Victory of Samothrace

Statue, white Parian marble; ship base, gray Lartos marble

▷ Size: 3.28 m. (10.76 ft.) high
▷ Provenance: Island of Samothrace (Samothraki, Greece; northeast Aegean Sea)
▷ Date: ca. 190 B.C.E.
▷ Present location: Louvre (Victory of Samothrace staircase, first floor, Denon Wing, section 8)
▷ Identification number: Ma 2369

This monument, the Winged Victory of Samothrace, is one of the three most famous exhibits in the great Louvre Museum, the other two being the Mona Lisa painting and the statue of Venus de Milo. The tens of thousands who view the statue each year often have little idea of its original location, nor of the mysterious sanctuary in which it stood. Its connection with the journeys of the apostle Paul is even more obscure.

This remarkable figure was discovered in 1863 by Charles Champoiseau, French vice-consul to Adrianople (Turkey) and amateur archaeologist. The head and arms of the statute are missing and have never been discovered, though various fragments have been located. The goddess of victory, Nike, stands on the prow of a ship that serves as the base of the statue, as though she had just descended from the heavens as a token of impending victory. The posture of the body suggests that the right arm was raised, perhaps to bring a trumpet to the lips announcing victory (as depicted on coins), or to cup its hand about the mouth for the same purpose. Other authorities have suggested that the right hand might have held a laurel wreath of victory. Ship monuments were frequently created in the ancient world (Rome, Lindos, Samos, Delos, etc.), both to commemorate naval victories and as an offering to the gods in thanks. (On the plateau just above the statue, and in sight of it, stood another such ship monument, one dedicated to Demetrius I Poliorcetes.)

This statue has been praised as perhaps the greatest example of Hellenistic sculpture, both for its dramatic form and its amazing execution. The style suggests the work of sculptors from the island of Rhodes at this time, and it may commemorate a naval victory by the Rhodian fleet at Side in 190 B.C.E. (Ceramic evidence at the site on Samothrace would suggest that the base was laid around 200 B.C.E., though authorities differ on the date.) The figure appears braced against a strong wind blowing against her wet, transparent garments, depicted with incredible lifelikeness in the smooth stone. The right side of the body is not worked with the same detail as the left side, suggesting that the

351

placement of the work expected it to be viewed from the front left-hand side. (The right wing of the figure in the Louvre is a plaster version of the left one, which is original.) Originally the monument stood in an imposing location above the theater at Samothrace, in a niche in the rock face of a hill, above an artificial reflecting pool across which the ship appeared to glide. As impressive as the statue is in its location today in the Louvre, it cannot approximate what must have been the total effect of that original setting.

The Greeks always regarded Samothrace as the most mysterious and remote of all the islands, as it certainly was such from ancient Athens. Samothrace was famed as the home of the Sanctuary of the Great Gods, and the ruins of its extensive and impressive temples and other structures even today give evidence of its impressive beauty in ancient times. The Great Gods were twin gods known as the Cabeiri, mysterious and much-feared volcanic gods of the underworld. Those who joined the cult of this mystery religion were promised well-being in this world and eternal life hereafter. Initiations, of course, were secretive, but they seemed to have been celebrated in midsummer when pilgrims came from great distances to join in the celebrations. Many famous people were initiated into the mysteries, including Herodotus, King Lysander of Sparta, and later, the emperor Hadrian. Likewise, it was on Samothrace that Philip II of Macedon met his future wife, Olympias, the mother of Alexander the Great, who was also attending the mysteries.

Today there is a small museum just off the main road at the foot of the sanctuary. Its small but interesting collection includes a plaster model of the Winged Victory, a marble stela prohibiting the uninitiated from entering the inner sanctum of the Anaktaron (hall of initiation) — similar to the warning at the temple in Jerusalem — oil lamps used in the initiations, and various architectural remains from the sanctuary.

Biblical Significance

Samothrace is mentioned once in the New Testament: "We set sail from Troas and took a straight course to Samothrace, the following day to Neapolis, and from there to Philippi, which is a leading city of the district of Macedonia and a Roman colony" (Acts 16:11-12). This occurred on Paul's second missionary journey after his vision in which a Macedonian man urged him, "Come over to Macedonia and help us" (Acts 16:9). Paul and his comrades then decided not to initiate work along the western coast of Asia Minor (modern-day Turkey) but to cross over into Macedonia instead, believing that they had been "forbidden by the Holy Spirit to speak the word in Asia" (Acts 16:6). So they went to Troas and took a ship bound for Neapolis, and it likely docked for the night at the small harbor of Samothrace. (If at all possible, ships avoided night crossings of the seas.) The breakwater, or harbor mole, of the ancient harbor of Samothrace is still visible just beneath the water. (That is not at the main harbor, though the locals may say so.) The ancient harbor was located on the same side of the island as its modern counterpart, but up the coast to the north, directly below the Sanctuary of the Great Gods.

There is no evidence that Paul visited the site, or even that he set foot on the island, though he may have done so. Travelers preferred to sleep on shore whenever possible rather than in crowded conditions on board ship. Sailors frequently carried small tents for that purpose, and as Paul was a tentmaker and often on ships, he may have had such a tent. (However, there is no mention of it in the Bible.) If he did go on shore, Paul's natural curiosity and the fame of the place may have led him the short distance uphill to the sanctuary, where the imposing statue of Nike immediately would have loomed large before him. As Paul had no superstitions concerning foreign gods or their images — he had no scruples against eating meat offered to idols, since, as he said, "no idol in the world really exists" (1 Cor. 8:4) — likely he would have had no hesitancy in going there. Apparently approaching the area of the monument would not have been forbidden. An inscription warned visitors not to enter the specific precinct of the Anaktaron where the initiations were conducted, so obviously visitors were expected in the general area of the site, and the Winged Victory monument lay outside the inner sanctuary. Nevertheless, the biblical text gives no indication of any of Paul's activities before the ship sailed the next day.

101. Statue known as "the Winged Victory," from the island of Samothrace, Greece

Statues of Artemis

Marble statue

▷ Size: Great Artemis — 2.92 m. (9.58 ft.) high; Beautiful Artemis — 1.74 m. (5.71 ft.) high
▷ Provenance: Ephesus (modern Selçuk, Turkey)
▷ Date: Great Artemis — first or early second century c.e.; Beautiful Artemis — second century c.e.
▷ Present location: Ephesus Museum (Room of Artemis Ephesia), Selçuk, Turkey
▷ Identification number: Great Artemis — 712; Beautiful Artemis — 718

According to Greek mythology, Artemis, one of the more popular Greek deities, was the twin sister of Apollo. Born on the island of Delos (or on the nearby island of Ortygia, according to some traditions), Artemis was the daughter of Zeus and Leto. Traditionally, she was the virgin goddess of the hunt, the protector of the young of all wild animals, and a goddess of human childbirth. Various animals were often associated with Artemis, including lions, bulls, rams, deer, and bees. In some locales, Artemis assumed the characteristics of a mother-goddess and was associated with fertility. The Romans identified Artemis with the goddess Diana. Although she was worshipped throughout Asia Minor, Greece, Syria, and even in Rome, Ephesus was one of the major centers in the ancient world for her cult.

As early as the eighth century B.C.E., a small temple to Artemis existed at Ephesus. In the late seventh or early sixth century, this temple was replaced with another temple. Around the middle of the sixth century B.C.E., a monumental marble temple was built at Ephesus for the worship of Artemis, which was destroyed by a disastrous fire in the fourth century B.C.E. Rebuilt a few decades later, this temple continued to be a center for the Artemis cult until it was abandoned sometime after the fourth century C.E., partially due to the growth of Christianity in Ephesus. The temple of Artemis (or, the Artemision), known as one of the seven wonders of the ancient world, drew visitors from throughout the Mediterranean world who came to offer sacrifices and bring gifts to Artemis.

Two large marble statues of Artemis Ephesia were found at Ephesus by excavators, both of which are displayed in the Room of Artemis Ephesia of the Ephesus Museum. These two statues depict Artemis in a style characteristic of the Ephesian Artemis cult, which was distinctive from the usual Hellenistic portrayal. Both statues were found in the ruins of the Prytaneion (the "city hall" of Ephesus), where they had been ritually buried, perhaps after the disastrous earthquake of the fourth century C.E. (They also might have been buried

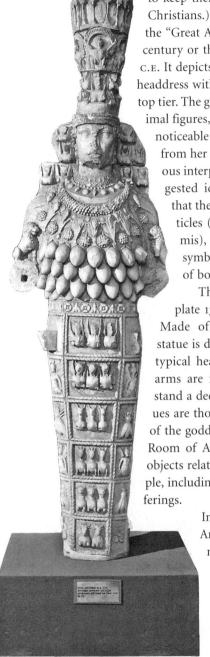

to keep them from being destroyed by zealous Christians.) One statue (number 712), known as the "Great Artemis," is usually dated to the first century or the beginning of the second century C.E. It depicts the goddess wearing a three-tiered headdress with representations of temples on the top tier. The goddess is decorated with various animal figures, including bees and bulls. Especially noticeable are the many oval objects projecting from her chest, which have given rise to various interpretations. The most frequently suggested identifications of these objects are that they represent eggs, breasts, or bull testicles (bulls were often sacrificed to Artemis), any of which would have served as symbols of fertility. Unfortunately, most of both arms of the statue are missing.

The other statue (number 718; see plate 13) is called the "Beautiful Artemis." Made of fine-grained white marble, this statue is dated to the second century C.E. The typical headdress is missing, but the statue's arms are intact. On each side of the statue stand a deer and a beehive. Both of these statues are thought to be modeled after the statue of the goddess that was in the Artemision. The Room of Artemis Ephesia also contains other objects related to Artemis and the Artemis temple, including architectural pieces and votive offerings.

In addition to the two large statues of Artemis Ephesia, other statues of Artemis were also found at Ephesus. Among these would be the statue of Artemis the hunter (inventory number 1572) that is on display in the Room of the Terrace Houses of the Ephesus Museum. This statue, from the first century B.C.E., depicts Artemis in the more typically Hellenistic representation of the

102. Statue known as "the Great Artemis," now in the Ephesus Museum

goddess in which she is portrayed as a girl or young woman in the role of the virgin hunter. She is usually dressed in a short skirt, carrying a bow and arrows. Sometimes she is accompanied by deer or by hunting dogs. This statue in the Ephesus Museum is missing part of the left arm in which she would have been holding the bow or quiver of arrows.

The British Museum has on display the base of one of the marble columns from the fourth-century B.C.E. temple of Artemis (GR 1872.8–3.9 [sculpture 1206]; located in room 22). The column drum is decorated with carved figures whose identity is disputed. This portion of the column is 1.84 meters (6.04 ft.) high and 1.97 meters (6.46 ft.) in diameter. Room 77 of the British Museum contains a variety of architectural fragments from both the temple of Artemis built in the mid-sixth century B.C.E. and the temple built in the fourth century B.C.E.

Statues of Artemis or Diana can be seen in many museums throughout the

103. Statue of Artemis/Diana, known as "Diana of Versailles"

world. A beautiful example of a sculpture of Artemis/Diana (MR 152; also numbered Ma 589), shown in figure 103, can be seen in the Louvre (room 17, ground floor, Sully Wing, section 7). Dated to the first or second century C.E., the statue is known as "Diana of Versailles" because during the seventeenth and eighteenth centuries it was on display in the palace at Versailles. This marble statue, discovered in Italy and showing the goddess with a deer, is thought to be a Roman copy based on a Greek statue from the fourth century B.C.E.

Biblical Significance

According to the account in the book of Acts of what is traditionally called Paul's third missionary journey, he spent more than two years in Ephesus, working to make converts to the Christian faith. His efforts, however, not only yielded new followers, but also aroused intense opposition from artisans in the city who made a living by selling silver shrines of Artemis. (The "shrines" were apparently miniature temples sold as souvenirs or for use as offerings in the temple. No silver miniatures of the Artemis temple have been found, although clay models have been discovered. Miniature silver images of Artemis, as well as gold and ivory ones, have been found at Ephesus.) Paul's activities were hurting their business, because he was convincing the people "that gods made with hands are not gods" (19:26). Demetrius, a silversmith who led the opposition to Paul, warned that not only would Paul's success be detrimental to their sales, "but also that the temple of the great goddess Artemis will be scorned, and she will be deprived of her majesty that brought all Asia and the world to worship her" (19:27). Enraged over the damage to their finances as well as the insult to Artemis, the people shouted, "Great is Artemis of the Ephesians" and rushed to the theater, dragging some of Paul's travel companions into the theater with them. Hearing of the outbreak, Paul wanted to rush to the theater to try to calm the crowd, but some of his friends, along with some of the city officials, convinced him not to do so. The episode ended without violence, and Paul soon departed from Ephesus.

Paul certainly would have been familiar with the temple of Artemis in Ephesus. Furthermore, he would have seen various statues and other representations of Artemis. Whereas Artemis is not mentioned elsewhere in the Bible, Ephesus is mentioned in several other places in the New Testament, usually in connection with Paul (Acts 18:19, 21, 24; 20:16-17; 1 Cor. 15:32; 16:8; 1 Tim. 1:3; 2 Tim. 1:18; 4:12). One of the letters in the New Testament attributed to Paul is known as the letter to the Ephesians, although serious questions are often raised about both its destination and its authorship. In addition, the church in Ephesus is one of the seven churches in the book of Revelation to which John of Patmos sent a letter to admonish and encourage the believers (Rev. 1:11; 2:1-7).

357

Theodotus Synagogue Inscription

Inscribed limestone tablet

▷ Size: 75 cm. (29.53 in.) high; 41 cm. (16.14 in.) wide
▷ Writing: Greek language
▷ Provenance: Jerusalem, Israel
▷ Date: First century C.E.
▷ Present location: Rockefeller Museum, Jerusalem (entrance gallery)
▷ Identification number: IAA S.842

From 1913 to 1914 the French scholar Raymond Weill excavated a part of Old Jerusalem south of the Temple Mount in the area known as the Ophel, or the City of David. In December 1913 he discovered a limestone tablet inscribed with ten lines of Greek text. The translation of the text reads:

> Theodotus son of Vettenus, priest and *archisynagōgos,* son of an *archisynagōgos* and grandson of an *archisynagōgos,* built the assembly hall *(synagōgē)* for the reading of the Law and for the teaching of the commandments, and the guest room, the chambers, and the water fittings, as an inn for those in need from foreign parts, (the synagogue) which his fathers founded with the elders and Simonides.[1]

When the stone tablet was first discovered it was dated prior to 70 C.E., a dating that was almost unanimously accepted. In recent years, however, this dating has been challenged by some scholars who would date the inscription as late as the third or fourth century C.E. Based upon several factors, however, including the archaeological level in which the stone was found and the style of Greek writing, a pre-70 C.E. dating still seems to be the most likely time period for this stone inscription. The stone slab was a building block, perhaps a foundation stone, for a synagogue.

Housed today in the Rockefeller Museum in Jerusalem, this inscribed block is important for several reasons (especially if the pre-70 C.E. date is correct, which seems likely). First, the text on this stone may provide inscriptional evidence of a first-century synagogue building in Palestine. The origin of synagogues as a Jewish institution is unclear. They may have originated as early as

---

1. John S. Kloppenborg, "The Theodotos Synagogue Inscription and the Problem of First-Century Synagogue Buildings," in *Jesus and Archaeology,* ed. James Charlesworth (Grand Rapids: Eerdmans, 2006), pp. 252-53.

the Babylonian exile as a place of worship, teaching, and community activities for Jews who were separated from their homeland. The earliest literary reference to synagogues appears in third-century B.C.E. Egyptian documents. The problem with these references, however, is that they may refer not to synagogues as buildings, but rather to a gathering of the people, since the Greek word for synagogue means "a gathering" or "a meeting." The earliest archaeological evidence for buildings in Palestine that perhaps were used as synagogues is from the first century C.E. Public assembly halls, dated prior to 70 C.E., have been found at Gamla, Masada, and the Herodium. (Similar claims have also been made about building remains discovered at Magdala, Jericho, Kiryat Sepher, and Capernaum.) Although the evidence is not decisive, some of the architectural and ornamental features of these buildings suggest their use for religious purposes, thus the conclusion that they were synagogues. The Theodotus Inscription clearly refers to a building in use as a synagogue. If its pre-70 C.E. dating is accurate, then this discovery provides solid evidence of a synagogue building in Jerusalem that was built during the end of the first century B.C.E. or early part of the first century C.E.

A second reason this inscription is significant is the title it uses for the synagogue official, *archisynagōgos*. Not only did Theodotus hold this office in the synagogue, but according to the inscription so did his father and his grandfather. If the traditional dating of the inscription is correct, then Theodotus's grandfather would have been *archisynagōgos* sometime during the first century B.C.E. This is the earliest known use of this title for the person who served as the leader of the Jewish synagogue, pre-dating by approximately fifty years other examples of a similar use of this term.

104. Inscription describing the synagogue built by Theodotus

The third reason scholars consider this inscription important is that it provides a description of some of the functions of early synagogues. The Theodotus Inscription states that the purpose of the synagogue was for "the reading of the Law and for the teaching of the commandments, and . . . as an inn for those in need from foreign parts." References in the New Testament (Matt. 4:23; 9:35; 13:54; Mark 1:21; 6:2; Luke 4:15-30; 6:6; 13:10; John 18:20; Acts 15:21) also depict the synagogue as a place where scripture reading and teaching were prominent activities.

Biblical Significance

Synagogues are mentioned numerous times in the New Testament, primarily in the Gospels and Acts. Several accounts describe Jesus teaching, preaching, and even healing in the synagogues of Galilee (Matt. 4:23; 9:35; 13:54; Mark 1:21-27, 39; 3:1; 6:2; Luke 4:14-37, 44; 6:6-11; 13:10-17; John 6:59; 18:20). The book of Acts portrays Paul as often going to the synagogues when he initially entered a city in order to share his gospel message first with his fellow Jews (13:5, 14-47; 14:1-7; 17:1-12, 17; 18:4, 19; 19:8). The results of his teaching and preaching in the synagogues were mixed. Some of his listeners received his message approvingly, while others refused to accept his teaching, at times forcing him to leave the synagogue and even the city. (The accuracy of the information in Acts about Paul's missionary activity among the Jews is suspect since Paul described himself as "an apostle to the Gentiles" [Rom. 11:13] who was sent to share the message with the Gentiles and not with the Jews [Gal. 2:9].)

Whereas in most cases in the New Testament the mention of a synagogue could be understood as a reference either to a specific building or simply to the gathered community that met in someone's home or elsewhere, in at least one case the term synagogue clearly refers to a building used as a religious meeting place. Luke 7 tells the story of a centurion who came to Jesus asking him to heal his slave who had become gravely ill. The centurion is identified as the one "who built our synagogue for us" (7:5). Some scholars have suggested that Luke's reference to a synagogue building is anachronistic, claiming that buildings used specifically for Jewish religious gatherings did not exist during the time of Jesus, but developed later. If the pre-70 c.e. dating of the Theodotus Inscription is correct, then this is evidence for at least one synagogue in Jerusalem during the time of Jesus. (Some scholars have tried to connect the Theodotus synagogue with the synagogue of the Freedmen mentioned in Acts 6:9, since both were apparently synagogues of Greek-speaking Jews. However, this claim has little evidence to substantiate it. Furthermore, the "synagogue of the Freedmen" does not necessarily refer to a building. It may designate only a community of former slaves who had been Diaspora Jews.)

Synagogue Inscription at Corinth

White marble cornice block

▷ Size: 93 cm. (36.61 in.) long; 42 cm. (16.54 in.) high; 22 cm. (8.66 in.) deep
▷ Writing: Greek language
▷ Provenance: Corinth, Greece
▷ Date: Fourth century c.e. (?)
▷ Present location: Archaeological Museum of Ancient Corinth (courtyard)
▷ Identification number: 123

In 1988 archaeologists from The American School of Classical Studies in Athens, led by Rufus Richardson, found an inscription on the underside of a white marble cornice block that apparently had been reused as the lintel over the doorway to an ancient Jewish synagogue. The damaged inscription read, "[Syna]gogue of the Hebr[ews]." Since Paul preached in a synagogue in Corinth, any evidence of such a synagogue is significant, and the discovery of this inscription created a worldwide sensation among New Testament scholars. Early optimistic reports on the stone, typically, had it dated to the first century. Subsequent epigraphic studies, based on the style of the inscription's irregular, badly cut lettering, have established that it comes from a period subsequent to the time of Paul. Precise dating still does not exist, and reputable authorities continue to date it anywhere from the second to the fifth centuries c.e.

The stone was discovered east of the Lechaion road, less than three hundred yards from the broad stairway and monumental propylaea (gateway) that led to the forum and a short distance north of the Fountain of Pirene. The first excavators speculated that the synagogue in which Paul preached must be located nearby because the size of the stone, they thought, made it unlikely it would have been moved far from its original location. Furthermore, later synagogues often were simply remodeled or rebuilt on the site of the earlier building. That conclusion has been called into question; first, because the stone is actually not so large to be unmanageable, and second, because the subsequent

105. Inscription from a synagogue at Corinth

attacks on Corinth by the tribes of the Herulians and Goths smashed and scattered stones everywhere in their rampage. (Nonetheless, it is difficult to imagine any of those invaders carrying such a stone from one location to another simply to relocate it. On the other hand, it certainly is possible that the synagogue of Paul's day, and the stone, originally might have been located in a different place.)

However, another curiosity in the inscription is also a factor in its identification. The word used for "Jews" is "Hebraioi" rather than "Ioudaioi," the common Greek term for Jews. Why the use of the archaic name? (Biblical scholars routinely use the term "Hebrews" to designate the people of Israel prior to the Babylonian captivity in 587 B.C.E. and use the word "Jews" for them after that.) The same usage of "Hebrews" is found on an ancient synagogue in Rome, and some scholars speculate that the synagogue in Corinth might have been an offshoot from it. Whether or not that is true, it may have been conventional for the first synagogue in any city to use the ethnic name, "Hebrews," while later synagogues would give themselves another appropriate name. In that case, this inscription would indicate the original synagogue of Corinth.

Another object with Jewish significance was discovered in the area of the theater, a marble impost, or capital, decorated with three menorahs (seven-branched candelabra) separated by palm branches *(lulav)* and citron *(etrog)*. The style of this subject suggests a date in the fifth century C.E. This find is unrelated to the previous inscription, but likely it was part of a subsequent synagogue. Today it is mounted in the courtyard of the museum in Corinth, just below the stone with the inscription.

Biblical Significance

Paul came to Corinth from Athens on the first of his three visits and apparently stayed there for eighteen months (Acts 18:11). Following his traditional pattern, he sought out a synagogue in which to begin his Christian missionizing. According to Acts 18:4, "Every Sabbath he would argue in the synagogue and would try to convince Jews and Greeks." Subsequently, conflicts over his attempts to persuade the Jews that "the Messiah was Jesus" (Acts 18:5) led to his expulsion from the synagogue. Paul then declared that he was turning his mission toward the conversion of Gentiles rather than Jews. Leaving the synagogue, he went to the house of Titius Justus, evidently a Roman "god-fearer" who worshiped the god of Israel but was not a Jew. This home was next door to the synagogue, perhaps even sharing a common wall with it. Though the text is not specific, the context seems to imply that Paul used this residence as the new site of his preaching. In spite of the continuing hostility from the Corinthian synagogue, Paul obviously had some success among the Jewish community. Crispus, called the "official" *(archisynagogos)* of the synagogue and "all of his household," a term that included his servants as well as his family, were converted (Acts 18:8). (In addition to Crispus, Acts 18:17 names Sosthenes also as an "official" of a synagogue, but whether he served the same synagogue, or there was more than one synagogue in Corinth, is uncertain.)

Even if this lintel stone is not from the synagogue of Paul's day, as authorities seem certain, it nonetheless reminds Christian visitors of the ministry of Paul in this vital center of the imperial Roman world.

Model Body Parts Dedicated to Asclepius

Terra-cotta models of parts of the body

- ▷ Size: Various
- ▷ Provenance: Ancient Corinth, Greece
- ▷ Date: Fourth century B.C.E. to first century C.E.
- ▷ Present location: Archaeological Museum of Ancient Corinth, Greece (Asclepion Room and room 2)

The small archaeological museum on the site of ancient Corinth contains one of the most curious collections of objects to be found in any museum in the world. In a room that is usually kept locked, the Asclepion Room, terra-cotta models may be found of virtually every part of the human body and many of its organs. (On request, the attendant usually will open the room to visitors. A few samples of these models are in a display case in room 2 of the museum.) Ancient Corinth had a notable center of healing, the Asclepion, named for Asclepius, the god of healing. In the four centuries that immediately preceded the New Testament era, Asclepius had moved from his place as a minor god of Thessaly (eastern Greece) to prominence among all of the gods of the Mediterranean world. More than three hundred temples to Asclepius in the region have been identified by archaeologists.

At the same time that great strides in medicine were being made under the school of Hippocrates, the ancient belief in the mysterious rituals of the cult of Asclepius did not waver among most people. Skepticism is evident among various sophisticated writers, but the common people were not dissuaded, and even into the Roman era the shrines were crowded with pilgrims seeking

106. Assortment of clay body parts dedicated to Asclepius

cures. Individuals from all walks of life came to the many temples around the Mediterranean dedicated to the god. Indeed, one of the most notable of these shrines, and certainly the most dramatic in its location, was on the island of Cos (Kos), and the medical school of Hippocrates itself was located on one of its terraces. Competition was keen between the priests of Asclepius and the newer physicians of that era, and though the physicians would eventually win out, at the time of the New Testament the devotion of the people to the rites of the Asclepion was still strong.

The Asclepion at Corinth, though certainly not as famous as the one at Cos or the central shrine at Epidaurus, just to the south of Corinth, was typical in its features. Located just outside the central area of the city in a quiet place with springs of water, the Asclepion functioned as a healing spa. It had rooms where its visitors could spend the night while waiting for a visitation from the god, as well as various dining rooms, gardens, and even a swimming pool, six feet deep. It was customary for those who believed themselves cured to leave a votive offering to the god in the form of a terra-cotta model of whatever part of the body had been healed. Evidence of workshops of the *koroplasts,* the Greek name for the workmen who made the models, has been found near most of the shrines. These offerings would be placed near the altar where the sacrifices to the god were conducted. The smaller models would be mounted on wooden plaques, with nails driven through holes in the casts for that purpose, and then hung on walls of the sanctuary. The larger models would be mounted directly to the walls.

The intense belief of people in the powers of the god is evidenced by the ten cubic meters of these life-size body parts that were unearthed during excavations at the shrine at Corinth. Most of these votives were found in seven deposits. They include: nine entire arms; three hands with arms to the elbows; more than twenty individual feet and nine feet that include the leg to the knee; ten legs that include the thigh; five ears; three eyes, two in one pair; eleven complete female breasts, and seventeen complete male genitals. Three torsos, two female heads, and four male heads also were found. The uniformity of the models indicates that they were professionally made, rather than being done by the donors themselves. The kind of healing desired by a person is usually self-evident from the particular organ or part of the body. The models of breasts or sexual organs, however, likely do not signify healing from cancer or other ailments, but rather an answer to prayers for a successful pregnancy or a cure for impotence.

Biblical Significance

Certainly, neither Christians nor Jews would have sought healing from Asclepius or dedicated terra-cotta votive offerings to him. However, the apostle Paul did spend eighteen months in Corinth, and his many sports analogies show him to have been a keen observer of life in that sports-mad area (1 Cor. 9:24-27). As at Athens, where he referred to an altar to an unknown god he had observed on his way to Mars Hill (Acts 17:22-31), Paul seems to have used references to local culture as a means of communicating his message. The church at Corinth was a real trouble spot in Paul's ministry, as evidenced in his two letters to them. Though the congregation was likely a relatively small one, it was fraught with divisiveness. Partisan divisions in the church centered upon attachment to various Christian leaders: Paul himself, Apollos, Peter, and even Christ (1 Cor. 1:12). Paul reminded them that the church was "the body of Christ" and that they were "members" of that body, each with valuable and unique gifts, just as the members of the human body have their own specialized functions and worth (1 Cor. 12:12-27). He makes no reference to the terra-cotta models dedicated to Asclepius, and we cannot know that he specifically had them in mind. Nevertheless, it is difficult to imagine any citizen of Corinth hearing the mention of individual parts of the body, whose functions are essential to the health of the body as a whole, without recalling the frequent sight of these models of body parts dedicated to Asclepius.

Politarch Inscription at Thessalonica

Inscribed stone slab

▷ Size: 1.8 m. (5.92 ft.) long; 82.5 cm. (32.5 in.) high
▷ Writing: Greek language
▷ Provenance: Thessalonica (Thessaloniki), Greece
▷ Date: Mid-second century C.E.
▷ Present location: British Museum (room 78)
▷ Identification number: GR 1877.5–11.1 (BM Inscriptions 171; IG 10/2 1.126)

Thessalonica was the capital of the Roman province of Macedonia. Situated on the Via Egnatia, the main Roman road that connected the Adriatic Sea on the west to Byzantium on the east, the city also had an excellent port on the Aegean Sea. The road, coupled with the port, helped Thessalonica to become a thriving commercial center. The modern city of Thessaloniki (or, Saloniki) is the second largest city in Greece today. An inscription from a Roman arch that was part of a gateway into the city of Thessalonica lists the names of the holders of public office at the time the arch was constructed. The date of the arch, part of the old Vardar Gate, cannot be precisely determined, but it was built sometime during the second century C.E. In addition to listing the city treasurer and the gymnasiarch (the person in charge of the gymnasium, which served as a social center, exercise facility, and educational institution), the inscription records the names of six (or seven; the wording is ambiguous) people who held the office of politarch. The politarchs, whose title literally means "ruler of the citizens," were the chief magistrates of the city and were appointed annually. The number of politarchs in a city varied from one location

107. Inscribed stone block mentioning city officials called "politarchs" in Thessalonica

to the next and at different time periods. During the mid-second century, when this stone block was inscribed, the usual number of politarchs in a city varied between three and seven. The politarchs performed administrative and executive functions, as well as exercising judicial authority. The chief magistrates of Hellenistic and Roman cities were known by various titles in different locales. The title "politarch" was widely used in Macedonia (northern Greece). Of the more than sixty known inscriptions that mention politarchs, three-fourths of them are from the Macedonian area of Greece, with approximately half being from Thessalonica itself.

When the Roman arch was torn down in 1876, the inscribed stone slab was saved and taken to the British Consulate in Thessalonica. The next year the British Consul General, J. E. Blunt, presented it to the British Museum, where it remains on display today. The last few letters of lines three and four are missing, since they were carved on the adjoining stone block, which was not preserved. Both Greek and Roman names appear in the list of politarchs. A translation of the Greek text of the inscription reads:

> Serving as politarchs: Sosipatros (son) of Kleopatra, and Lucius Pontius Secundus, son of Aulus Avius Sabinus, Demetrios (son) of Faustus, Demetrios (son) of Nikopolis, Zoilos (son) of Parmenion, also known as Meniskos, (and) Gaius Agilleius Potitus; treasurer of the city: Tauros (son) of Ammia, also known as Reglus; serving as gymnasiarch: Tauros son of Tauros, also known as Reglus.[1]

The first word in the Greek inscription, ΠΟΛΕΙΤΑΡΧΟΥΝΤΩΝ (*poleitarchountōn*), is a participial form of the verb that means to serve as a politarch.

Biblical Significance

The earliest New Testament letter written by Paul was probably the letter to the church at Thessalonica that is now known as 1 Thessalonians. In the letter, written around 50 C.E., Paul spoke very warmly and appreciatively of the community of Christians there, calling them his "glory and joy" (1 Thess. 2:20). According to Acts, Paul first visited the city during his so-called second missionary journey, which was his first venture onto European soil. Arriving there shortly after having spent time at Philippi, Paul shared his Christian faith with inhabitants of the city, both Jew and Gentile alike. Although he attracted some

---

1. Translation by the author (Reddish). Greek text given in B. F. Cook, *Greek Inscriptions, Reading the Past*, vol. 5 (Berkeley and Los Angeles: University of California Press/British Museum, 1987), pp. 22-23.

followers and started a church there, his activities aroused the ire of some of the locals. Not able to find Paul or Silas, his traveling companion, the angered citizens dragged Jason, who had hosted Paul as a guest, and other Christians before the politarchs (NRSV: "city authorities"; 17:6) and accused them of acting against Roman decrees. As a result of this trouble, Paul left the city and continued his travel to southern Greece (Acts 17:1-10).

The author of Acts correctly labeled the magistrates of the city as politarchs, indicating his familiarity with the office title used in that region. Interestingly, four of the names in the inscription are also attested in the New Testament: Sosipatros (Sosipater) and Lucius were the names of two of Paul's co-workers mentioned in Romans 16:21 (cf. "Sopater," a shortened form of Sosipater, mentioned in Acts 20:4); individuals named Secundus (from Thessalonica) and Gaius (from Derbe) traveled with Paul at the end of his third missionary journey (Acts 20:4); apparently a different Gaius, this one from Macedonia, also traveled some with Paul (Acts 19:29). The individuals named in the inscription are obviously not the same as the biblical persons bearing those names. The presence of these names in the inscription and in the biblical texts attests to the popularity of these names at that time.

Relief of Praetorian Guard

Marble relief

- ▷ Size: 1.59 m. (5.22 ft.) high; 86 cm. (33.89 in.) wide
- ▷ Provenance: Puteoli (modern Puzzuoli), Italy
- ▷ Date: 102 C.E.
- ▷ Present location: Collection of Classical Antiquities, Pergamum Museum, Berlin (room 18)
- ▷ Identification number: Sk 887

The Praetorian Guard was the special group of soldiers who served as body-guards for the Roman emperor. Augustus had nine cohorts of Praetorian Guards, each cohort consisting of nearly five hundred soldiers. Under later emperors the number of cohorts fluctuated from nine to twelve to as many as sixteen (under Vitellius), and the size of each of the cohorts was increased to one thousand guards. Finally, under Domitian the size was set at ten cohorts, which became the standard number of cohorts of the guard. The members of the Praetorian Guard served for sixteen years and received a much better salary and had a more pampered lifestyle than regular soldiers. The Praetorians not only served as imperial bodyguards, but also at times went on military campaigns with the emperor. During the time of the Julio-Claudian emperors (from Augustus to Nero), their duties were mainly ceremonial, serving as guards at the palace of the emperor in Rome and appearing in parades and on various state occasions. The Praetorian Guard eventually became a powerful political force, involved in removing and even assassinating emperors. In 312 C.E., Constantine disbanded the Praetorian Guard.

A soldier of the Praetorian Guard is depicted in this marble relief found at Puteoli, Italy. The soldier is holding a spear in his right hand, a small shield in his left hand, and has a sword in its sheath at his side. This relief was part of an arch erected in 102 C.E. at Puteoli to honor the military accomplishments of the emperor Trajan (98-117 C.E.). Another marble slab (MS 4916) that was part of this arch is in the University of Pennsylvania Museum of Archaeology and Anthropology (room 18). The relief on this slab shows three members of the Praetorian Guard (one soldier is partial). One of the soldiers carries a spear against his shoulder; another is carrying a large oval shield (the embossed flowers and scorpion on the shield identify the soldiers as members of the elite Praetorian Guard); and the third wears a sheathed sword at his waist. The back

side of this slab originally contained an inscription celebrating the accomplishments of the emperor Domitian (81-96 C.E.). A paranoid and cruel emperor, Domitian was finally assassinated. After his death, the senate officially condemned his memory and ordered that his name and inscriptions be erased. As a result of this *damnatio memoriae,* the honorific inscription on this marble slab was chiseled off.

108. Marble slab with a relief of a Roman soldier who was a member of the Praetorian Guard

Biblical Significance

The closing chapters of the book of Acts describe Paul's arrest in Jerusalem, his imprisonment for two years in Caesarea, his appeal for his case to be heard before the emperor in Rome, and his travel to Rome as a prisoner. When Paul arrived in Rome, he "was allowed to live by himself, with the soldier who was guarding him" (Acts 28:16). Paul was apparently under house arrest, likely chained to a Roman soldier. The end of Acts states that "he lived there two whole years at his own expense" (28:30). The soldiers who guarded Paul while he was under house arrest awaiting trial before the emperor were possibly members of the Praetorian Guard, for the imperial guard was sometimes used for this purpose.

When Paul wrote his letter to the church at Philippi, he mentioned that he was in prison at the time (Phil. 1:13). Concerned that some of the Christians in Philippi might be worried about him, Paul assured them that his imprisonment "has actually helped to spread the gospel, so that it has become known throughout the whole imperial guard and to everyone else that my imprisonment is for Christ" (1:12-13). The word that is translated here as "imperial guard" is the Greek word *praitōrion,* which is a loanword from the Latin *praetorium.* The word could refer to the Praetorian Guard, to the emperor's military headquarters in Rome, or to the residence of Roman governors in the empire. (The word occurs in Acts 23:35 also, where it clearly refers to the governor's residence: the *praetorium* of Herod.) The translation of the term is affected by the question of where Paul was imprisoned at the time of writing the letter. If he was imprisoned in Rome when he wrote to the church at Philippi (which is the traditional view), then the term likely refers to the Praetorian Guard. If he was imprisoned elsewhere, such as Caesarea or Ephesus (the leading contenders to a Roman imprisonment), the term probably denotes the residence of the provincial governor. (Even if the imprisonment was outside Rome, the term could possibly still refer to the Praetorian Guard, since imperial guards were sometimes stationed in cities outside Rome.) Scholarship is divided over the question of the location of Paul's imprisonment at the time Philippians was written, and thus over the correct understanding of the term in Philippians 1:13 as well.

Head of Nero

Bronze equestrian statue

▷ Size: 35 cm. (13.78 in.)

▷ Provenance: Cilicia, Asia Minor (present-day Turkey)

▷ Date: Third quarter of first century C.E.

▷ Present location: Louvre (room 24, ground floor, Denon Wing, section 8)

▷ Identification number: Br 22

This representation of Nero, which dates to near the end of his reign, is one of a comparatively limited number of images of the emperor that still exist after the *damnatio memoriae* against him by the Roman Senate following his death in 68 C.E. (an official order to obliterate all traces of someone's existence; literally, "cursing of the memory"). In addition to this bronze portrait head, part of a large equestrian statue, a portion of one arm and hand also remain (Br 23; 46.5 cm. [18.31 in.] long). Only the portion of the left arm below the biceps exists, but from the position of the fingers, it appears that this hand held the reins of the horse. A trace of a draped garment is visible on the left side of the neck and prob-

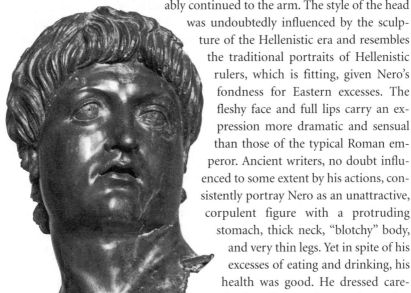

ably continued to the arm. The style of the head was undoubtedly influenced by the sculpture of the Hellenistic era and resembles the traditional portraits of Hellenistic rulers, which is fitting, given Nero's fondness for Eastern excesses. The fleshy face and full lips carry an expression more dramatic and sensual than those of the typical Roman emperor. Ancient writers, no doubt influenced to some extent by his actions, consistently portray Nero as an unattractive, corpulent figure with a protruding stomach, thick neck, "blotchy" body, and very thin legs. Yet in spite of his excesses of eating and drinking, his health was good. He dressed carelessly at times and strangely at other times (including wearing women's clothes and shoes when it pleased him). He curled his thick hair (as is

109. Head from a bronze equestrian statue of Emperor Nero

371

evident in this sculpture) rather than cut it short across the forehead, as was the custom for men of the upper classes.

As a young man Nero was said to have a handsome face and a strong body, and to be particularly adept at wrestling. His mind was quick, and he was tutored by the philosopher Seneca. He had a life-long interest in poetry, music, art, and architecture — his famous Golden House pioneered the use of vaulted rooms in Roman design — and his only noteworthy contribution to the empire was as a patron of the arts. He saw himself as a poet and musician; he could play the lyre and fancied himself a singer, though his voice was weak, but those who literally were forced by the Praetorian Guard to attend his concerts would feign death or even leap from the walls of the theatre to escape hearing him. Nero also loved the games and chariot races and competed, both in Italy and Greece, in Olympic-style contests. Unsurprisingly, he won every time, even once when he fell from his chariot and did not cross the finish line. But his real loves were poetry, singing, and the herald contests, and again, he never failed to win a gold medal.

Nero was acclaimed emperor at the age of seventeen upon the death of Claudius, thanks to the support of Agrippina, his powerful mother; Burrus, the praetorian prefect; and Seneca, his tutor. Typical of many of the emperors, his first years were politic and moderate. Claudius was deified by the senate, with the full backing of Nero, although Nero's funeral oration "honoring" him was so full of wry sarcasm that laughter broke out continuously among the listeners. (Seneca produced a satirical version of the deification, or *apotheosis*, which he called the *Apocolocyntosis* — the "Pumpkinification" of Claudius.) In these early years the emperor seemed to try to win over the senate through various means, but Nero's ruthless extermination of enemies and imagined rivals doomed that possibility: he poisoned Britannicus, his brother, whom he saw as a threat, at his own dinner table — bad form, even for a Roman emperor; eventually, his sister, his father, his mother, his aunt, and two wives were murdered or forced to commit suicide. His mother, Agrippina, had tried to dominate him, and in fact, rule, but when at last that grew unbearable for him, he had her killed (after two botched attempts). His two wives, Olympia and Poppaea, certainly anything but saints themselves, were disposed of. Nero banished and then executed Olympia; he killed Poppaea in a rage by kicking her in the abdomen, though she was six months pregnant. This list of victims does not include countless other individuals, high and low, whom he executed or had murdered for one reason or another.

Nero was always suspected in the great fire of Rome (64 C.E.) that destroyed half the city, but even Seneca doubted that he did it. He probably enjoyed it, however. He was suspected because he had already begun rebuilding projects in the poorer sections, and the fire destroyed much substandard housing. Furthermore, it cleared the area upon which he would build his unbelievable Domus Aurea, the Golden House of Nero, which he built on one hundred twenty-five acres after the fire. This personal residence featured a colossal statue of himself more than one hundred twenty feet tall (approximately the height of a twelve-story building), triple colonnades of more than a mile in front of the palace, one room with a ceiling that revolved and another with an ivory ceiling, and vast gardens complete with every kind of animal.

Money, as always — or the lack of it — was a principal reason for his fall. Nero was lavish and profligate in everything: gifts to friends and the populace, festivals and games, and construction projects. His trip to Greece with a great entourage was enormously expensive. There he had begun the often-attempted enterprise of cutting a canal through the Isthmus of Corinth using the labor of slaves, including some six thousand Jewish captives from the recent wars in Judea. Nero insisted on carrying off the first basket of earth on his own shoulders, after first singing a hymn of praise to the gods (which must have been as painful to the Jews as the labor). But money problems soon brought all such work to an abrupt halt. Nero desperately tried to staunch the financial hemorrhaging by increasing taxes on the already overburdened provinces but, as a result, Britain and Judea had broken out in riots and eventually both revolted against the empire. Instabilility abroad matched instability at home.

Much of the unrest in Rome was due to the personal habits of the emperor himself. Nero has always been notorious in history for his sexual excesses and that of his court. His sexual appetites knew no bounds, and no kind of sexual activity with anyone of any sex was considered below him. He surrounded himself with actors, freedmen, and certain lowborn persons who suited his tastes. He was as happy portraying the mistress as the master in a homosexual liaison. The extravagant parties he gave in his gardens defined the word orgy in Roman society; there nothing, including rape and incest, sometimes forced, was forbidden. Perhaps the crowning blows to his reign, as far as the senate and nobility were concerned, were his two homosexual marriages, one to a young slave that he had castrated for the purpose.

As more and more Romans fell victim to the emperor's fears — he had killed his three leading generals at one time, several key governors, and even his old tutor, Seneca — his scant support evaporated. When certain leading senators (and most especially, when the new head of the Praetorian Guard) decided enough was enough, Nero fled the city in terror, accompanied by his secretary. But as the troops drew near, Nero clumsily stabbed himself in the neck and died. Among his last words reputedly were these: "I — such an artist! — perish!" (Suetonius, *Nero* 49.1).

Biblical Significance

Nero blamed the fire of Rome on the Christians. Suetonius says that they were a new and dangerous sect, but does not say why they were dangerous. Tacitus, in his comments about the fire, says that Christians were blamed to throw suspicion away from Nero. Many were rounded up and arrested, and under torture some confessed and pointed to others (whether their confessions related to "incendiarism" or to being Christians is not clear). Their deaths were performed in a particularly barbaric manner: some were sown in animal skins and set upon by dogs, while others were crucified and set on fire to serve as torchlights along the roads and in Nero's gardens. This cruelty toward them was so savage, Tacitus says, that many citizens of Rome felt sympathetic toward them. Subsequent persecutions under Nero must have been limited and infrequent, since Pliny the Younger, governor of Bithynia, will say later in his correspondence with Trajan that he is unfamiliar with any trials or legislation concerning Christians, and his experience in Rome made him well aware of Roman legal precedents. These accounts are important historically for two reasons: first, because they document the first known official persecution of Christians; and second, because they prove that by the year 64 C.E. Christians were a distinct sect (distinct from the Jewish religion), sufficiently known to be scapegoats for the fire.

A second significance of Nero to the biblical record is the fact that he was the emperor, unfortunately, to whom Paul, as a Roman citizen, appealed for justice (Acts 25:21; 28:19) when he felt that plots against him in Jerusalem would ultimately result in his death. After languishing in prison in Rome — even though it was his own hired house with a Roman guard, paid for by himself — Paul disappears. History has concluded by the silence of the record, and in the absence of further writings by Paul, that he had been executed by the Romans. As a Roman citizen he could not have been crucified, but most likely would have been killed by the sword. Whether the outcome would have been different under another emperor of the era is impossible to know. However, many modern scholars are convinced, based on historical developments at the time, that if Paul had not appealed to Rome he might well have survived.

Menorah and Burnt House

Menorah — drawing incised on plaster;
Burnt House — one of several Jewish dwellings of the Upper City, Jerusalem

▷ Size: Reconstructed drawing — 32 cm. (12.6 in.) high; 32 cm. (12.6 in.) wide

▷ Provenance: Modern Jewish Quarter, Jerusalem

▷ Date: ca. 37 B.C.E.–70 C.E.

▷ Present location: Menorah drawing — Bronfman Archaeology Wing, Israel Museum, Jerusalem; Burnt House — the Herodian Quarter and Wohl Archaeological Museum, Jerusalem

▷ Identification number: Menorah drawing — IAA 1982-1055

When the Roman army burst into the city of Jerusalem on August 9, 70 C.E., the Upper City, known historically as the dwelling place of the wealthy aristocracy of Jerusalem, was the last part of the city to fall. It managed to hold out for another month after the destruction of the temple before being destroyed by fire and the onslaught of the legions. According to Josephus, many people who escaped the initial onslaught in the lower part of the city fled up into this section, but the subsequent slaughter of the populace there was horrific:

> Pouring into the alleys, sword in hand, they [the Roman soldiers] massacred indiscriminately all whom they met, and burnt the houses with all who had taken refuge within. Often in the course of their raids, on entering the houses for loot, they would find whole families dead and the rooms filled with the victims of the famine, and then, shuddering at the sight, retire empty-handed. Yet, while they pitied those who had thus perished, they had no similar feelings for the living, but, running everyone through who fell in their way, they choked the alleys with corpses and deluged the whole city with blood, insomuch that many of the fires were extinguished by the gory stream. (Josephus, *Jewish War* 6.404-406 [Thackeray, Loeb Classical Library])

Even taking into account the usual hyperbole of Josephus, there is no doubt that the slaughter of the people and the devastation of the city of Jerusalem was terrible and complete. Evidence of this destruction in the Upper City, an area about which virtually nothing had been known previously, came to light in the excavations conducted in the Jewish Quarter following the Six-Day War (June 1967). Professor Nahman Avigad of the Hebrew University was asked to look for any archaeological remains that might be uncovered in the rebuilding

110. Drawing of a menorah incised on plaster from a first-century house in Jerusalem

work going on in the Upper City. Excavation in the area began in 1969 and continued for fourteen years, virtually around the clock, through 1983. His work brought to light numerous dwellings that verified the historical accounts of the Upper City as the place of residence for the wealthy of Jerusalem, including the former palaces of the Hasmonean kings, the palace of King Herod, and the homes of the Sadducees and high priests, including that of the high priest Caiaphas.

The homes that were found were remarkable, fully the equal of the most luxurious Roman villas, complete with ornate mosaic floors (only in geometric patterns, rather than including animal depictions, according to the prohibitions in the Torah against such "graven images"), numerous mikvehs (pools for ritual cleanliness), and wall frescoes in the popular "Pompeian red." Some of the walls uncovered remain standing to a height of eleven feet. But evidence of burn marks on the walls, as well as charred cedar timbers from the ceilings, showed the effect of the conflagration that swept through the quarter. A unique find in the area was the oldest depiction ever found of a menorah, the seven-branched candelabra that stood in the temple, inscribed on a plaster fragment from the wall of a house that once stood only a few hundred yards away from the temple itself (see fig. 110). To the right of the menorah are two paritally preserved rectangular objects, which are likely the incense altar and the table of the bread of the Presence (or, "showbread"). The drawing, as reconstructed, is 32 cm. (12.6 in.) high and 32 cm. (12.6 in.) wide. This object is now on display in the Bronfman Archaeology Wing of the Israel Museum.

Several of these homes are now preserved in the Wohl Archaeological Museum. The first of these, known as the Western House, is near the museum entrance; from there a corridor leads to the Middle Block, which apparently encompasses rooms from two houses. To the left is the Peristyle Building, the only known example in Israel of a home with a courtyard surrounded by columns. Past it lies the largest of these residences, the Palatial Mansion. This opulent home had a floor space of six hundred square meters (over two thousand square feet) on two ground levels, and in addition it had an upper story overlooking the lower city and the Temple Mount. Stone tables of unusual quality and other luxury furnishings were found throughout the house, including rare glassware. Because of the large number of mikvehs found in the home, more than would be expected even in such a luxurious residence, initial speculation regarded this house as the home of the Jewish high priest, possibly Caiaphas himself. But no specific evidence has emerged to validate this claim. A model of the home in the museum provides visitors with an excellent idea of the size and luxury of the house.

These discoveries in themselves would have been sensational. Yet the most historic find was a small object found in a house a short distance to the north that came to be known as the "Burnt House." The floor space of this home covered approximately fifty-five square meters (180 feet; much of the original area of the home could not be excavated because it lay under existing buildings). The remains consisted of a courtyard paved with stone, four workrooms, with a portion of one or two ovens in each room; a mikveh (pool for ceremonial cleansing); and a small kitchen with floors of beaten earth that showed the sunken bases of three clay ovens. This level apparently served as the basement of the home; the upper stories of the home had been totally destroyed. Many objects were found here: stone tables; mortars and pestles; heavy grinding stones; various large vases, bowls and cups also made of stone; jars, cooking pots, and other pottery vessels; and a quantity of perfume vases. Whatever work was done here involved grinding, perhaps the making of incense for temple use.

These objects found in the Burnt House were in exactly the same place where they had been the day that the Roman invaders ransacked the place. Also, against one wall in the kitchen was found evidence of the human toll taken by the Romans' vengeance. The skeletal remains of the complete forearm and hand of a young woman approximately seventeen years of age, perhaps a serving girl, still reached for a step in the kitchen as she attempted to flee when the house collapsed. (The rest of the skeleton seems to have been somehow scattered or destroyed over the centuries.) In one of the rooms an iron spear, never used, was found leaning in a corner where it apparently had been placed for protection. But the most sensational discovery was yet to come. Here, under the debris of the collapsed walls and ceiling, a round stone weight was found, ten centimeters (4 in.) in diameter, which bore the Aramaic inscription "Bar Kathros," son of Kathros. (The stone weight is in a display case in the Burnt House.) The "House of Kathros" was known as one of the high priestly families in the first century. For the first time, not only was a home of one of the aristocracy uncovered, but it also gave evidence of possibly being the residence of one of the high priests of Israel.

Biblical Significance

According to the Gospels, when Jesus was arrested he was escorted by both Roman and Jewish guards to the home of the high priest for questioning. But who was the high priest at that time, Caiaphas or Annas? Both are identified as such in various places in the Gospels. To whose house was he taken, and where was it?

The succession of high priests in the time of Jesus is complex, as is the use of the title in the Gospels. John 18:19 refers to Annas as high priest, but he had been deposed in 14 C.E. during the reign of Tiberius by Valerius Gratus, the fourth Roman prefect over Judea, who preceded Pontius Pilate. Gratus then appointed Ismael, son of Phiabi (15-16 C.E.), who was immediately succeeded by Eleazar (16-17 C.E.) and Simon (17-18 C.E.). Gratus then appointed Caiaphas to the office in 18 C.E., and he served for eighteen years, an unusually long period of time, until he was deposed by Vitellius, Roman governor of the region of Syria (which included Palestine) in 36 C.E. The Acts account of the arrest of Peter and John for preaching the resurrection of the dead in the temple area (a doctrine denied by the Sadducees, though embraced by the Pharisees) also names Annas as high priest: "The next day their rulers, elders, and scribes assembled in Jerusalem, with Annas the high priest, Caiaphas, John, and Alexander, and all who were of the high-priestly family" (Acts 4:5-6). In Matthew, however, it is Caiaphas rather than Annas who is the chief actor. According to his account, it was in the courtyard of his house that a meeting of the high priests and elders convened to find a charge on which to arrest Jesus (Matt. 26:3), and it was to his house that Jesus was taken following his arrest (Matt. 26:57). Yet according to John, Jesus was taken first to Annas's house after his arrest and then was brought to Caiaphas (John 18:12-24). Luke, on the other hand, names both Annas and Caiaphas as high priests at the beginning of the ministry of John the Baptist: "During the high priesthood of Annas and Caiaphas, the word of God came to John son of Zechariah in the wilderness" (Luke 3:2). These and other verses show the confusion in the question.

No really satisfactory harmonization of these accounts has ever been agreed upon by biblical interpreters, but some useful suggestions have been made. First, according to Jewish tradition the office of high priest was a lifetime position. Therefore a former, living high priest may well have been still considered a "high priest." Second, five of the sons of Annas, as well as a grandson, later served in the office of high priest. Additionally, according to John, Caiaphas was the son-in-law of Annas (John 18:13), so obviously the influence of Annas continued long after his term of office. This may partially explain the prominence of his role in the Gospel accounts. Finally, many commentators have concluded that both priests were involved in some way in the last events of the life of Jesus, but that Caiaphas indeed was the official high priest at the time. (See the article "Ossuary of the High Priest Caiaphas.")

How is the Burnt House or the family of Kathros connected with all of this? There is no doubt that the Kathros family belonged to one of only a few aristocratic families whose sons occupied the office of high priest under the Romans. Among these high priestly families were the House of Boethus, the House of Annas, and the House of Phiabi. These names appear in a folk-song preserved in the Babylonian Talmud and in the Tosefta, but certainly not in a positive light (italics added):

> Woe is me because of the house of Boethus, woe is me because of their staves. Woe is me because of the House of Hanan, woe is me because of their whisperings. *Woe is me because of the House of Kathros, woe is me because of their pens.* Woe is me because of the House of Ishmael ben Phiabi, woe is me because of their fists. For they are high priests and their sons are treasurers and their sons-in-law are trustees and their servants beat the people with staves. (*b. Pesahim* 57:1; *t. Menahot* 13:21)[1]

These verses, written in the sixth century c.e., attack these high priestly families for various offenses, including violence, slander, and other abuses. "Hanan" here is the same as the Greek "Annas." Some scholars have also suggested that the roots of the names "Caiaphas" and "Kathros" bear such close similarities phonetically that they may well belong to the same family. Whether or not that is true, and whether either the Burnt House or the Palatial Mansion is the original residence of the high priest at the time of the trial of Jesus, these homes nevertheless give a profound insight into the luxurious dwellings of the aristocratic Sadducees and priestly class during that era.

1. Translation from M. Stern, "Chapter 11: Aspects of Jewish Society: The Priesthood and Other Classes," in *The Jewish People in the First Century,* vol. 2, edited by S. Safrai and M. Stern in co-operation with D. Flusser and W. C. van Unnik, Compendia Rerum Iudicarum ad Novum Testamentum, Section One (Assen/Maastricht: Van Gorcum; Philadelphia: Fortress, 1987), pp. 603-4.

Head of Vespasian and Statue of Titus

Vespasian: Head from a marble statue

▷ Size: 45.5 cm. (17.72 in.) high
▷ Provenance: Carthage (modern Tunisia)
▷ Date: 70-80 C.E.
▷ Present location: British Museum (room 70)
▷ Identification number: GR 1850.3–4.35

Titus: Marble statue

▷ Size: 198 cm. (78 in.) high
▷ Provenance: Found (1828) in a garden of the Lateran in Rome
▷ Date: 79-81 C.E.
▷ Present location: Braccio Nuovo, Vatican Museums, Vatican City
▷ Identification number: 2282

The emperors Vespasian and Titus, father and son, are remembered in the history of Rome for solidifying the empire after a tumultuous period of civil war. In biblical history, however, they are remembered for something entirely different — the destruction of Jerusalem and the burning of the temple in 70 C.E. The two images of the emperors displayed here represent the aspects of their careers as leaders of the Roman Empire. The head of Vespasian (fig. 111) gives a sense of the mature emperor as a canny administrator. The statue of Titus pictured here (fig. 112) shows him in his toga as he would have appeared before the Roman senate or on the streets of Rome. Another impressive statue of Titus (shown in plate 14), which was made shortly after the final collapse of Judea, portrays him as a battlefield commander dressed in his full uniform as a general of the army. This statue (inventory number 6059) is owned by the National Archeological Museum of Naples, Italy. Unfortunately, it is not on permanent display, but is occasionally displayed in special exhibitions in the Naples museum or on loan to other museums. Both images are true to history.

Vespasian was born in 9 C.E. into an equestrian family; his father was a prosperous tax collector and moneylender. He began his public career as an aedile (a city administrator) in Rome, but not on an auspicious note. Caligula not only once rebuked him for not keeping the city streets clean, but also dropped him into a muddy street to reinforce the fact. Under Claudius, things took a turn for the better. Vespasian served with the army in Germany and then commanded the Second Legion in southern Britain. He was named con-

111. Head from a marble statue of Vespasian

sul of Rome in 51 C.E., and later governed North Africa. He also accompanied Nero on his famous tour of Greece, but his success as a general was far superior to his career as a courtier. Vespasian was in the habit of leaving the room whenever Nero was singing, and finally, when he slept through Nero's reading of one of his own poems, he was banished from court circles. After retiring to an obscure town for a while, afraid for his life, he was surprised to receive command of the army in Judea, which was engaged in running battles with Jewish rebels. Nero may have been angered over the slights of Vespasian, but he knew him to be a shrewd, experienced general in such siege warfare as they were waging in Judea. Vespasian entered Judea in 66 C.E. and quickly won several battles against the Jews. One of his captives was Josephus, general of the Jewish rebel army in Galilee, who later became the famous chronicler of the history of the Jews. The wily Josephus told the ever-superstitious Vespasian that soon he would become emperor. When that turned out to be true, Vespasian released him, and Josephus became an apologist for the Romans as well as a historian of the Jewish people.

After the death of Nero in 68 C.E., the empire was plunged into chaos. Galba, Otho, and Vitellius all briefly held the title of emperor in the year 69 C.E., and all died; Galba and Vitellius were murdered, and Otho committed suicide. It was left to the armies to settle the raging civil war. The legions in the east, beginning with those in Egypt, hailed Vespasian as emperor, and the armies in the west soon followed their example. Vespasian therefore left the conduct of the war to his son, Titus, and returned to Rome to accept the acclamation of the senate (69 C.E.). The war had dragged on during 67-68 C.E. due to the conflicts at home, but with Vespasian stabilizing Rome, Titus laid siege to Jerusalem and reduced it to rubble in 70 C.E. Upon his return, he joined his father in a spectacular triumph through the streets of Rome. The famous Arch of Titus, still standing in the ancient forum of Rome, celebrates their victory.

Vespasian's reign as emperor (69-79 C.E.) was altogether successful. Immediately upon taking power, he began numerous reforms. Abuses in the law courts, the military, and the imperial court itself were ended. The infamous "law of treason," used to eliminate political enemies and seize their wealth, was revoked. The treasury was strengthened, though not always to the satisfaction of the wealthy, because taxes were increased, sometimes doubled. Vespasian instituted a tax on the Jews of a half-shekel to repair the Capitoline temple, damaged in the civil wars, and likely also to punish the Jews by reminding them that they no longer had a temple to which to pay the same tax. He also placed a tax for the first time on the use of public urinals, and Titus objected on the grounds that such a tax was beneath the dignity of their court. Vespasian, noted for his sense of humor, held a coin under Titus's nose and asked if it smelled differently, since it had come from that tax. He angered the young men of the upper classes by prohibiting moneylenders from allowing sons to borrow against their future inheritances. Though he developed a reputation as personally greedy for his many taxes, he lived a conservative life by the standard of other emperors. He would not live in the imperial palace (the infamous Domus Aurea — the Golden House — of Nero), which he used for public building projects, but had his own house in a park in the city.

On the other hand, Vespasian was popular with many of the common people because of his generosity and his common ways. He was plain spoken and his speech was peppered with profanity (think Lyndon Johnson). Once when a young officer who was wearing too much perfume approached him, he revoked the officer's command. Vespasian also was the emperor who began construction on the vast Coliseum of Rome, though it was left to Titus to complete it in 80 C.E. After a long life, he died quietly at his country home in Renate, the same town in which he had been born. When he felt the onset of his illness, he was said to quip, "Oh no! I think I am becoming a

112. Marble statue of Titus, now in the Braccio Nuovo, Vatican Museums

god!" (Suetonius, *Vespasian* 23.4). In fact, he was — at least by official Roman standards — as he was subsequently deified by the senate.

The administration of Titus (79-81 C.E.) was even more popular, perhaps because it only lasted a little over two years. He was said to have an exceptional memory and to read Latin and Greek fluently. Titus had a reputation also as an excellent soldier. Once his horse was killed out from under him, and he took the horse of the man fighting next to him. Suetonius says that in the final attack on Jerusalem he killed twelve defenders with twelve arrows, and that the city was taken on his daughter's birthday, much to the delight of his troops. Titus seemed genuinely to court the friendship of the people of Rome and did his best to grant requests, whenever possible. Once when his staff criticized him for promising more than he could deliver, he was said to reply that no one should leave a conversation with the emperor feeling unhappy. On a day when he had not given anything to anyone, he said to his dinner guests, "Friends, I have lost a day" (Suetonius, *Titus* 8.1 [Rolfe, Loeb Classical Library]). The infamous informers who sought to ruin others were particular targets, and Titus banished many of them to remote islands, while others were beaten with whips and rods in the forum and then exhibited in the arena.

In spite of his general good nature, Titus was overly fond of drink and his passions led to many courtesans, both male and female. He carried on a torrid affair with Queen Berenice of Judea, daughter of Agrippa I, who had first come to Rome in 75 C.E. and returned when Titus became emperor; but when the situation became notorious, he sent her away from Rome, though, according to Suetonius, neither of them wished it. He was often ruthless in dealing with enemies who exceeded his patience. Nonetheless, Titus added to his favorable reputation by his swift and effective response to calamities in the empire. During his reign, Mount Vesuvius erupted and buried Pompeii and Herculaneum, and a fire erupted in Rome that burned for three days and nights. The emperor donated statues from his own estate to various public buildings that had been destroyed, and he provided financial and medical assistance to the victims of the volcanic eruption.

The reign of Titus was cut short by his sudden death due to a fever, September, 81 C.E. He was forty years old. Like his father, he, too, was deified by the senate.

Biblical Significance

The lives of Vespasian and Titus are as intertwined in their relation to the Bible as in their public lives. Both of them spent time as military commanders in Israel during the years of rebellion that led up to the destruction of Jerusalem, and Titus had taken part in four successful sieges against cities in Judea prior to the storming of Jerusalem (Jotapata, Japha, Tarachaeae, and Gamla). In some ways, these two emperors may have affected Judaism more than any other rulers in history.

Judea had suffered from onerous taxes in the past, as well as from other abuses at the hands of the Romans. Yet the Jewish people and their religion had steadfastly continued. But with the destruction of the temple under the bloody and relentless siege of Titus — which may well have come in reprisal for the heavy losses of the Romans, in spite of the statements of Josephus to the contrary — Judaism was permanently altered. With no temple, the sacrificial system and its offerings collapsed. So did the traditional priesthood. The Sadducees, the party of the aristocracy, and the Sanhedrin, the religious ruling body of Israel, likewise vanished. Only the Pharisees, a lay organization, and the synagogue survived. With no intent and even less interest, the total annihilation of the Jewish religious structure by Vespasian and Titus led to the eventual development of modern Judaism. In other respects, the emperors showed no signs of being anti-Semitic in their administrations, the temple tax of Vespasian notwithstanding. Taking the treasures from the temple in Jerusalem (which was enormously wealthy due to its taxes and the moneys left for safekeeping in its possession) was standard practice for the Romans. On the inside walls of the Arch of Titus these treasures, including its golden menorah and the silver trumpet-shaped offering containers, are depicted, providing a first-century look at these objects.

Likewise, in a sidebar of the campaign, the capture of Josephus in Galilee would result in the only detailed history of the Jews during this period that would ever be produced. From it, almost exclusively, we learn of the Pharisees and Sadducees, as well as of the minor parties and many religious divisions of the day. Without the writings of Josephus, religious scholarship would be crippled in understanding the times, both the Hellenistic and Roman periods.

Judea Capta Coin

Bronze sestertius coin

▷ Size: ca. 35 mm. (1.38 in.) diameter
▷ Writing: Latin language
▷ Provenance: Rome
▷ Date: ca. 71 C.E.
▷ Present location: British Museum (room 70)
▷ Identification number: CM BMC Vespasian 342

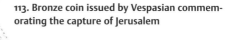

**113. Bronze coin issued by Vespasian commem-
orating the capture of Jerusalem**

To commemorate the Roman victory over Judea in the First Jewish
Revolt (66-74 c.e.), which was cli-
maxed by the destruction of Jerusalem and the burning of its temple, the
emperor Vespasian issued a large series
of coins that bore the legend "Judea
Capta" ("Judea vanquished"). The campaign
originally was led by Vespasian, but when he left Judea to accept the acclamation of the senate as the new emperor of Rome, he put his son, Titus, in charge
of the war. It was Titus who subsequently achieved the final victory (see the article "Head of Vespasian and Statue of Titus"). This series of coins would continue for twenty-five years under Vespasian and his sons who succeeded him
as emperor, Titus and Domitian. The coins were issued in various denomina-
tions of silver and gold as well as bronze. The majority of them were minted in
Rome, but they were produced also in more than forty mints across the empire, including one in Caesarea in Judea. Only bronze coins were minted in
Judea. The coins produced in Rome had Latin inscriptions; those produced
elsewhere in the empire generally were inscribed in Greek. (The Greek term
for Judea Capta on the coins was "Ioudias Ealokuias," with the same meaning.)

This particular coin shows two figures on either side of a date palm. The
seated woman on the left represents Judea in mourning. The standing figure is
a captured Jewish male with his hands tied behind his back. He stands before
armor captured in the war. The inscription "SC" beneath the figures is an abbreviation for S[enatus] C[onsulto], "by the decree of the senate." Many other
varieties of these coins were produced. Sometimes the victorious emperor is
portrayed, along with the Jewish woman in mourning; on other coins, only a
seated captive with hands bound behind his back is pictured. New designs
were developed under both Titus and Domitian. Some coins of Domitian picture the goddess Nike writing on a shield, or the goddess Minerva with a spear,
shield, and trophy.

These commemorative coins were particularly important to Vespasian for a
number of reasons. The war in Judea had dragged on for several years at great
expense to the nation, and sharp questions were being raised about the empire's inability to subdue such a tiny nation. For the Flavian family, the new
imperial house, conquering Judea was an important trophy. Extraordinary
celebrations were held in Rome in 71 c.e., and a spectacular triumph was held

for both Vespasian and Titus. Later, Titus would dedicate the great Arch of Titus as a monument to the victory, and it still stands in the Roman Forum today. The inner walls of the arch show reliefs of Roman soldiers bearing spoils from the temple in Jerusalem, including the golden menorah that stood in the temple. Finally, these coins also served as propaganda to other nations, warning them against the futility of resisting Roman imperial power.

The Romans produced similar coins following their victories over other nations, including Egypt, the Germans, the Dacians (Romania and Moldova), and the Spanish tribes. Augustus issued the Egyptian coin after his conquest of Egypt in 28 B.C.E. This coin carried a similar legend to the Judea Capta coin: "Aegupto Capta" ("Egypt vanquished"). On one side it depicted a crocodile.

Biblical Significance

The conquest of Judea portrayed on these coins totally altered the Jewish religion forever. Virtually all of the well-known institutions of first-century Israel vanished. The temple disappeared and was never replaced. Eventually the Jews were totally banished from their own capital city, and this prohibition would last until the end of the fourth century. The emperor Hadrian replaced Jerusalem with a totally Roman city, Aelia Capitolina, with a temple to a Roman god, Jupiter Capitolinus, built over the former site of the Jewish temple. This meant that the synagogue would grow in importance as an institution for sustaining the Jewish community. The sacrificial system ceased to exist, and a renewed emphasis on the study of the Torah resulted. Likewise, the upper priesthood with its high priest was no more, and the ecclesiastical judicial system of the Jews known as the Sanhedrin ended. Along with them went the aristocratic politico-religious organization known as the Sadducees. Only the Pharisees, the devout separatists connected with the synagogue, survived. The favored status Jews once enjoyed at the hands of the early imperial courts was severely compromised. Nero sent six thousand Jewish slaves from Judea to Corinth in an attempt to dig through the Isthmus of Corinth and create a canal for shipping. The attempt was unsuccessful, but doubtless many of the slaves remained in that area.

Christians, great numbers of whom were Jewish, were affected also. They suffered along with their Jewish neighbors in the attack on the city and its aftermath. No doubt many of them also were scattered from Judea as a result of its conquest. Some Christians saw the destruction of Jerusalem as fulfillment of the words of Jesus as given in Matthew 24:1-2:

> As Jesus came out of the temple and was going away, his disciples came to point out to him the buildings of the temple. Then he asked them, "You see

all these, do you not? Truly I tell you, not one stone will be left here upon another; all will be thrown down."

Others would have remembered the words of the prophet Isaiah:

> For Jerusalem has stumbled
>   and Judah has fallen,
> because their speech and their deeds are against the Lord,
>   defying his glorious presence.
> . . . .
> Your men shall fall by the sword
>   and your warriors in battle.
> And her gates shall lament and mourn;
>   *ravaged, she shall sit upon the ground.* (Isa. 3:8, 25-26; italics added)

It must have been virtually impossible for any former citizen of Jerusalem, Jewish or Christian, to look upon the images depicted on the Judea Capta coin and not remember the vivid imagery of the prophet's words.

The Great Altar of Pergamum

Monumental marble altar

▷ Size: Base of the original altar — ca. 36.44 m. (119.55 ft.) long; ca. 34.2 m. (112.2 ft.) deep; 9.66 m. (31.69 ft.) high
▷ Provenance: Pergamum (Bergama, in modern Turkey)
▷ Date: First half of the second century B.C.E.
▷ Present location: Collection of Classical Antiquities, Pergamum Museum, Berlin (room 2)

In 1871 the German engineer Carl Humann, who was in Germany as a supervisor for a construction firm, discovered marble architectural pieces and fragments of reliefs that had been reused in a section of the Byzantine city wall at Pergamum. As a result of these discoveries, several excavation campaigns were started by the Berlin Museum in 1878, with Humann as one of the expedition leaders. During the excavations, Humann discovered the remains of the Great Altar, including its foundations, 132 relief panels and hundreds of relief fragments, statues, busts, inscriptions, and other architectural pieces. These pieces of the Great Altar were shipped to Germany, where the altar was partially reconstructed with the assistance of these recovered remains. This magnificent reconstruction is now on display in the Pergamum Museum in Berlin. The remains of the marble base of the altar (a five-stepped platform) can be seen today on the acropolis of Pergamum.

The marble base of the Great Altar was almost a square, 36 meters (119.55 ft.) by 34.2 meters (112.2 ft.). This five-stepped base (or, crepidoma) surrounded the altar on all four sides. On top of this was a large platform shaped like a "square horseshoe" that extended along the north, east, and south sides. On the west side was a twenty-meter-wide (65.62 ft.) flight of marble stairs that led to the upper part of the structure. Running around the midsection of this platform was a relief frieze measuring 2.3 meters (7.55 ft.) high and 113 meters (370.73 ft.) long. This frieze contained more than one hundred larger-than-life-size figures. The scenes on the frieze depicted the mythological battle between the Giants and the Greek gods and goddesses. A colonnaded stoa ran along the top of the platform and across the top of the stairs, thus creating an open court in the middle of the structure. In the middle of this open court was the altar for burnt offerings. On the three walls inside this court that surrounded the altar was another series of carved relief panels. This frieze por-

114. Reconstruction of the Great Altar of Pergamum

trayed the story of Telephus, the son of Hercules and the legendary founder of Pergamum.

Often called the Great Altar of Zeus, the altar likely actually served as the altar for both the temple of Athena and the temple of Zeus, both of which at the time were located nearby. The Great Altar was built by Eumenes II, who also remodeled the sanctuary of Zeus and the sanctuary of Athena. Eumenes II was king of Pergamum from 197 to 159 B.C.E. The Great Altar, constructed of marble with Ionic columns, elaborately carved friezes, and a monumental stairway, was one of the most impressive as well as one of the most important structures in ancient Pergamum. Located on a prominent position on the southern slope of the acropolis, the Great Altar would have been visible from a considerable distance away and would have been the dominant sight on the acropolis. Unfortunately, as with several other building projects started by Eumenes, the Great Altar was not completely finished at his death. His brother and successor, Attalus II, chose not to complete his brother's unfinished projects.

The city of Pergamum was the capital of one of the most powerful kingdoms in Asia Minor during the third and second centuries B.C.E. At one time, much of Asia Minor was under the control of the Pergamum kingdom. The time of Eumenes II was the height of the power and glory of Pergamum. Not only was the kingdom politically and militarily strong, but it also fostered and nurtured the arts. Renowned for its impressive library (supposedly containing 200,000 volumes and second only to the great library at Alexandria, Egypt), its sculpture, and the magnificent architecture of its buildings, Pergamum was one of the leading cultural centers of the Mediterranean world. A careful examination of the reconstructed Great Altar will suggest that Pergamum's reputation was well deserved. The Attalid kingdom of Pergamum ended in 133 B.C.E. with the death of Attalus III, who had bequeathed the kingdom in his will to the Romans. Under Roman rule, Pergamum's fortunes fluctuated. The city experienced periods of prestige and growth, coupled with eras of decline. At one point it seems to have been the capital of the Roman province of Asia Minor, although it was often overshadowed by Ephesus as the leading city of the area.

In the Pergamum Museum in Berlin the complete altar has not been rebuilt. The entire front (west) side, with its broad staircase, was reconstructed. Visitors can admire the panels of the frieze that decorate the walls, climb the stairs, and walk through the colonnade at the top of the altar. Even in its partially reconstructed state, the Great Altar is still awe-inspiring.

Also in the Pergamum Museum (Collection of Classical Antiquities, room 8) is the reconstructed marble propylon (entrance way) of the Sanctuary of Athena from the acropolis at Pergamum. Athena was the chief goddess of the city of Pergamum. Her sanctuary on the acropolis of the city contained a temple set within a sacred enclosure that was surrounded on three sides by stoas. This monumental, two-story gate was the main entrance to the sanctuary and was added in the second century B.C.E. The Greek inscription on the upper portion of the lower story reads, "King Eumenes to Athena Bringer of Victory."

Biblical Significance

In chapters 2 and 3 of the book of Revelation, the author, John of Patmos, penned messages to churches in seven cities of Asia Minor. One of those churches was located in the city of Pergamum. Revelation 2:13, addressed to the Pergamum church, states, "I know where you are living, where Satan's throne is." Several suggestions have been offered concerning the identity of "Satan's throne," including that it is a reference to the Asclepion (a sanctuary/healing center of Asclepius, the god of healing) or to the temple to the emperor Augustus (the remains of which have not been found, but whose existence is mentioned in ancient writings and is depicted on ancient coins).

For many interpreters, the most plausible suggestion, however, is that "Satan's throne" is a reference to the temple complex at Pergamum that contained the Great Altar and the temples to Zeus and Athena (or perhaps to the Great Altar alone). For John, the worship of Zeus (or of any other god besides the God of the Bible) was tantamount to worshipping Satan, the archenemy of God. The Great Altar was the center of the worship of Zeus (and likely Athena, as well) at Pergamum. Thus, this was his "seat," his power base, his "throne." (The shape of the Great Altar could also have suggested the metaphor of a large throne.) Furthermore, since the Roman emperor was sometimes thought to be the earthly manifestation, or at least the representative, of Zeus, then the reference to the "throne of Satan" at Pergamum may encompass both the worship of Zeus and the worship of the emperor. Faithfulness to God had already cost the life of at least one of the Christians at Pergamum — "Antipas my witness, my faithful one, who was killed among you, where Satan lives" (2:13). The rest of the church at Pergamum had also been faithful, refusing to compromise their commitment to God, even though they lived in the very shadow of "Satan's throne."

Head and Arm of a Statue of Domitian

Marble statue

▷ Size: Head — 1.25 m. (49.21 in.) high; arm — 1.75 m. (68.90 in.) long
▷ Provenance: Ephesus (modern Selçuk, Turkey)
▷ Date: End of first century C.E.
▷ Present location: Ephesus Museum (Imperial Cult Room), Selçuk, Turkey
▷ Identification number: Head — 1/76/92; hand — 2/76/92

During the first and second centuries C.E., the city of Ephesus was probably the third or fourth largest city in the Roman Empire, with a population estimated at 225,000 to 250,000. Serving as the capital of the Roman province of Asia (in western Turkey), Ephesus proudly boasted of being the first and greatest metropolis of Asia. On at least four occasions the city was honored with the title of *neokoros,* or temple warden, for its temples for the imperial cult. One of these temples was the temple of the Flavian Sebastoi (sometimes called the temple of Domitian), built toward the end of the first century C.E. during the reign of Domitian as emperor (81-96 C.E.). The temple stood on a terrace structure in the middle of the city and was dedicated to Domitian and his predecessors, Titus (his brother) and Vespasian (his father). These three emperors were known as the Flavian Sebastoi. (*Flavius* was their "family name" and *sebastoi* is the Greek equivalent of "augustus," a title given to the Roman emperors.) Nothing much remains of the temple today, except the terrace on which it was built.

The terrace was constructed over a vaulted substructure. When archaeologists excavated this substructure of the temple terrace, they discovered the remains of a colossal marble statue of an emperor. The most impressive remains of the statue that were recovered were the head and the left forearm (see fig. 115). The head is turned slightly to the left; the upraised arm likely originally held a spear. Parts of the feet and fingers were also found. This statue, which probably stood more than 7 meters (23 feet) tall, has usually been identified as a statue of Domitian. Some scholars, however, have argued that the statue represented his brother Titus. The head, arm, and left big toe of the statue are on display in the Imperial Cult Room. On the opposite side of the room are relief panels from an altar (inventory number 373) that stood in front of the temple of the Flavian Sebastoi. The reliefs on the front panels and one of the side panels depict military paraphernalia (helmets, shields, armor, swords, and sheaths); the other side panel shows a bull beside an altar prior to being sacrificed.

Emperor worship involved the offering of divine honors, including sacrifices, to the Roman emperors. Although the custom developed slowly and was variously tolerated or promoted by different emperors, by the end of the first century C.E. the imperial cult was widely established in the Roman Empire, and particularly strong in Asia Minor. Cities vied for the honor of being allowed to build a temple to one or more emperors and, consequently, to be designated a *neokoros,* or temple warden. In many of the cities, festivals were held to honor the emperors on their birthdays, to celebrate their military victories, or to commemorate important events in the life of the emperor or their families. These festivals, which often lasted for days, included public feasts, athletic contests, processionals, and sacrifices to the gods. Social pressure to participate in emperor worship would have been strong. To be a part of the civic life of the cities of the empire, particularly in Asia Minor, meant being involved in the imperial cult. Participation in the worship of the emperor was a way of showing loyalty to the ruler and to the Roman Empire. Although there does not seem to have been any empire-wide enforcement of participation in emperor worship, overzealous local officials may have emphasized emperor worship as a way of ingratiating themselves to the Roman rulers.

In addition to these objects related to the imperial temple, the Ephesus Museum also displays an interesting variety of material goods uncovered from the archaeological excavations of the ancient city. These well-displayed objects in the museum provide an insightful glimpse into the political, social, and religious life of the inhabitants of this important city in ancient Asia Minor.

Although many of the ancient representations of Domitian were destroyed or reworked to depict other emperors after the *damnatio memoriae* against him (see below), various museums around the world display sculptured images of Domitian, including the National Archaeological Museum in Naples, the Vatican Museums in Rome, the National Archaeological Museum in Athens, and the Museum of Fine Arts in Boston. Many museums also display coins minted by Domitian that are stamped with his image. The coin shown in plate 15 (CM 1872.7–9.506; BMC Domitian 371), on display in room 70 of the British Museum, was made to celebrate Domitian's German campaign between 85 and 89 C.E. The coin is a bronze sestertius, minted in Rome.

The Delphi Archaeological Museum in Delphi, Greece, displays a dedicatory inscription from Domitian commemorating repairs he made to the temple of Apollo at Delphi in 84 C.E. (room 12; inventory numbers MD 1128, 1173, 1680, 1709). The inscription reads, "Emperor Caesar Domitian, son of the divine Vespasian, Augustus Germanicus, Pontifex Maximus, three times holder of tribunician power, father of the fatherland, acclaimed emperor seven times, consul ten times, designated consul eleven times, repaired the temple of Apollo at his own expense."

Titus Flavius Domitianus (Domitian) became emperor in 81 C.E. when his brother Titus died unexpectedly from a fever, after having served as emperor for only two years. Domitian's reign was portrayed by the Roman historians (such as Tacitus, Suetonius, Pliny the Younger, and Dio Cassius) as tyrannical and ruthless, especially in his latter years. His relationship with the senate was particularly difficult. He alienated the senate and aristocracy by intimidating and punishing them and confiscating power. He exiled several of his senatorial opponents and even had some of them put to death. As presented by the ancient writers, the latter part of Domitian's reign was a time of intimidation and fear, brought about by an emperor who was paranoid, cruel, and self-aggrandizing. Anyone who was perceived as a threat to Domitian's power or even failed to show proper respect and reverence for the emperor risked persecution or death. Dio tells of one woman who "was tried and put to death be-

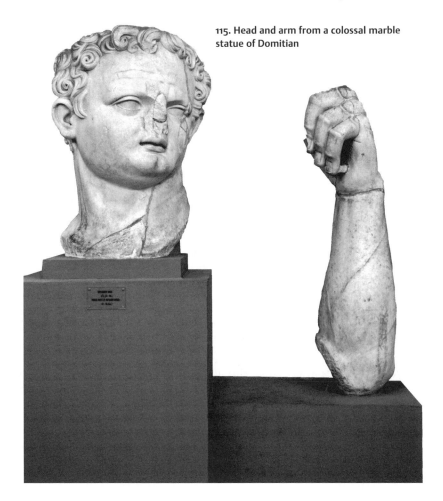

115. Head and arm from a colossal marble statue of Domitian

cause she had undressed in front of an image of Domitian" (Dio Cassius, *Roman History* 67.12.2 [Cary, Loeb Classical Library]). As a further example of Domitian's exaggerated self-importance, Suetonius claimed that the emperor sent out a circular letter in the name of his procurators that began with the words, "Our Master and our God bids that this be done" (Suetonius, *Domitian* 13.1-2). Furthermore, Dio says that Domitian insisted that he be considered a god and took pride in being called "master" and "god" (Dio Cassius, *Roman History* 67.4.7). The use of these titles for Domitian, however, has not been found on any coin or inscription, or in any contemporary writing.

Early Christian tradition remembered Domitian as one of the early persecutors of the church. Evidence for such persecutions, however, is difficult to find. At most, one can point to a few isolated situations in which a handful of Christians were persecuted. Even in those cases, they likely were punished not simply because they were Christians, but because they were thought to be guilty of other charges. (The letters between Pliny the Younger and the emperor Trajan suggest that merely assembling as a group, which seems to have been banned at that time in the eastern Roman provinces, could bring Christians into trouble with the authorities. See the article "Statue of Trajan.")

In spite of these extremely negative portrayals of Domitian by his contemporaries, modern historians have often assessed Domitian's reign more favorably. The evaluations by the ancient historians are suspected of being overblown and biased, since the writers were members of the aristocracy who were in opposition to Domitian. Granted, he was a tyrant and a persecutor, especially of the senatorial class, but he was possibly the victim of caricature and exaggeration. In some ways he was a successful emperor. He initiated many building programs throughout the empire; he was successful in defending the empire from outside attacks and was popular with the troops; he provided entertainment and games for the populace; and, surprisingly, he was reported to have been meticulously strict and fair in the administration of justice. His administration of the provinces was especially commendable. Even Suetonius, who despised Domitian, says of him, "He took such care to exercise restraint over the city officials and the governors of the provinces, that at no time were they more honest or just" (Suetonius, *Domitian* 8.2 [Rolfe, Loeb Classical Library]).

Eventually the fear, suspicion, and unpopularity engendered by Domitian led to at least three attempts to eliminate him, the last of which was successful when a group of his freedmen, likely supported by more powerful figures, stabbed him to death on September 18, 96 C.E. Following his death, the senate passed a *damnatio memoriae* (obliteration of his memory) against Domitian, which called for the erasure of the name of the despised emperor from all public monuments (see the article "Relief of Praetorian Guard.")

Biblical Significance

According to the evidence of the New Testament, the apostle Paul spent a considerable amount of time in the city of Ephesus. The book of Acts portrays Paul making a brief stop at Ephesus at the end of his second missionary journey (18:19-21) and then spending more than two years there during his third journey (19:10). On his final trip to Jerusalem he bypassed Ephesus, but sent for the leaders of the church there to meet with him at Miletus (Acts 20:17). Paul, himself, in 1 Corinthians 15:32 and 16:8, refers to his visits to Ephesus. Later traditions, whose authenticity has been questioned, also associate Paul, as well as Timothy, with the city (1 Tim. 1:3; 2 Tim. 1:18). One of the letters in the New Testament traditionally attributed to Paul is known as the letter to the Ephesians, although its authorship and its recipients are strongly disputed (the location "in Ephesus" does not appear in the earliest and best extant texts of Ephesians). Not only does the city have a strong connection with the Pauline tradition, but the church in Ephesus is also one of the seven churches to which the author of Revelation sent a message in Revelation 2 and 3. In fact, Ephesus has the distinction of being the only city visited by Paul that is also mentioned in Revelation.

In addition to the general information about the city of Ephesus that the museum objects offer, the items from the temple of the Flavian Sebastoi (the altar, and the head and arm from the statue) provide insight into the cult of emperor worship that is a part of the background of the book of Revelation. One of the concerns of John of Patmos was the involvement by the Christians of Asia Minor in the worship of the emperor. Apparently some of the people in the churches of Asia Minor were taking a lax approach to the issue, perhaps justifying their involvement as simply a matter of civic or social responsibility. For John, however, involvement in the imperial cult, regardless of the justification, was incompatible with the idea of the sole sovereignty of God. To participate in emperor worship was to render to a human being the worship and allegiance that were due to God alone. Revelation 13 portrays the Roman Empire and its emperors as "a beast rising out of the sea" and the imperial cult that promoted emperor worship as a "beast that rose out of the earth." John attempted to persuade his readers that the emperor, rather than being divine, was a beastly evil that should be resisted. Like Antipas who was martyred in Pergamum (2:13), the Christians were urged to remain faithful in their commitment to God, even if such faithfulness required the ultimate sacrifice of martyrdom.

Although disagreement over the question exists, the likely date for the writing of the book of Revelation was during the reign of Domitian as emperor. Thus the temple of the Flavian Sebastoi at Ephesus, with its altar and imperial statue (possibly of Domitian), has particular relevance for the book of Revelation.

Statue of Trajan

Marble sculpture

- ▷ Size: Life-size
- ▷ Provenance: Gabies (Pantano), Italy
- ▷ Date: ca. 108 C.E.
- ▷ Present location: Louvre (room B, Daru Gallery, ground floor, Denon Wing, section 8)
- ▷ Identification number: MR 360 (also numbered Ma 1150)

Unfortunately, less is known about the career of Trajan (98-117 C.E.) than is known about his predecessors. Suetonius gives no biography of him, and Tacitus speaks very little of him. What is known comes mostly from the writings of Pliny the Younger, governor of the Roman province of Bithynia in Asia Minor (modern-day Turkey); his exchange of letters with the emperor is especially valuable to Christian history. Nonetheless, the later writings of Dio Cassius, as well as various monumental inscriptions and other historical fragments, do provide an outline of his career.

The future emperor Trajan was born at Italica, Spain (53 C.E.), and thus became the first emperor from one of the Roman provinces, though it is likely he came from an old Roman family. (Some recent sources have questioned that opinion.) His father had served with distinction in the armies of Vespasian and Titus in Judea, and he later became governor of Syria and afterward proconsul of Asia. Trajan served under his father as legionary legate in Syria and later as legate of the Seventh Legion in Spain. He was sent to Germany in 89 C.E. on Domitian's orders to crush a rebellion along the Rhine River. His fidelity earned him a consulship in 91 C.E. and the governorship of Germania Superior followed, with headquarters at the site of modern-day Mainz, Germany. The then-current emperor, Nerva, in trouble at home, decided he needed to bring a powerful and attractive figure into his regime, so he adopted Trajan in 97 C.E. Trajan was said to be a tall, handsome man, a "soldier's soldier," popular with his troops. All of these personal characteristics — but more especially, Trajan's legions — would be assets to Nerva. However, the emperor died before Trajan reached Rome, and his transition to power was untroubled as the senate and people welcomed him as the new emperor.

One of Trajan's first acts when he arrived in Rome in 98 C.E. was the deification of his predecessor, an action designed to solidify his position in Rome. Immediately, however, he was forced to become preoccupied with foreign affairs. The situation with the tribes beyond the Danube was always unsettled and getting worse. Two wars were fought against them in the next five years, culminating in the beheading of their king, Decebalus, and the annexing of Dacia (modern Romania). In 107 C.E. Trajan led in the annexing of Arabia, though details are scanty, and in 116 C.E. he launched an invasion against the Parthians. Armenia fell to the Romans, and Trajan likewise had considerable success in Mesopotamia, though the region was never satisfactorily pacified. The capital city of the Parthians was captured, but the Romans never really gained political control. Trajan, like Alexander, then pressed on toward the Persian Gulf. However, revolt broke out all over the eastern territories of Rome, and the Jewish communities of the Diaspora in Cyprus, Egypt, and Judea were at the center of it. Trajan was forced to change his plans. He moved into Arabia to oppose rebel forces massing at the desert city of Hatra, but his army was repulsed. As he rode about the walls, he himself narrowly escaped death when an arrow fired at him struck a cavalry officer next to him. While there his health began to fail, and he left the man who would become his successor, Hadrian, in charge of the command in the east. Trajan wished to return home, but his condition worsened and he died in Selinus of Cilicia in 117 C.E. Like many others who imitated Alexander's adventures in the east, Trajan found the area to be vast and complete control impossible. The portrait carving of Trajan as an older man, in the Museum of Anatolian Civilizations in Ankara, Turkey (museum

116. Marble statue of Trajan, now in the Louvre

inventory number 10345; see plate 16), made not long before his death, shows the effects of the stress of his latter years. The sculpture is in the form of a tondo with the relief carving of Trajan's head projecting from the round medallion. Located on a wall on the ground floor of the museum, the sculpture measures 63.8 cm. (25.12 in.) in diameter.

Trajan was known in his administration for fair dealings with the people and good relations with the senate. His victories in Dacia enriched the Roman treasury, and he was able to complete numerous building enterprises, including an aqueduct, modernized harbors, and most especially, the Forum of Trajan, which dwarfed the similar efforts of his predecessors. This vast complex of magnificent buildings extended for some two thousand yards and included a law court, two libraries, various market areas, an equestrian statue of Trajan, and his spectacular memorial, the Column of Trajan, which still stands in Rome today. A procession of carved figures depicting his wars against the Dacians winds around the column in serpentine fashion. After Trajan's death, his ashes were deposited in the column's base.

Biblical Significance

Though our historical sources for the career of Trajan are limited, the record of Pliny the Younger's correspondence with him concerning Christians is an unequaled treasure. Pliny was serving at that time (111-113 C.E.; some authorities favor 109-111 C.E.) as governor of Bithynia and Pontus (westward of modern-day Istanbul), and he exchanged correspondence with the emperor to ask his advice concerning the proper means of dealing with a sect that had been called to his attention. What was he to do with these people who were called Christians? (Italics added.)

> I have never been present at an examination [the Latin word indicates a formal trial] of Christians. Consequently, I do not know the nature or the extent of the punishments usually meted out to them, nor the grounds for starting an investigation and how far it should be pressed. Nor am I at all sure whether any distinction should be made between them on the grounds of age, or if young people and adults should be treated alike; whether a pardon ought to be granted to anyone retracting his beliefs, or if he has once professed Christianity, he shall gain nothing by renouncing it; and whether it is the mere name of Christian which is punishable, even if innocent of crime, or rather the crimes associated with the name.
>
> For the moment this is the line I have taken with all persons brought before me on the charge of being Christians. I have asked them in person if they are Christians, and if they admit it, I repeat the question a second and

third time, with a warning of the punishment awaiting them. *If they persist, I order them to be led away for execution;* for, whatever the nature of their admission, I am convinced that their stubbornness and unshakeable obstinacy ought not to go unpunished. There have been others similarly fanatical who are Roman citizens. I have entered them on the list of persons to be sent to Rome for trial.

Now that I have begun to deal with this problem, as so often happens, the charges are becoming more widespread and increasing in variety. An anonymous pamphlet has been circulated which contains the names of a number of accused persons. Among these, I considered that I should dismiss any who denied that they were or ever had been Christians when they repeated after me a formula of invocation to the gods and had made offerings of wine and incense to your statue (which I had ordered to be brought into court for this purpose along with the images of the gods), and furthermore had reviled the name of Christ: *none of which things, I understand, any genuine Christian can be induced to do.*

Others, whose names were given to me by an informer, first admitted the charge and then denied it; they said that they had ceased to be Christians two or more years previously, and some of them even twenty years ago. They all did reverence to your statue and the images of the gods in the same way as the others, and reviled the name of Christ. They also declared that the sum total of their guilt or error amounted to no more than this: *they had met regularly before dawn on a fixed day to chant verses alternately among themselves in honour of Christ as if to a god, and also to bind themselves by oath, not for any criminal purpose, but to abstain from theft, robbery and adultery, to commit no breach of trust and not to deny a deposit when called upon to restore it.* After the ceremony it had been their custom to disperse and reassemble later to take food and of an ordinary, harmless kind; but they had in fact given up this practice since my edict, issued on your instructions, which banned all political societies. *This made me decide it was all the more necessary to extract the truth by torture from two slave women, whom they called deaconesses* [Latin: *ministrae*]. I found nothing but a degenerate sort of cult carried to extravagant lengths.

I have therefore postponed any further examination and hastened to consult you. The question seems to me to be worthy of your consideration, especially in view of the number of persons endangered; for *a great many individuals of every age and class, both men and women, are being brought to trial,* and this is likely to continue. It is not only the towns, but villages and rural districts too which are infected through contact with this wretched cult. I think though that it is still possible for it to be checked and directed to better ends, for there is no doubt that people have begun to throng the

399

temples which had been almost entirely deserted for a long time; the sacred rites which had been allowed to lapse are being performed again, and the flesh of sacrificial victims [animals] is on sale everywhere, though up till recently scarcely anyone could be found to buy it. It is easy to infer from this that a great many people could be reformed if they were given an opportunity to repent. (Pliny, *Letters* 10.96 [Radice, Loeb Classical Library])

This inquiry from a provincial governor to the emperor contains an incredible amount of unique information regarding first-century Christians in the Roman world. Notice the following: Pliny says he is unaware of the correct procedure to follow, because he has never been present in any trials concerning Christians. Since Pliny had extensive experience in the courts of Rome, most scholars believe his statement implies that previous persecutions were rare or nonexistent. (On the other hand, his statement simply says that *he had never been present* at any trials of Christians, not that they had not occurred, and that he did not know the punishments *usually meted out to them.* So the matter seems at least inconclusive.)

Pliny also says that he has executed Christians prior to his letter to the emperor, not because he found them guilty of crimes against the state, but because they had stubbornly refused to correct an insult, as Pliny saw it, to the emperor and imperial Rome. Once he began investigating reports of the group, a pamphlet giving the names of many Christians was circulated anonymously. Having heard that Christians would not sacrifice to the gods or the emperor, Trajan ordered the suspects to do so, and, especially, he ordered them to curse Christ — *all things he had been told a real Christian would not do.* Some of those investigated claimed to been members of the movement once but to have renounced the faith. Note that a few of the people had become associated with Christianity as long as twenty years before (as early as 90 C.E.).

After his investigations, Pliny came to the conclusion not only that Christianity was a movement harmless to the state, but also that Christians were peace-loving, law-abiding, family-honoring people who were true to their word in business. Their only "crime" was to meet regularly before dawn to sing a hymn to Christ, "as to a god," and later (an evening service) to have an innocent meal together. This account is the most extensive information concerning Christian worship and practice at this time that exists from any source.

Nevertheless, Pliny blocked this harmless assembly, following the instructions of Trajan to prevent political associations. Just how extensive those instructions were is revealed in another exchange of correspondence in which Pliny requests Trajan to grant permission for a volunteer fire brigade to be formed after a fire had swept through their city (Nicomedia). The emperor denied the request, saying that such gatherings might begin as a society for fire protection but would quickly turn into an assembly of political dissidents. (Societies of any sort seem to have been banned in the eastern provinces.) If a fire brigade could not be allowed to assemble, what chance was there that a peculiar religious sect would be allowed such a privilege?

Pliny's information was obtained under torture from two "ministrae" of the church, two women who served the church. (In difficult cases, the Romans never believed that truth had been obtained without the use of torture.) This translation interprets the word *ministrae* as "deaconesses," although it could mean anything from the leaders of the church — even pastors — to anyone who served the church. However, since these two women slaves were chosen by the governor to provide him with conclusive information to send to the emperor, it seems certain that he selected those he considered the most authoritative and knowledgeable about the local Christian church.

Finally, Pliny's comments make clear that this was no minor, localized sect. In fact, prior to his interrogation of Christians, the movement had spread across the countryside to the extent that *the temples were almost deserted* and the demand for sacrificial animals had virtually ceased.

Trajan's reply to Pliny's questions is equally fascinating (italics added):

> You have followed the right course of procedure, my dear Pliny, in your examination of the cases of persons charged with being Christians, for it is impossible to lay down a general rule to a fixed formula. *These people must not be hunted out;* if they are brought before you and the charge against them is proved, they must be punished, but in the case of anyone who denies that he is a Christian, and makes it clear that he is not by offering prayers to our gods, he is to be pardoned as a result of his repentance however suspect his past conduct may be. But pamphlets circulated anonymously must play no part in any accusation. They create the worst sort of precedent and are quite out of keeping with the spirit of our age. (Pliny, *Letters* 10.97 [Radice, Loeb Classical Library])

The emperor affirmed the actions of Pliny, but added the following important modification: Christians should not be sought out. In other words, no official persecution of the sect was to be conducted, and anonymous evidence must not be allowed. (Apparently, Trajan was not happy with the report of the anonymous pamphlet, as no emperor wanted that sort of thing on himself.) Trajan had taken great pains in Rome to avoid the appearance of being a persecutor of either nobility or plebs, and he saw any campaign against this religious sect as "a dangerous precedent." No doubt, he wanted to avoid the reputation — and the fate — of Domitian.

Altogether, Christian history is indebted in a strange way to this governor and this emperor who persecuted Christians, for their letters provide a unique insight into the worship practices and ethical standards, as well as the courage, of early Christians in the Roman world.

Ancient Biblical Texts

Silver Scroll Amulets: The Oldest Biblical Text Ever Discovered

Silver scroll amulets

▷ Size: 3.9 cm. (1.54 in.) long; 1.1 cm. (.43 in.) high (IAA 1980-1495); 9.7 cm. (4 in.) long; 2.7 cm. (1 in.) high (IAA 1980-1496)
▷ Writing: Hebrew
▷ Provenance: Ketef Hinnom, Israel (near Jerusalem)
▷ Date: Seventh century B.C.E.
▷ Present location: Israel Museum, Jerusalem (Bronfman Archaeology Wing)
▷ Identification numbers: IAA 1980-1495; IAA 1980-1496

In 1979, while excavating burial caves across the Hinnom (Gehenna) Valley from Mt. Zion and the Old City of Jerusalem, Gabriel Barkay discovered one cave that had not been plundered. In Cave 4 he found the bones of nearly one hundred people that had been placed there over several centuries. Among the many objects discovered there — more than one hundred pieces of jewelry, two hundred fifty complete pottery vessels, forty arrowheads, and numerous incised ivory pieces — he found two small silver scrolls designed to be worn on a cord about the neck. The one pictured here is the smaller of the two (IAA 1980-1495). Both contained this portion of the familiar words from the "Priestly Blessing" found in Numbers 6:24-26:

> May Yahweh bless and keep you;
> May Yahweh cause his face to shine upon you and grant you peace.

The complete quotation as found in the New Revised Standard Version of the Bible reads:

> The Lord bless you and keep you;
> the Lord make his face to shine upon you, and be gracious to you;
> the Lord lift up his countenance upon you, and give you peace.

This inscription was written in Paleo-Hebrew with cursive lettering by someone who clearly was not a professional scribe. Deciphering the writing on the scrolls was impossible at first because the lettering had been incised so lightly and the scrolls themselves contain numerous breaks. Translation was at last made possible, thanks to modern computer imaging techniques. This research confirmed the archaeologists' original estimate of the date of the scrolls, firmly placing the objects in the late seventh century B.C.E.

Biblical Significance

The discovery of these silver scrolls deserves to be known as one of the most important events in the history of biblical archaeology. The inscription found on them is the oldest quotation of a biblical text ever discovered, more than four hundred years older than the Dead Sea Scrolls. To place the amulets in context, when their inscriptions were written, King Josiah of Judah may well have been upon the throne (640-609 B.C.E.). The discovery of the book of Deuteronomy had recently been celebrated, and a spirit of spiritual renewal was sweeping over the country after the disastrous, fifty-five-year reign of the idolatrous King Manasseh (697-642 B.C.E.). Perhaps the possessor(s) of this scroll was participating in such a renewal by the wearing of this prayer. Obviously, its wearer regarded it as one of his most prized possessions, as it was included with him in burial. In a few short years (assuming the owner died previous to 587 B.C.E.), the Babylonians would lay siege to Jerusalem, destroy the temple, and carry thousands of the citizens of Judea into captivity.

In one sense, it is not entirely correct to refer to this inscription as "the oldest quotation from the Bible." In fact, it may even be older than that. These scrolls with their inscription predate the formal writing of the biblical book which contains the quotation (Numbers), and thus they belong to the earlier period of oral

117. Silver scroll amulet (IAA 1980-1495) inscribed with words from Numbers 6:24-26

history and transmission. This priestly benediction was a traditional prayer, well-known over many centuries. It is still in use in Jewish liturgy today, as well as by parents to bless their children on the Sabbath. Christian churches also use its words as a benediction with which to close their worship. The many strands of tradition in the book of Numbers make this blessing exceedingly difficult to date, but it clearly predates the formal style of the post-exilic period in which its introduction (Num. 6:22-23) is written. To find a copy from this early century of a benediction that later would become a much-loved verse in the Hebrew Scriptures and the Christian Old Testament is to find a treasure indeed.

The Isaiah Scroll from the Dead Sea Scrolls

Leather scroll

- ▷ Size: ca. 22-25 cm. (8.7-9.8 in.) high; 7.34 m. (24.08 ft.) long
- ▷ Writing: Hebrew language
- ▷ Provenance: Near Qumran, Israel
- ▷ Date: Latter half of the second century B.C.E.
- ▷ Present location: Shrine of the Book Museum, Israel Museum, Jerusalem
- ▷ Identification number: IMJ 95.57/22

During the winter of 1946-47, three bedouin young men were tending their sheep and goats in the area around the northwestern shore of the Dead Sea. One of the young men wandered off in search of a lost sheep (or goat). Spying a cave in the cliffs above, he picked up a rock and tossed it into the opening of the cave. Hearing a breaking sound, he returned to his companions and excitedly told them what had happened, thinking that there might be something of value hidden in the cave. Soon afterwards, one of the other young men went to the cave, climbed in, and found ten pottery jars. All were empty except two. One of the jars contained nothing but dirt. In the other jar, however, he found three leather scrolls, two of which were wrapped in linen. Disappointed at not finding a treasure of silver, gold, or other recognizably valuable items, he reported his find to the other two bedouin. They retrieved the three scrolls and took them back to their camp. Even though they were unaware of the significance of the musty, old scrolls they had discovered, the three young men had just completed the first part of what would come to be called "the most important archaeological discovery of the century."

118. The major Isaiah Scroll (1QIsaᵃ) found in cave 1 at Qumran. The two complete columns (cols. 33-34) in the portion pictured here contain Isaiah 40:2-41:23.

A few months after this initial discovery, two of the young men helped find four additional scrolls in the cave. These first seven scrolls, however, were only the beginning of the amazing discovery of what is now known as the Dead Sea Scrolls. Ultimately, between various bedouin searchers and archaeologists, eleven caves were discovered from 1947 to 1956 that contained scrolls, scroll fragments, or, in some cases, ostraca (broken pieces of pottery used for writing). Altogether, the approximately twenty-five thousand scroll fragments represent parts of nearly nine hundred scrolls that had been hidden in the caves near the Dead Sea.

Although the connection of these scrolls to the ruins located nearby known as Qumran is disputed, the most widely accepted view is that the Qumran settlement was a community of very devout Jews who withdrew from mainstream society and the Jerusalem temple, whose high priest they saw as corrupt. Retreating to this area near the Dead Sea, they established a strict communal settlement that tried to follow the requirements of the Jewish Torah as they interpreted them. At Qumran, the inhabitants made copies of biblical scrolls and other writings, primarily for their own use, but perhaps also to sell to other individuals. The people at Qumran are traditionally seen as a part of the larger Jewish group known as the Essenes, who were discussed by the Jewish writers Philo and Josephus, as well as by Pliny the Elder, the Roman writer. According to the traditional view, the Qumran community began during the latter half of the second century b.c.e. and lasted until 68 c.e., when the settlement was destroyed by the Romans during the first Jewish-Roman war. In order to keep the Roman soldiers from finding and looting or destroying the scrolls, the community hid the scrolls in the nearby caves for safekeeping. For some unknown reason, the scrolls were never retrieved from the caves until their chance discovery nearly two thousand years later.

The scrolls that were found in those eleven caves were of various types. Approximately a quarter of them were copies of books that now comprise the Hebrew Bible. In fact, with the exception of the book of Esther, a portion of every book in the Hebrew Bible has been found among the Dead Sea Scrolls. (No portion of Nehemiah or 1 Chronicles has been found either, but Ezra-Nehemiah was considered one book and written on the same scroll, and 1-2 Chronicles was considered one book, the book of Chronicles.) In addition to biblical texts, other scrolls contained rule books (or, community manuals), expansions or revisions of biblical stories, commentaries on biblical books, poetic or wisdom literature, and miscellaneous works (such as the *Copper Scroll* and the *War Scroll*).

One of those first three scrolls found in Cave 1 by the bedouin was a copy of the book of Isaiah, known as 1QIsa[a]. (The number "1" indicates the scroll was found in Cave 1. "Q" identifies the scroll as having been discovered at Qumran. "Isa" is an abbreviation for the book of Isaiah, and the superscript "a" means that this scroll was the first copy of Isaiah found in the caves.) The book of Isaiah was one of the most prevalent writings found at Qumran, with twenty copies of this prophetic text having been recovered from the Qumran caves. Only one of these, 1QIsa[a], is a virtually complete manuscript of the book. (A few words and letters are missing because of some holes in the text.) Several of the other Isaiah scrolls, however, have survived in substantial portions. Of these copies of Isaiah, 1QIsa[a] is the most important because it is so well preserved. Copied around 125 b.c.e., this scroll is the oldest manuscript of a complete book of the Bible. The scroll consists of fifty-four columns of Hebrew text and is one of the longest of the scrolls found at Qumran. Seventeen pieces of leather were stitched together to form the scroll.

The Isaiah Scroll (1QIsa[a]) is housed today in the Shrine of the Book Museum, a building designed and constructed specifically for the exhibition of the Dead Sea Scrolls and related artifacts. The Shrine of the Book Museum is a part of the Israel Museum in Jerusalem. Along with the Isaiah Scroll, several other important Dead Sea Scrolls are on display in the Shrine of the Book Museum, including a portion of the *Temple Scroll* (11Q19), a portion of the *Thanksgiving Scroll* (1QH[a]), a portion of the *Rule of the Community* (1QS), a portion of the Psalms Scroll (11Q5), a portion of the *War Scroll* (1Q33), a portion of an Exodus scroll (4Q22), and several others. In order to protect the fragile scrolls from damage, the documents on display rotate every three to six months. In the center of the room on the main floor is a display case designed to look like a scroll wrapped around a scroll handle. Initially this case contained the entire 1QIsa^a scroll on display. However, due to concerns over damage to the scroll, it was removed and replaced with a replica. A portion of the original scroll is in one of the several display cases around the wall of the room.

The entrance hall of the Shrine of the Book slopes downward and narrows slightly, intended to give the visitor the feel of entering a cave. Both sides of the entrance hall are lined with display cases containing various artifacts found in the caves near Qumran, including fragments of some of the scrolls from the caves, one of the scroll jars from Cave 1, pottery, limestone cups, an oil lamp, sheep-shearing scissors, phylactery cases, charred dates, and silver coins.

Most of the Dead Sea Scrolls that were discovered are stored in the basement of the Rockefeller Museum in Jerusalem and are not available for public viewing. One of the most intriguing texts of the Dead Sea Scrolls is the *Copper Scroll*, discovered in Cave 3. Inscribed on a sheet of copper, the text of this scroll consists of a list of sixty-four locations of supposed buried treasure. The authenticity of the list of treasures, as well as the scroll's connection to the community at Qumran and to the rest of the Dead Sea Scrolls, is strongly debated. Today, this scroll, which had to be cut into strips before it could be read because the heavily oxidized scroll could not be unrolled, is displayed in the Jordan Archaeological Museum in Amman, Jordan.

Biblical Significance

One of the primary reasons the discovery of the Dead Sea Scrolls was such a momentous find is the new information the scrolls provide scholars about the wording and arrangement of biblical texts. Prior to the discovery of the Dead Sea Scrolls, the earliest known copies of the books of the Hebrew Bible (in Hebrew) were written in the ninth and tenth centuries C.E., including the Cairo Codex of the Prophets, dated to ca. 895 C.E., and the Aleppo Codex (about one third of which is missing), dated to ca. 930 B.C.E. According to most scholars, the last book of the Hebrew Bible to be written was the book of Daniel, composed around 165 B.C.E. Thus, prior to the discovery of the Dead Sea Scrolls, the earliest known copy of the Hebrew Bible was separated from the writing of the books by nearly eleven hundred years, and in the case of some of the biblical books, by approximately two thousand years. (Daniel was not considered one of the prophets and was not included in the Cairo Codex.) The discovery of the Dead Sea Scrolls, however, moved us approximately a thousand years closer to the originals. The benefit of having these earlier texts is that in some cases the Dead Sea Scrolls provide a better wording of the biblical writings, a wording that is likely closer to the original wording of the texts. Modern editions of the Hebrew Bible (or, the Christian Old Testament) have profited greatly from the discovery of these ancient biblical texts.

The Dead Sea Scrolls also provide a wealth of information about one of the many groups in early Judaism. Whether the persons who copied and preserved the scrolls were actually the Essenes or some otherwise unknown group, the scrolls give us a virtual "library" of the writings of this Jewish group. The information in the scrolls sheds light on the history of this community, its organization, its beliefs and practices, and its approach to biblical interpretation. The scrolls reveal the richness and diversity of Judaism during this time period. Furthermore, the specific works found at Qumran and the nature of those works reveal that the shape and contents of the Jewish canon were not firmly established by the first century C.E. Exactly what works comprised the Jewish Scriptures was still fluid.

In the early years after the discovery of the scrolls, several attempts were made to connect Jesus or the early Christian community to the scrolls. Eventually, those endeavors were seen to be misdirected. Almost all scholars now agree that the Dead Sea Scrolls are Jewish documents, with only tangential connections to Christianity. The importance of the Dead Sea Scrolls for the study of early Christianity lies not in the identification of any of the scrolls as Christian works (which they are not), but in the background information they provide for the development of early Christianity. Christianity originated and developed as a first-century Jewish movement. Thus, the more information one can gain about first-century Judaism, the better one can understand certain aspects of early Christianity. Some of the ideas and practices of the Qumran community likely influenced early Christianity — and even some of the New Testament writings — not because the early Christians were a part of the Qumran community, but because these ideas and practices were a part of the mosaic of first-century Judaism. The Dead Sea Scrolls, such as the great Isaiah Scroll 1QIsa[a], are a tangible connection to one Jewish group who tried to adhere faithfully to their understanding of what it meant to be the people of God.

The Aleppo Codex

Parchment codex (manuscript in book form) of the Hebrew Bible

▷ Size: 33 cm. (13 in.) high; 26.5 cm. (10.43 in.) wide
▷ Writing: Hebrew language
▷ Provenance: Aleppo, Syria
▷ Date: Tenth century c.e.
▷ Present location: Shrine of the Book Museum, Israel Museum, Jerusalem
▷ Identification number: IMJ 96.85/221A

The Aleppo Codex, often known in Hebrew as the *Keter* ("crown") of Aleppo, is one of the most important manuscripts of the Hebrew Bible. Written during the first half of the tenth century b.c.e., the codex originally contained around 490 leaves (980 pages), of which 295 leaves have survived. The text is written on parchment in brown ink, with three columns of text per page (except for the books of Job, Psalms, and Proverbs, which are written in two columns per page). Each column contains twenty-eight lines of text. As was customary, before the writing was begun a faint line was inscribed across the columns for each line of text in order to insure that the writing was straight. The scribe who produced the Aleppo Codex wrote each word beneath the lines, so that the letters, in effect, hang from the inscribed lines (sometimes called "pendant writing"). Although ancient biblical manuscripts, like other works, often contained ornamented letters or decorations, none of the extant pages of the Aleppo Codex have any ornamentation or decoration.

The earliest Hebrew texts were produced with a consonantal writing, that is, the writing contained no vowels. As long as Hebrew continued to be the everyday language of the Jewish people, reading the consonantal texts was not a problem. Once Aramaic became the standard language of the Jews, however, fluency in reading Hebrew became more difficult. Because of that situation, a method of indicating vowel sounds was developed that involved a system of dots and dashes that were written above, below, or inside consonants to indicate the vowel sounds that followed. This method of indicating pronunciation of the texts was called pointing the text. In addition to vowel signs (or points), the scribes added various symbols to the text to indicate syllable stress and intonation. Finally, scholars annotated the texts, adding notes at the top and bottom of the pages and in appendices, as well as abbreviations in the margins. These notes were known as *masora* (Hebrew: "tradition" or "transmission"), and the scholars who were responsible for these additions to the text during the sixth to the eleventh centuries c.e. were known as the Masoretes. A copy of the Hebrew Bible that contains these notes and additions by the Masoretes is called a "Masoretic text." In a more technical sense, the term "Masoretic Text" is used to refer to the standard text of the Hebrew Bible that was derived from the work of the Masoretes at Tiberias. (Copies of the Hebrew Scriptures that were intended for public reading in worship were not written with these additions to the text and were not written in codex form. Rather, they were always unadorned texts written on scrolls.)

The Aleppo Codex is an example of the Masoretic Text. This copy of the Hebrew Scriptures was written around 930 C.E. in the city of Tiberias in Israel by the scribe Shlomo ben Buya'a. The scholar Aaron ben Asher supplied the vowel marks and accent signs, as well as the masoretic notes for the Aleppo Codex. The codex apparently passed into the possession of the Karaite Jewish community in Jerusalem, after which the scroll was looted and eventually transferred to the Jewish community in Cairo at the end of the eleventh century. At the end of the fourteenth or beginning of the fifteenth century, the codex was deposited with the Jewish community in Aleppo, Syria, where it was

119. The page of the Aleppo Codex containing Amos 4:6–5:19

413

kept in the synagogue for over five hundred years. The codex was stored in a chest in a niche called the Cave of Elijah in the synagogue.

In December of 1947, following the United Nations' approval of the resolution that established the modern nation of Israel, riots erupted against the Jewish community in Aleppo. During the violence, the rioters broke into the synagogue, threw the codex on the floor, and set the synagogue afire. The codex disappeared and was assumed to have perished in the flames. For ten years, however, the manuscript was apparently hidden by individuals in Syria to protect it. In January 1958, the codex reappeared, having been smuggled out of Syria, and was brought to Jerusalem. Today this important manuscript of the Hebrew Bible is on display in the lower floor of the Shrine of the Book Museum, which is part of the Israel Museum. The fate of the missing pages of the codex (more than a third of the manuscript) is unknown. Since examination of the manuscript has revealed no fire damage, the missing pages were apparently torn out of the codex, either intentionally or accidentally. In 1982, one of the missing leaves was handed over by a Jewish family who had migrated from Aleppo to Brooklyn, New York. An additional fragment, containing verses from Exodus 8, was donated in 2007 to the Ben-Zvi Institute in Jerusalem, which is responsible for the Aleppo Codex. The fragment came from the family of a man who had picked up the piece from the floor of the synagogue in Aleppo after the riots. He later moved to Brooklyn, New York, keeping the fragment in his wallet until he died in 2000.

Biblical Significance

The Aleppo Codex is widely considered the most important copy of the Masoretic Text of the Hebrew Bible. It is not the most complete surviving early copy — that distinction belongs to the Leningrad Codex, written in 1008 C.E. and containing the entire Hebrew Bible. Neither is it the earliest example of the Masoretic Text. The Cairo Codex, a manuscript produced ca. 895 C.E. that contains the books of the prophets, is earlier than the Aleppo Codex. Rather, the significance of the Aleppo Codex is that it is the oldest surviving codex that originally contained the entire Hebrew Bible. Earlier codices, such as the Cairo Codex and others, only contained parts of the Hebrew Bible. The Aleppo Codex, on the other hand, is the earliest known example of a book containing all the works that comprise the Hebrew Bible as it exists today. Unfortunately, part of the codex is missing, specifically Genesis 1:1–Deuteronomy 28:16 at the front of the codex, a few pages from some of the prophets in the middle of the codex, and part of the end of the codex, including the last part of the Song of Solomon and the entire books of Ecclesiastes, Lamentations, Esther, Daniel, and Ezra/Nehemiah.

In addition to being the earliest originally complete text, the Aleppo Codex also seems to be the text that was used to correct many later manuscripts. A colophon at the end of the Leningrad Codex states that the scribe who produced the codex "wrote and pointed and provided with Masora this codex of the Holy Scriptures from the corrected and annotated books prepared by Aaron ben Moses ben Asher the teacher, may he rest in the Garden of Eden! It has been corrected and properly annotated."[1] (A colophon is text, usually at the end of a manuscript, that provides information about the writing of the manuscript.) The great Jewish scholar of the twelfth century, Moses Maimonides, also appears to be referring to the Aleppo Codex as a model text used for checking certain aspects of other manuscripts. He wrote, "The Torah scroll on which we have relied in these matters is the scroll well known in Egypt containing the twenty-four books, which was in Jerusalem until recently, and which was used to check other scrolls. All relied on it, since Ben Asher corrected it, examined it carefully for many years, and checked it many times, whenever it was copied. I relied on it when I wrote a correct Torah scroll."[2]

Papyrus 52: Oldest Fragment of the New Testament

Papyrus fragment of the Gospel of John

▷ Size: ca. 8.9 cm. (3.50 in.) high; 5.8 cm. (2.83 in.) wide
▷ Writing: Greek language
▷ Provenance: Original, unknown; earliest known location, Alexandria, Egypt
▷ Date: ca. first half of the second century C.E.
▷ Present location: John Rylands University Library, University of Manchester, England
▷ Identification number: P. Ryl. Gk. 457

The papyrus fragment shown here is the oldest copy of any part of the New Testament ever discovered. (None of the original autographs, or manuscripts, of the Bible has ever been found.) It contains portions of the Gospel of John, chapter 18:31-33 and 37-38. This tiny leaf is the upper corner of one page from a biblical codex (that is, a writing in book form rather than a scroll) and is writ-

---

1. Ernst Würthwein, *The Text of the Old Testament,* trans. Erroll F. Rhodes, 2d ed. (Grand Rapids, Mich.: Eerdmans, 1995), p. 180.

2. *The Code of Maimonides,* Book 2, *The Book of Love,* Treatise 3, "Laws Concerning Tefillin, Mezuzah, and the Torah Scroll" 8.5, trans. Menachem Kellner. Yale Judaica Series, vol. 32 (New Haven, Conn.: Yale University Press, 2004), p. 100.

120. The recto of the papyrus fragment known as p⁵² containing a part of the text of the Gospel of John

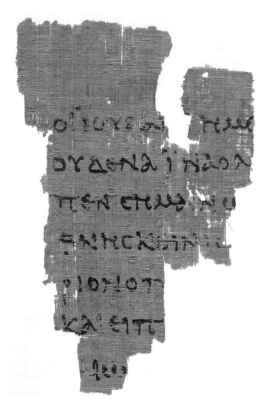

ten on both the front and the back. The letters on this unique document are written in dark ink on light-colored papyrus of fine quality, likely by someone who was not a professional scribe. The codex is estimated to have originally comprised approximately one hundred thirty pages and consisted solely of the Gospel of John. Portions of seven lines remain on each side; on the front side (recto), three verses, 18:31-33, and on the back side (verso), two verses, 18:37-38:

18:31-33: "[We] are not permitted to put [anyone] to death." (This was to fulfill what Jesus had said [when he indicated] the kind of death he was to [die].) Then Pilate entered the headquarters again, summoned Jesus, and asked him, "Are you the King of the [Jews]?"

18:37-38: "For this I was born, and for [this] I [came into the world], to testify to the truth. Everyone who [belongs to the truth] listens to my voice." Pilate asked him, "What is truth?" After he had said [this], he went out to the Jews again and told them, "I find [no] case against him." (Translation from the NRSV; brackets indicate missing words.)

This text was among many papyrus fragments obtained in Egypt by Bernard Grenfell in 1920 for the John Rylands Library at the University of Manchester, England. It may have come originally from the ruins of the ancient city of Oxyrhynchus, Egypt, the famous site where Grenfell and Arthur Hunt, both Fellows of Queens College, Oxford, at that time, also found three papyri now known simply as "Sayings of Jesus." (With the discovery in 1945 of the *Gospel of Thomas* at Nag Hammadi, Egypt, the same verses were found in that document. See the article "The *Gospel of Thomas* from the Nag Hammadi Writings.") These fragments were among more than 40,000 other pieces of papyri — biblical, classical, and secular — of unmatched historical value.

Grenfell may have found this historic document, but its meaning and value had not yet been discovered. For many years it rested among hundreds of similar fragments awaiting translation. Then in 1934, a twenty-four-year-old Fellow of St. John's College at Oxford, C. H. Roberts, picked up the fragment as he was sorting through the collection. He was excited to recognize the few Greek lines as being from the Gospel of John. Immediately he wrote a booklet, *An Unpublished Fragment of the Fourth Gospel in the John Rylands Library* (Manchester, 1935), which analyzed the find and gave a translation of the verses. This document was republished, with slight alterations, in the *Bulletin of the John Rylands Library* 20 (1936). As Roberts analyzed the style of writing on the document and compared it with other papyri, he found its closest match in the writings of the Hadrianic era (117-138 C.E.). Consequently, he estimated the date for the fragment to be the first half of the second century.

Considerable scholarly debate has ensued since that time over this date. A few authorities would put the writing into the late first century, some, nearly a century later, and others remain firmly agnostic over the possibility of arriving at any specific date without further evidence. Those who question the date have raised two considerations. First, some doubt that a codex form of writing (a bound book) would exist so early in Egypt. If so, it is a notable exception to the usual scrolls. Second, skepticism also exists over the possibility of accurately dating a Greek document by epigraphical (handwriting) evidence alone, without either archaeological evidence (from the stratum in which it was found) or further clues in the text of the document itself. Scholarly consensus, however, has remained in general agreement with the original estimate, though some continue to favor the middle of the second century or somewhat later. Nevertheless, the authenticity of this document is not in question, and in any case it remains the earliest text of any portion of the New Testament ever found.

Biblical Significance

Naturally, any manuscript that can be authenticated as the oldest portion of the New Testament is highly significant for biblical research. The brevity of the text on the papyrus, unfortunately, yields little value for interpretive studies in John. But this document, if anything, has yielded an even more surprising and totally unexpected piece of information. For many years, many textual critics had regarded the date of the Gospel of John, universally agreed to be the last writing of the New Testament Gospels, as approximately 160 C.E. (F. C. Baur, et al.). Yet, this portion of the Gospel of John was in circulation in Egypt by the middle of the second century, if not before, and not in a great urban center such as Rome or Alexandria, but in a provincial Egyptian town approximately 120 miles south of modern Cairo. If the Gospel of John was written in Ephesus, as many authorities believe, then it is remarkable that it could have reached so far into Egypt by this time. (If it were written from Antioch or Alexandria, as some have proposed, the time necessary for its transmission, of course, would have been less.) Wherever it was written, a late date for the Gospel of John is now rejected by modern scholars. Based on the evidence of this papyrus fragment, known as p^{52}, John's Gospel is now generally dated to the end of the first century C.E., if not a decade earlier.

Codex Sinaiticus

Parchment codex (manuscript in book form) of the Christian Bible

▷ Size: ca. 38.1 cm. (15 in.) high; 34.5 cm. (13.5 in.) wide
▷ Writing: Greek language
▷ Provenance: St. Catherine's Monastery, Sinai Peninsula
▷ Date: Fourth century C.E.
▷ Present location: British Library (Sir John Ritblat Gallery)
▷ Identification number: Add. MS 43725

Along with Codex Vaticanus and Codex Alexandrinus, Codex Sinaiticus is one of the three most important early copies of the New Testament (and arguably, the most important of the three). The manuscript is not in the form of a scroll, like most earlier manuscripts, but is formed by leaves fastened together as in a modern book. This type of bound volume, known as a codex, seems to have developed around the second century C.E. and quickly gained in popularity, particularly among Christian scribes. Codices have many advantages over scrolls, such as they are more convenient to use and are cheaper, since one can write on both sides of the leaves (each page). Written in Greek in pale brown ink, the text of Codex Sinaiticus is in four columns per page, with each column consisting of forty-eight lines. The handwriting in the manuscript belongs to what is known as the uncial form of handwriting. The uncial script was a formal style of writing with carefully written, separated letters, similar to capital letters. The text contains no spaces between the words.

121. The page of Codex Sinaiticus containing the end of the Gospel of Mark and the beginning of the Gospel of Luke

Scholars have dated the manuscript to the fourth century C.E. and have identified (by handwriting styles) three scribes as being responsible for its production. In addition to corrections made to the manuscript by the original scribes, several other scribes made various corrections, perhaps in the seventh century. Various proposals have been made for the location where the codex was first copied, including Alexandria (Egypt), Constantinople, or Caesarea (Palestine). Codex Sinaiticus originally consisted of over 1460 pages and contained the entire Old Testament (Septuagint version with the Apocrypha), the New Testament, and two additional Christian writings (the *Epistle of Barnabas* and the *Shepherd of Hermas*). Today, only 804 pages remain, with the vast majority (694 pages) in the British Library. Of the remaining pages, 86 are in the Leipzig University Library, 24 pages and 14 fragments are at St. Catherine's Monastery, and fragments of 6 pages are in the National Library of Russia in St. Petersburg. The entire New Testament is preserved (all of which is in the British Library), but unfortunately, slightly more than half of the Old Testament has been lost, including almost all of the Torah.

The discovery of Codex Sinaiticus is one of the most intriguing stories in the history of biblical manuscripts. In 1844 the German scholar Constantin von Tischendorf traveled throughout the Middle East in search of ancient biblical manuscripts. While visiting St. Catherine's Monastery at the foot of Mt.

Sinai in the Sinai Peninsula, Tischendorf saw a basket in the monastery library that was filled with pages of old parchments that were destined to be burned. Having been told by the librarian that two similar piles of old, moldy parchments had already been thrown into the fire, Tischendorf examined the basket of manuscripts and was amazed to find among the parchments in the basket several sheets of the Septuagint (the Old Testament written in Greek). The librarian agreed to let him have forty-three of the sheets, but no more, having become suspicious at Tischendorf's excitement over the discovery. Upon his return to Europe, Tischendorf deposited those forty-three leaves, which contained portions of 1 Chronicles, Jeremiah, Nehemiah, and Esther, in the library of the University of Leipzig.

Hoping to recover more pages of the manuscript, Tischendorf returned to St. Catherine's in 1853. Much to his disappointment, however, this trip was unsuccessful. In 1859, this time with the financial backing of the czar of Russia, Tischendorf returned once more to St. Catherine's. After a few days of searching at the monastery with no success, Tischendorf was planning to depart when his fortune unexpectedly changed. One of the monks invited him to his room and during their discussions about the Septuagint, the monk told Tischendorf that he, too, had read a copy of the Septuagint. He then took from a corner of his room a manuscript wrapped in a red cloth. Concealing his excitement, Tischendorf nonchalantly asked if he could take the manuscript back to his room to examine. Once he had the manuscript in his room, Tischendorf could hardly contain his enthusiasm, as he found not only the pages he had seen fifteen years earlier but also other portions of the Old Testament, the complete New Testament, and two other Christian writings, the *Epistle of Barnabas* and the *Shepherd of Hermas*.

After prolonged and complicated negotiations, including travel to Cairo, Jerusalem, and Constantinople, Tischendorf eventually succeeded in gaining permission to borrow the manuscript to take it back with him in order to make a copy of it. In 1862, on the one thousandth anniversary of the founding of the Russian Empire, Tischendorf presented to Czar Alexander II of Russia a grand, four-volume copy of the manuscript that he had printed at Leipzig. The details of the story are unclear at this point. One version of the account claims that Tischendorf, based on his suggestion and with the approval of the monks, made a gift of Codex Sinaiticus to the czar. In return, the czar sent several gifts to the monastery. The monks' version of the story, however, differs. They claim that they had only given Tischendorf permission to borrow the manuscript and expected him to return it. Understandably they were upset when it was not returned. (In 1990 the authors visited St. Catherine's Monastery. While touring the monastery, they asked one of the monks if he could point out the room in which Codex Sinaiticus was found. When the monk looked puzzled, he was told, "Tischendorf . . . Codex Sinaiticus . . . he found it here?" "Yes, and stole it!" replied the monk, ending the conversation. Apparently, the loss of Codex Sinaiticus is still a sore subject.)

After the Russian Revolution, the Russian government, needing money, agreed to sell the manuscript to the British Museum for one hundred thousand British pounds. In 1933, the manuscript was transferred to the British Museum. Today, Codex Sinaiticus is on permanent display in the British Library. An additional discovery related to Codex Sinaiticus occurred in 1975 when, in a previously unknown recess in a wall at the Monastery of St. Catherine, some monks discovered a large quantity of manuscripts and manuscript fragments. Among this assortment of materials were discovered twelve complete leaves (twenty-four pages) of Codex Sinaiticus, along with some additional fragments.

Biblical Significance

Codex Sinaiticus, usually designated by the Hebrew letter ℵ ("aleph," the first letter of the Hebrew alphabet), is the earliest surviving complete copy of the New Testament, as well as the only complete copy of the New Testament written in the uncial script. In addition to being one of the most important witnesses of the text of the New Testament, Codex Sinaiticus also contains some of the earliest and best copies of some of the books of the Old Testament. One example of the importance of Codex Sinaiticus is the evidence it provides for the ending of the Gospel of Mark. The majority of extant early Greek manuscripts contain verses 9-20 at the end of chapter 16 of Mark. (Some manuscripts have a different, shorter ending.) Codex Sinaiticus, on the other hand, along with Codex Vaticanus and a few additional minor witnesses, ends at verse 8 of chapter 16. Based partially on the evidence of Codex Sinaiticus, most textual critics today are convinced that the Gospel of Mark originally ended at 16:8 (or perhaps the remainder of the Gospel was lost). Figure 121 shows a page (folio 228) from Codex Sinaiticus containing the last verses of the Gospel of Mark (16:2b-8) and the beginning verses of the Gospel of Luke (1:1-18a).

Codex Alexandrinus

Parchment codex (manuscript in book form) of the Christian Bible

▷ Size: 32.1 cm. (12.64 in.) high; 26.4 cm. (10.39 in.) wide
▷ Writing: Greek language

▷ Provenance: Original, unknown; earliest known location, Alexandria, Egypt

▷ Date: Early fifth century C.E.

▷ Present location: British Library, London (Sir John Ritblat Gallery)

▷ Identification number: MS Royal 1 D. VIII

The earliest provenance of Codex Alexandrinus is unknown. A thirteenth or fourteenth century note in Arabic on the first folio, signed by "Athanasius the humble," says the codex was committed to the "patriarchal cell" in the fortress of Alexandria, Egypt, and threatens excommunication to anyone who removes it. Another note in Latin by Cyril Lucar, the Eastern Orthodox Patriarch of Alexandria (1602-1621; later patriarch of Constantinople, 1621-1638), says that the manuscript was written by Thecla the martyr, a noble lady of Egypt, shortly after the Council of Nicaea (325 C.E.), but this attribution clearly is spurious. Most scholars date Alexandrinus to the first half of the fifth century C.E., although some scholars would argue for the late fourth century. Apparently Cyril Lucar brought the manuscript with him from Alexandria to Constantinople and offered it in 1624 to Sir Thomas Roe, the English ambassador, as a gift to King James I. The patriarch's gift was motivated by assistance given him by the

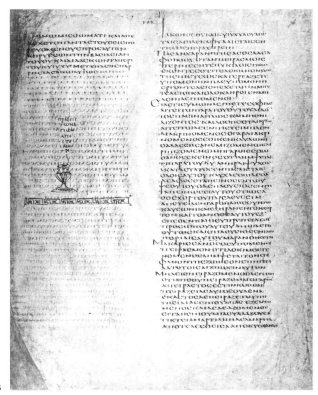

122. The page of Codex Alexandrinus containing the end of the book of Acts and the beginning of the book of James

British during a complex struggle with the Turkish authorities, the Roman Catholic Church, and his own subordinates. The codex was actually presented in 1627 to King Charles I (James I having died in 1625), only sixteen years after the printing of the King James Bible. This volume immediately became the showpiece of the Royal Library (now the British Library) and was pored over by the world's leading biblical scholars. Because of its connection with Alexandria, it has always been known as Alexandrinus (abbreviated "A" in textual studies).

The text is written on parchment in two columns of uncial script (from the Latin *uncialis,* "inch-high"; capital, or block letters) in brown ink, with no spacing between words. Each column contains between forty-six and fifty-two lines per column, with twenty to twenty-five letters per line. The beginning line of each book is written in red ink. Some letters at the beginning of lines are written somewhat larger than the others. The handwriting gives evidence of having come from five different scribes. At the present time, 773 pages of the codex exist from the approximately 822 original pages. These contain all of the books of the Old Testament, although a few pages are lost from Genesis, 1 Kings, and Psalms. The books of Tobit, Judith, and 1-4 Maccabees are also included. The New Testament has all the books of the New Testament, as well as 1 Clement and 2 Clement, but with some significant portions missing. It lacks almost all of Matthew (from 1:1 to 25:6), John 6:50–8:52, and 2 Corinthians 4:13–12:6. The preface to the codex lists the Psalms of Solomon also, but it is missing, and the space between its listing and that of the other books suggests that the scribe did not regard it as part of the accepted canon.

The page from the codex shown in figure 122 (folio 76) contains the ending of the book of Acts (28:30-31) and the beginning of the book of James (1:1-15). As is the case in many ancient manuscripts, in Codex Alexandrinus the General (or, Catholic) Epistles, which are comprised of James, 1 and 2 Peter, 1, 2, and 3 John, and Jude, are placed immediately after the book of Acts. Note the decorations the scribe has added at the end of the book of Acts.

Biblical Significance

This codex was the first of the great manuscripts of the Bible to be discovered. Probably no other manuscript has had such an influence on modern textual studies. Following its discovery, and the widespread scholarly attention it received, the science of textual criticism may be said to have begun. Alexandrinus is considered a complex, "mixed" text — one from various textual traditions — and somewhat less "pure," particularly in the Gospels, than the other two great texts, Sinaiticus and Vaticanus. (See the article "Codex Sinaiticus.") Nevertheless, it has had significant influence in the development of modern translations of the Bible. It preserves one of the best texts of Deuteronomy and Revelation, and it is the oldest manuscript of the second and third books of Maccabees. Its text of the Old Testament is considered one of the most valuable witnesses to the Septuagint, the Greek translation of the Old Testament. In the New Testament, Alexandrinus has the so-called longer ending of Mark (16:9-20), in contrast to the two earliest codices, Sinaiticus and Vaticanus. Since Mark ends so abruptly in some manuscripts — the original ending may have been lost at some stage of transmission or, more likely, the Gospel originally ended abruptly — early interpreters may have wished to provide a more satisfying conclusion to the work. Scholarship is virtually unanimous today in rejecting these verses as original to the Gospel, but at an early date Christians clearly accepted its account of further appearances of Jesus after his resurrection.

The *Gospel of Thomas* from the Nag Hammadi Writings

"Sayings of Jesus" document on papyrus

▷ Size: ca. 28 cm. (11.02 in.) high; 15 cm. (5.91 in.) wide
▷ Writing: Coptic language
▷ Provenance: Nag Hammadi, Egypt
▷ Date: ca. fourth century c.e.
▷ Present location: Coptic Museum, Cairo, Egypt
▷ Identification number: NH Codex II,2; museum number 10544

In December of 1945 an Arab peasant, Muhammad Ali, accidentally found thirteen leather-bound volumes of papyrus documents hidden in a jar that had been buried not far from the village of Nag Hammadi in Upper Egypt. Muhammad and his brother were digging for a type of soil used to fertilize their crops when they uncovered a pottery vessel approximately three feet tall. They broke it open hoping to find gold or other treasures, but were disappointed to find only books and some loose papyrus leaves. Returning home, they threw the books and loose pages on a pile of straw beside the oven. Their mother later admitted that she had burned several of the leaves along with the straw used to start a fire in the oven.

What they had found proved to be one of the most sensational archaeological discoveries of the twentieth century. The thirteen volumes contained a virtual library of Gnostic writings. Although the Gnostics were a sect long known to scholars, virtually nothing of their earliest writings had ever been discovered. The subsequent history of the codices resembles that of the Dead

Sea Scrolls in the delay in their publication and the right of scholarly access to them. In the forefront of the conflict was the so-called Jung Codex, a volume that was taken out of Egypt (under more than dubious circumstances) and offered for sale in the United States. Eventually it was purchased for the Jung Institute in Zurich, Switzerland, as a gift to the famous psychoanalyst Carl Jung who had a lifelong interest in Gnostic philosophy as it pertained to an understanding of the self. This particular volume contained one of the earliest documents of Gnosticism, the *Gospel of Truth,* considered to be either an original work of Valentinus, an Alexandrian teacher of Gnostic concepts who broke with the Christian church while in Rome (ca. 136 C.E.), or its revision by one of his early disciples. A work by the same title is attributed to Valentinus by Irenaeus. Other important Gnostic writings among the fifty-two documents in this collection include the *Apocryphon* ("secret book") *of John,* the *Gospel to the Egyptians,* the *Apocryphon of James,* and the *Apocalypse of Paul.* Another Gnostic work subsequently discovered and recently published, the *Gospel of Judas,* has attracted worldwide attention.

123. A portion of Codex II of the Nag Hammadi writings, including the closing lines from the *Gospel of Thomas*

Nevertheless, among all of the Nag Hammadi writings, the *Gospel of Thomas* remains the subject of the greatest interest, among both scholars and non-scholars alike. This document was so unlike any of the others that its translation immediately aroused popular curiosity and intense scholarly interest (not to mention heated scholarly bickering and debate), as well as a new field of research. The *Gospel of Thomas* purports to be 114 sayings of Jesus, and indeed it bears more resemblance to the canonical Gospels than do any other of the apocryphal gospels. Many scholars believe that the original version of the sayings was written in Greek and originated in Syria, though these conclusions have been disputed. A papyrus had already been found in the 1800s at Oxyrhynchus, Egypt, with a few of these sayings in Greek, although positive identification of their source was only made possible by the Nag Hammadi discoveries. (See the article "Papyrus 52.")

The bound volume itself (Codex II) consists of thirty-eight folios sewn through the fold with two separate stitches of flax thread. Its cover is made of goat leather painted a rose color and decorated with rows of heart-shaped leaves, spirals, meander patterns, and an *ankh* (the hieroglyph for "life"). Double flaps of leather enclosed the open side of the codex and leather thongs secured the volume. Along with the *Gospel of Thomas,* this codex contains several other writings, including the *Gospel of Philip,* noted for its attributing of a special relationship between Jesus and Mary Magdalene.

Based on an analysis of the papyrus used to reinforce the board covers of the volume, the manuscript can be dated to approximately 350-400 C.E. The date of the original writings themselves, however, remains a subject of debate. Estimates range from the end of the first century to the beginning of the third century. Some scholars insist that portions of these works may go back even further, perhaps even to the middle of the first century.

The photograph included here (fig. 123) shows the page from Codex II that contains the ending of the *Gospel of Thomas* (comprising sayings 110-114) and the beginning of the *Gospel of Philip.* (The title of the *Gospel of Thomas* appears at the end, not the beginning, of the work.)

Biblical Significance

The *Gospel of Thomas* has been at the forefront of the sharp disagreements over the date of these writings, with two strongly held, divergent viewpoints. One group of scholars is convinced that this work may be so early that it even predates the canonical Gospels. They would place its writing in the latter half of the first century, perhaps in the 60s or 70s, making their composition contemporaneous with, or even prior to, some of the other Gospels. Few authorities, however, believe that any of the sayings of Jesus as recorded in the canonical Gospels are dependent on these sayings.

The Jesus Seminar, a group of scholars who debated the historicity of the sayings of Jesus, identified virtually every item in the other apocryphal gospels as "black," that is, the majority believe Jesus did not say them. But in the *Gospel of Thomas,* they identified five sayings as "red," that is, Jesus undoubtedly said the passage or something closely similar. Yet only two of the sayings truly unique to *Thomas*, not duplicated in the canonical Gospels, were judged "possibly" to have come from Jesus (Logion [saying] 97, the parable of the broken jar of meal; and Logion 98, the parable of the assassin) and none "red," or assured. Overall, however, they were so impressed by the *Gospel of Thomas* that they published a work entitled *The Fifth Gospel*, regarding this writing as an early, independent attestation of the canonical sayings of Jesus. They count thirty-two instances of sayings in Thomas that parallel verses in the biblical Gospels.

As an example of many sayings in the *Gospel of Thomas* that are virtually identical with those in the New Testament, the following may be given as examples:

Logion 20: The disciples said to Jesus, "Tell us what the kingdom of heaven is like."

He said to them, "It is like a mustard seed. It is the smallest of all seeds. But when it falls on tilled soil, it produces a great plant and becomes a shelter for birds of the sky."

Logion 54: "Blessed are the poor, for yours is the kingdom of heaven."

Logion 96: Jesus said, "The kingdom of the father is like [a certain] woman. She took a little leaven, [concealed] it in some dough, and made it into large loaves. Let him who has ears hear."[1]

Other scholars are equally convinced that the *Gospel of Thomas* is a derivative writing; that is, it is merely a later Gnostic overlay on the original Gospel sayings. For instance, in the opening lines, or preface, of the writing, the sayings listed are identified as "secret," a notable emphasis in Gnosticism on hidden knowledge, possessed by the few: "These are the secret sayings which the living Jesus spoke and which Didymos Judas Thomas wrote down." In the canonical Gospels, on the other hand, Jesus teaches publicly and sends his disciples to teach others. Likewise, the first of the sayings in the *Gospel of Thomas*, while virtually parallel to a saying in the Gospel of John (John 8:51), shows an example of another key difference between the emphasis of the *Gospel of Thomas* and the canonical Gospels: "And he said, 'Whoever *finds the interpretation of the sayings* will not experience death.'" On the other hand, the Gospel of John says, "Whoever *keeps my word* will never taste death" (emphasis

---

1. All quotations from the *Gospel of Thomas* are from "The Gospel of Thomas (II,2)," introduced by Helmut Koester, translated by Thomas O. Lambdin, in *The Nag Hammadi Library*, ed. James M. Robinson, 3rd ed. (San Francisco: Harper & Row, 1988), pp. 124-138.

added). Whereas faith and obedient living are stressed in the canonical Gospels, Gnostic writings emphasize knowledge and the understanding of hidden truths.

Among those sayings in *Thomas* that show the strongest tendencies toward Gnostic philosophy may be listed the following examples:

Logion 13: And he took him [Thomas] and withdrew and told him three things. When Thomas returned to his companions, they asked him, "What did Jesus say to you?"

Thomas said to them, "If I tell you one of the things which he told me, you will pick up stones and throw them at me; a fire will come out of the stones and burn you up."

Logion 114: Simon Peter said to them, "Let Mary leave us, for women are not worthy of life."

Jesus said, "I myself shall lead her in order to make her male, so that she too may become a living spirit resembling you males. For every woman who will make herself male will enter the kingdom of heaven."

This peculiar final saying likely means that if women wish to enter the kingdom of heaven they must renounce the physical world, especially sexuality, including childbearing, since procreation continues the evil, material world created by the evil demigod (of Gnostic myth); sexual differentiation likewise was seen by Gnosticism as a similar product of the work of this evil demigod.

Sensational Finds:
Genuine or Forgery?

The James Ossuary, the Ivory Pomegranate, and the Baruch Bulla

Archaeology has experienced many instances of forged objects in its history and many more claims of such fraud. Unfortunately, the field known historically as "biblical" archaeology seems to have had more than its share of these controversies. The very nature of objects important to the faith of a religion leads to increased controversy, as well as the temptation for some unscrupulous individuals to forge such items for the market. These controversial "finds" are rarely those artifacts that are unearthed on a dig at a biblical site, but rather they are anonymous objects from unknown provenances "discovered" on the antiquities market.

Recently the world of biblical research has experienced one of the most dramatic and extensive charges of fraud in its history. At the center of this controversy are three items, with numerous others on the periphery of the charges: an ossuary claimed to be the burial box of James, the brother of Jesus; a tiny ivory pomegranate, perhaps part of a ceremonial scepter, believed to date to the first temple of Israel; and a bulla, or clay seal, alleged to contained the name of Baruch (Berechiah), secretary of the prophet Jeremiah.

The James Ossuary

During the first century C.E., it was the custom of wealthy Jews in Palestine to bury their dead in a cave for one year, then remove the bones and place them in an ossuary (burial box). Many such ossuaries have been found, both with and without descriptions. At a press conference held in October of 2002, the discovery of an ossuary bearing the inscription "James son of Joseph, brother of Jesus" was announced. This object was first examined by André Lemaire of the Sorbonne University in Paris, in the home of a private collector, Oded Golan, an Israeli engineer who lived in Tel Aviv. He claimed to have obtained it from an Arab antiquities dealer in Jerusalem some fifteen years earlier but to have been unaware of its significance. Initial reports by experts, though not unanimous, generally concluded that the object and its inscription were authentic. Nevertheless, doubts continued to be raised about the authenticity of the inscription. A lengthy study then was conducted by the Israeli Antiquities Authority, directed by paleographers and geologists, on both the writing and the material of the box itself. They concluded that the ossuary was authentic, but that the inscription, or at least the last portion of it ("brother of Jesus"), was not. The box itself was covered with an authentic patina, material deposits left from centuries of ground water and atmospheric deposits on its surface. But in the case of the inscription, deposits found within the incised letters proved to be a newer, chalky substance, which the experts believed was applied in a wash to the forged inscription to conceal its newness. Subsequently, an indictment of antiquities fraud was brought against Oded Golan, who was charged with being the mastermind of a counterfeiting ring of five men responsible for fabricating antiquities over a period of more than fifteen years. Recently his attorney has claimed to have photographs dating to the 1970s showing the ossuary in Golan's possession at that time and therefore nullifying the government's claims against him. The authenticity of the inscription from a scholarly point of view remains a matter of divided opinion.

The Ivory Pomegranate

This tiny object (IMJ 88.80.129; see fig. 124), just 43 mm. (1.69 in.) high, initially achieved renown as the only artifact ever discovered from the first temple of Jerusalem (Solomon's Temple). The words, "Holy to the priests, Temple of [Yahwe]h," were engraved upon it. The use of this object was uncertain, but scholars believed it to be either the top of a ceremonial scepter carried by the priests or one of the decorative elements in the temple. It first appeared in a Jerusalem antiquities shop in 1979 and was declared authentic by André Lemaire, French epigrapher, who published an article on it in 1981. Its location after that was uncertain until 1987, when it was offered for sale to the Israel Museum by a tour

124. Small ivory pomegranate previously alleged to be from Solomon's temple in Jerusalem

guide on behalf of its anonymous owner. After the famed Israeli archaeologist and epigrapher Nahman Avigad certified the authenticity of the pomegranate, the museum purchased it for $550,000. It has been on display at the museum since 1988. But in 2004 the museum suddenly announced that the object was fraudulent, on the basis of the findings of a committee from the Israel Antiquities Authority that the museum had requested to examine the pomegranate's authenticity. A new examination with an environmental scanning electron microscope, which did not exist at the time of the original examination, revealed synthetic material in the inscription between the external patina and the ivory. As a result of these findings, the museum now considers the inscription to be forged. Furthermore, the museum is now dating the object itself to the Late Bronze Age (14th-13th century B.C.E.). It will remain on display, according to the museum, to acquaint the public with the ongoing process of authentication of archaeological materials.

The Baruch Bulla

Another object has been declared inauthentic by the Israel Antiquities Authority, a clay bulla attributed to Baruch (or Berechiah, the longer form of the name), secretary to the prophet Jeremiah (see Jer. 36:4). A bulla is a stamped piece of clay that was used to seal a papyrus document. This stamp reads, "Belonging to Berekayahu, son of Neriyahu, the scribe." It is written in three lines of pre-exilic Hebrew linear script separated by double horizontal lines, with a single line bordering the oval impression. Two such bullae were found in Israel. One has a portion of a fingerprint on it in addition to the words; another one, otherwise identical, is in the Israel Museum (IMJ 76.22.2299). The museum's bulla measures 1.7 × 1.6 cm. (.69 in. by .63 in.). This seal appeared in the 1970s in the collection of a noted Israeli collector, Dr. Reuben Hecht, and the artifact became known after it was described in an article by Nahman Avigad. Its provenance is unknown. At this point the Israel Antiquities Authority has declared only the fingerprint bulla (which is in the collection of Shlomo Moussaieff, a well-known collector who lives in London) to be a forgery, perpetrated by two of the men claimed to be part of the forgery ring associated with the James Ossuary. One authority on the examining commission said that tests of the bulla showed fluoride in the water used to make the wet clay — scarcely an ancient ingredient in water. Thus far nothing has been said concerning the bulla in the Israel Museum.

Bibliography

Abells, Zvi, and Asher Arbit. "Some New Thoughts on Jerusalem's Ancient Water Systems." *Palestine Exploration Quarterly* 127 (1995): 2-7.

Aharoni, Yohanan, in cooperation with Joseph Naveh and contributions by A. F. Rainey, M. Aharoni, B. Lifshitz, M. Sharon, and Z. Gofer. *Arad Inscriptions.* Translated by Judith Ben-Or. Edited and revised by Anson F. Rainey. Jerusalem: The Israel Exploration Society, 1981.

Aharoni, Y[ohanan]. "Hebrew Ostraca from Tel Arad." *Israel Exploration Journal* 16 (1966): 1-7.

Albenda, Pauline. Adaptation into French by Annie Caubet. *The Palace of Sargon, King of Assyria: Monumental Wall Reliefs at Dur-Sharrukin, from Original Drawings Made at the Time of Their Discovery in 1843-1844 by Botta and Flandin.* Paris: Editions Recherche sur les Civilisations, 1986.

Albright, W. F. "The Discovery of an Aramaic Inscription Relating to King Uzziah." *Bulletin of the American Schools of Oriental Research* 44 (1931): 8-10.

Alföldy, Géza. "Pontius Pilatus und das Tiberieum von Caesarea Maritima." *Scripta classica israelica* 18 (1999): 85-108.

Allen, Lindsay. *The Persian Empire.* Chicago: University of Chicago Press, 2005.

Alster, Bendt. *The Instructions of Suruppak.* Mesopotamia. Copenhagen Studies in Assyriology, vol. 2. Copenhagen: Akademisk Forlag, 1974.

———. *Proverbs of Ancient Sumer: The World's Earliest Proverb Collections.* 2 vols. Bethesda, Md.: CDL Press, 1997.

———. *Studies in Sumerian Proverbs.* Mesopotamia. Copenhagen Studies in Assyriology, vol. 3. Copenhagen: Akademisk Forlag, 1975.

Alston, Richard. *Aspects of Roman History AD 14-117.* London: Routledge, 1998.

Athas, George. *The Tel Dan Inscription: A Reappraisal and a New Interpretation.* Sheffield: Sheffield Academic Press, 2003.

Avigad, N[ahman]. "The Epitaph of a Royal Steward from Siloam Village." *Israel Exploration Journal* 3 (1953): 137-52.

———. "Excavations in the Jewish Quarter of the Old City of Jerusalem, 1969/70 (Preliminary Report)." *Israel Exploration Journal* 20 (1970): 1-8.

————. *The Herodian Quarter in Jerusalem, Wohl Archaeological Museum.* Jerusalem: Keter Publishing House, n.d.

Avigad, Nahman. Rev. and completed by Benjamin Sass. *Corpus of West Semitic Stamp Seals.* Jerusalem: The Israel Academy of Sciences and Humanities; the Israel Exploration Society; The Institute of Archaeology, The Hebrew University of Jerusalem, 1997.

AvRutick, Sharon, ed. *The Israel Museum, Jerusalem.* New York: Harry N. Abrams, 2005.

Aynard, Jeanne Marie. *Le prisme du Louvre AO 19.939.* Bibliothèque de l'École des hautes études. Section des sciences historiques et philologiques, fasc. 309. Paris: H. Champion, 1957.

Barnett, Richard D. *Ancient Ivories in the Middle East and Adjacent Countries.* Qedem, vol. 14. Jerusalem: The Institute of Archaeology, The Hebrew University of Jerusalem, 1982.

————. *Sculptures from the North Palace of Ashurbanipal at Nineveh (668-627 B.C.).* London: British Museum Publications, 1976.

Barnett, Richard D., with a supplement by Leri Glynne Davies. *A Catalogue of the Nimrud Ivories.* 2nd ed. London: British Museum Publications, 1975.

Barrett, C. K., ed. *The New Testament Background: Writings from Ancient Greece and the Roman Empire That Illuminate Christian Origins.* Rev. ed. San Francisco: HarperSanFrancisco, 1989.

Bauckham, Richard, ed. *The Book of Acts in Its Palestinian Setting.* Vol. 4, *The Book of Acts in Its First Century Setting.* Grand Rapids: Wm. B. Eerdmans, 1995.

Beyerlin, Walter, ed. *Near Eastern Religious Texts Relating to the Old Testament.* The Old Testament Library. Philadelphia: Westminster, 1978.

Bickerman, Elias J. "The Warning Inscriptions of Herod's Temple." *The Jewish Quarterly Review* 37 (1946-47): 387-405.

Biran, Avraham. *Biblical Dan.* Jerusalem: Israel Exploration Society, Hebrew Union — Jewish Institute of Religion, 1994.

Biran, Avraham, and Joseph Naveh. "An Aramaic Stele Fragment from Tel Dan." *Israel Exploration Journal* 43 (1993): 81-98.

————. "The Tel Dan Inscription: A New Fragment." *Israel Exploration Journal* 45 (1995): 1-18.

Boardman, John, ed. *The Cambridge Ancient History.* Plates to Volume 3. New ed. Cambridge: Cambridge University Press, 1984.

Boardman, John, et al., eds. *The Cambridge Ancient History.* Vol. 3, pt. 2, *The Assyrian and Babylonian Empires and Other States of the Near East, from the Eighth to the Sixth Centuries B.C.* 2nd ed. Cambridge: Cambridge University Press, 1991.

Boardman, John, et al., eds. *The Cambridge Ancient History.* Vol. 4, *Persia, Greece and the Western Mediterranean c. 525 to 479 B.C.* 2nd ed. Cambridge: Cambridge University Press, 1988.

Borger, Riekele. *Die Inschriften Asarhadons Königs von Assyrien.* Archiv für Orientforschung. Beiheft 9. Graz: Im Selbstverlage des Herausgebers, 1956.

Bron, François, and André Lemaire. "Les inscriptions araméennes de Hazaël." *Revue d'assyriologie et d'archéologie orientale* 83 (1989): 35-44.

Chavalas, Mark W., ed. *The Ancient Near East: Historical Sources in Translation.* Malden, Mass.: Blackwell, 2006.

Clermont-Ganneau, Charles. *Archaeological Researches in Palestine during the Years 1873-1874.* 2 vols. London: Committee of the Palestine Exploration Fund, 1896-1899.

Clifford, Richard J. *Creation Accounts in the Ancient Near East and in the Bible.* The Catholic Biblical Quarterly Monograph Series 26. Washington, D.C.: The Catholic Biblical Association of America, 1994.

Coogan, Michael D. *The Oxford History of the Biblical World.* New York: Oxford University Press, 1998.

————, ed. and trans. *Stories from Ancient Canaan.* Philadelphia: Westminster, 1978.

Cook, B. F. *Greek Inscriptions.* Reading the Past, vol. 5. Berkeley and Los Angeles: University of California Press/British Museum, 1987.

Cook, J. M. *The Persian Empire.* New York: Schocken Books, 1983.

Craigie, Peter C. *Ugarit and the Old Testament.* Grand Rapids: Wm. B. Eerdmans, 1983.

Curtis, J. E., M. R. Cowell, and C. B. F. Walker. "A Silver Bowl of Artaxerxes I." *Iran: Journal of the British Institute of Persian Studies* 33 (1995): 149-53.

Curtis, J. E., and J. E. Reade, eds. *Art and Empire: Treasures from Assyria in the British Museum.* New York: The Metropolitan Museum of Art, 1995.

Curtis, John, and Nigel Tallis. *Forgotten Empire: The World of Ancient Persia.* London: The British Museum Press, 2005.

Dalley, Stephanie. *Myths from Mesopotamia: Creation, the Flood, Gilgamesh, and Others.* Oxford: Oxford University Press, 1989.

Daltrop, Georg, Ulrich Hausmann, and Max Wegner. *Die Flavier: Vespasian, Titus, Domitian, Nerva, Julia Titi, Domitilla, Domitia.* Abteilung 2, band 1, *Das römische Herrscherbild,* ed. Max Wegner. Berlin: Verlag Gebr. Mann, 1966.

Dandamaev, M. A. *A Political History of the Achaemenid Empire.* Translated by W. J. Vogelsang. Leiden: E. J. Brill, 1989.

Davies, G. I., assisted by M. N. A. Bockmuehl, D. R. de Lacey, and A. J. Poulter. *Ancient Hebrew Inscriptions: Corpus and Concordance.* Cambridge: Cambridge University Press, 1991.

Dearman, Andrew, ed. *Studies in the Mesha Inscription and Moab.* Archaeology and Biblical Studies, no. 2. Atlanta: Scholars Press, 1989.

de Genouillac, Henri. *Textes religieux sumeriens du Louvre.* 2 vols. Paris: Musée de Louvre, 1930.

Delaporte, Louis. *Catalogue des cylinders, cachets et pierres gravées de style oriental.* 2 vols. Paris: Librairie Hachette, 1920-23.

Dietrich, Manfried, Oswald Loretz, and Joaquín Sanmartín. *The Cuneiform Alphabetic Texts from Ugarit, Ras Ibn Hani, and Other Places* (KTU: second, enlarged edition). Münster: Ugarit-Verlag, 1995.

Dio Cassius. *Roman History.* 9 vols. Translated by Earnest Cary. Loeb Classical Library. Cambridge, Mass.: Harvard University Press, 1914-27.

Donner, H., and W. Röllig. *Kanaanäische und aramäische Inschriften.* 3 vols. 2nd ed. Wiesbaden: Harrassowitz, 1966-69.

Driver, G. R. *Canaanite Myths and Legends*. Old Testament Studies, no. 3. Edinburgh: T&T Clark, 1956.

Ephʿal, Israel, and Joseph Naveh. "Hazael's Booty Inscriptions." *Israel Exploration Journal* 39 (1989): 192-200.

Erdemgil, Selahattin, et al. *Ephesus Museum*. Translated by Christine M. Thomas. Istanbul: Do-Gü Press, n.d.

Evans, Craig A. *Ancient Texts for New Testament Studies: A Guide to the Background Literature*. Peabody, Mass.: Hendrickson, 2005.

Fant, Clyde E., and Mitchell G. Reddish. *A Guide to Biblical Sites in Greece and Turkey*. New York: Oxford University Press, 2003.

Fitzmyer, Joseph. "Paul." In *The New Jerome Biblical Commentary*, edited by Raymond E. Brown, Joseph A. Fitzmyer, and Roland E. Murphy, pp. 1329-1337. New York: Prentice Hall, 1990.

Fleischer, Robert. *Artemis von Ephesos und verwandte Kultstatuen aus Anatolien und Syrien*. Leiden: E. J. Brill, 1973.

Foster, Benjamin R. *Before the Muses: An Anthology of Akkadian Literature*. 2 vols. Bethesda, Md.: CDL Press, 1993.

Frahm, Eckart. *Einleitung in die Sanherib-Inschriften*. Archiv für Orientforschung, supplement 26. Vienna: Institut für Orientalistik der Universität Wien, 1997.

Frame, Grant. *Rulers of Babylonia: From the Second Dynasty of Isin to the End of Assyrian Domination (1157-612 BC)*. The Royal Inscriptions of Mesopotamia. Babylonian Periods, vol. 2. Toronto: University of Toronto Press, 1995.

Freedman, David Noel, ed. *The Anchor Bible Dictionary*. 6 vols. New York: Doubleday, 1992.

Frerichs, Ernest S. and Leonard H. Lesko, eds. *Exodus: The Egyptian Evidence*. Winona Lake, Ind.: Eisenbrauns, 1997.

Galter, Hannes, et al. "The Colossi of Sennacherib's Palace and Their Inscriptions." *Annual Review of the Royal Inscriptions of Mesopotamia Project* 4 (1986): 27-32.

Gibson, John C. L. *Textbook of Syrian Semitic Inscriptions*. 3 vols. Oxford: Clarendon, 1971-82.

Glassner, Jean-Jacques. *Mesopotamian Chronicles*. Edited by Benjamin R. Foster. Society of Biblical Literature Writings from the Ancient World, no. 19. Atlanta: Society of Biblical Literature, 2004.

————. "Le récit autobiographique de Sargon." *Revue d'assyriologie et d'archéologie orientale* 82 (1988): 1-11.

Goetze, A., and S. Levy. "Fragment of the Gilgamesh Epic from Megiddo." *Atiqot* 2 (1959): 121-28.

Gordon, Edmund I., with a chapter by Thorkild Jacobsen. *Sumerian Proverbs: Glimpses of Everyday Life in Ancient Mesopotamia*. New York: Greenwood, 1968.

Goshen-Gottstein, M. H. "The Aleppo Codex and the Rise of the Massoretic Bible Text." *Biblical Archaeologist* 42 (1979): 145-63.

Gray, John. *The Legacy of Canaan: The Ras Shamra Texts and Their Relevance to the Old Testament*. Supplements to Vetus Testamentum, vol. 5. Leiden: E. J. Brill, 1957.

437

Grayson, A. Kirk. *Assyrian and Babylonian Chronicles.* Locust Valley, N.Y.: J. J. Augustin, 1975.

―――. *Assyrian Rulers of the Early First Millennium* BC *I (1114-859* BC *).* The Royal Inscriptions of Mesopotamia. Assyrian Periods, vol. 2. Toronto: University of Toronto Press, 1991.

―――. *Assyrian Rulers of the Early First Millennium* BC *II (858-745* BC *).* The Royal Inscriptions of Mesopotamia. Assyrian Periods, vol. 3. Toronto: University of Toronto Press, 1996.

Green, Peter. *Alexander of Macedon, 356-323* B.C.: *A Historical Biography.* Berkeley and Los Angeles: University of California Press, 1991.

Gunter, Ann C., and Paul Jett. *Ancient Iranian Metalwork in the Arthur M. Sackler Gallery and the Freer Gallery of Art.* Washington, D.C.: Smithsonian Institution, 1992.

Haas, N. "Anthropological Observations on the Skeletal Remains from Giv'at ha-Mivtar." *Israel Exploration Journal* 20 (1970): 38-59.

Hallo, William W., gen. ed., and K. Lawson Younger Jr., assoc. ed. *The Context of Scripture.* 3 vols. Leiden: E. J. Brill, 1997-2002.

Harper, Prudence O., Joan Aruz, and Françoise Tallon, eds. *The Royal City of Susa: Ancient Near Eastern Treasures in the Louvre.* New York: The Metropolitan Museum of Art, 1992.

Heidel, Alexander. *The Babylonian Genesis.* Chicago: University of Chicago Press, 1942.

―――. *The Gilgamesh Epic and Old Testament Parallels.* 2nd ed. Chicago: University of Chicago Press, 1949.

Herdner, Andrée. *Corpus des tablettes en cunéiforms alphabétiques découvertes à Ras Shamra-Ugarit de 1929 à 1939.* 2 vols. Mission de Ras Shamra, vol. 10. Paris: Imprimerie Nationale, 1963.

Hess, Richard S., and David Toshio Tsumura, eds. *"I Studied Inscriptions from before the Flood": Ancient Near Eastern, Literary, and Linguistic Approaches to Genesis 1–11.* Sources for Biblical and Theological Study. Winona Lake, Ind.: Eisenbrauns, 1994.

Hoffmeier, James K. *Israel in Egypt: The Evidence for the Authenticity of the Exodus Tradition.* New York: Oxford University Press, 1996.

Inan, Jale, and Elisabeth Rosenbaum. *Roman and Early Byzantine Portrait Sculpture in Asia Minor.* London: Oxford University Press, 1966.

Jacobsen, Thorkild. *The Harps That Once . . . : Sumerian Poetry in Translation.* New Haven: Yale University Press, 1987.

―――. *The Sumerian King List.* Chicago: University of Chicago Press, 1939.

Jakob-Rost, L., et al. *Das Vorderasiatisches Museum Berlin.* Mainz am Rhein: Philipp von Zabern, 1992.

Josephus. *The Jewish War.* 3 vols. Translated by H. St. J. Thackeray, et al. Loeb Classical Library. Cambridge, Mass.: Harvard University Press, 1927-28.

Kaiser, Otto. *Isaiah 13–39: A Commentary.* Old Testament Library. Philadelphia: Westminster, 1974.

Kitchen, K. A. "A Possible Mention of David in the Late Tenth Century BCE, and Deity *Dod as Dead as the Dodo?" *Journal for the Study of the Old Testament* 76 (1997): 29-44.

Kloppenborg, John S. "The Theodotos Synagogue Inscription and the Problem of First-Century Synagogue Buildings." In *Jesus and Archaeology*, edited by James Charlesworth, pp. 252-53. Grand Rapids: Wm. B. Eerdmans, 2006.

Kraeling, Carl H., and Lucetta Mowry, "Music in the Bible." In *Ancient and Oriental Music*, edited by Egon Wellesz, pp. 283-312. *The New Oxford History of Music*, vol. 1. London: Oxford University Press, 1957.

Kramer, Samuel Noah. *From the Poetry of Sumer: Creation, Glorification, Adoration.* Berkeley and Los Angeles: University of California Press, 1979.

———. *From the Tablets of Sumer.* Indian Hills, Colo.: Falcon's Wing, 1956.

———. *Sumerian Mythology: A Study of Spiritual and Literary Achievement in the Third Millennium B.C.* Rev. ed. Philadelphia: University of Pennsylvania Press, 1972.

———. *The Sumerians: Their History, Culture, and Character.* Chicago: University of Chicago Press, 1963.

Kramer, Samuel Noah, and John Maier. *Myths of Enki, the Crafty God.* New York: Oxford University Press, 1989.

Lambert, W. G. *Babylonian Wisdom Literature.* Oxford: Clarendon, 1960.

Lambert, W. G., and A. R. Millard. *Atra-ḫasīs: The Babylonian Story of the Flood.* Oxford: Oxford University Press, Clarendon Press, 1969.

Lambert, W. G., and Simon B. Parker. *Enuma Eliš. The Babylonian Epic of Creation: The Cuneiform Text.* Oxford: Clarendon, 1966.

Late Babylonian Astronomical and Related Texts. Copied by T. G. Pinches and J. N. Strassmaier. Prepared for publication by A. J. Sachs with the co-operation of J. Schaumberger. Providence, R.I.: Brown University Press, 1955.

Layard, Austen Henry. *Nineveh and Its Remains.* 2 vols. New York: George P. Putnam, 1849.

Lemaire, André. "'House of David' Restored in Moabite Inscription." *Biblical Archaeology Review* 20 (1994): 30-37.

Lémonon, Jean-Pierre. *Pilate et le gouvernement de la Judée: Textes et monuments.* Paris: J. Gabalda, 1981.

Lewis, Brian. *The Sargon Legend: A Study of the Akkadian Text and the Tale of the Hero Who Was Exposed at Birth.* American Schools of Oriental Research Dissertation Series, no. 4. Cambridge, Mass.: American Schools of Oriental Research, 1980.

Lichtheim, Miriam. *Ancient Egyptian Literature: A Book of Readings.* Vol. 2, *The New Kingdom.* Berkeley and Los Angeles: University of California Press, 1976.

Lindenberger, James M. *Ancient Aramaic and Hebrew Letters.* Edited by Kent Harold Richards. Society of Biblical Literature Writings from the Ancient World, no. 14. 2nd ed. Atlanta: Society of Biblical Literature, 2003.

Ling-Israel, Pnina. "The Sennacherib Prism in the Israel Museum — Jerusalem." In *Bar-Ilan Studies in Assyriology,* edited by Jacob Klein and Aaron Skaist. Ramat Gan: Bar-Ilan University Press, 1990.

Lloyd, Seton. *The Archaeology of Mesopotamia: From the Old Stone Age to the Persian Conquest.* Rev. ed. London: Thames and Hudson, 1984.

Luckenbill, Daniel David. *Ancient Records of Assyria and Babylonia.* 2 vols. Chicago: University of Chicago Press, 1926-27. Reprint, New York: Greenwood Press, 1968.

————. *The Annals of Sennacherib*. The University of Chicago Oriental Institute Publications, vol. 2. Chicago: University of Chicago Press, 1924.

Luukko, Mikko, and Greta Van Buylaere, eds. *The Political Correspondence of Esarhaddon*. State Archives of Assyria, vol. 16. Helsinki: Helsinki University Press, 2002.

Maimonides, Moses. *The Code of Maimonides*. Book Two: The Book of Love. Translated by Menachem Kellner. Yale Judaica Series, vol. 32. New Haven: Yale University Press, 2004.

Mallowan, M. E. L. *Nimrud and Its Remains*. 3 vols. New York: Dodd, Mead & Co., 1966.

Matthews, Victor H., and Don C. Benjamin. *Old Testament Parallels: Laws and Stories from the Ancient Near East*. 3d ed., fully rev. and exp. New York: Paulist, 2006.

Mitchell, T. C. *The Bible in the British Museum: Interpreting the Evidence*. London: The British Museum Press, 1988.

Moorey, P. R. S. *Ancient Mesopotamian Materials and Industries: The Archaeological Evidence*. Oxford: Clarendon, 1994.

Moran, William L., ed. and trans. *The Amarna Letters*. Baltimore: The Johns Hopkins University Press, 1987.

Moret, Alexandre M. "Légende d'Osiris à l'époque thébaine d'après l'hymne à Osiris du Louvre." *Bulletin de l'Institut français d'archéologie orientale* 30 (1931): 725-50.

Murnane, William J. *Texts from the Amarna Period in Egypt*. Edited by Edmund S. Meltzer. Society of Biblical Literature Writings from the Ancient World Series, no. 5. Atlanta: Scholars Press, 1995.

Murphy-O'Connor, Jerome. "Paul and Gallio." *Journal of Biblical Literature* 112 (1993): 315-17.

Mykytiuk, Lawrence J. *Identifying Biblical Persons in Northwest Semitic Inscriptions of 1200-539 B.C.E.* Atlanta: Society of Biblical Literature, 2004.

Na'aman, Nadav. "Three Notes on the Aramaic Inscription from Tel Dan." *Israel Exploration Journal* 50 (2000): 92-104.

Nougayrol, Jean. "Une version ancienne du 'juste souffrant.'" *Revue biblique* 59 (1952): 239-50.

Oates, Joan, and David Oates. *Nimrud: An Assyrian Imperial City Revealed*. London: The British School of Archaeology in Iraq, 2001.

Parpola, Simo, ed. *Letters from Assyrian and Babylonian Scholars*. State Archives of Assyria, vol. 10. Helsinki: Helsinki University Press, 1993.

Parrot, André. *The Arts of Assyria*. Translated by Stuart Gilbert and James Emmons. New York: Golden Press, 1961.

Pasinli, Alpay. *Istanbul Archaeological Museums*. 4th enlarged printing. Istanbul: A Turizm Yayinlari, 2005.

Pitard, Wayne. *Ancient Damascus: A Historical Study of the Syrian City-State from Earliest Times until Its Fall to the Assyrians in 732 B.C.E.* Winona Lake, Ind.: Eisenbrauns, 1987.

Plassart, A. "L'inscription de Delphes mentionnant le proconsul Gallion." *Revue des Études grecques* 80 (1967): 372-78.

Pliny. *Letters and Panegyricus.* 2 vols. Translated by Betty Radice. Loeb Classical Library. Cambridge, Mass.: Harvard University Press, 1969.

Priese, Karl-Heinz, et al. *Pergamon and Bode Museum: The Ancient World on Museum Island.* Antike Welt: Zeitschrift für Archäologie und Kulturgeschichte. Mainz: Philipp von Zabern, 1991.

Pritchard, James B. *The Ancient Near East in Pictures Relating to the Old Testament.* 2nd ed. with Supplement. Princeton: Princeton University Press, 1969.

————, ed. *Ancient Near Eastern Texts Relating to the Old Testament.* 3rd ed. with Supplement. Princeton: Princeton University Press, 1969.

Rahmani, L. Y. *A Catalogue of Jewish Ossuaries in the Collections of the State of Israel.* Jerusalem: The Israel Antiquities Authority, The Israel Academy of Sciences and Humanities, 1994.

Reynolds, Frances, ed. *The Babylonian Correspondence of Esarhaddon and Letters to Assurbanipal and Sin-šarru-iškun from Northern and Central Babylonia.* State Archives of Assyria, vol. 18. Helsinki: Helsinki University Press, 2003.

Robertson, A. T. *A Grammar of the Greek New Testament in the Light of Historical Research.* 4th ed. Nashville: Broadman, 1934.

Robinson, James M., gen. ed. *The Nag Hammadi Library.* 3rd ed. San Francisco: Harper & Row, 1988.

Roth, Martha T., with a contribution by Harry A. Hoffner Jr. *Law Collections from Mesopotamia and Asia Minor.* Edited by Piotr Michalowski. Society of Biblical Literature Writings from the Ancient World, no. 6. 2nd ed. Atlanta: Scholars Press, 1997.

Russell, John Malcolm. *The Final Sack of Nineveh: The Discovery, Documentation, and Destruction of King Sennacherib's Throne Room at Nineveh, Iraq.* New Haven: Yale University Press, 1998.

————. *Sennacherib's Palace without Rival at Nineveh.* Chicago: University of Chicago Press, 1991.

————. *The Writing on the Wall: Studies in the Architectural Context of Late Assyrian Palace Inscriptions.* Winona Lake, Ind.: Eisenbrauns, 1999.

Sachs, A. J., T. G. Pinches, and J. N. Strassmaier. *Late Babylonian Astronomical and Related Texts.* Providence, R.I.: Brown University Press, 1955.

Sasson, Victor. "The Siloam Tunnel Inscription." *Palestine Exploration Quarterly* 141 (1982): 111-17.

Schaudig, Hanspeter. *Die Inschriften Nabonids von Babylon und Kyros' des Grossen.* Alter Orient und Altes Testament, vol. 256. Münster: Ugarit-Verlag, 2001.

Schniedewind, William M. "Tel Dan Stela: New Light on Aramaic and Jehu's Revolt." *Bulletin of the American Schools of Oriental Research* 302 (1996): 75-90.

Scholz, Suzanne. "Reconstructing Rape for the 'Olden Days': The Challenge of Biblical Rape Laws in Biblical Studies." Paper presented at the conference on "The Rhetorics of Identity: Place, Race, Sex and the Person," University of Redlands, Redlands, Calif. January 21, 2005.

Sefati, Yitschak. *Love Songs in Sumerian Literature: Critical Edition of the Dumuzi-Inanna Songs.* Ramat Gan: Bar-Ilan University Press, 1998.

Select Papyri. Vol. 1. Translated by A. S. Hunt and C. C. Edgar. Loeb Classical Library. Cambridge, Mass.: Harvard University Press, 1932.

el-Shahawy, Abeer. Photographs by Farid Atiya. *The Egyptian Museum in Cairo: A Walk through the Alleys of Ancient Egypt.* Cairo: Farid Atiya, 2005.

Skeat, T. C. "The Last Chapter in the History of the Codex Sinaiticus." *Novum Testamentum* 42 (2000): 313-15.

Slingerland, Dixon. "Acts 18:1-18, The Gallio Inscription, and Absolute Pauline Chronology." *Journal of Biblical Literature* 110 (1991): 439-49.

Smith, George. *Assyrian Discoveries: An Account of Explorations and Discoveries on the Site of Nineveh, during 1873 and 1874.* New York: Scribner, Armstrong & Co., 1875.

Sparks, Kenton L. *Ancient Texts for the Study of the Hebrew Bible: A Guide to the Background Literature.* Peabody, Mass.: Hendrickson, 2005.

Stager, Lawrence E. "When Canaanites and Philistines Ruled Ashkelon." *Biblical Archaeology Review* 17 (1991): 24-37, 40-43.

Stern, M. "Chapter 11: Aspects of Jewish Society: The Priesthood and Other Classes." In *The Jewish People in the First Century,* vol. 2, edited by S. Safrai and M. Stern in cooperation with D. Flusser and W. C. van Unnik, pp. 561-630. Section 1, Compendia Rerum Iudicarum ad Novum Testamentum. Assen/Maastricht: Van Gorcum; Philadelphia: Fortress, 1987.

Stolper, Matthew W. "Some Ghost Facts from Achaemenid Babylonian Texts." *The Journal of Hellenic Studies* 108 (1988): 196-98.

Suetonius. *The Lives of the Caesars.* 2 vols. Translated by J. C. Rolfe. Loeb Classical Library. Cambridge, Mass.: Harvard University Press, 1914.

Tacitus. *The Annals.* 4 vols. Translated by John Jackson. Loeb Classical Library. Cambridge, Mass.: Harvard University Press, 1931-37.

Thomas, D. Winton, ed. *Documents from Old Testament Times: Translated with Introductions and Notes by Members of the Society for Old Testament Study.* New York: Harper & Row, Harper Torchbooks, 1958. Reprint, with new foreword and bibliography by K. C. Hanson, Eugene, Ore.: Wipf & Stock Publishers, Ancient Texts and Translations, 2005.

Thureau-Dangin, F., et al. *Arslan-Tash.* 2 vols. Paris: Librairie Orientaliste Paul Geuthner, 1931.

Torczyner, Harry, et al. *Lachish I: The Lachish Letters.* The Wellcome Archaeological Research Expedition to the Near East, vol. 1. London: Oxford University Press, 1938.

Tufnell, Olga, with contributions by Margaret A. Murray and David Diringer. *Lachish III: The Iron Age.* The Wellcome-Marston Archaeological Research Expedition to the Near East, vol. 3. London: Oxford University Press, 1953.

Tzaferis, V. "Jewish Tombs at and near Giv'at ha-Mivtar, Jerusalem." *Israel Exploration Journal* 20 (1970): 18-32.

Ussishkin, David. "Gate 1567 at Megiddo and the Seal of Shema, Servant of Jeroboam." In *Scripture and Other Artifacts: Essays on the Bible and Archaeology in Honor of Philip J. King.* Edited by Michael D. Coogan, et al. Louisville: Westminster/John Knox, 1994.

————. "The Necropolis from the Time of the Kingdom of Judah at Silwan, Jerusalem." *Biblical Archaeologist* 33 (1970): 34-46.

Van De Mieroop, Marc. *A History of the Ancient Near East ca. 3000-323 BC.* Blackwell History of the Ancient World. Malden, Mass.: Blackwell, 2004.

Verbin, John S. Kloppenborg. "Dating Theodotos (CIJ II 1404)." *Journal of Jewish Studies* 51 (2000): 243-80.

Weinfeld, Moshe. "Job and Its Mesopotamian Parallels — A Typological Analysis." In *Text and Context: Old Testament and Semitic Studies for F. C. Fensham,* edited by W. Claassen, pp. 217-26. Journal for the Study of the Old Testament Supplement Series 48. Sheffield: Sheffield Academic Press, 1988.

Wesselius, Jan-Wim. "The First Royal Inscription from Ancient Israel: The Tel Dan Inscription Reconsidered." *Scandinavian Journal of the Old Testament* 13 (1999): 163-86.

Wiseman, D[onald] J. *Chronicles of Chaldean Kings (626-556 B.C.) in the British Museum.* London: Trustees of the British Museum, 1961.

————. *Illustrations from Biblical Archaeology.* London: Tyndale Press, 1958.

————. *Nebuchadrezzar and Babylon.* London: Oxford University Press, 1985.

————. "A New Text of the Babylonian Poem of the Righteous Sufferer." *Anatolian Studies: Journal of the British Institute of Archaeology at Ankara* 30 (1980): 101-7.

Woolley, Sir Leonard. *Excavations at Ur.* New York: Thomas Y. Crowell, Co., n.d.

Younger, K. Lawson, Jr. *Ancient Conquest Accounts: A Study in Ancient Near Eastern and Biblical History Writing.* Journal for the Study of the Old Testament Supplement Series 98. Sheffield: Sheffield Academic Press, 1990.

Zias, Joseph, and Eliezer Sekeles. "The Crucified Man from Giv'at ha-Mivtar: A Reappraisal." *Israel Exploration Journal* 35 (1985): 22-27.

Credits and Permissions

Excerpts

Our thanks to the various publishers for permission to use excerpted material from the following works (pages on which the excerpts appear are given in brackets):

All quotations from the Bible are from the New Revised Standard Version Bible, copyright 1989, Division of Christian Education of the National Council of the Churches of Christ in the United States of America. Used by permission. All rights reserved.

Alster, Bendt. *Proverbs of Ancient Sumer: The World's Earliest Proverb Collection,* vol. 1. Bethesda, Md.: CDL Press, 1977. [pp. 242-43]

Avigad, N[ahman]. "The Epitaph of a Royal Steward from Siloam Village." *Israel Exploration Journal* 3 (1953): 137-52. [p. 156]

Biran, Avraham, and Joseph Naveh. "The Tel Dan Inscription: A New Fragment." *Israel Exploration Journal* 45 (1995): 1-18. [p. 104]

Brown, Raymond E., Joseph A. Fitzmyer, and Roland E. Murphy, eds. *The New Jerome Biblical Commentary.* 1st Edition, New York: Prentice Hall, © 1990. Reprinted by permission of Pearson Education, Inc., Upper Saddle River, N.J. [pp. 336-37]

Chavalas, Mark W., ed. *The Ancient Near East: Historical Sources in Translation.* Malden, Mass.: Blackwell, 2006. [pp. 24-25, 58, 218]

Clifford, Richard J. *Creation Accounts in the Ancient Near East and in the Bible.* The Catholic Biblical Quarterly Monograph Series 26. Washington, D.C.: The Catholic Biblical Association of America, 1994. [p. 11]

Foster, Benjamin R. *Before the Muses: An Anthology of Akkadian Literature.* 2 vols. Bethesda, Md.: CDL Press, 1993. [pp. 48, 260-61, 262]

Glassner, Jean-Jacques. *Mesopotamian Chronicles.* Edited by Benjamin R. Foster. Society of Biblical Literature Writings from the Ancient World, no. 19. Atlanta: Society of Biblical Literature, 2004. [pp. 210, 229-30]

Hallo, William W., gen. ed., and K. Lawson Younger Jr, assoc. ed. *The Context of Scripture.* 3 vols. Leiden: E. J. Brill, 1997-2002. [pp. 4, 5, 6, 10, 13-14, 61, 62, 64, 72, 89-90, 92, 117-18, 121, 122, 131, 145, 161-62, 193, 194, 206, 207, 213, 214, 215, 224-25, 230, 233, 244-45, 248-49, 257, 268]

Josephus, *Jewish War*. Reprinted by permission of the publishers and the Trustees of the Loeb Classical Library from *Josephus*, volume IV, Loeb Classical Library, translated by H. St. J. Thackeray, Cambridge, Mass.: Harvard University Press, Copyright © 1930, by the President and Fellows of Harvard College. The Loeb Classical Library © is a registered trademark of the President and Fellows of Harvard College. [pp. 326, 327-28, 375]

Kloppenborg, John S. "The Theodotos Synagogue Inscription and the Problem of First-Century Synagogue Buildings." In *Jesus and Archaeology*, edited by James Charlesworth, pp. 252-53. Grand Rapids: Wm. B. Eerdmans, 2006. [p. 358]

Lichtheim, Miriam. *Ancient Egyptian Literature: A Book of Readings*. Vol. 2, *The New Kingdom*. Berkeley and Los Angeles: University of California Press, 1976. [pp. 245-46, 252-54, 254-55]

Moran, William L., ed. *The Amarna Letters*. © 1992 The Johns Hopkins University Press. Reprinted with permission of The Johns Hopkins University Press. (Excerpts from pp. 305 and 340-341.) [pp. 41-42]

Pliny, *Letters*. Reprinted by permission of the publishers and the Trustees of the Loeb Classical Library from *Pliny: Letters, Panegyricus*, volume II, Loeb Classical Library, translated by Betty Radice, Cambridge, Mass.: Harvard University Press, Copyright © 1969, by the President and Fellows of Harvard College. The Loeb Classical Library © is a registered trademark of the President and Fellows of Harvard College. [pp. 398-400, 401]

Pritchard, James. *Ancient Near Eastern Texts Relating to the Old Testament*. 3rd ed. with supplement. © 1950, 1955, 1969, renewed 1978 by Princeton University Press. Reprinted by permission of Princeton University Press. [pp. 19, 20, 21-22]

Robinson, James M., gen. ed. *The Nag Hammadi Library in English*, 3rd, completely revised ed. Copyright © 1978, 1988 by E. J. Brill, Leiden, The Netherlands. Reprinted by permission of HarperCollins Publishers. (Excerpts from pp. 126, 127, 128, 132, 136, and 138.) [pp. 427, 428]

Roth, Martha T., with a contribution by Harry A. Hoffner Jr. *Law Collections from Mesopotamia and Asia Minor*. Edited by Piotr Michalowski. Society of Biblical Literature Writings from the Ancient World, no. 6. 2nd ed. Atlanta: Scholars Press, 1997. [pp. 62, 63, 68, 69, 70]

Select Papyri. Reprinted by permission of the publishers and the Trustees of the Loeb Classical Library from *Select Papyri*, volume I, Loeb Classical Library, translated by A. S. Hunt and C. C. Edgar, Cambridge, Mass.: Harvard University Press, Copyright © 1982, by the President and Fellows of Harvard College. The Loeb Classical Library © is a registered trademark of the President and Fellows of Harvard College. [p. 340]

Thomas, D. Winton, ed. *Documents from Old Testament Times: Translated with Introductions and Notes by Members of the Society for Old Testament Study*. New York: Harper & Row, Harper Torchbooks, 1958. Reprint, with new foreword and bibliography by K. C. Hanson, Eugene, Ore.: Wipf & Stock Publishers, Ancient Texts and Translations, 2005. [pp. 95, 99-100]

Photographs

Appreciation to the sources named for permission to publish the following black and white photographs and color plates:

Photographs of two objects in the Archaeological Museum of Corinth, Greece (photographs are by the authors)
Figures 105 and 106

The Archaeological Museum, Istanbul, Turkey (all photographs are by the authors)
Figures 18, 26, 44, 81, 82, and 94

The Ashmolean Museum of Art and Archaeology, University of Oxford, Oxford, England. (Accession number AN 1923.444)
Figure 5

Ben-Zvi Institute, Jerusalem, Israel
Figure 119

Bildarchiv Preussicher Kulturbesitz/Art Resource, New York
Figures 100 and 114

Bildarchiv Preussicher Kulturbesitz/Art Resource, New York (photographs are by the authors)
Figures 17, 63, 83, 87, 97, and 108. Plate 7

© The British Library Board, London, England. All Rights Reserved. (Shelfmarks: Add. 43725, f.228; and Royal 1 D. VIII, f.76)
Figures 121 and 122

© Copyright the Trustees of The British Museum, London, England (all photographs are by the authors)
Figures 1, 3, 4, 6, 7, 8, 11, 13, 32, 33, 34, 35, 38, 39, 47, 48, 49, 50, 51, 53, 55, 56, 58, 61, 65, 66, 67, 75, 96, 99, 107, 111, and 113. Plates 1, 3, 5, 6, 11, 12, and 15

© The British Museum/Art Resource, New York
Figure 54

The Delphi Archaeological Museum, Delphi, Greece (photograph by the authors)
Figure 97

The Ephesus Museum, Selçuk, Turkey (all photographs are by the authors)
Figures 102 and 115. Plate 13

Eric Lessing/Art Resource, New York
Figures 9, 30, 31, 46, 52, 59, 88, 89, and 93. Plate 10

Freer Gallery of Art, Smithsonian Institution, Washington, D.C., Purchase, F1974.30
Figure 79

Collection of the Israel Antiquities Authority
Figures 20, 21, 28, 37, 45, 60, 62, 90, 91, 92, 104, 110, and 117

446

© The Israel Museum, Jerusalem, Israel
Figures 20, 21, 28, 37, 42, 45, 60, 62, 90, 91, 92, 104, 110, 117, 118, and 124

The John Rylands University Library, The University of Manchester, Manchester, England. Reproduced by courtesy of the University Librarian and Director.
Figure 120

© Jürgen Liepe, Berlin
Figure 19

The Louvre, Paris, France (all photographs are by the authors)
Figures 2, 15, 22, 23, 24, 25, 27, 29, 40, 41, 43, 64, 68, 73, 74, 76, 78, 80, 95, 101, 103, 109, and 116. Plates 4, 8, and 9

© Michael C. Carlos Museum of Emory University. Courtesy of the Michael C. Carlos Museum
Figure 57

The Museum of Anatolian Civilizations, Ankara, Turkey (photograph by the authors)
Plate 16

The Museum of the Ancient Orient, Istanbul, Turkey (all photographs are by the authors)
Figures 14, 16, 36, 69, and 71

The National Archaeological Museum, Athens, Greece (photograph by the authors)
Figure 85

The National Archaeological Museum, Naples, Italy (photograph by the authors)
Plate 14

Collection of the Oriental Institute of The University of Chicago (photographs are by the authors)
Figures 70, 77, and 84. Plate 2

Réunion des Musées Nationaux/Art Resource, New York
Figure 72

Scala/Art Resource, New York
Figures 10, 12, 112

The State Hermitage Museum, St. Petersburg, Russia (photograph by the authors)
Figure 86

Zev Radovan, www.BibleLandPictures.com
Figure 123

Index of Subjects

Index of Biblical Citations

Index of Objects by Museum

Altes Museum, Berlin
Antiochus IV, marble head of, 293-96

Archaeological Museum, Istanbul
Alexander the Great: marble head of, 289-93; statue of, 289-93
Augustus, head and busts of, 299
Gezer Calendar, 95-97
Hezekiah's Tunnel inscription, 144-48
New Hittite Laws tablet, 69-70
Temple in Jerusalem warning inscription, 327-29

Archaeological Museum of Ancient Corinth, Greece
Menorah carving on marble capital, 362
Model body parts dedicated to Asclepius, 363-65
"Synagogue of the Hebrews" inscription, 361-63

Ashmolean Museum of Art and Archaeology, Oxford
Amarna tablet, 38
Sennacherib, relief panel from palace at Nineveh, 171
Sumerian King List (Weld-Blundell Prism), 22-26

British Library
Codex Alexandrinus, 421-24
Codex Sinaiticus, 418-21

British Museum
Alexander the Great, head of, 289

Amarna tablets, 37-42
Artaxerxes I, silver bowl of, 280
Artaxerxes II, column base fragments inscribed with name of, 284
Artemis temple at Ephesus: architectural fragments of, 356; column base of, 356
Ashurbanipal: autobiography of, 183; clay tablet commemorating rebuilding temple of Sin, 183; clay tablets from library of (legend of Etana, legend of Ishtar, omen tablet), 184; Prism F of, 183; stelae of, 182-85; wall reliefs from palaces of, at Nineveh, 185-90
Ashurnasirpal II, Kurkh Monolith of, 117
Atrahasis Epic ("The Babylonian Story of the Flood"), 12-16
Augustus, bronze head of, 299
Babylonian Chronicle, 616-609 B.C.E., 195-99
Babylonian Chronicle, 605-595 B.C.E., 208-11
Balawat Gates, 122-23
Birth Legend of Sargon of Akkad, 47-49
Claudius, bronze head of, 333-36
Cyrus Cylinder, 267-70
Darius: cylinder seal of, shooting lions, 273; glazed brick relief panel of a guard with spear from Susa, 273

461

Index of Objects by Museum Number